D1216888

The Two
World Wars

The Two World Wars

A Guide to Manuscript Collections in the United Kingdom

S. L. MAYER & W. J. KOENIG

BOWKER
London & New York

First published 1976 in Great Britain by Bowker Publishing Company Limited, Epping, Essex and in the United States of America by R. R. Bowker Co., 1180 Avenue of the Americas, New York, NY 10036.

ISBN 0 85935 014 2

Library of Congress catalog card number 74-9187

Printed and bound in Great Britain
by Redwood Burn Limited
Trowbridge & Esher

Introduction

The study of the diplomatic, military, economic, political and social impact of the two world wars increases with each passing year. In the case of World War II, the vast amount of primary material available to the scholar, ever increasing as official restrictions are removed, gives broad scope for original research drawing on previously inaccessible resources. It is often surprising to realise that so little is known about the two greatest cataclysms of modern times, and the principal historical events of the twentieth century. There is hardly an aspect of life anywhere in the world which was not altered directly or indirectly as a result of the world wars. Nations were created and destroyed. Tens of millions of lives were lost. War machines were built in each of the major industrial countries and the aftermath of the wars left societies as well as economies transformed. Most of all, men's thinking on almost every subject imaginable was altered. National self-determination, the military-industrial complex, racism, nationalism, imperialism, socialism, communism, education and the role of the military in an industrial society were ideas and movements thrown up by the wars. Issues were raised by World War II in particular which remain problems decades after 1945. The guns of August 1914 sounded the birth of a new and more violent century than the world had ever seen, made even more frightening by the inventive genius of modern science.

The importance of the British role in both world wars is inestimable. As the ranking colonial and naval power in 1914, Britain's declaration of war on Germany on 4 August 1914 guaranteed the fact that the war, arising largely out of Central and Eastern European controversies, would be fought all over the world. Britain's command of the seas, however challenged, was retained throughout the war, although the effect of German submarines raised many fundamental questions, particularly in 1917. Britain's imperial allies, above all the Dominions — Canada, South Africa, Australia and New Zealand — fought against Germany and the Ottoman Empire in Europe, the Middle East,

Southeast Asia and Africa. For the first time in her history, Britain made a massive commitment of millions of men, raised first through volunteers and later through widespread conscription, to the continent of Europe. The British Expeditionary Force rose from five divisions in the first weeks of the war to an army of millions in France, Belgium, Italy, the Balkans and the Middle East. It can be argued that the British blockade of the Central Powers and British effort on the left wing of the 400-mile long Western Front from Flanders to the Swiss border finally broke the back of the German war machine. Although the introduction of American forces in the last months of the war made a critical difference, and although the sacrifice of French troops on their own soil and elsewhere was enormous, the impact of British arms on the outcome of World War I was vital.

The war against Germany which began in September 1939 once again saw Britain as the principal naval power leading its continental allies against a central European coalition. Britain's continental commitment in World War II was curtailed by the fall of France in June 1940. For the next year of the war, Britain fought virtually alone against Germany and Italy in the skies over the British Isles and in the North Sea, the Mediterranean and the Atlantic. When the war in Asia came to involve the Western colonial powers in December 1941, British forces fought and were beaten by Imperial Japan.

As in World War I, the British effort was crucial to the outcome of the war. British bombers flew daily and later nightly over Germany. British and Commonwealth troops forced back the Afrika Corps and the Italians from the gates of Alexandria to Tunisia. When the desert campaign came to an end in May 1943, British and American troops invaded Sicily and then Italy, forcing their way up the peninsula in a campaign lasting almost two years. After D-Day, 6 June 1944, Britain and her allies cleared France and Belgium and, after the Ardennes offensive, plunged into Germany. In the Far East, British arms were less dramatic and effective, taking a secondary position to those of the United States in the war against Japan. But in that theatre of operations, the British Army bore the brunt of the reconquest of Burma and in the latter stages of the war, British naval forces helped the US Navy at Okinawa and elsewhere. After the cessation of hostilities, the British forces liberated most of Southeast Asia from the Japanese.

As the war progressed, the war effort of Britain, though massive was dwarfed by the scale of American and Soviet operations. But, as in World War I, British diplomatic and political efforts were crucial throughout World War II. As the leader of a still vast empire, Britain participated fully in the Yalta and Potsdam Conferences which had the same effect as the Paris Peace Conference had in a more formal framework in 1919. The diplomacy and politics of the war were thus a concomitant of the military and naval operations.

We have attempted in this work to limit the scope of the material covered to the area of military history and to the political and diplomatic history of the world wars only insofar as these impinged on the military domain. What was and was not directly relevant to the military course of the wars was a constant question during the compilation of material and the answers often had to be quite broad. As economic warfare was as much a military tool as a tank or a bomber, for example, we have tried to include some of the more important material in this area. Britain itself came under attack in both wars, hence the civilian population had to be mobilized both for defence and survival. Civil Defence, air raid precautions, evacuation, and Home Guard records have therefore been included.

This book has posed far more problems than its predecessor, *European Manuscript Sources of the American Revolution* (London: Bowker, 1974). In our previous work, other historians and compilers had paved the way and it was also clear that few materials of major significance were likely to be discovered suddenly after 200 years. The amount of documentation in the eighteenth century was also but a fraction of the volume of paper produced by governments in the twentieth century. Our first attempt at surveying original sources for a specific event in history was thus a considerably simpler task, making it possible to combine in one volume coverage of all the European powers affecting the course of the American Revolution. The sheer magnitude of the material relating to the world wars and the fact that important new material is steadily entering the public domain soon indicated the need to limit this work to British manuscript sources.

With the relaxation in 1972 of the 30-year rule concerning official records, the amount of primary material available to the student has vastly increased. With some exceptions, the full resources of the most important repository for the study of the world wars, the Public Record Office in London, are now available for the first time. Many other official records have been released to county and local record offices and libraries. The quantity of private papers in public hands is also growing rapidly. In addition to the traditional repositories for private papers such as the British Library, the Bodleian Library, the National Libraries of Scotland and Wales, and some of the university libraries, a number of special archives for private papers have developed important collections. Among these are the Imperial War Museum, the National Army Museum, the National Maritime Musuem, the Royal Air Force Museum, Churchill College at Cambridge, the Liddell Hart Centre for Military Archives of King's College in London, the Cambridge South Asian Archive, Rhodes House Library and the Middle East Library of St. Antony's College in Oxford. There are also many untapped resources in the museums of the various branches of the British Army and in the one hundred or so regimental museums.

Although students have had the benefit of various bibliographies and bibliographic essays dealing with secondary sources concerning military history in general and the world wars in particular, there has been no work covering primary source material. This lack has been lessened recently with the appearance of C. Hazlehurst and C. Woodland, *A Guide to the Papers of British Cabinet Ministers 1900-1951* (London: Royal Historical Society, 1974), which locates and describes the surviving papers of 323 cabinet ministers, thus giving vital coverage to the top echelon of government. A related work has now been published which further extends the coverage begun by Hazlehurst and Woodland. This is C. Cook *et al, Sources in British Political History 1900-1951* (London: MacMillan, 1975): vol. I, *A Guide to the Archives of Selected Organisations and Societies*; vol. II, *A Guide to the Private Papers of Selected Public Servants.* This last provides coverage of the private papers of some 1,500 diplomats, civil servants, colonial administrators, and senior Air Force, Army and Navy personnel. Yet to appear are volumes III and IV covering Members of Parliament and other figures not in public service. Thus some much needed control has been established for the student over the realm of the private papers of public figures.

There are, however, many other records relating to the wars and the papers of many individuals which have not found their way into any published compilation. The primary material covered in the present volume concentrates on military and naval records in the public domain as well as the diplomatic and political records which impinge directly on the course of the wars themselves. With one or two exceptions, material still in private ownership has not been included. The most important of this privately owned material has been covered in Hazlehurst and Woodland and Cook *et al.* The intention of the present volume is thus not to be a comprehensive guide to the currently available material but rather to offer the student an introduction to the holdings of the more important repositories so that research can be more effectively planned. This book is really a *point d'appui* and time-saver, a tool to be used to identify repositories and the nature of their contents in relation to the wars and to locate certain types of information and documents.

Our approach was to survey the holdings of the main repositories and libraries of London, Cambridge, Edinburgh and Oxford through visits. The special archives were all surveyed *in situ* as well. Surveys were also conducted of selected military repositories such as the Royal Artillery Institution and the Royal Marines Museum and Archives. Such work yielded not only the bulk of the material in the book but also the most important. The county and local record offices and libraries were in most cases surveyed by post since it was neither possible nor valuable to undertake a programme of visits to all of them. Nevertheless, a considerable amount of valuable information was obtained by this method.

A mail survey of regimental museums was undertaken with varied results. Over one hundred museums received letters and about seventy ultimately responded. Some reported collections of material which was listed or catalogued and forwarded copies of their lists. About thirty reported no holdings at all or holdings of no interest, while the majority was found to have unlisted material. A few museums in the last category were visited but the results were not found to justify the time and expense involved for the purposes of this volume. In view of the fact that the National Army Museum is currently gathering information for a catalogue of the documents and photographs held by regimental museums, it was decided not to pursue this line of endeavour. It is hoped that eventually this catalogue will be in a form which will allow consultation by researchers.

Due to the sheer magnitude of its holdings, the Public Record Office presented a special problem. Any attempted summary of the relevant records in this repository would have encountered difficulties of consistency, accuracy and length. Since the Public Record Office has various guides, both published and unpublished, and has recently published its own summary of material relating to World War II, it was decided to discuss it only in general terms and to list some of the private office and deposited papers of public servants involved in the wars in various capacities.

Many people have assisted in the preparation of this book. We are exceptionally grateful to the many librarians and archivists who contributed information by post and also to the keepers of the various special archives for their assistance. We wish to thank Brian Bond for commenting on the entire manuscript of the book and Richard Holmes and John Keegan for their contributions. Our special thanks go to Michael Armstrong and Joel Goldberg for their visits to regimental museums and to Pam Holmes and Eileen Clarke for much appreciated clerical support.

It is our hope that the information brought together in this volume will ease the path of students of the two world wars to the location of original material and encourage them to embark on new studies of these two important events.

S. L. *Mayer*
W. J. *Koenig*

London
10 December 1975

Abbreviations

ADC, Aide-de-camp
AEAF, Allied Expeditionary Air Force
AFHQ, Allied Force Headquarters
ALFSEA, Allied Land Forces Southeast Asia
AOA, Air Officer in charge of Administration
AOC, Air Officer Commanding
AOC-in-C, Air Officer Commanding-in-Chief
ARP, Air Raid Precautions
ASC, Army Service Corps
ASV, Air to Surface Vessel (radar device)
ATC, Air Training Corps
ATS, Auxiliary Territorial Service
BEF, British Expeditionary Force
BGS, Brigadier General Staff
CCRA, Commander Corps Royal Artillery
CID, Committee for Imperial Defence
CIGS, Chief of the Imperial General Staff
C-in-C, Commander-in-Chief
CO, Commanding Officer
COSSAC, Chief of Staff to Supreme Allied Commander
CQMS, Company Quartermaster-Sergeant
CSM, Company Sergeant Major
DAAG, Deputy Assistant Adjutant-General
DCNS, Deputy Chief of Naval Staff
EEF, Egyptian Expeditionary Force
FAA, Fleet Air Arm
GHQ, General Headquarters
GOC, General Officer Commanding
GOC-in-C, General Officer Commanding-in-Chief
GSO, General Staff Officer
HQ, Headquarters

IEF, Indian Expeditionary Force

MAUD, Sub-committee of the Committee for the Scientific Survey of Air Warfare, to investigate the atomic bomb

NCO, Non-commissioned Officer

NSDAP, Nationalsozialistische Deutschlands Arbeiterpartei (National Socialist German Workers' Party)

OC, Officer Commanding

OC-in-C, Officer Commanding-in-Chief

OKH, Oberkommando des Heeres (German Army High Command)

OKW, Oberkommando der Wehrmacht (German Armed Forces High Command)

OTC, Officers' Training Corps

POW, Prisoner of War

QMAAC, Queen Mary's Army Auxiliary Corps

RA, Royal Artillery

RAF, Royal Air Force

RAFVR, Royal Air Force Volunteer Reserve

RAMC, Royal Army Medical Corps

RAOC, Royal Army Ordnance Corps

RASC, Royal Army Service Corps

RDC, Rural District Council

RE, Royal Engineers

RFA, Royal Field Artillery

RFC, Royal Flying Corps

RHR, Royal Highland Regiment

RINVR, Royal Indian Navy Volunteer Reserve

RMA, Royal Marine Artillery

RMLI, Royal Marine Light Infantry

RN, Royal Navy

RNAS, Royal Naval Air Service

RNVR, Royal Naval Volunteer Reserve

RNVR(A), Royal Naval Volunteer Reserve (Air)

SACSEA, Supreme Allied Commander Southeast Asia

SEAC, Southeast Asia Command

SHAEF, Supreme Headquarters, Allied Expeditionary Force

SOE, Special Operations Executive

SS, Schutzstaffel (Nazi Security Force)

TA, Territorial Army

TAF, Tactical Air Force

UDC, Urban District Council

UNRRA, United Nations Relief and Rehabilitation Administration

USAAC, United States Army Air Corps

VAD, Voluntary Aid Department

WAAC, Women's Army Auxiliary Corps

WFSt., Wehrmachtführungsstab (German Armed Forces Operations
   Staff)
WRAC, Women's Royal Army Corps
WRAF, Women's Royal Air Force
WRNS, Women's Royal Naval Service
W/T, Wireless telegraphy
WVS, Women's Voluntary Services

*Aberdeen City Library, Rosemount Viaduct, ABERDEEN
AB9 1GU*

WORLD WAR I

Cpl. Harry Robertson, Gordon Highlanders, holograph diary containing
a day-to-day account of the battle of the Somme, July — December
1916.
Douglas Stephen, account of his experiences with the 401st Company,
RE, in France and Belgium, 1915-18, 12 pp., ts., 1970.

*The Gordon Highlanders, Regimental Headquarters,
Viewfield Road, ABERDEEN AB1 7XH*

There is a collection of diaries, letters and maps, most of which have
been published in the official regimental history and regimental
magazine. Enquiries should be made to the Commandant.

*Manuscript and Archives Section, University Library, King's
College, ABERDEEN AB9 2UB*

Sir George Arthur D. Ogilvie Forbes (1891-1954)
Correspondence and papers including: **bundle 28,** letters relating to the
Mesopotamian campaign, 1914-16, where he served as ADC to Lt. Gen.
Sir F. S. Maude, C-in-C Mesopotamia; **boxes 38-41,** private papers as
Counsellor, British Embassy in Berlin, 1937-9, and similarly at the
British Legation in Oslo, 1939; and his draft annual report on
conditions in Germany, 1939.

*Department of Manuscripts, National Library of Wales,
ABERYSTWYTH, Dyfed SY23 3BU*

The manuscript collections fall into two broad groups: the National
Library of Wales MSS, and other collections consisting of bequests,
deposits and donations. The former are described in the *National
Library of Wales Journal: Supplements — Handlist of Manuscripts in
the National Library of Wales.* The other collections are covered in
some detail in the *Annual Reports* of the Library. The following brief
survey is based on the foregoing publications.

NATIONAL LIBRARY OF WALES MSS

2143E. Collection of letters, circulars and memoranda from government departments and local authorities received by Evan Evans, clerk of Cardiganshire County Council, 1914-18.

5564-5565. 11th Service Battalion, Welch Regiment, minutes and correspondence of the Comforts Committee, 1915-16.

6079-6080A. Royal Welch Fusiliers. D Company, 20th Battalion and E Company, 16th Battalion, roll books, 1915.

9472E. Papers and reports by Charles E. Breese regarding employment of soldiers for harvesting in Anglesey, Caernarvon and Merioneth, 1916.

9982E. Circulars, correspondence, accounts and other papers relating to Belgian refugees, farm produce for the armed forces, etc. in Llan-iuta-Harlech, 1914-18.

10436E. Royal Welch Fusiliers, 15th Battalion war diary, 1 December 1915 − 30 January 1918.

10850. Letter to E. W. Evans from D. R. Daniel of Camberwell concerning recruiting for WWI, n.d.

12104B. Exercise book containing poems written by J. Thomas Llangwyllog during service in France, WWI.

12674B. Various letters, including one holograph letter from the Rev. John Owen Thomas referring to his work among Welsh and English soldiers in France, 1917.

12699B. Telegram from the Press Association to the *Cambrian News,* Aberystwyth, September 1939, concerning unconfirmed *Associated Press* reports of fighting in Danzig and the bombing of Polish towns; a *Reuters* statement regarding a broadcast by Hitler and Danzig's proclamation of itself as part of Germany; and unconfirmed reports from Paris relating to the beginning of the German offensive.

20403-20493. Some 3,500 letters of David Lloyd George to his wife and other members of his family.

OTHER COLLECTIONS

A. R. Andrews
Log books, 1940-5, of Air Raid Warden Post No. 7, Llanbadarn Fawr and subsidiary papers.

Breconshire and Radnor Territorial Association
Minute books, 1908-68.

Maj. Gen. W. R. Cox
Finely bound copy of *The History of the 53rd (Welsh) Division in the Second World War.*

Sir Alfred Davies (1861-1949)
Permanent Secretary of the Welsh Department of the Board of Education and originator of the British POWs Book Scheme. There is various material referring to the scheme, including Davies' fully documented ts. account of the movement, various letters and reports on the treatment of POWs, etc.

R. J. S. Davies
Various papers, including *inter alia* two army field books of (?)Capt. K. R. Davies of the Yorkshire and Lancashire Regiment, recording regimental routine while on active service, 1916-17.

Edward, Prince of Wales
Holograph letter of 1915 from the future Edward VIII, of the Guards Division in France, to Gen. Sir James Hills-Johnes.

Emrys Evans
Account of experiences with the RAMC in Salonika during WWI, an English version of 39 pp. and a Welsh version of 13 pp.

Julian Franklyn
'Copy their virtues, being a memoir of the Welsh Horse (Lancers)', 1957, and material gathered for the account. The latter is not available until AD 2022.

Dr George H. Green
Papers, including *inter alia* a file of drawings, water-colours, photographs, letters, etc. relating to his army service in Egypt, 1915-17.

R. O. Jenkins
Papers referring to service as a captain attached to the White Russian forces in the Archangel district, 1919, consisting of a few military documents and maps, and a number of letters in Russian and English. Cyclostyled reports, based on documents and memoranda compiled in 1945, regarding the Japanese occupation of Malaya, 1942-5, with particular reference to conditions in prison and internment camps.

Richard Idwal Mervyn Jones (1885-1937)
Papers of this poet and playwright, including *inter alia* letters, 1915-19, mainly from East Africa and military hospitals in England.

Maesmawr Collection
The collection includes a 95 pp. ts. of the personal diary of Col. Cecil Allanson, kept as GSO 1, 57th Division in France, 16 February — 19 July 1917. There is also a ts. summary of his career.

Montgomeryshire County Council
ARP Committee records, 1938-41.

Iwan J. Morgan
A collection including *inter alia* the papers of Brig. Gen. Edward A.
Herbert (1866-1946) regarding his military career which included
service in WWI.

Chirk Castle Muniments
This large collection contains *inter alia* 156 items, 1940-2 and n.d.,
relating to the 6th Battalion, Denbighshire Home Guard and more
particularly D Company.

Owen and Colby Papers
Correspondence and other items referring to Maj. Lawrence Colby
(1880-1914), Grenadier Guards, consisting of letters to his parents prior
to and subsequent to embarkation for France, August – October 1914;
notification of his death near Gheluvelt, 24 October 1914; and letters
from fellow officers and other ranks describing the circumstances of
death, etc.

Maj. W. G. Rowlands
Commanding officer of B Company, 1st Battalion, Cardiganshire Home
Guard. Album of photographs, short list of the battalion and related
miscellaneous papers from WWII.

Sir Geoffrey Shakespeare
Financial Secretary to the Admiralty during the appointment of
Winston Churchill as 1st Sea Lord, 1939-40. A dossier of papers
regarding this appointment, consisting of memoranda, minutes,
instructions and correspondence with Churchill on various issues.

D. A. Thomas Papers
350 letters of David Alfred Thomas, Viscount Rhondda (1856-1918),
Minister of Food Control, 1917-18.

W. Emyr Williams
Papers, including *inter alia* files concerning service in Palestine and
Egypt during WWI, consisting of photographs, maps, and letters home,
1915-19. There are also some printed items such as issues of the
Palestine News, April – November 1918.

*Airborne Forces Museum, Depot The Parachute Regiment
and Airborne Forces, Browning Barracks, ALDERSHOT,
Hampshire GU11 2DS*

WORLD WAR II

Some 200 files on the wartime build-up and subsequent actions of the
1st and 6th Airborne Divisions.
Diary of Gen. Sir Gerald Lathbury as a temporary brigadier in the
Oxfordshire and Buckinghamshire Light Infantry at Arnhem, 17
September — 23 October 1944. There is a photocopy in the Imperial
War Museum.
Corps and unit histories:
2nd Parachute Brigade in Operations HISTORY, DRAGOON and
MANNA.
2nd Parachute Brigade, MS war diary.
3rd Parachute Brigade, MS history.
5th Parachute Brigade, souvenirs and pictures from the Far East.
1st Parachute Battalion, MS diary of events at Arnhem by Lt. Col.
Dobie.
2nd Parachute Battalion, MS diary of events at Arnhem Bridge.
3rd Parachute Battalion, short MS history.
4th Parachute (West Country) Battalion, short MS history.
5th Parachute (Scottish) Battalion, short MS history.
6th Parachute (Royal Welch) Battalion, short MS history.
7th Parachute (Light Infantry) Battalion, short MS history.
8th Parachute Battalion, short MS history.
9th Parachute Battalion, MS history and notes on the Merville Battery.
10th Parachute Battalion, short MS history.
11th Parachute Battalion, short MS history.
12th Parachute (Yorkshire) Battalion, short MS history.
13th Parachute Battalion, short MS history.
15th Parachute Battalion, short MS history.
151/156 Parachute Battalion, short MS history.
17th Parachute Battalion, short MS history.
22nd Independent Company, Operation VARSITY reports by the OC.
1st (Canadian) Parachute Battalion, short MS history.
Royal Ulster Rifles, report on operations in Normandy, 6 — 16 June
1944.
Oxford and Buckinghamshire Light Infantry, 2nd Battalion, capture of
Pegasus Bridge.

Royal Army Medical Corps Historical Museum, Keogh
Barracks, Ash Vale, ALDERSHOT, Hampshire GU12 5RG

The documents at this Museum are now housed in the Muniment Room
of the Royal Army Medical College, London (see p. 196).

Intelligence Corps Museum, Headquarters Intelligence Corps,
Templer Barracks, ASHFORD, Kent TN23 3HH

The Intelligence Corps Museum holds various records but no material or
listing will be released until completion of the writing of the *History of*
the Intelligence Corps.

Buckinghamshire Record Office, County Hall, AYLESBURY,
Buckinghamshire HP20 1UA

TERRITORIAL ARMY COLLECTION

Records of the Buckinghamshire Territorial Forces Association and
other Buckinghamshire military records acquired by the Association.
Territorial Army Association, 1908-68, correspondence, financial
records, committee minutes, printed annual reports, MS of 'Citizen
Soldiers of Buckinghamshire' by Swann (1931), and related items.
1st Buckinghamshire Battalion, TA, 1908-54, MS battalion history,
charts, photographs, cuttings, musters, day-to-day record for 1914-18,
war history by Wright, battalion orders from 1915-18, trench log at
Hébuterne in 1915, war diary for 1942, orders from 1939-45, etc.
2nd Buckinghamshire Battalion, TA, 1914-46, battalion history for
1914-18 by Swann, roll of honour from 1914-18, recruitment papers in
1914, etc.
Buckinghamshire Yeomanry, miscellaneous records, 1794-1968,
including: order book, 3rd Line Depot, April 1915; action report, E. L.
Mughar, 1917; ts. record of service, 1914-18; and WWII papers
comprising **RFA 393-394**, batteries muster and 99th Field Regiment
reform after Dunkirk.
Oxfordshire and Buckinghamshire Light Infantry, 1908-68, consisting
of printed histories, 1741-1927 and 1914-15, and roll of honour,
1914-19.
Volunteer Defence Corps, 1914-20, comprising muster book,
correspondence and orders, Mid-Buckinghamshire Battalion, 1915-18;

similarly, 2nd Battalion, 1916-18; papers referring to formation of the corps, 1914-16; papers regarding 3rd Battalion, 1916-17; and brigade orders, 1915-16.

Home Guard records, 1940-6, correspondence, accounts, enrolments, training, battalion orders, Aylesbury defence scheme, register of personnel, photographs, and related items.

WORLD WAR I

Diary of a visit to the front in France as representative of the Ministry of Munitions by W. H. Grenfell, 1915. **Desborough Collection, D/86/8.** Files of papers and correspondence regarding Lord Cottesloe's service as Musketry Officer, 21st Division, 1914-15, including divisional orders, etc.; plans, circulars and the like, relating to the provision of rifle ranges for the training of Territorial Forces, 1914-15, with photographs; letters of Lord Cottesloe to his wife and a diary of his visit to France, 1916; correspondence with soldiers invalided in Wistow Hospital, Leics., 1916-20; and miscellaneous correspondence of the Cottesloe family during the war period. **Fremantle Collection.**

Museum of the Royal Army Chaplains' Department, Royal Army Chaplains' Department Centre, Bagshot Park, BAGSHOT, Surrey

The Curator reports that there is no original material of any historical value relating to WWI but some manuscripts and personal diaries of limited historical value referring to WWII.

Bedfordshire & Hertfordshire Regiment Association Museum, Kempston Barracks, BEDFORD MK42 8AJ

Enquiries should be addressed to the Curator.

WORLD WARS I AND II

Brig. C. N. Barclay, MS 'History of The Bedfordshire and Hertfordshire Regiment, 1914-1945'.

Bedfordshire County Record Office, County Hall,
BEDFORD MK42 9AP

WORLD WAR I

Home Guard. **H.G.**
War Agricultural Committee. **W.A.**
Nursing, hospitals, VAD. **W.N.**
War Pensions Committee. **W.P.**
Secret and confidential, including official diaries. **W.S.C.**
County Appeal Tribunal. **S.T.**
File relating to Bedford teachers' military service, 1915-16. **E.B.V. 14.**
File regarding taking over of elementary schools as hospitals, etc.
E.B.V. 36.
Letters from John Longuet Higgins of 13th London Regiment, in the
trenches, France, 1914-15. **H.G. 12/10/113-138.**
Letters from Kenneth Longuet Higgins, Royal Marine, killed in the
Dardenelles, 1915. **H.G. 12/10/152-157.**
Correspondence about German prisoners at Tempsford Hall, 1917-19.
W.Y. 919, 920.
Pvt. Benson's wounding at Foucacourt on the Somme, account; his
pocket book; and photograph of his family, with bullet hole, 1915.
X 399/1-3.
Bagshawe deposit, two papers regarding the Ministry of Munitions,
1916. **B.G. 5/1.**
Testimonial to Mayoress from Bedford War Hospital Supply Depot
members, book, photographs, etc., 1916-19. **A.D. 3959.**
File of maps showing German order of battle, 1917-18. **X 405/58.**

WORLD WAR II

ARP: correspondence, circular, letterbooks, minutes, area arrange-
ments. **W/A.R.P.**
Central register of accommodation. **W/C.R.A.**
Evacuation correspondence. **W/Ev. C.**
Evacuation, various. **W/Ev. V.**
Fire Guards, various. **W/F.G.V.**
Home Guard Battalion orders. **W/H.G.B.**
Home Guard nominal rolls. **W/H.G.N.**
Home Guard, various. **W/H.G.V.**
Invasion Committee. **W/I.N.V.**

WVS. **W/W.V.S.**
Various. **W/V.**
Willington records. **W/W.**
Files relating to schools, etc. in wartime, evacuees, and ARP in schools, Bedford, 1939-40. **E.B.V. 37-40, 48.**
Papers, etc. regarding London children evacuated to Bedfordshire, 1939-44. **E.V. 102-106.**
Correspondence concerning ARP equipment., *c.* 1939. **Z 209/27.**
Northill Invasion Committee records, 1939-45. **P 10/28/3.**
Wartime tank production at Britannia Iron Works, photographs and press-cuttings from the 1940s. **BR 82/5.**
Requisitioning of York Street Mission Hall, belonging to St. Cuthbert's, for Civil Defence purposes. **P 120/6/10.**
Navigation logs, personal file, etc. of F/O Godber, 1942-5. **X 489.**
Firewatchers' log books, list books, and a list and payment book for St. Mary's Church, Bedford, 1941-4. **X 56/17-18.**

Public Record Office of Northern Ireland, 66 Balmoral Avenue, BELFAST BT9 6NY

This listing includes only a few of the more important collections and is not comprehensive.

WORLD WARS I AND II

Sir Edward Henry Carson
Baron Carson (1854-1935). Attorney-General, May — November 1915; 1st Lord of the Admiralty, December 1916 — July 1917; and Minister without Portfolio, 1917 — January 1918. The collection includes general correspondence, 1896-1937; Cabinet papers and memoranda, 1915-17; and Admiralty papers, 1916-17, with about 200 subject files.

James H. H. Pollock (b. 1893)
This collection includes his correspondence as District Commissioner, Haifa, 1939; Galillee, 1942; and Jerusalem, 1944-8.

Lt. Col. Sir Wilfrid Spender (1876-1960)
Spender served as GSO 1, General Staff, Ulster and 31st Divisions, and later with GHQ during WWI. There are papers relating to his career between 1912 and 1944.

Regimental Headquarters, King's Own Scottish Borderers
Regimental Museum, The Barracks,
BERWICK-UPON-TWEED

There are two typed summary lists of the records held by the
Regimental Museum and Library, prepared by the County Archivist in
1975. Enquiries should be made to the Regimental Secretary.

2nd Battalion, KOSB, digest of service, 7 November 1859 – 5 July
1942. **13.**

'Historical Records, 1st Battalion, KOSB, Vol. 2', covering 13 May
1828 – 10 September 1940, and including loose letters, papers and
historical notes. **16.**

'Letters relative to Badges and Devices, the KOSB', album of letters,
1858-1961. **27.**

Photographs collected by Col. E. D. Jackson, 1913-53. **114.**

Depot KOSB scrapbook, 1916-42. **134.**

WORLD WAR I

1st Battalion, KOSB, digest of service, 21 September 1910 – 18 March
(?)1939. **18.**

2nd Battalion, KOSB, digest of service, 1 April 1910 – 11 March 1939.
19.

'War Diary: Extracts for Inclusion in Digest of Service, 1st Battalion,
KOSB', 11 September 1914 – 2 April 1919, ts. copy. **20.**

3rd Battalion, KOSB, account book of the Regimental Fund, 1894-
1924. **26.**

1st and 2nd Battalions, KOSB, large folio scrapbook, 1913-38. **54.**

1st Battalion, KOSB, cuttings book, 1760-1915, taken from miscellaneous books. **62.**

Honours Vol. 1, copies of recommendations for military honours by
the CO, 1 March 1917 – 22 February 1918. **65.** Similarly, 8 March – 4
November 1918. **66.**

1st Battalion, KOSB, scrapbook and photographs, 1918-37. **109.** Also
scrapbook, 1911-49. **108.**

Depot KOSB, scrapbook, 1896-1915. **125.**

1st Battalion, KOSB, photographs, 1914. **130.**

3rd Battalion, KOSB, photographs, 1915-17. **133.**

4th (Border) Battalion, KOSB, Roll of Honour, 1914-19. **163.**

WORLD WAR II

File of correspondence with Allied Battalions, 1944-54. **42.**

List of officers and other ranks killed in WWII, file. **67.**
Photographs of senior officers, 1925-45. **110.**
KOSB, press-cuttings, 1939-45. **138, 142, 159-162.**
Depot KOSB, scrapbooks, 1939-63. **140, 143-145.**
1st Battalion, KOSB, scrapbook, 1939-40. **139.**

Humberside County Record Office, County Hall, BEVERLEY, North Humberside

Yorkshire East Riding Territorial and Auxiliary Forces Association, records, 1907-68. **ref. TAF.**

WORLD WAR I

Private deposits: letter mentioning Goole steamships returned from Germany and Goole POWs coming home, WWI. **ref. DDX/7/45;** and autobiography of R. W. Shooter, WWI in vol., 1902-20. **ref. DDX/163/1.**
Lieutenancy: correspondence file relating to East Riding Territorial Force Association, 1907-15. **ref. LT/4/40.**

WORLD WAR II

ARP and Civil Defence records, including statistics, returns, reports, incident records and circulars, 1939-50. **ref. CD.**
Plan showing positions of pumping stations, reservoirs and towers in the East Riding belonging to Hull Corporation, ARP, 1938. **ref. MP23.**
Home Guard, nominal rolls and company books, 1940-4. **ref. HG.**
Church of England: Mappleton, file on war damage repairs to church and vicarage, 1948-53. **ref. PR/1206;** Flamborough, notices on distribution and examination of gas-masks, 1938-9. **ref. PR/2362;** and Hull, Drypool (a heavily bombed parish in WWII), correspondence and accounts relating to war damage and military occupation, 1939-49. **ref. PR in process.**

Archives and Museum, Bexley Public Libraries, Hall Place, Bourne Road, BEXLEY, Kent DA5 1PQ

WORLD WAR II

Civil Defence incident logs.

Central Library, Borough Road, BIRKENHEAD, Cheshire
L41 2XB

WORLD WARS I AND II

Birkenhead Corporation, ARP and Civil Defence files from the Town
Clerk's private office, 1939-45.
Civil Defence, large collection of records, including registers of
personnel, etc.
Rolls of Honour, WWI and WWII, with some supporting documentation
for the latter.
Wallasey Home Guard, small collection of privately donated papers.
Cheshire Regiment, set of photograph albums.

Birmingham Public Libraries, Reference Library,
BIRMINGHAM B3 3HQ

WORLD WAR I

Capt. Arthur E. Impey, diary of a gunner in WWI, 1918. **430000.**

WORLD WAR II

Letters sent to old boys of King Edward's Grammar School, Aston,
during WWII by Frank Jones, late Second Master of the school,
duplicated ts. sheets. **639329.**
Sector C21.52 Fire Fighting Group, Whitehall Road and part of
Broughton Road, Handsworth, Birmingham, minute book, 1941-5,
including MS. **662464.**

Sutton Coldfield Branch Library, Local History Department,
Lower Parade, BIRMINGHAM B72 1YA

Records from the Operations Room of the Sutton Coldfield ARP, as
yet unsorted or listed. Enquiries should be made to the Local History
Librarian.

University of Birmingham, The Main Library, P.O. Box 363,
BIRMINGHAM B15 2TT

Sir (Joseph) Austen Chamberlain (1863-1937)
Secretary of State for India, 1915-17, and member of the War Cabinet,

April 1918 — January 1919. Personal letters to 1937; and political papers, 1905-37, including political and military aspects of WWI, India, etc. There are many papers relating to military operations in Mesopotamia.

(Arthur) Neville Chamberlain (1869-1940)
Prime Minister, 1937 — May 1940. Personal papers to 1940; political papers, 1916-40, especially in relation to European affairs, 1936-40; and some correspondence and papers relating to his post as Director General of the National Service Department, December 1916-17.

Regimental Museum, The South Wales Borderers and Monmouthshire Regiment, The Barracks, BRECON, Powys

Enquiries should be made to the Curator.

WORLD WAR I

War diaries, 1914-18 of 1st, 2nd, 4th, 5th, 6th, 7th, 8th, 10th, 11th and 12th Battalions.
2nd Battalion, war diary, 1913-23, and at Tsingtao, 1914.
English translation of a German soldier's diary at Tsingtao, August — September 1914.
Lance Cpl. W. A. Wilson, 1st Battalion, diary for 4 August — 21 September 1914.
Drummer W. G. E. Wilson, MS diary, 16 March — 19 July 1915, and ts. copy, 16 March 1915 — January 1917.
Maj. Gen. K. F. D. Gattie, MS diary of the second battle of Ypres, May 1915.
Brig. Gen. A. J. Reddie, WWI diary with notes, photographs and press-cuttings.
Part of diary believed to have belonged to Herbert Herbert, killed at Llangemark, 19 December 1914.
Sgt. W. Peacock, 'History of the Great War', MS.
Capt. W. A. Burns, two diaries kept in Salonika, 1916.
2nd Lt. A. B. G. Biggerton-Evans, subaltern's diary kept in Gallipoli, 1915.
Mr Buchanan, copy of diary kept in Gallipoli, 1915.
Sketch map and notes regarding an engagement on 8 May 1915 during the second battle of Ypres.
MS recollections of WWI, composed by a member of the 2nd Brecknock Battalion.

Message sent by Lt. Col. Burleigh-Leach, OC 1st Battalion, to Col.
Pereira at the battle of Gheluvelt, 31 October 1914.
Capt. J. Farrow, letter of 16 February 1916 on service with the 4th
South Wales Borderers in Mesopotamia.

WORLD WAR II

2nd Battalion, war diary from D-day to VE-day, 1944-5.
Capt. J. N. Somerville, MS diary of service with the 2nd Battalion, 3
June 1944 — 22 January 1945.
Letter outlining the activities of the 1st Battalion, October 1939 —
November 1945.
Letter referring to the Rundwick Raid by the 2nd Battalion, 21-22
March 1945.

University Library, University of Sussex, BRIGHTON, East Sussex BN1 9QL

Maj. Gen. Thomas W. Rees (1898-1959)
Commander of the 10th Indian Division in Iraq and North Africa,
1942, and the 19th Indian Division in Burma, 1944-5. Private papers,
including some relating to his WWII activities.

Bristol Record Office, The Council House, College Green, BRISTOL BS1 5TR

127th (Bristol) Heavy Battery, Royal Garrison Artillery, pamphlets on
its history.

WORLD WAR I

Bristol Recruiting Committee, minutes, 1915.
Letters from a chaplain serving aboard a hospital ship based at
Alexandria, 1914-18. **Dakin MSS.**
Leaflets, etc., referring to recruitment and anti-conscription campaigns,
1914-18. **Trades Council.**
Album of news-cuttings regarding Bristol and WWI, especially the
treatment of wounded soldiers.

WORLD WAR II

Official: war diary, 1939-45; indexes to ARP and Home Security circulars; operational guide; and news-cuttings of the Emergency Committee, 1939-45.
Committees: ARP, minutes, 1941-5, and deed and agreements, 1938-42; Emergency (Civil Defence), minutes, 1939-45; West Bristol Defence, minutes, 1941-2; and Lord Mayor's War Services, minutes, 1939-45, and correspondence, receipts, and payments, 1947-52.
German invasion map of the Bristol area, *c.* 1940.
Prof. C. M. MacInnes (1891-1972), documents relating to various aspects of his work during and in connection with WWII. MacInnes served as Emergency Information Officer for the City of Bristol, 1941-5, and wrote *The British Empire at War* (1941) and *Bristol at War* (1962).

Bromley Public Libraries, Central Library, BROMLEY, Kent BR1 1EX

WORLD WAR II

Civil Defence records: bomb maps of 'P' Division and the Orpington UDC area; administrative and operational records for Beckenham, Bromley, Orpington and Penge, 1939-45, two boxes; and W. T. Redgrave, 'Warden's Service in Bromley', ts., 1971.
Home Guard records: various pamphlet histories of local units, some in duplicated ts.; and Col. F. W. Chamberlain, papers as commander of 'P' Division, Home Guard (access restricted until cataloguing is complete).
Royal Observer Corps records: Bromley HQ Control papers; and J. F. Wilson, 'Royal Observer Corps: a brief history . . . and some memories of the Bromley Group No. 19', ts., 1975.

Suffolk Record Office, Bury St. Edmunds Branch, Schoolhall Street, BURY ST. EDMUNDS, Suffolk IP33 1RX

WORLD WAR I

Alice Frances Theorora Harvey, Marchioness of Bristol, scrapbook labelled 'War Scrap Book 1914-1918'. **816/5.**
Roll of Honour, 1914-18. **D12/21/1.**
National Service, local tribunals' applications for exemption, 1916-18. **D12/22.**

WORLD WAR II

13th Essex (35th GPO) Battalion HQ, nominal roll of members of E Company, Bury St. Edmunds. **D12/2/3.**

C. Dudley Bright, Observer Officer, No. 14 Group Centre, Royal Observer Corps. Narrative history, 1937-45, with organisation chart and Air Ministry 'Stand Down' order, 8 May 1945. **D12/2/7.**

Suffolk Home Guard, 2nd Battalion, records, 1939-45. **598.**

Suffolk Home Guard, 2nd (Bury St. Edmunds) Battalion, nominal roll, 30 December 1944. **D12/2/1.**

Suffolk Home Guard, 3rd Battalion, nominal roll at stand down, 1945. **D12/2/2.**

Files relating to ARP, evacuation and other matters, 1939-45. **616.**

Civil Defence papers, including report on air raids on Norwich, 1942, and a combined Civil and Military Defence scheme for Bury St. Edmunds, 1942. **676.**

ARP, Bury St. Edmunds Control Centre, in and out messages, June 1942 – February 1945. **D12/4/1.**

Borough Defence, information officers, 1939-45. **D12/7.**

Women's Auxiliary Service, 1939-45. **D12/11.**

Letter of 20 April 1941 from Field-Marshal Lord Wilson to Bury St. Edmunds Borough Council. **665.**

Suffolk Regimental Association, The Keep, Gibraltar Barracks, BURY ST. EDMUNDS, Suffolk

The material held by the Association is largely uncatalogued and may be seen by appointment only. All records listed below relate to the Suffolk Regiment unless otherwise indicated. Enquiries should be made to the Regimental Secretary.

Army Lists, Suffolk Regiment, 1889-1950.

WORLD WAR I

Cambridgeshire Regiment, 1st Battalion, war diary, 1 March 1915 – 10 May 1919, and papers relating to the regiment, 1914-18.

2nd Battalion, war diary, 4 August 1914 – 30 April 1919; mobilisation orders; war diary, March 1915 – March 1916; operation orders and report on battle for Infantry Hill, Mondy-le Freux, 12 – 19 June 1916; and desiderata of the battalion's WWI participation.

8th Battalion, maps of Lille-Ostend, WWI.

Lt. Huffield, 2nd Battalion, war diary, August 1916 – December 1917.

Lt. Col. A. Taylor, 2nd Battalion, war diaries, 1914-18.
Capt. E. F. Ladward, 2nd Battalion, war diary, March 1915 — March 1916.
Lt. Col. Frederick W. Turner, 4th Battalion, personal diary, 2 August 1914 — 21 May 1916.

WORLD WAR II

2nd Battalion, digest of service, especially concerning the Arakan and Burma campaigns; and maps of Kohima, Imphal, etc., 1944.
Minutes of mass meetings, 1939-45.
Translation of the diary of a Japanese POW.
Copy of a diary written by Mr Grant entitled 'My Escape from Singapore', written by 2nd Lt. Anindell and Privates Fox and Martin, 4th Battalion, with notes by CSM Quinn.
CSM James Leatherland, history of the Suffolk Regiment at D-day, Sword Beach.

Gwynedd Archives Service, Caernarvon Area Record Office, County Offices, CAERNARVON, Gwynedd LL55 1SH

Anglesey, Caernarvonshire, Merioneth and Montgomeryshire Territorial and Auxiliary Forces Association, minutes and financial records, 1907-68.

WORLD WAR I

Vaynol Papers, records of the Caernarvonshire Motor Battalion (Caernarvonshire Volunteer Regiment), 1914-18.
Mariah Chapel Records, lists of servicemen who were members of the Chapel, 1916-18, prepared for sending parcels.
Acting Sgt. D. Arthur Jones, diary in Welsh describing journey aboard HM Army Transport *Nestor* and German prize ship *Huntsgreen*, from England to India, December 1916 — March 1917.
Caernarvon Borough, soldiers' bathing parade record book, 1917-18.

WORLD WAR II

Caernarvonshire Home Guard, 3rd Battalion, papers, 1940-5.
Caernarvon Borough, WVS correspondence and papers mainly concerning comforts for troops, 1940-4; and minute book of various

committees, including Evacuation, ARP and Reconstruction, 1944.
Menai Bridge UDC, five files and vols. relating to ARP and evacuation, 1939-47.
Amlwich UDC, 26 files relating to billeting, evacuation, Home Guard, Civil Defence, ARP, etc., 1938-57.
Holyhead UDC, nine files relating to billeting, evacuation, ARP, the POW Camp Hostel at Llangefni, Territorial Army, etc., 1939-45.
Twrcelyn RDC, 11 files relating to evacuation, 1940-50.
Valley RDC, eight files relating to proposed Anti-aircraft artillery camp at Llanwyfa, billeting, etc., 1939-54.
Anglesey CC, two vols. and one file relating *inter alia* to war zone courts.
Llanfairfechan UDC, 13 files and books relating *inter alia* to ARP and evacuation, 1939-48.
Penmaenmawr UDC, 48 files relating *inter alia* to ARP, evacuation, the Ministry of War Transport, etc., 1938-53.
Criccieth UDC, two vols. relating to Civil Defence and ARP warnings received, 1939-41.
Bethesda UDC, four files relating to ARP, billeting, etc., 1938-54.
Portmadoc UDC, seven files relating to ARP and evacuation, etc., 1939-48.
Lleyn RDC, eight files relating to evacuation, POW hostels, ARP, TA, Women's Land Army, and war service, 1939-50.
Nant Conway RDC, 11 files relating to evacuation, 1940-50.
Gwyfrai RDC, 64 files relating to ARP and evacuation, 1939-46.
Dolgellau UDC, two files relating to WVS and the POW camp, Sattelite B Dolgellau, 1939-48.
Bala UDC, ten files relating to evacuation, deaths due to war operations, etc., 1938-50.
Barmouth UDC, 16 files relating to evacuation, refugees, ARP, civilian deaths, etc., 1938-52.
Penllyn RDC, 17 vols. and files relating to evacuation, refugees, ARP, Civil Defence, etc., 1939-46.
Deudraeth RDC, three letter books relating to evacuation, 1939-43.
Merioneth CC, six files relating to air attack structural protection, the Anti-aircraft practice camp at Tonfannau, evacuation, etc., 1939-53.

Royal Military College Museum, Sandhurst, CAMBERLEY, Surrey

Enquiries should be made to the Curator.

WORLD WARS I AND II

Captain George Paterson, 34th Sikh Pioneers. War diary and letters to his wife, covering service on the Western Front, August 1914 — March 1916; in Mesopotamia, April 1916 — August 1918; and Persia and India, August 1918 — September 1919. There are also press-cuttings and photographs.

Maj. L. E. L. Maxwell, Hodson's Horse. Personal war diary, covering service in Iraq, October 1941 — April 1943; Syria, May 1943 — March 1944; Syria and Lebanon, March 1944 — April 1945; and extra-regimental employment in Persia, India, Singapore and repatriation to the UK, May 1945 — September 1946.

C. R. Pawsey, Deputy Commissioner, Naga Hills. Narrative and correspondence referring to events in Nagaland, including the battle of Kohima, 1941-5. Subjects covered include intelligence reports concerning Japanese and Indian National Army movements, relations with local tribesmen, liaison with USAAC posts, the Assam Rifles and the Labour Corps.

Staff College Library, CAMBERLEY, Surrey

Operations, orders, and administrative material relating to British land operations in France and Belgium 1940, the Mediterranean and Middle East 1940-5, North-West Europe 1944-5, and the Far East 1941-5.

These are typewritten and/or duplicated reports of operations which are also to be found in the Imperial War Museum. The collection obtains 28 boxes, which contain 5-10 pieces and about 50 individual pieces, most of which is located in the Public Record Office in original form. This collection contains no diaries, no photographic material and no personal material.

CAMBRIDGE

As one of the leading university cities in Britain, Cambridge is exceptionally rich in manuscript and documentary material for modern British history. Although the University Library and various college libraries hold important papers for leading figures of modern times, the centre of contemporary documentation at Cambridge is Churchill College, which holds the voluminous personal papers of arguably the greatest and certainly the best documented of public figures in modern British history, Winston Churchill. For a discussion of and short guide to Cambridge libraries, see A. N. L. Munby, *Cambridge College Libraries* (Cambridge, Heffer, 1962).

Churchill College, CAMBRIDGE CB3 0DS

One of the newest colleges of the university, Churchill College has sought to draw together the papers of other leading figures from Churchill's time and now possesses a substantial collection. Many of the deposits have restrictions on their use, and researchers must first write to the Keeper of the Archives to learn any conditions of access. Permission from the Keeper is necessary for admission to the archives.

Winston Spencer Churchill (1874-1965)
Churchill was Prime Minister, 1940-5 and 1951-5; 1st Lord of the Admiralty, 1911-15 and 1939-40; Chancellor of the Duchy of Lancaster, 1915; Minister of Munitions, 1917-18; and held other Cabinet offices in the pre-war and inter-war periods.

The papers are closed to the public until completion of the multi-volume biography begun by Randolph Churchill and continued by Martin Gilbert. They are divided into three categories. 'Chartwell' covers the period to 27 July 1945, the end of Churchill's first term as Prime Minister. 'Churchill' covers the period from 27 July 1945 to his death in 1965. 'Premier' covers the papers of the Prime Minister's private office, 1940-5, and are in the possession of the Public Record Office which will retain them in perpetuity. The current principle of access is that those papers with which Martin Gilbert is finished may be viewed on a restricted basis.

A. V. Alexander
Albert Victor Alexander, Earl Alexander of Hillsborough (1885-1965). 1st Lord of the Admiralty, 1929-31 and 1940-6. 61 boxes of political papers, 1920-64.

C. R. Attlee
Clement Richard Attlee, Earl Attlee (1883-1967). Leader of the Labour Party, 1935-56; Deputy Prime Minister, 1941-5; and Prime Minister, 1945-51. Correspondence with Winston Churchill, 1941-5, and drafts for his autobiography, As It Happened.

Rear Admiral T. P. H. Beamish (1874-1951)
Naval Assistant to the 1st Sea Lord, August — November 1914; command of HMS Invincible, November 1914 — March 1915, including the battle of the Falkland Islands; command of HMS Cordelia, April 1915 — May 1917, including the battle of Jutland; and Admiralty Staff, 1917-19. Eight boxes of papers, with special conditions of access.

Ernest Bevin (1881-1951)
Minister of Labour and National Service, 1940-5. 36 boxes of Ministry of Labour papers, 1940-5.

J. Burgon Bickersteth
Academic in Canada and associate of many British politicians and civil servants. Xerox copies of correspondence and reports to Sir Maurice Hankey, Secretary to the Cabinet, on Canadian affairs, 1932-40.

Gen. Sir Charles Bonham-Carter
WWI diaries, and correspondence and papers as Governor of Malta, 1936-40.

Reginald Brett
Reginald Brett, 2nd Viscount Esher (1852-1930). Member of CID and intimate of Edward VII and George V. Diaries, correspondence and papers, 1868-1934.

Lawrence Franklin Burgis (1892-1972)
WWI service with the Black Watch, and Assistant Secretary of the War Cabinet, 1918 and 1939-45. Memoirs.

Sir Alexander George Montagu Cadogan (1884-1968)
Permanent Under-Secretary for Foreign Affairs, 1938-46. 20 boxes of diaries and papers, 1909-66.

Sir James Chadwick (1891-1974)
Nuclear physicist. 36 boxes of scientific and personal papers, with special conditions of access.

Group Capt. Malcolm Grahame Christie (1881-1971)
Air engineer and traveller in Europe, especially Germany, 1933-40. Eight boxes of correspondence and reports, 1928-44.

Hugh Clausen (1888-1972)
Naval armaments engineer. Technical papers and lectures, 1938-69.

Sir John Douglas Cockcroft (1897-1967)
Nuclear physicist. Chief Superintendent, Air Defence, Research and Development Establishment, Ministry of Supply, 1941-4; and Director, Atomic Energy Division, National Research Council of Canada, 1944-6.

Capt. John Creswell, RN
Naval historian and author. Naval papers, 1912-70.

Henry Page Croft
Henry Page Croft, 1st Baron Croft of Bournemouth (1881-1947). Commanded the 68th Infantry Brigade at the Somme, 1916; Parliamentary Under-Secretary of State for War, 1940-5; and a close associate of Winston Churchill. Political papers, 1908-47.

Sir Philip Cunliffe-Lister
Sir Philip Cunliffe-Lister, 1st Earl of Swinton (1884-1972). Army service, 1914-17; Joint Secretary of the Ministry of National Service, 1917-18; Secretary of State for Air, 1935-8; Cabinet Minister resident in West Africa, 1942-4; and Minister of Civil Aviation, 1944-5. Personal and political papers, 1914-70.

Admiral Andrew Browne Cunningham
Admiral of the Fleet Andrew Browne Cunningham, 2nd Viscount Cunningham of Hyndhope (1883-1963). Deputy Chief of Naval Staff, 1938-9; C-in-C Mediterranean, 1939-42; Head of British Admiralty delegation to Washington, 1942; Naval C-in-C, Expeditionary Force, North Africa, 1942; and 1st Sea Lord and Chief of Naval Staff, 1943-6. Four boxes of correspondence, and material from various sources for a biography covering 1928-67.

Admiral Sir Charles Daniel (b. 1893)
Service in HMS *Orion,* 1912-18, including the battle of Jutland. One box of diaries of the Second Battle Squadron, 1914-16.

Admiral Sir Reginald Plunkett-Ernle-Erle (1880-1967)
Service with the Grand Fleet in HMS *Lion,* 1914-18, including action at Heligoland, Dogger Bank and Jutland; C-in-C, The Nore, 1939-41; Home Guard, 1941-3; and Commodore of Ocean Convoys, 1943-5. 28 boxes of naval and political papers, 1902-65.

Admiral Sir John Hereward Edelsten (1891-1966)
Senior Naval Officer, operations against Italian Somaliland, 1940-1; Chief of Staff to C-in-C Mediterranean, 1941-2; Assistant Chief of Naval Staff (U-boat warfare and trade), 1942-4; and Rear Admiral (Destroyers), British Pacific Fleet, 1945. Two boxes of papers, 1931-52.

Admiral Sir Ralph Edwards (1901-63)
Midshipman with Grand Fleet, 1917; and Chief of Staff, Eastern Fleet and Captain of HMNZS *Gambia,* WWII. Four boxes of diaries and papers.

Paul Einzig (b. 1897)
Economist; Political Correspondent, *Financial News,* 1939-45; and author of many publications relating to international affairs, economic warfare, and WWII. 32 boxes of papers.

Air Vice-Marshal Sir Thomas Walker Elmhirst (b. 1895)
Service with HMS *Indomitable* in the Dardanelles and at Dogger Bank, 1914-15; RNAS, 1915-18; Air Commodore, HQ Fighter Command, 1940, during battle of Britain; AOC RAF, Egypt and the Desert campaigns, 1941-2; AOA, TAF North Africa, 1943; and Second in Command, British Air Forces Northwest Europe, Normandy-Germany campaign, 1944-5. 17 boxes of memoirs and papers, 1904-64.

Farrelly Papers
Frank Farrelly, driver in the Royal Engineers, account of the evacuation of Dunkirk, 1940. Sister Francis Mary (Farrelly), account of internment by the Japanese in Borneo, 1942.

Sir William Farren (1892-1970)
Aeronautical engineer. Director of Technical Development, Ministry of Aircraft Production, 1940-1; and Director, Royal Aircraft Establishment, Farnborough, 1941-6. Five boxes of papers, with special conditions of access.

Maj. H. Fowle, RA
Journal of a voyage to Malta, 1941.

Edward Francis Williams
Edward Francis Williams, Baron Francis-Williams (1903-70). Writer and journalist, he was Controller of News and Censorship at the Ministry of Information, 1941-5. 42 boxes of MSS and ts. published works, and correspondence, 1960-70. Special conditions of access.

Godfrey Alexander French
Four boxes of naval papers.

Admiral John Henry Godfrey (1888-1971)
Service in the Dardanelles, 1915; on staff of the C-in-C Mediterranean, 1916-17; Director of Naval Intelligence, 1939-42; and Flag Officer Commanding Royal Indian Navy, 1943-6. Two boxes of memoirs.

Capt. Russell Grenfell, RN
Three boxes of correspondence and drafts for his works on naval history.

Sir Percy James Grigg (1890-1964)
Service with Royal Garrison Artillery, 1915-18; Permanent Under-Secretary of State for War, 1939-42; and Secretary of State for War, 1942-5. 29 boxes of official and personal papers, 1901-64.

Admiral Sir (William) Reginald Hall (1870-1943)
Director of the Intelligence Division, Admiralty War Staff, 1914-18. One box of memoirs and papers, 1915-33.

Sir Maurice Hankey
Sir Maurice P. A. Hankey, 1st Baron Hankey of the Chart (1877-1963). Secretary to the War Cabinet, 1916, and to the Imperial War Cabinet, 1917-18; Secretary to the Cabinet, 1919-38; Minister without Portfolio, 1939-40; and Paymaster General, 1941-2. 135 boxes of official and personal papers, 1890-1963.

Capt. G. C. Harper, RN (1894-1962)
Three boxes of diaries, 1914-20.

Theodor Harris, alias Feodor Minoŕsky
Diaries and memoirs of the French Foreign Legion, 1940-2.

Brig. Gen. Sir Harold Hartley (1878-1972)
Chemist. Chemical Adviser to the 3rd Army, 1915-17; Assistant Director, Gas Services, GHQ France, 1917-18; and Controller of Chemical Warfare Department, Ministry of Munitions, 1918-19. 385 boxes of personal, official and scientific papers, 1890-72, with special conditions of access.

Sir Ralph (George) Hawtrey (b. 1879)
Economist. Director of Financial Enquiries, Ministry of the Treasury, 1919-45; and author of many publications relating to international economic matters. 60 boxes of papers.

Prof. A. V. Hill (b. 1886)
Physiologist. Attaché with British Embassy in Washington, 1940; member of the War Cabinet Scientific Advisory Committee, 1940-6; and member of various air defence committees. 12 boxes of memoirs, personal and scientific papers.

Wing Commander Sir (Eric) John Hodsoll (b. 1894)
Assistant Secretary of State, Home Office, for ARP, 1935-7; and Inspector-General of Civil Defence, 1938-47. 37 boxes of Civil Defence papers and other official papers, 1930-65.

Admiral Sir Horace Hood (1870-1916)
Naval Secretary to 1st Lord of Admiralty, 1914; Admiral in Command, Dover Patrol, 1914; and Admiral in Command, 3rd Battle Cruiser Squadron, 1915-16, killed at Jutland. Six boxes of naval and family papers.

H. Hyde Montgomery (b. 1907)
Author. British Army Staff, USA, 1942-4; SHAEF, 1944; and Allied Commission for Australia, 1944-5. Seven boxes of papers.

Sir Thomas Inskip
Sir Thomas Inskip, 1st Viscount Caldecote (1876-1940). Minister for the Co-ordination of Defence, 1938-40. Extracts from his diaries, 1938-40.

R. W. A. Ivermee, RAF
Photographs of the surrender of the German High Seas Fleet and Allied intervention in North Russia, 1918-19.

Wing Commander Sir Archibald James (b. 1893)
Memoirs of the RFC and RAF expansion, 1931-6.

Storm Jameson, Mrs Guy Chapman
Five letters from Sir Basil Liddell Hart, 1943-68.

Admiral Lord Keyes
Admiral of the Fleet Roger John Brownlow Keyes, 1st Baron Keyes (1872-1945). Commodore in charge of Submarine Service, 1910-14; Chief of Staff, Eastern Mediterranean Squadron, 1915; Grand Fleet Captain and Rear Admiral, 1916-17; Director of Plans, Admiralty, 1917; Acting Vice-Admiral in command of the Dover Patrol, 1918; commended operations against Zeebrugge and Ostend, 23 April 1918; Special Liaison Officer to the King of Belgium, 1940; and Director of Combined Operations, 1940-1. 96 boxes of papers, 1905-45, with special conditions of access.

Capt. H. N. Lake, RN
Accounts of the battle of the Atlantic, 1940 and 1943.

Field-Marshal Frederic Rudolph Lambart
10th Earl of Cavan (1865-1946). Command of the 4th (Guards) Brigade in France and Flanders, 1914; Guards Division in Flanders, 1915; 14th Corps in France, 1916-17; and all British troops in Italy, 1917-18. Memoirs.

Sir John Lennard-Jones (1894-1954)
Physicist. Flying Officer, RFC, WWI, and Chief Superintendent of
Armament and Research, Ministry of Supply, 1940-5. Four boxes of
personal and scientific papers, with special conditions of access.

Sir Shane Leslie (1885-1971)
Author of several memoirs on generals and a book on Jutland. Special
conditions of access.

Sir George Ambrose Lloyd (1879-1941)
Sir George Ambrose Lloyd, 1st Baron Lloyd of Dolobran (1879-1941).
Secretary of State for the Colonies and Leader of the House of Lords,
1940-1. 148 boxes of political and private correspondence, 1879-1940.

Oliver Lyttelton
Oliver Lyttelton, 1st Viscount Chandos (1893-1972). Adjutant, 3rd
Battalion, Grenadier Guards, 1915-18; Brigade Major, 4th Guards
Brigade, 1918; and Minister of State resident in the Middle East,
1941-2. Two boxes of WWI letters and correspondence from Egypt,
1941-2.

Reginald McKenna (1863-1943)
Secretary of State for Home Affairs, 1911-15, and Chancellor of the
Exchequer, 1915-16. 17 boxes of political correspondence, 1906-20.

Donald MacLachan (1908-71)
Author and journalist. One box of material for his *Room 39: A Study
in Naval Intelligence* (1968).

Commander A. A. F. MacLiesh, RN
Gallipoli diaries, letters and photographs, 1914-16.

H. D. R. Margesson
Henry David Reginald Margesson, 1st Viscount Margesson of Rugby
(1890-1965). Chief Government Whip, 1913-40, and Secretary of State
for War, 1940-2. One box of political correspondence, 1924-50.

Capt. C. Marsden, RN
Two boxes of memorials of HMS *Southampton* at Jutland.

Sir David Maxwell Fyfe
Sir David Maxwell Fyfe, 1st Earl of Kilmuir (1900-67). Solicitor
General, 1942-5, and Deputy Chief Prosecutor at the Nuremberg Trials.
27 boxes of personal and political papers, 1922-65.

Prof. Lise Meitner (1878-1968)
Nuclear physicist. Personal and scientific papers, with special conditions of access.

Admiral G. B. Middleton
Two letters to his wife describing D-day, 1944.

Admiral Sir Dudley Burton Napier North (1881-1961)
Served in the battle cruiser *New Zealand* at Heligoland and commanded her at the Dogger Bank and Jutland; Admiral Commanding North Atlantic Station, 1939-40; and Flag Officer-in-Charge, Great Yarmouth, 1942-5. Four boxes of naval papers.

Sir Eric Clare Edmund Phipps (1875-1945)
Diplomatist. 1st Secretary to the British Embassy in Paris 1916-19; British Secretary to the Paris Peace Conference, 1919; Assistant Secretary at the Foreign Office, 1919-20; and Ambassador Extraordinary and Plenipotentiary at Berlin, 1933-7, and Paris, 1937-9. 23 boxes of diplomatic papers, 1921-40.

A. J. H. Pollen (1866-1937)
Inventor, naval engineer and journalist. 20 boxes of technical papers and articles, 1901-30.

Vice-Admiral Sir (Arthur) Francis Pridham (b. 1886)
Gunnery officer in HMS *Weymouth, Shannon* and *Marlborough* during WWI; Flag Officer, Humber Area, 1939-40; and President of the Ordnance Board, 1941-5. Memoirs, 1886-1945, and war diaries, 1914-19.

Field-Marshal H. S. Rawlinson
Field-Marshal Henry Seymour Rawlinson, 1st Baron Rawlinson of Trent (1864-1925). Commanded the 7th Division and 3rd Cavalry Division in Belgium, 1914; 4th Corps, 1914-15; 1st Army, 1916-18; British Military Representative on the Supreme War Council, 1918; and commander of the 4th Army, 1918. Seven boxes of diaries and papers, 1914-19.

Admiral of the Fleet Sir John Michael de Robeck (1862-1928)
Second in command and then commander, Naval Forces in the Dardanelles, 1915; commander of the 9th Cruiser Squadron in the North Atlantic, 1914-15; and Vice-Admiral of the 2nd Battle Squadron, 1916-19. 30 boxes of personal and naval papers, 1875-1927.

Capt. Stephen Wentworth Roskill (b. 1903)
Historian. Historical and family papers, 1912-70, with special conditions of access.

Arthur Michael Samuel
Arthur Michael Samuel, 1st Baron Mancroft (1872-1942). Assistant to the Director of Army Contracts, War Office, 1914-15, and Staff Assistant, Ministry of Munitions, 1915-16. Press-cuttings, books and speeches, 1916-41.

Basil Sanderson
Basil Sanderson, 1st Baron Sanderson of Ayot (1894-71). GSO 3, 1st Infantry Division; Brigade Major, 126th Infantry Brigade; and GSO 2, 41st Infantry Division. WWI diaries.

Capt. R. A. I. Sarell, RN
RNAS daily reports, June 1915.

George Saunders (1859-1922)
Correspondent for *The Times* in Berlin, 1897-1908; similarly in Paris, 1908-14; and served in the Department of Political Information and other war departments, 1915-18.

S. J. Sime
Petty Officer, naval memoirs, 1928-45.

Sir Archibald Sinclair
Sir Archibald Henry MacDonald Sinclair, 1st Viscount Thurso (1890-1970). Leader of the Liberal Party, 1935-45, and Secretary of State for Air, 1940-5. 197 boxes of papers, with special conditions of access.

Admiral of the Fleet Sir James Fowne Somerville (1882-1949)
Service in the Dardanelles, 1915-16; communications officer to various admirals during WWI; OC Force H at Gibraltar, 1940-2; C-in-C Eastern Fleet, 1942-4; and head of the British Admiralty Delegation to Washington, 1944-5. 24 boxes of naval and personal papers, 1891-1949, with special conditions of access.

Maj. Gen. Sir Edward Spears (1886-1974)
Head of the British Military Mission to Paris, 1917-20; Prime Minister's personal representative with the French Prime Minister and Minister of Defence, May — June 1940; head of the British mission to Gen. Charles de Gaulle, June 1940; and head of missions to Syria and Lebanon, 1942-4. Papers, with special conditions of access.

Sir Cecil Spring Rice (1859-1918)
Diplomatist. Official and personal papers, 1860-1918.

Capt. C. S. B. Swinley (b. 1898)
Service in HMS *New Zealand*, 1916-18; at evacuation of Odessa, 1919; command of HMS *Codrington* and the Dover Patrol destroyers, 1939-40; various ship commands, 1940-2; Chief of Staff to the Admiral commanding Malta, 1942; and Director of Service Conditions, 1943-5. 53 boxes of papers, with special conditions of access.

Sir George Paget Thomson (b. 1892)
Nuclear physicist. Chairman of the 1st British Committee on Atomic Energy and Scientific Adviser to the Air Ministry, 1943-4. One box of MAUD Committee papers, with special conditions of access.

Admiral W. Tompkinson (1877-1971)
Six boxes of naval papers.

Robert Vansittart
Robert Gilbert Vansittart, 1st Baron Vansittart of Denham (1881-1957). Permanent Under-Secretary of State for Foreign Affairs, 1930-8, and Chief Diplomatic Adviser to the Foreign Secretary, 1938-41. 11 boxes of papers.

William Douglas Weir
William Douglas Weir, 1st Viscount Weir (1877-1959). Scottish Director of Munitions, 1915-16; Controller of Aeronautical Supplies and member of the Air Board, 1917-18; Director General of Aircraft Production, 1918; Secretary of State and President of the Air Council, 1918; Director General of Explosives, Ministry of Supply, 1939; and Chairman of the Tank Board, 1942. 89 boxes of papers.

Group Capt. Hugh Alexander Williamson (b. 1885)
Service in WWI, and Calshot Pembroke Dock and Air Ministry, 1939-43. Four boxes of memoirs and naval aviation papers, with special conditions of access.

Sir Henry Urmston Willink (1894-1973)
Service with the RFA in France, 1914-19, and Minister of Health, 1943-5. Two boxes of personal papers and memoirs, with special conditions of access.

Prof. C. T. R. Wilson (1869-1959)
Physicist. Two boxes of papers relating to studies of the effects of thunderstorms on balloons and airships, 1918-40.

Leonard Wincott
Naval mutineer, 1931, memoirs.

Edward Wood
Edward Frederick Linley Wood, 1st Earl of Halifax (1881-1959). Secretary of State for Foreign Affairs, 1938-40, and British Ambassador to Washington, 1941-6. Two reels on microfilm of part of the Hickleton papers.

Economics Faculty Library, Sidgwick Avenue, CAMBRIDGE CB3 9DA

John Maynard Keynes Papers
Economic papers of John Maynard Keynes, Baron Keynes (1883-1940). Joined the Treasury in 1915 and became head of the External Finances Department in 1917; adviser to the Treasury on war finance, 1940; and played a leading role in economic negotiations with the United States and at Bretton Woods, 1944.

King's College, CAMBRIDGE

John Maynard Keynes Papers
Literary papers of John Maynard Keynes.

Trinity College, CAMBRIDGE

Edwin Montagu Papers
Papers of Edwin Samuel Montagu (1879-1924). Financial Secretary to the Treasury, 1914-16; Minister of Munitions, 1916; and Secretary of State for India, 1917-22. Six boxes of papers mostly relating to his work at the India Office, 1910-14 and 1917-22, but also some other papers regarding the Cabinet Committee on Food Supplies, 1914-16, memoranda and correspondence with David Lloyd George, 1917-22, etc.

Richard Austen Butler Papers
Richard Austen Butler, Baron Butler of Saffron Walden, Under-

Secretary of State for Foreign Affairs, 1938-41, and Minister of Education, 1941-5. He ultimately intends to house his papers at Trinity College.

University Library, West Road, CAMBRIDGE CB3 9DR

There is no published catalogue of the modern manuscript holdings of the University Library but see A. E. B. Owen, *Summary Guide to Accessions of Western Manuscripts since 1867* (Cambridge, University Library, 1966). The following is a listing of the major collections which are relevant to the two world wars, together with some miscellaneous items, but is not comprehensive.

Edgar Abraham Papers
Papers of Edgar Gaston Furtado Abraham (1880-1955). Service with the Royal Garrison Artillery in France; Assistant Secretary, War Cabinet, January – May 1918; Supreme War Council, Versailles, May 1918-19; and Supreme Council, Paris Peace Conference, 1919-20. The papers are mainly sets of minutes and memoranda of the War Cabinet, Supreme War Council and the Paris Peace Conference, with little unofficial or personal material.

Stanley Baldwin Papers
Papers of Stanley Baldwin, 1st Earl Baldwin of Bewdley (1867-1947). Joint Financial Secretary to the Treasury, June 1917 – April 1919; President of the Board of Trade, 1921-2; Chancellor of the Exchequer, 1922-3; and Prime Minister, 1923 – January 1924, November 1924-9, and June 1935 – May 1937. The collection is mainly concerned with his first two administrations and contains only three miscellaneous items prior to 1923. There is no material regarding his work at the Treasury, no family or personal papers, and no official or departmental papers for 1935-7. See A. E. B. Owen, *Handlist of the Political Papers of Stanley Baldwin, 1st Earl Baldwin of Bewdley* (Cambridge, University Library, 1973).

Marquess of Crewe Papers
Papers of Robert Offley Ashburton Crewe-Milnes, 1st Marquess of Crewe (1858-1945). Lord President of the Council, 1905-8 and 1915-16; Lord Privy Seal, 1908 and 1912-15; and Secretary of State for India, 1910-15. 150 boxes of material including papers relating to the Dardanelles Commission, Cabinet committees, Indian affairs, and much printed material.

Hardinge of Penshurst Papers
Papers of Charles Hardinge, 1st Baron Hardinge of Penshurst (1858-1944). Permanent Under-Secretary of State for Foreign Affairs, 1906-10 and 1916-20, and Viceroy of India, 1910-16. The collection contains *inter alia* important and unduplicated memoranda regarding the peace negotiations. See N. J. Hancock, *Handlist of Hardinge Papers at the University Library, Cambridge* (Cambridge, University Library, 1968).

Sir Charles Des Graz Papers
Papers of Sir Charles Louis Des Graz (1860-1940). Minister to Serbia, 1914-20. There is a diary for 1914-16, and correspondence and papers, 1893-1940.

Jan Christian Smuts
Microfilms of private papers of Jan Christian Smuts (1870-1950). Minister without Portfolio and member of the War Cabinet, 1917-19, and Prime Minister of South Africa, 1919-24 and 1939-48. The papers consist mainly of private correspondence, some parliamentary papers, papers referring to the South African National Party, 1912-34, and the United Party, as well as writings, speeches and broadcasts. **Ref. Microfilm 666-766, 773-782, 832-854.**

Viscount Templewood Papers
Papers of Sir Samuel John Gurney Hoare, Viscount Templewood (1880-1959). Foreign Secretary, 1935; 1st Lord of the Admiralty, 1936-7; Home Secretary, 1937-9; Lord Privy Seal and member of the War Cabinet, 1939 — April 1940; and Ambassador to Spain on Special Mission, 1940-4. 115 boxes of material, including Cabinet papers, political papers, cuttings and scrapbooks.

Miscellaneous
Col. Edward Davenport Ridley (1883-1934). War diaries and letters, 1914-18. **Add. 7065-7070.**
Letters from servicemen to Mrs Prime of Cambridge, 1914-18. **Add. 7660.**
English translations of letters from Indian soldiers in Palestine, 1918. **Add. 6170.**

German Naval Archives
The University Library also holds on microfilm parts of the German Naval Archives. See *Catalogue of Selected Files of the German Naval Archives microfilmed at the Admiralty . . .*, two folio ts. vols. (London, 1959-64).

University Archives, c/o University Library, West Road,
CAMBRIDGE CB3 9DR

Wartime Administration
Papers relating to ARP, emergency arrangements, National Service, accommodation of London colleges in Cambridge, special courses for the armed forces and for American forces, the Hankey Radio Training Scheme, etc., 1939-46.

Cambridge South Asian Archive, Centre of South Asian
Studies, Laundress Lane, CAMBRIDGE CB2 1SD

The Cambridge South Asian Archive was established in 1967 by the Centre of South Asian Studies to collect the papers of those who had served during the period of British rule in the former Indian Empire and Ceylon. Prospective users must present an academic letter of introduction or other evidence of academic standing. The following entries were drawn from Mary Thatcher, ed., *Cambridge South Asian Archive* (London, Mansell, 1973). The archive contains many unpublished autobiographies of former colonial officials which touch upon the wars but only those of more direct importance have been included here.

Abraham Papers
Details of a tour made by Maj. W. E. V. Abraham in Burma, March 1942, when accompanying Gen. Alexander to Rangoon as liaison officer; various papers relating to the defence of Burma, 1939-45; budget papers, India, 1943-4; and papers on India during WWII.

Allsop Papers
Miscellaneous papers of F. Allsop: speeches and articles of Sir R. H. Dorman-Smith and F. Burton Leach; 'Blue print for Burma. Report by certain Conservative Members of Parliament on the future of Burma', December 1944; Khin Myo Chit, 'Three years under the Japanese', 1945; and confidential report of the District Administration (Reconstruction) Committee (Burma), Simla, 1944.

Anonymous Papers (2)
Various notes on the Frontier Corps of Scouts/Militia dealing with officers, ethnic composition of the units, equipment, and changes brought about by WWII.

Baker Papers
Letters and diaries of E. B. H. Baker who served in the Indian

administration, 1927-47. From 1940, Baker was Additional Secretary to the Governor of Bengal. His diaries for the war years contain detailed accounts of the progress of the war, defence measures, the effect of the war on India, and criticisms of the Viceregal Staff.

Barkeley Smith Papers
Memoirs of Rupert Barkeley Smith, 1908-22, including his experiences with Indians during WWI and the war's effect on them.

Bell Papers
Papers of J. M. G. Bell, Indian Civil Service, 1940-58. Items of possible interest are: tour diaries and notes made during tours in Chandpur, Kalimpong and Chittagong, 1940-3; secret report of July 1943 on civilian appreciation of the military situation on the Arakan front; report to Civil Defence Commissioners at Calcutta concerning the air raid on Chittagong, 20 December 1943; and several reports on Japanese atrocities.

Bor Papers
Dr N. L. Bor, Director of Assam Relief Measures. Ts. copy of a 47 pp. 'Report of Relief Measures in Assam', which was a result of the Japanese campaign of 1944.

Carter Papers
MS and ts. memoirs by M. O. Carter of the Chittagong District, including the political situation, 1942-3; the 1943 famine; and the war in 1944, especially the capture of Akyab.

Crofton Papers
Ts.197 pp. description of civil service life in India, 1925-47, by Lady Olive Crofton, including wartime life in India, WVS work, conditions for the soldiers and staff in the canteens on the Burma front, Wavell as Viceroy, etc.

Davis Papers
Letters and journals, 1915-47, of D. Davis, subaltern in 1/7th Hampshire Regiment, September 1914 — February 1919. The journals describe service in Aden, January — May 1918, including the fighting in the desert with Sheikh Othman.

Gimson Papers
Notes by C. Gimson, 1940-3, on the war in Manipur, the bombing of Imphal, civilian relations with the army, relief measures, etc.

Hailes Papers
Journals of Lt. Col. W. L. Hailes, 1914-40, describing *inter alia* his service in Mesopotamia, 1914-18, with good accounts of army life.

Hall Papers
Autobiography of Capt. G. F. Hall of the Public Works Department in Orissa and Bihar, 1911-47, containing some material on India during WWII, relations with the army, and refugees from Burma.

Hutchings Papers
Sir Robert Hutchings, Indian Civil Service, ts. report on the evacuation of Burma, 1942.

MacDonald Papers
Ts. 72 pp. account entitled 'Royal Indian naval coastal forces', 1942-5, by T. MacDonald, describing operations against the Japanese along the Burma coast, destruction of Myebon, anti-submarine activity, Arakan operations, the assault on Akyab, etc. There is another copy in the India Office Manuscripts, **Photo Eur. 91** (see p. 134).

MacLean Papers
A. MacLean, several reports of the Evacuee Welfare and Rehabilitation Department, Government of Burma, 1942-5; one folder and one notebook of letters of people who walked out of Burma; confidential letter and questionnaire from the Chief Secretary's Office, Government of Burma, 19 August 1942, on the civil aspect of war in Burma; and various cuttings on the war in Burma.

Martin Papers
Memoirs of O. H. Martin, Indian Civil Service, 1913-45, including his service with the 14th Lancers, Indian Cavalry in Iraq, 1917-18, and his post as Chief Secretary to the Governor of Bengal during WWII. The later section of the memoirs deals with the outbreak of war, deficiencies of the Indian Army, terrorism, the economic effects of the war, Burma refugees, the Bengal famine, etc.

Pawsey Papers
Six boxes of papers, cuttings and pamphlets of Sir Charles Pawsey. **Box 3** contains various articles and cuttings on Burma and Assam in WWII.

Rule Papers
Diary of Lt. Col. D. G. Rule, January 1914 – June 1915, in the

Northwest Frontier Province, including the recruiting, training and sending of regiments to the war, especially Egypt.

Stephens Papers

The papers of I. M. Stephens, containing *inter alia* a ts. report by. Norman Devine, staff reporter and correspondent of *The Statesman,* on a press conference of 9 April 1943 by Lt. Gen. N. M. Irwin, Commander of the Eastern Army. This occurred amidst a controversy about the Arakan campaign, described on pp. 112-21 of I. M. Stephens, *Monsoon Morning.*

Stewart Papers

These papers contain notes by C. Gimson on WWII in Manipur and an extract from the Manipur State Administration Report for 1943-4.

Taylor Papers

Letters and diary of Mrs. A. W. Taylor, wife of the civil surgeon of Manipur, Cachar and Burma, 1940-2. There is also a letter from Dr Taylor to his wife, 17 April 1942, from Kalewa, Burma, concerning cholera among the refugees, the general health management of Kalewa, the Japanese advance, and the military occupation.

Tottenham Papers

Memoirs of Sir Richard Tottenham discussing *inter alia* the Indian National Congress and WWII, the Andaman Islands during the war, the Indian National Army, and the Viceroys and Commanders-in-Chief, Willingdon, Linlithgow, Wavell, Birdwood and Chetwode.

Whyte Papers

19 pp. of notes, comments and criticisms of the evacuation of Burma scheme, 19 March – 16 May 1942, by V. C. Whyte; sketch map of the evacuation area; two pages of accounts for part of the evacuation; various notes and instructions to evacuation personnel; and cuttings relating to the evacuation.

Wiles Papers

The papers of Sir Gilbert Wiles, containing minutes of a meeting held at the Secretariat, 7 June 1940, about the setting up of District War Committees, Government of Bombay, Home Department. There are also confidential telegrams from June 1940, on the same subject and the war situation.

Williamson Papers
European War, financial adjustments with the War Office. Review of the general situation by W. Robinson, 16 October 1916.

Cambridgeshire Record Office, Shire Hall, Castle Hill, CAMBRIDGE CB3 0AP

Cambridgeshire Territorial and Auxiliary Forces Association, minutes, 1908-68, and annual reports, 1914-19.

WORLD WAR I

Swaffham Prior, Roll of Honour, notes and correspondence regarding serving men, 1915-29, and Zeppelins over villages, 1915-16. **P150/3/10, 13.**
Royston and District Volunteer Training Corps, papers relating to Thriplow, Fowlmere and Foxton detachments. **R53/4/193.**
Volunteer Training Corps, defence of Cambridgeshire papers, 1915-16. **R58/6/8.**
Volunteer Training Corps, register of enrolled men. **P17/28/2.**

WORLD WAR II

Cambridgeshire Regiment, minutes of meetings on POWs, 1944-6; files, 1929 and 1939-46; and history of the regiment in 1939-42 and 1945.
Home Guard, 4th Cambridge Battalion, papers, 1939-44.
Duxford Invasion Committee, minutes and correspondence, 1941-3.
County Council, ARP, papers and instructions, 1938-43.
Firewatchers' log books, St. Paul's, Cambridge, 1941-4.

The Buffs Regimental Museum, Poor Priests' Hospital, Stour Street, CANTERBURY, Kent

The Museum contains two war diaries of the Buffs Regiment kept by Col. Bertram R. Mitford:
86 Vol. V, 1 January 1914 — 26 December 1915.
87 Vol. VI, 1 January 1916 — 31 December 1917.
Enquiries should be made to the Curator of the City of Canterbury Museums.

*Cathedral Archives and Library, CANTERBURY, Kent
CT1 2EG*

WORLD WAR II

Canterbury Corporation records: Emergency Committee minutes,
1939-46; Civil Defence records, 1939-45; casualty records; and Civil
Defence Centre, working records.

Cardiff Central Library, The Hayes, CARDIFF CF1 2QU

WORLD WAR I

South Wales Borderers, MS names and addresses of officers and warrant
officers who served with the 6th Battalion (Pioneers) on active service
in France and Flanders, 1915-18. **2.1201.**
Monmouthshire Regiment, ts. copy of the minutes of the Officers' Mess
of the 3rd Battalion in France, 4 April 1916. **3.456.**

WORLD WAR II

Cardiff Civil Defence: Air Raid Wardens Service news-cuttings, October
1938 – September 1941; locally issued circulars, 1940-4; and miscellaneous records, notices, training manuals, etc.
Civil Defence, Sub-control, Bridgend, 1939-45. Staff souvenirs and
history written by R. G. Williams, ts. **3.868.**
British Legion: documents, letters and news-cuttings regarding British
Legion Volunteer Police for service in Czechoslovakia, 1938, MS and ts.
4.767.

*Cumbria Record Office, The Castle, CARLISLE, Cumbria
CA3 8UR*

TTAF Territorial and Auxiliary Forces Association for Cumberland and
Westmorland, minute books, 1908-68.

WORLD WAR I

Penrith UDC. Ministry of National Service, official and local correspondence, 1917-18, including seven recruiting posters for the Women's Land Army, 1917. Military Service Tribunal, minute books, 1915-18; registers of cases with decisions, 1916-18; applications for exemptions and supporting letters, 1918, etc. **SUDP.**

Whitehaven Union, Whitehaven Rural Local Tribunal for Exemption from Military Service, minute book, 1915-18. **SPUW.**

Kirkbampton Civil Parish Council, minute book, including *inter alia* 'Formation of a recruiting committee', 1915. **SPC/34.**

Wigton Parish Records; **311,** letter from George Scott, a teacher at the Wigton National Mixed Schools regarding war service, 1916. **DB/21/40.**

Hodbarrow Mine, Millom, papers referring to army men directed to work in the mines 1915, and list of soldiers returned to work on munitions n.d. (1914-16). **PR/36.**

Star Cinema, Denton Holme, three letters from two soldiers in France and the Army of the Rhine, containing mostly personal news, 1915-19. **DB/51.**

Lonsdale Battalion Papers, mainly 1914-16, including official and internal correspondence, training circulars and regulations, nominal rolls, battalion orders, registers of in-letters and orders received, station orders, company employ books, CO's letters, telegrams and vouchers, and general files. **D/Lons/L.**

Catherine Marshall MSS: letters from H. G. Marshall, stationed at Peshawar, India, to his parents, 1916-18; No Conscription Fellowship, 1916-20; various Pacifist bodies, 1914-19; and correspondence, etc. **D/M.**

Fletcher-Vane (Lord Inglewood), of Hutton in the Forest; **Acc. 2136, Box 3** contains an album labelled 'The War 1914-18 and My Other Crimes', containing press-cuttings, photographs and comments from Sir Frederick Vane, chiefly relating to Ireland. **D/Van.**

'A Spectator at the Battle of Jutland', MS notes by Adam Potts, former Royal Marines, n.d., including a photograph of the author and two photographs of the German battle cruiser *Derfflinger.* **DX/170.**

Letters of Pvt. Joe Moscrop on active service with the Border Regiment, including service in England, 1914 – July 1915; with the BEF, France, July 1915 – September 1916; and convalescence in Malta, from September 1916. **DX/180/3** and **DX/291/6.**

Record of the 11th (Lonsdale) Battalion, Border Regiment, compiled by 'V.M.' from notes by the CO and officers, September 1914 – 1 July 1916. The battalion served in France from 23 November 1915, at and near Longpre, Bouzencourt, Albert and Aveluy, and suffered two thirds casualties in an attack at the Somme in June 1916. **DX/416.**

Letters to Miss S. Lowther from sailors aboard HMS *Sappho* in the North Sea thanking her for gifts, February 1915. **DX/475.**

J. H. Wood's proposals for fitting depth charges, etc. to merchant

shipping to improve protection against submarines and raiders, which he sent to the Board of Invention, and the Board's reply, 1917. **DX/557.**
Dr Crerar of Maryport, map of the South Devon coast, Sidmouth to Lyme Regis, taken from the wardroom of the German battle cruiser *Kaiser* when raised from Scapa Flow in 1929. **D/CR.**

WORLD WAR II

ARP Committee, minute books, 1938-41. **CC.**
Highways Committee, plans referring to the construction of military defences in Cumberland, 1940-1. **CCH.**
Civil Defence ledger, 1941-46. **Civil Defence.**
Clerk's Files: ARP files relating to the report and control centre, local defence volunteers, air raids general, and wardens' whistles, 1939-45. **CC.**
Civilian casualties files, 1940-3. **CC/PH (Casualty Bureau).**
Carlisle City: ARP files, letters, reports, etc., 1938-40; Home Guard, nominal roll, orders and correspondence, 1941-4. **Ca.**
Penrith UDC, ARP Committee minute book, 1938-9. **SUDP.**
Wigton RDC modern files, general files including Naval Air Station, Anthorn, April 1944 – March 1945.
Cockermouth RDC, Clerk's Department, modern files: no. 91 is ARP, September 1938 – May 1944.
Warwick Parish records; **40**, Roll of the Fallen, 1939-45. **PR/42.**
Brampton; **21**, eyewitness account and official record of the crash of an RAF Lancaster bomber returning to Crosby Airport, Carlisle, from a mission on Kirkby Moor near Crosby, 9 January 1943, in the *Brampton Newsletter,* January 1973. **PR/60.**
Friends of the Lake District; **30**, file regarding the Seaplane factory at Calgarth Park, Windermere, including correspondence with Lord Beaverbrook at the Ministry of Aircraft Production, 1940-1, and one letter from Sir Stafford Cripps, 1944. **DSO/15.**
Carlisle Monthly Meeting; **61**, conscientious objectors, correspondence and papers, 1939-40, including a transcript of proceedings before the tribunal at Carlisle, 1939. **DFC/F/2.**

Dyfed Archives, County Record Office, County Hall, CARMARTHEN, Dyfed SA31 1JP

Carmarthenshire Territorial Army Association, minutes, etc., 1907-68.

Catalogues, reports, pamphlets, etc., referring to POWs, the Battle of Britain, etc., 1886-1945. **Taliaris 159.**
Military photographs, 1870-1945. **Taliaris Maps 1.**

WORLD WAR I

Press copy book of letters written by the Belgian Refugees Committee, 1915-19. **Antiquarian Society B35.**
Maj. M. S. Legh, army officer's notebook and army field message book; and 2nd Lt. R. U. Peel, RA war diary, *c. 1914-18.* **Taliaris 428.**

WORLD WAR II

Letter of 10 June 1942 to Lord Dynevor concerning Ammanford Home Guard. **Dynevor 133/1270.**

Royal Engineers Corps Library, Institution of Royal Engineers, CHATHAM, Kent

The Library contains some war diaries of RE units in WWI. Enquiries should be made to the Librarian.

Essex Record Office, County Hall, CHELMSFORD, Essex CM1 1LX

WORLD WAR I

Printed maps used on the Western Front, 1916-18. **D/DU 346/9/8.**
Ts. list of Downham parishioners serving in the war. **D/P 257/28/1.**
Old age pensioners' recollections. **T/Z 25/596-691** and *passim.*
G. H. Rose, personal diaries relating to wartime experiences in Egypt, restricted access. **D/DU 418.**
Essex Constabulary: set of Home Office circulars, chief constable's memoranda, posters issued by military authorities, and recruiting posters and emergency announcements, 1915-16. **J/P 5/4,5.**
Essex Constabulary war records: circulars concerning restrictions on aliens, 1914-18; investigation of aliens; ARP notices, 1915-18; circulars and correspondence regarding firearms, lighting and Defence of Realm regulations, 1914-18; local emergency committees, circulars and correspondence, 1914-19; and Zeppelin raids, 1916-17. **J/P 12.**

Little Clacton, parish activities, including invasion preparations. **D/P 80/28/2.**

Stow Maries, Emergency (Invasion) Committee, 1914-15. **D/P 391/30/1.**

Witham District Emergency Committee printed instructions, 1915. **D/DU 252/3.**

Colchester, printed notices referring to possible evacuation and black-out, 1915-16. **D/DU 689/15.**

Great Oakley, Invasion Committee papers, 1914 and 1916. **D/P 47/28/6.**

Wakes Colne, Emergency Committee papers, 1915-17. **D/P 88/28/3.**

Brentwood District Emergency Committee printed regulations, 1915. **Library folder Brentwood.**

Ardleigh, printed evacuation instructions, 1915. **Newscuttings Library, 71.**

Log book of the SS *Kalgan* of the China Navigation Company, chartered by the Admiralty, including rumour of a German raider off the China coast, 26 March 1917. **D/DMb B2.**

Letter of Agnes Baines, with the American Ambulance Unit, Neuilly-sur-Seine, 1915. **D/DVz 372.**

WORLD WAR II

List of residents in the armed forces, Bradwell-Juxta-Mare. **D/P 251/28/9.**

Similarly, Hythe, Colchester, Peldon. **D/P 245, 287.**

Pebmarsh evacuation surveys, 1938-9. **D/Z 32.**

Stebbing evacuation surveys, 1938-40. **D/Z 50.**

Chelmsford, map showing location of bomb incidents. **D/Z 65.**

Feering Parish Invasion Committee minutes, 1942-3. **D/P 231/30/23.**

Birchanger, Stansted Mountfitchet and Ugley Parish Invasion Committee minutes, 1942-3. **D/P 109/28/12.**

Danbury Parish Invasion Committee minutes and papers, 1941-3. **D/Z 12/1.**

Manuden Parish Invasion Committee papers, 1941-3. **D/Z 12/2.**

Rawreth Air Raid Warden's log, 1940-4. **D/Z 13.**

Home Guard, 53rd Essex Battalion, registers, 1941-4. **D/Z 10/1-3.**

Home Guard record of officers, *c.* 1942. **D/Z 10/4.**

Home Guard register of non-commissioned officers, B Company, 54th Essex Battalion, *c.* 1942. **D/Z 10/5.**

County ARP Control, records, 1939-45. **C/W 1.**

Leyton and Walthamstow, Group 7 (London Civil Defence Region) records, 1939-45. **C/W 2.**

Essex County Council committees: ARP Committee, 1936-50; ARP Emergency Sub-committee, 1939-42; ARP Metropolitan Sub-committee, 1939-45; similarly, Emergency Sub-committee, 1939-49; Extra-Metropolitan ARP Special Committee, 1942-5; Civil Defence Committee, August 1939 – June 1942; and Civil Defence Emergency Committee, April 1941 – June 1942.

Cheshire Record Office, The Castle, CHESTER CH1 2DN

WORLD WAR II

DDX 328. Luftwaffe briefing papers for targets in Stalybridge and Weston Point: briefing with plans on 1 inch and 6 inch scales for the electric power station, Stalybridge, October 1939; and briefing with plan on 6 inch scale and air photograph for dock installations at Weston Point, Weston in Runcorn, January 1940. They were found on the airfield at Nantes, France after the German evacuation in 1944.
County Emergency Committee minutes, 1939-46.
ARP Committee minutes, 1935-46.
ARP Committee, correspondence files, 1939-45.

Chester City Record Office, Town Hall, CHESTER CH1 2HJ

OFFICIAL ARCHIVES

Chester County Borough Council, Emergency Committee minute books, 1932-45. **CCB/200-201.**
Town Clerk's Department: ATC, correspondence file, 1938-47 **24D/1, box 416**; war damage, public utility undertakings, correspondence file, 1940-9 **230/12, box 464.**

DEPOSITED ARCHIVES

Cheshire Volunteer Regiment, Chester Company, minute book, 1914-16, and handbill of weekly orders, 27 September 1915. **CR 12/1-2.**
Caldwell Family Papers: three letters from Alexander Caldwell relating to experiences in the army in Gibraltar, 1917; one letter from Alfred John Caldwell concerning his service in the hospital ship HMHS *Dunluce Castle,* 1915; and two letters from Frank Caldwell referring to his army service, 1915 and 1917. **CR 103/3-5, 10, 17-18.**

Chester ARP, weekly orders issued by the Chief Warden, 1939-45. **CR 166/2-3.**
Chester Home Guard, duplicated ts., 'The Home Guard' by F. C. Saxon.

Chesterfield Library, Corporation Street, CHESTERFIELD, Derbyshire S41 7TY

WORLD WAR II

Derbyshire Home Guard, 6th (Chesterfield Borough) Battalion, file of correspondence and photographs, c. 1938-44, compiled by a former member of the battalion.

Royal Military Police Museum, Regimental Headquarters, Royal Military Police, Rousillon Barracks, CHICHESTER, West Sussex

The archives of the Royal Military Police are in the process of being catalogued and are not available for outside inspection.

West Sussex Record Office, County Hall, CHICHESTER, West Sussex PO19 1RN

WORLD WAR I

Citation concerning command at the battle of the Somme and at Arras, 1919. **Add. MS. 1551.**
Letters from C. E. Bland while on active service in Northern France, 1915-16. **Add. MS. 16,945.**
Albums of press-cuttings relating to the war. **MP 882-885.**
Photographs and autographs of wounded soldiers at the Royal West Sussex Hospital, 1915-16. **MP 864.**
Copy of a letter from a soldier at the front in France, 1915. **MP 1148.**

Gen. Sir Frederick Ivor Maxse (1862-1958)
Maxse commanded the 1st Guards Brigade at the Mons, Marne and Aisne in 1914; the 18th Division, 1915-16; XVIII Corps, 1917; and was Inspector-General of Training in France, 1918. His private papers are deposited under a 50-year restriction. Other papers are in the Imperial War Museum (see p. 106).

WORLD WAR II

Action Officers' minute books, 1940-5. **Add. MSS. 1316,1317.**
Home Guard records, 1940-4. **Add. MSS. 14,996-15,028.**
ARP diaries, Chidham area, 1940-4. **Add. MSS. 15,029-15,032.**
Miscellaneous ARP records. **Add. MSS. 15,033-15,038.**
Map of Sussex showing flying bomb attacks. **MP 80.**
Official pamphlets concerning general civilian procedure in wartime and methods of protection against air and gas attacks, fire and the invader, 1938-42. **MP 486.**
German propoganda leaflet concerning losses to British shipping, (?)1940-1, and photographic supplement, reputedly from an American journal, entitled "Dieppe, We and British Invade France", also possibly propaganda. **MP 715.**
Map of feeding centres on the South Downs, 1942. **MP 1138.**
War diary, 1939-41. **Mitford MSS. 1272,1273.**
Fire Watchers' log books, Rudgwick Parish, 1941-3. **Par. 160/7/12,13.**

Coventry City Record Office, 9 Hay Lane, COVENTRY, West Midlands CV1 5RF

WORLD WAR I

Warwickshire Volunteer Regiment, Associations 4 and 5, records.
Roll of Honour: The Great War, 1914-18. **A276.**
The Great War, 1914-18, a record of those people employed by the Corporation who served in HM Forces. **A277.**
Coundon minute book, including official papers on the recruitment campaign of 1915. **Acc 420.**
Map of the Western Front. **Acc 615.**

WORLD WAR II

1. Three bound vols. of papers relating to the war years, mostly press-cuttings referring to air raids, ARP material and other home front matters.
2. Miscellaneous war papers:
A. List of miscellaneous national papers, including ARP handbooks, memoranda, training bulletins, booklets, and circulars on incendiaries, gas, decontamination, home protection, equipment maintenance, etc.
C. Miscellaneous Civil Defence papers, including stock-taking returns of the Civil Defence, the Development Officer's papers, lists of shelters,

first aid and ARP posts, ARP Depot papers, provisions made by industrial and business concerns for incendiary bombs, fire guard, training, rescue services and shelters.

F. Miscellaneous papers of air raid damage and post-raid assistance, including rest centres, handbooks and pamphlets.

I. Miscellaneous papers relating to ARP in industrial firms, 1938 and 1939.

L. Miscellaneous Civil Defence reports and papers regarding air raid sirens.

3. Lists of war dead.

4. War damage photographs, two albums and one box.

6. Committee minute books: **A.** ARP, 1938-9; and **H.** National Emergency, 1939-45.

7. Maps, mainly of war damage and ARP matters.

Private Accessions:

Two German war target maps, 1940 and 1941. **Acc. 41.**

Large German war target map of Coventry, 1940. **Acc. 95.**

Information to the public following the air raids. **Acc. 170.**

Private papers of an air raid warden, 1940-4. **Acc. 408.**

Home Guard, personal files and circulars from 1941. **Acc. 430.**

Land Defence Volunteers, circulars, 1940. **Acc. 456.**

ARP Organisation Report on the air raid of 14-15 November 1940, which is the fullest account of the raid. **Acc. 501.**

Coventry and Warwickshire Collection, including a collection of war target maps, circulars and pamphlets, and a collection of bomb damage photographs.

Central Library, Katherine Street, CROYDON, Surrey CR9 1ET

WORLD WAR II

Home Guard, 33rd Surrey Battalion, A Company, ts. accounts of the history and training of the Croydon Town Hall Home Guard, list of discharges, etc., 1945.

Home Guard, 32nd Surrey Battalion, photographs of activities compiled by members of the battalion, 1940-4.

Tenterden Fire Watchers log book, 1941-4.

Gwent County Record Office, County Hall, CWMBRAN, Gwent NP4 2XH

Monmouthshire Territorial and Auxiliary Forces Association: minute books, 1912-67; and press-cuttings, 1908-64.

WORLD WAR I

South Wales Borderers (1st Gwents), 10th (Service) Battalion, ts. copy
of war diary, 1915-18.
Military Service Act of 1916: Brynmawr Local Tribunal, correspondence, circulars and case papers, *c.* 1916-18; and Chepstow Tribunal
minute book, 1916-18.

WORLD WAR II

Monmouthshire County Council: Civil Defence Committee minutes,
1942-68; ARP Committee minutes, 1935-42; and air raid messages,
1939-42.
Newport County Borough Council, Emergency Sub-committee,minutes,
1940-6.
District Council records contain much information relating to ARP and
Civil Defence, but these are as yet unscheduled.

Clwyd Record Office, The Old Rectory, Hawarden,
DEESIDE, Clwyd CH5 3NR

Denbighshire and Flintshire Territorial and Auxiliary Forces Association, records, 1908-68.

WORLD WAR I

Godsal of Iscoyd Park MSS
265. File of letters and papers relating to the naval career of Alfred E.
Godsal, including training certificates, commissions, letters to his
parents during his war service (with references to attacks on Ostend),
letters of condolence on his death, press-cuttings and photographs,
1904-21.
267. Vol. of copy letters to his parents, from Philip Godsal as a POW at
Burg-bei-Magdesburg and later Mainz, with references to camp conditions, routine and the death of Basil Philips of Rhual, 1914-15.
268. Christmas cards received by Mr and Mrs Godsal from the front,
1916-18.
266, 319 and **320.** Letters to parents from France, diaries, papers, maps
and plans of trenches, press-cuttings, etc., of Maj. Walter H. Godsal,
Durham Light Infantry, November 1914 — January 1919.

321. Notes on 'The Godsal Rifle Action' in *The Outpost,* magazine of the Highland Light Infantry, July 1915.

322. *Bulletin des Armées de la République,* réservé à la zone des Armées, 5 December 1917.

323. Printed English and French maps of France and Belgium used by Maj. W. H. Godsal at the front, with secret military instructions in French and English for the 1st Army, and plan of Nieuport, 1917, five items.

Report on munitions of war, resources of the North Wales area, 1915, and papers referring to an anti-German riot in Rhyl, 1915-16. **FC/C.**

WORLD WAR II

Papers and photographs concerning a Parliamentary delegation to Buchenwald Concentration Camp, April 1945. **Morris Jones MSS.**

Capt. R. D. Griffiths, papers relating to the sinking of SS *Willesden* and imprisonment in Japan, 1941-5. **D/DM/389.**

Leaflet, as dropped over Germany, in German. **D/DM/130/13.**

Register of air raids and alarms, 1940-2. **FP/5/21.**

There are numerous references to ARP and evacuation in various classes of official records and the minute books of district councils.

The Dorset Military Museum, The Keep, DORCHESTER, Dorset DT1 1RN

Enquiries should be addressed to the Secretary, Dorset Regiment Association, at the above address.

WORLD WAR I

Dorset Regiment, War diaries:

1st Battalion, 1914-18.

2nd Battalion, August 1914 — May 1919 (missing November 1915 — July 1916 and February 1919).

1/4th Battalion, 1916-19.

2/4th Battalion, 1917-19.

5th Battalion, 1915-19 and Composite Battalion 'Norsets', February — July 1916.

6th Battalion, 1915 — May 1919.

Personal diaries:

Officer's diary with 1/4th Battalion in India, 1914-15.

Officer's diary in the Mesopotamia campaign, 1914-15.

Officer's diary with the Queen's Own Dorset Yeomanry in France, 1914-18.
Warrant Officer's diary as a POW in Europe, 1914-18.

WORLD WAR II

Dorset Regiment, War diaries:
1st Battalion in Sicily and Italy, 1939-44.
2nd Battalion, June 1940-6.

Dorset Record Office, County Hall, DORCHESTER, Dorset

RECORDS OF THE QUEEN'S OWN DORSET YEOMANRY

Order books:
Regimental, 1914-15. **6/1-2.**
1/1st Battalion, 1915-19. **7/1-14.**
2/1st Battalion, 1915-17. **8/1-4.**
94th Field Regiment, RA, later 94th Dorset and Hants. Field Regiment, RA, 1939-44. **A 9/1-9.**
Correspondence:
Duplicate telegram book, 1914. **D 5.**
Letter book, 1916. **D 6.**
Rolls and returns:
Record of officers' services, 1794-1915. **E 1.**
Nominal rolls, 1915 and 1917-19. **E 4,5.**
Field returns by O/C Unit, 1915-18, and numerical roll, 1st Battalion, 1919. **E 6.**
Miscellaneous:
Printed regulations for mobilisation, 1910-13; papers relating to mobilisation, 1914; and miscellaneous letters and papers, 1914-20. **F11.**
Letters regarding formation of a 3rd Line depot, 1915. **F 12.**
Papers concerning the regiment in Gallipoli, Egypt, Palestine and on manoeuvres, including letters and press-cuttings relating to the battle of Agagia and the cavalry charge against the Senussi, 1916. **F 13.**
1/1st Battalion, casualty books, 1915-18; reports of deaths on field service, 1916-18; and war diary, 1918-19. **F 14·16.**
Printed items:
'Water in Southern Palestine', 1st and 2nd provisional editions, 1917. **G 11.**
'A Brief Record of the Advance of the Egyptian Expeditionary Force under the Command of Sir Edward H. H. Allenby', 1919. **G 12.**

WORLD WAR I

Account of the men of Rampisham who went to war. **P111/MI1.**
Letters, etc. referring to the death of J. N. Williams at the Dardanelles, 1915. **D289/C32.**
Membership and attendance register of National Volunteers, Whitchurch Canonicorum Company, 1914, and list of parishioners serving in the forces. **P278/MI4, 5.**
Letter from Ernest MacDermot in France, 1916. **D359/F32.**
Copy letters of Capt. B. W. Fagan, Oxon and Bucks Light Infantry, from France, 1914-18. **D302/1.**

WORLD WAR II

Civil Defence records, County Control, and also assorted papers from some boroughs.
Report on damage to property of Sherbourne Almshouse by air raids, 1940-1, and correspondence about ARP and the war effort, 1940-2. **D204/E44, 105** and **C145-6, 149, 152, 154-5.**
Stalbridge Local Defence Committee, minutes, 1941-3, and Stalbridge war book, *c.* 1942. **P208/MI9, 10.**
Dorset Home Guard, history of 1st (Bridport) Battalion, 1940-5. **LB1.**
Flying Officer D. Mansel-Pleydell, RAFVR, war diary, 1943-4. **MR 46.**

Manx Museum Library, Kingswood Grove, DOUGLAS, Isle of Man

Enquiries should be made to the Curator.

WORLD WAR I

Knockaloe Internment Camp, journals (sample official records), 1914-19.
Photograph collection of Knockaloe and Douglas Internment Camps, WWI, including photographs and negatives of unnamed prisoners.

WORLD WAR II

History of the Manx Home Guard, ts., 1969. **Ref. MD 475.**
Territorial and Auxiliary Forces Association of the Isle of Man, minute books, 1938-68, and General Purposes Committee minute books, 1938-68. **Ref. MD 15035/1-8.**

Ewart Library, Catherine Street, DUMFRIES DG1 1JB

Culvennan Papers
Four MS notebook diaries of Lt. Col. L. A. C. Gordon, 4th Brigade, Royal Field Artillery, covering mobilisation in India, 1914; service in France to December 1915; service in Mesopotamia, 1916 — Spring 1917; and return to France to study 'recent developments'. Plans and photographs are included.

Durham County Record Office, P.O. Box, County Hall, DURHAM DH1 5UL

Durham County Territorial and Auxiliary Forces Association:
Association meetings' minutes, 1908-68. **D/Ta 1,2.**
Committee meetings' minutes, 1908-68. **D/Ta 3-14.**

Londonderry Papers
In and out letters of the Chief Londonderry Agent, Mr Malcolm Dillon, including some personal letters from the front. **D/Lo/C 277.**
Letters to members of the Londonderry Family:
33 letters from France, 1914-15. **D/Lo/C 628.**
Three letters from Gerald Archibald Arbuthnot, 1913-15. **D/Lo/C 634.**
Five letters from Walter Carson with accounts of naval activities, 1914-16. **D/Lo/C 642.**
50 letters from Lord and Lady Beresford regarding naval affairs, 1907-18. **D/Lo/C 645-646.**
Two letters from Richard E. Onslow, 3rd Viscount Long, concerning the campaign in Egypt, 1915. **D/Lo/C 664.**
Eight letters from E. Dorothea Spence referring to her son's military activities, 1915-18. **D/Lo/C 674.**
Three letters from Sir Arthur Stanley concerning Red Cross affairs, 1914 and 1917. **D/Lo/C 675.**
Personal correspondence of Charles, 7th Marquess of Londonderry (1878-1949), including comments on the war in France. **D/Lo/C 682.**
Miscellaneous letters from various correspondents, mainly of a personal and social nature but including comments on WWI. **D/Lo/C 684.**
193 letters from soldiers, mainly referring to gifts but some including accounts of the fighting, 1914-18. **D/Lo/C 688.**
Ts. account of the bombardment of Hartlepool, 1914. **D/Lo/F 609.**
Notices issued at Seaham Harbour, including some relating to Zeppelin raids, blackouts, etc., *c.* 1912-26. **D/Lo/F 704.**
87 letters to newspapers, mainly lists of gifts sent to troops of the Durham Light Infantry in France, 1914-16. **D/Lo/F 1130.**

Press bureau accounts of fighting in France and the Dardanelles, 1915, three papers. **D/Lo/F 1141.**
'Reality, the World's Searchlight on Germany', 1917, one paper. **D/Lo/X 48.**
Report of the Parliamentary Committee considering the supply of horses for military purposes, 1915, and file. **D/Lo/X 129.**
Letter from the Marquess of Londonderry explaining his attitude to Germany, 1937. **D/Lo/X 129.**

Headlam Papers
Personal papers of Lt. Col. Sir Cuthbert Morley Headlam, 1st Bt. (1876-1964). Service with the Bedfordshire Yeomanry and on the General Staff in France, 1914-18; editor of *Army Quarterly,* 1920-42; and Parliamentary Secretary to several ministries in the 1920s and 1930s. The papers comprise:
Diaries for 1890, 1895-7, 1899, 1902-4, 1910-15, 1919-45 and 1947-51. **D/He 1-46.**
1169 letters to his wife, mostly written while serving with the British Army in France and containing many comments on political and military affairs, August 1914 and June 1915 — January 1919. **D/He 50.**
Letters from various correspondents, including Neville Chamberlain, 1937-9, and Field-Marshal Sir John Dill, 1936-40. **D/He 47/1-253.**

Edleston of Gainford (2nd deposit)
Correspondence of R. H. Edleston with the printer of his booklet, *The Republic of San Marino, Italy and the War,* with a proof copy of the pamphlet, 1918. **D/Ed 1.**
Papers of the Great Britain to Poland Fund, 1915-18. **D/Ed 2.**
Union of Democratic Control (magazine), 1916-19, 25 issues; and pamphlets including *The Origins of the Great War* by H. N. Brailsford, *Shall this War end German Militarism?* and *The Prussian in Our Midst* by Norman Angell, *Parliament and Foreign Policy* by Arthur Ponsonby, *War and the Workers* by J. R. MacDonald, and *A League of Nations* by J. A. Hobson. **D/Ed 2.**

Miscellaneous
Scrapbook of newspaper cuttings, etc., relating to WWI, indexed, 1914-18. **UD/Sea 36.**
'How young soldiers were trained 20 years ago', ts. account of Charles Laughton's army career in WWI, 1938. **UD/Sea 45.**
List of Germans dying of influenza at Harperley Station POW Camp, November 1918. **EP/Ham 28.**
List of volunteers from Washington Parish, 1914. **EP/Wa 55.**

Log book of Middleton St. John's School where one child was killed in the attack on Hartlepool, 1914. **E/SE 14.**

Copy letters of Col. W. D. Lowe of the 18th Durham Light Infantry to Col. Burden, describing fighting at Meteren, 1918. **D/Sa/X 132.**

Copy of a letter from J. H. Mawson at Gallipoli to 'Mr. Blackburn', 1915. **D/WSS 93.**

4th Battalion, Durham Light Infantry, official war diary during posting at Barnard Castle, 1914-19. **D/Bo No. 40.**

Copies of newspaper cuttings regarding the bombardment of Whitby and Hartlepool, 1914. **D/Ph 22/1-9.**

Article by John Wilson, MP on *The War: its Origins and Situation,* 1914. **D/X188/12.**

Under Shell-fire: The Hartlepools, Scarborough and Whitby under Shell-fire, by Frederick Miller, 1917. **D/X 202/11.**

Vol. of press-cuttings collected by Col. Rowland Burdon of Castle Eden concerning the Volunteer Battalion, later the 18th Durham Light Infantry, 1914-38. **D/X 210/1.**

Ts. diary kept by an unidentified soldier in C Company, 2nd Battalion, Durham Light Infantry, August 1914 — October 1916. From October 1914, this soldier was a German POW. **D/X 402/1.**

Dr J. R. MacDonald, diary with the RAMC, 1940-5. **D/X 348/1.**

Hetton ARP Committee minutes, 1938-41. **UD/He 115.**

Jarrow ARP Committee minutes, 1938-45. **MB/Ja 65, 66.**

Maj. Maurice Pease, letters to his mother while on service in the Middle East, October 1942 — February 1943. Ts. copies with notes by Pease. **D/X 171/1-2.**

Durham Light Infantry Museum and Arts Centre, Aykley Heads, DURHAM

Enquiries should be made to the Keeper in Charge.

WORLD WAR I

War Diaries:

1st Battalion, in India, 1914-35. **2218.**

2nd Battalion, on the Western Front, 1914-18. **2221.**

2/5th Battalion, Western Front and Macedonia, 1914-19. **2219/3.**

9th Battalion, on the Western Front, 1916-17. **1487.**

1/9th Battalion, on the Western Front, February — December 1918. **2219/1.**

2/9th Battalion, on the Western Front, July 1917 — January 1920. **2219/2.**

13th Battalion, Western Front and Italy, 1914-18. **2015/1.**
20th Battalion, on the Western Front, 1915-19. **796.**
22nd Battalion, on the Western Front, 1916-18. **1974/9.**
151st Brigade, battle of the Aisne, 1918. **2224.**
Other Material:
J. F. Fleming, ts. memoir, 'By land and sea to India'. **1178.**
Sgt. F. G. Stone, diary and other documents concerning the 2nd Battalion, 1914-15. **2222-2223.**
Sgt. I. Plews, 2nd Battalion, diary, 1915. **2250.**
Lt. J. Harter, 2nd Battalion, letter of October 1914 relating to the battle of Ennetières. **1827/1.**
Lt. Col. D. L. Brereton, 2nd Battalion, letters and reports regarding the Marchies sector, March 1918. **1527/2.**
Chaplain J. H. G. Birch, 5th Battalion, diary, 1914-18. **866;1167.**
Capt. W. Marley, 5th Battalion, diary, August — September 1915. **2111/1.**
Cpl. G. Thorpe, 2/6th Battalion, anecdotes of service, 1918. **1125.**
Sgt. T. Marshall, 8th Battalion, letters and documents as a POW and internee, 1915-18. **1230-1236.**
Lt. Col. H. H. S. Morant, 10th Battalion, correspondence book, 1917. **97.**
2nd Lt. J. W. Gamble, 14th Battalion, letters, 1915-16. **2154-2155.**
Lt. H. Goodley, 20th Battalion, diary relating to the Western Front and Italy, 1917-18. **2092/1.**
Telegram concerning the outbreak of war, to 1st Battalion in India, 1914. **503.**
Telegram regarding mobilisation, to the Durham Light Infantry Depot, 1914. **68.**
15th Battalion, orders, bulletins, etc., 1914-18. **99.**

WORLD WAR II

Telegram regarding the outbreak of war, 1939. **977.**
CSM T. Waterman, 2nd Battalion, diary of march into captivity and POW documents, 1940. **2014.**
6th Battalion, orders for D-day, 1914. **410.**

Department of Manuscripts, Durham University Library, Palace Green, DURHAM DH1 3RN

Lt. Col. Angus Alexander MacFarlane-Grieve (1891—1970)
Served with the Highland Light Infantry from 1914 and commanded

the 2nd Battalion, Seaforth Highlanders in France from March 1918. War diary, 1914-18. **MS 940.42 m2.**

Sir Harold MacMichael (1882-1969)
High Commissioner, Palestine and Transjordan, 1938-44, and Special Representative in Malaya, 1945. Large deposit of papers relating to his career.

The Rt. Hon. The Earl of Balfour, Whittinghame Tower,
EAST LOTHIAN

NRA—Scotland 0012

WORLD WAR I

The relevant papers of Arthur James Balfour, 1st Earl Balfour:
18. Correspondence with Lord Derby from the Paris Embassy regarding French politics, Anglo-French relations and international affairs generally. Also included is Derby's detailed diary and a confidential letter on relations between Lloyd George and Clemenceau, 1918.
58. War Cabinet agenda, 11 December 1916; Cabinet papers on President Wilson's peace initiative (draft) and Belgian exports; and draft rules of procedure for the War Cabinet.
75. Papers, 1914-17, including some relating to US opinion, Austrian peace moves, Vatican mediation in 1917, Balfour at the Calais Conference of 1915, etc.
166. Letter from Oswald Balfour to Frances Balfour on the formation of public school battalions, shortage of rifles, conditions at his regimental depot, etc., 1915.
250. Letters from Oswald Balfour and Edward Lascelles at the Western Front and from Lt. Col. Earle in a POW camp, September 1914 — June 1915.
251. Letters describing the bombardment of Scarborough and Zeppelin raids on London, Hull and Guildford, 1914-15.
252. Letters from Dr Maclagan Wedderburn, Maj. Gen. Egerton, Capt. Diggle RN, Constantine Brown and an anonymous midshipman on board submarine *E7*, relating to the Dardanelles, May — November 1915.
253. Letters from Neville Lytton at GHQ and Edward Lascelles with the 55th Division, relating to the German breakthrough on the Western Front, March — April 1918. Also letters from Frank Balfour and L. Palmer regarding operations in Mesopotamia, January — April 1918.

254. Letter from Rosalind Benson describing an attack by a German submarine on MacBrayne's steamer *Plover* in the Minch, July 1918.

255. Letters and diaries of Oswald Balfour and other officers of the 60th Rifles from the Western Front, September 1914 — February 1915, and from Salonika, February 1915.

256. Letters from Frank Balfour in the Sudan, 1915, and as a political officer in Mesopotamia.

257, Letters from Capt. W. Balfour at the Western Front, September 1914 — September 1915.

258. Various letters and diaries referring to the Western Front, the Falkland Islands, the Dogger Bank, etc.

259. Letters from Sir Charles Fergusson describing the operations of the 5th Division on the Western Front, August 1914 — May 1915.

260-261. Miscellaneous letters and anecdotes concerning various aspects of the war.

268. A few letters from various people on active service in France.

270. Letter from Arthur James Balfour in Paris, regarding the French Army, 8 June 1918.

Middlesex Regimental Association, T & A Centre, Deansbrook Road, EDGWARE, Middlesex HA8 9BA

Enquiries should be made to the Regimental Secretary.

WORLD WAR I

War diaries:
1st Battalion, August 1914 — November 1918.
2nd Battalion, November 1914 — November 1918.
3rd Battalion, December 1914 — March 1919.
4th Battalion, August 1914 — November 1918.
1/7th Battalion, February 1915 — October 1919, also standing orders, maps and recommendations for awards.
1/8th Battalion, June 1915 — December 1917, also orders of the day, maps, telegrams and miscellaneous papers.
1/9th Battalion, November 1917 — March 1919.
2/7th Battalion, January — September 1915 and January — December 1917.
2/10th Battalion, August — September 1915 and November 1915 — December 1917, also maps and miscellaneous papers regarding the Palestine campaign.
3/10th Battalion, June 1917 — February 1918.
11th Battalion, June 1915 — March 1918.

12th Battalion, July 1915 – February 1918, also operations orders and miscellaneous rolls of officers.

13th Battalion, September 1915 – October 1919.

16th Battalion, November 1915 – February 1918, also miscellaneous orders.

17th Battalion, December 1915 – February 1918, also miscellaneous orders of the day.

18th Battalion, November 1915 – September 1918.

19th Battalion, May 1916 – January 1920.

20th Battalion, May 1916 – June 1919, also operations orders, rolls of officers, recommendations for awards and miscellaneous papers.

21st Battalion, May 1916 – August 1918, also maps and miscellaneous operations orders.

23rd Battalion, May 1915 – November 1919, also miscellaneous operations orders.

26th Battalion, August 1916 – November 1919.

32nd Battalion, July – November 1915.

1st Labour Company, March 1917 – January 1918.

2nd Labour Company, April – November 1917.

1st Special Company, May – September 1919, also operations orders, sketch maps and miscellaneous papers.

WORLD WAR II

1st Battalion, ts. history, 1944-5.

1st Battalion, A Company: war diaries, June 1944 – May 1945; operational standing orders, 1944; and miscellaneous papers.

1st Battalion, C Company, war diary, 1944-5.

1st Battalion, D Company, ts. 'The Company History in Europe', 1944-5.

2nd Battalion, ts. history by Commander P. K. Kemp RN.

Lists of honours and awards, Middlesex Regiment, 1939-45.

1st Battalion, Princess Louise's Kensington Regiment: roll of officers, 1944-6, and brief narrative of movements, May 1943 – September 1945.

2nd Battalion, Princess Louise's Kensington Regiment, war diaries, May – July and September – December 1944.

MISCELLANEOUS

Minutes of meetings of the Regimental History Committee, 1955.

Miscellaneous papers and correspondence referring to the preparation of the regimental history.

EDINBURGH

As the capital of Scotland, Edinburgh is the seat of the main repositories for the study of the Scottish role in the world wars, apart from the Public Record Office in London. The National Library of Scotland and the Scottish Record Office each contain important collections of the papers of public figures as well as official papers. Perhaps the most complete military museum in Britain, the Scottish United Services Museum has extensive collections documenting the often disproportionately large role played by Scottish regiments in most British campaigns overseas. The student of either world war will, therefore, find Edinburgh an important locale for research. The libraries of Edinburgh, and of Scotland in general, are well described in Colin Smith and R. S. Walker, *Library Resources in Scotland* (Glasgow, Scottish Library Association, 1973, 2nd ed.).

Edinburgh Central Library, George IV Bridge, EDINBURGH EH1 1EG

Ethel M. Moir
Scottish Women's Hospital, Dr Elsie Inglis' Serbian-Russian unit in Rumania and Russia. One vol. of letters, August 1916 – April 1917; one vol. of photographs; and jottings from her diary, February 1918 – February 1919.

Lilias M. Grant
Uncensored diary of the Scottish Women's Hospital, Dr Elsie Inglis' Serbian-Russian unit in Rumania and Russia, August 1916 – April 1917.

Lt. R. L. Mackay
Argyll and Sutherland Highlanders. Diary, September 1916 – January 1919.

National Library of Scotland, Department of Manuscripts, George IV Bridge, EDINBURGH EH1 1EW

Barnton Sector Fire Fighting Leaders
Three minute books, 1942-4. **Acc. 4303.**

Rev. Prof. David Cairns
Diary as padre with the 131st Field Regiment, RA, 1944-5, and related

military maps; and paper on the state of the reformed churches in Germany, 1945. **Acc. 5931-2.**

Maj. Gen. Sir John H. Davidson (1876-1954)
Papers, mostly 1918, as Director of Military Operations in France. **Acc. 3679.**

Rear Admiral Robert K. Dickson (1898-1952)
Correspondence and other papers of Admiral Dickson and Midshipman A. W. Dickson. Admiral Dickson served at the Falkland Islands, 1914; Gallipoli, 1915; Jutland, 1916; with the Grand Fleet destroyers; and in South Russia, 1917-18. In WWII he was Duty Captain of the Admiralty War Room, 1939-40; commander of the fast minelayer HMS *Manxman*, 1940-2; Deputy Director of Plans of the Naval Staff, 1943-4; and Chief of Naval Information, 1944-6. **Acc. 2670, 2676.**

Arthur Cecil Murray
3rd Viscount Elibank (1879-1962). Correspondence and papers, 1909-62, covering military, political and diplomatic matters. Murray served as Private Secretary to Sir Edward Grey at the Foreign Office, 1910-14; in France with 2nd King Edward's Horse, 1914-16; and as Assistant Military Attaché in Washington, 1917-18. **MSS. 8801-24.**

Admiral Sir Angus Cunninghame Graham
Notes on life in the Grand Fleet, 1914 – June 1916, and précis of a lecture, 'The submarine and anti-submarine war 1914-1918', delivered at the Royal Air Force College, Andover, 1934. **Acc. 4317, 5705.**

C. M. Grieve
Letter to Helen Cruikshank referring to his wartime activities, 1943. **Acc. 5929.**

Field-Marshal Douglas Haig
1st Earl Haig (1861-1928). Letters, diaries, military notebooks and textbooks, photographs, maps, orders, press-cuttings, etc., 1882-1928, covering all aspects of his career. Haig commanded the 1st Army in France, 1914-15, and was C-in-C Expeditionary Forces in France and Flanders, 1915-19. The papers may only be consulted with the permission of the present Lord Haig. **Acc. 3155.**
Copies of these papers are in the Scottish Record Office (see p. 63).

51st Highland Division
Letters regarding the division and copies of its news sheet, 1944-5. **Acc. 4549.**

Gen. Sir James Aylmer Lowthorpe Haldane (1862-1950)
Diaries, autobiography, letters and war maps. Haldane commanded the 3rd Division on the Western Front, 1914-16, and the 6th Army Corps, 1916-19. **Acc. 2070.**

Richard Burdon Haldane
Viscount Haldane (1856-1928). Papers and correspondence of Viscount Haldane and his family, 1830-1937. Haldane was Secretary of State for War, 1905-12, and Lord Chancellor, 1912 — May 1915. There is much correspondence giving detailed impressions of events and contemporaries, and his role in the Anglo-German negotiations to 1914. **MSS. 5901-6108.**

Home Guard
Records of the service of the Home Guard, 1940-5, partly histories and statements compiled after demobilisation and partly original war diaries, orders, etc. **MS. 3816** is Scottish Command HQ, Home Guard Branch; **3818** West Scotland, District I—Lanarkshire, Glasgow, Wigtownshire, and Dumfriesshire; **3819** West Scotland, District II—Stewartry of Kirkcudbright, Dunbartonshire, Argyll, Stirlingshire and Clackmannanshire, Renfrewshire and Bute, and No.2 Transport Column; **3820** East Scotland, District I—Edinburgh City, Scottish Border, Lothians and Peeblesshire, and 2nd East Lothian Battalion; **3821** East Scotland, District II—Midlothian, West Lothian, Peeblesshire, Angus, Dundee, Perthshire, Kinross-shire, Independent Company, Fife and No. 1 Transport Column; and **3822** Anti-aircraft. **MSS. 3816-22.**

Sapper Jack of Blackhall, Midlothian
Journal describing service in the RE in South Africa and German East Africa, 1916-17. **Acc. 3607.**

Col. (later Brig. Gen.) Sydney Bellinghame Jameson
Some 200 letters to his wife, 1914-20. **Acc. 3433.**

Gen. Sir Herbert A. Lawrence (1861-1943)
Five folders of papers, mostly 1918. Lawrence served in the Dardanelles, 1915; Egypt, 1916; and France, 1917-19. From January 1918, he was Chief of Staff, HQ, British Armies in France. **Acc. 3678.**

W. A. L. Mann
Papers concerning his military service, particularly on the Burma-Thailand Railway and in Changi Prison Camp, Singapore, with explanatory notes, 1941-50. **Acc. 4549.**

Frederick C. Brown
Miscellaneous letters and papers, 1574-1923, including letters of Frederick C. Brown, Royal Marines, serving on the east coast of Africa, 1914-18. **Acc. 3998.**

Anton Mussert
Copy of a letter from Mussert, founder of the Dutch Nazi Party, to Mussolini in 1939, and two letters to Mussert from J.L. and Lucia Pierson, 1939 and n.d. **Acc. 3138.**

Naval Affairs
Nine vols. of correspondence and collections relating to naval affairs, especially the escape of the *Goeben* and *Breslau,* 1914. **Acc. 4321.**

Lance Cpl. George Ramage
War diary with the 1st Battalion, Gordon Highlanders, on the Western Front, 1915-16. **MSS. 944-947.**

James Roy
Xerox copy of his 'Recollections of an Intelligence Officer', 1914-19. **Acc. 5415.**

Miss M. MacKenzie Scott
Diaries regarding her experiences during the siege of Budapest and at home after the war, 1940-66. **Acc. 5385.**

Lt. Chilton L. Addison Smith
Papers, 1909-36, including letters, notes, memoranda and an autobiography, relating to service with the Seaforth Highlanders and incidents in WWI. **Acc. 6027-31.**

Miss Mary Stewart-Richardson
Diary and notes relating to nursing service in France, 1914-15. **Acc. 5729.**

Western Front 1914-19
Graph of the British front in France and Belgium, January 1916 – November 1918, showing its length, fighting strengths, number of Americans with British divisions, casualties and prisoners taken. The graph was kept by RE staff at GHQ. **MSS. 3016.**

Scottish Record Office, H.M. General Register House EDINBURGH EH1 3YY

Douglas Mackinnon Baillie Hamilton Cochrane
12th Earl of Dundonald (1852-1958). Distinguished service in WWI. The papers include engagement diaries, 1886-1930; papers relating to conscientious objectors; letters referring to WWI; and papers used in his autobiography, *My Army Life* (1926). **GD 233/139-141.**

Lt. Col. A. D. Greenhill Gardyne
Microfilm copies of diaries with the Gordon Highlanders, covering *inter alia* service in France and Belgium during WWI.

Field-Marshal Douglas Haig
Duplicate copies of the papers held by the National Library of Scotland (see p. 58). **GD 1/381.**

Lt. Col. Archibald Hay
Diary of the Dardanelles and Mesopotamian campaigns, 1915-16. **GD 73/2/26.**

Marquis of Lothian
Philip Kerr, 11th Marquis of Lothian (1882-1940). The papers contain Kerr's general correspondence, 1918-39; much material relating to the Dardanelles in 1916-17; war aims and reparations, conscientious objectors, peace negotiations, etc. from his tenure as Private Secretary to David Lloyd George, 1916-1920; and his private correspondence as Ambassador to the USA, 1939-40. **Lothian Muniments GD 40, section 17.**

Steel-Maitland MSS
Papers of Sir Arthur Herbert Drummond Ramsay Steel-Maitland (1876-1935), covering every aspect of his career. He was Parliamentary Under-Secretary of State for the Colonies, May 1915 — September 1917; Joint Parliamentary Under-Secretary of State for Foreign Affairs and Parliamentary Secretary to the Board of Trade as Secretary to the Overseas Trade Department, 1917 — April 1919. **GD 193.**

Ministry of Defence: Territorial and Auxiliary Forces
Records of the Territorial and Auxiliary Forces Associations:
Roxburgh, Berwickshire and Selkirkshire, 1908-68. **MD/1.**
Lanark, 1908-68. **MD/2.**
Dumfriesshire, Kirkcudbrightshire and Wigtownshire, 1908-68. **MD/3.**

City of Aberdeen and Aberdeenshire, Banffshire and Kincardineshire, 1907-68. **MD/4.**
Ayrshire, Renfrewshire and Bute, 1901-60. **MD/5.**
Stirlingshire, Clackmannanshire and Kinross-shire, 1907-60. **MD/6.**
City of Dundee, Angus, Fife and Perthshire, 1859-60. **MD/7.**
Elgin, Moray, Ross and Cromarty, Inverness-shire, Nairn, Sutherland and Caithness, 1907-53. **MD/8.**
Argyll and Dunbarton, 1916-68. **MD/9.**

La Bassée, France
Three documents referring to military operations in the La Bassée area of France, May 1917. **GD 1/731.**

Scottish Record Office, West Register Office, Charlotte Square, EDINBURGH

WORLD WAR I

HH/31. 1914-18 War Files (Scottish Office). The following are some of the more relevant files:
2. Ships and fisheries, 1914.
5. News and newspapers, limited access, 1914-16.
6. German aircraft and suspected aircraft in the north of Scotland.
10. Alien enemies, alien restrictions and POWs, 1914-16.
11. Illegal trading with the enemy, case of W. Jacks and Co, limited access.
13. Suspected craft, coast patrol and submarines in home waters, 1914.
20-21. Emergency arrangements, air raids, precautions, etc.
22. Munitions, etc., closed access.
34. Peace propaganda, closed access.
35. Censorship warrants.

WORLD WAR II

HH/50. 1939-45 War Files (Scottish Office). The following are some of the more relevant files:
1-5. Air raids.
6. Sinking of SS *Athenia.*
7-10. Ministry of Home Security.
11-13. Casualty Hospital Service.
14. Civil Defence.
15-20. Miscellaneous.

21-47. Emergency powers of war legislation.
48-51. Evacuations of civilians.
52-53. Financing of Civil Defence expenditure.
55-63. Emergency powers for Scotland.
64-66, 78-79, 115. Civil Defence.
91-103. Heavy air attacks, Clydeside.
104-114. Evacuations.
119-125. Protected areas.
159. War diary of a clerk in the Scottish Office. **36370/46.**
160-165. Record of high explosives, missiles and incendiary bombs dropped on Scotland during the war.

Scottish United Services Museum, Crown Square, The Castle, EDINBURGH EH1 2NG

Use of the documents is by appointment only. Enquiries should be made to the Keeper.

GENERAL

Maj. Gen. E. G. Miles, 'Blue Bonnets O'er the Border', a short history of the King's Own Scottish Borderers, 1659-1953, written *c.* 1954. **25.954.1.**
Maj. O. G. W. White, ts. entitled 'The Dorsetshire Regiment 1881-1951'. **39/54.881.1.**
Admiral Sir Murray Anderson, 21 documents relating to his career. **1959-32.**
Rear Admiral Robert K. Dickson (1898-1952). Autobiographical notes, 1914-52. Dickson's papers are in the National Library of Scotland, under which entry a biographical note is given (see p. 58).
Maj. Gen. Granville Egerton (1859-1951). Commander of the Lowland Division, 1914-15; service in the Dardanelles, 1915; and Inspector of Infantry, 1916. One box of letters and documents relating principally to the Seaforth Highlanders. **2262.** The contents are as follows:
.5.a-e Reports referring to Gallipoli.
.7. Remarks by Gen. Sir Ian Hamilton, dated 30 December 1926, relating to the musketry training of the British Army before 1914.
.8c. Action on the Menin Road, 25-27 July 1917.
.8f. Report on assault demonstrations at Auxi-le Cateau by Maj. Gen. Egerton, 31 July 1917.
.8j. Report of a visit made to the BEF by Brig. Gen. A. J. Chapman and Brig. Gen. D. A. Macfarlane for the inspection of training depots and schools of instruction, 28 February 1916.

.9. Letters concerning the Seaforth Highlanders, 1941-44.

.17. Brief account of the Seaforth Highlanders in the Sicilian campaign, July — August 1943, with photographs.

52nd Lowland Division, ten documents relating to the division's Army Medical Services. **RAMC.918.1.1951-1628.**

Maj. Gen. Sir (Henry) Hugh Tudor (1871-1965), ts. entitled 'The Fog of War'.

WORLD WAR I

Collections of pamphlets, charts, etc., relating to the RA in WWI. **R.A. 914.2.**

Letter of 12 March 1958 from Mr McK. Annand regarding the uniforms of the Tientsin Volunteer Corps in WWI. **958.1.**

Proclamation by the Government of Australia concerning conscription, 16 November 1917. **958.103.**

Trench maps of the 51st (H) Divisional Sector in WWI. **R.E.914.1.**

Sapper J. Gregor, RE, small book, 25 October 1915. **R.E.915.1.**

Letter from K. A. Bippes, 5th Baden Field Artillery Regiment, relating to the 'Testament' of a Scots Guardsman who died on 28 January 1915 near Auchy-la-Basse, France. **3.G.915.1.**

Maj. A. F. Purvis, Scots Guards: documents, maps, etc. referring to the White Russian campaign, 1918-19; instruction manual in Russian for the Lewis gun; and rules and notes for guidance, South Russia. **3.G.918.1.1959/30.**

Three trench maps of the Beaumont-Hamel sector, 1916. **I.F.V.916.1.**

Pvt. Robert Burton, various documents giving details of his service in the Lancashire Fusiliers, 1914-16; his wounding, and the shipwreck of HMS *Royal Edward,* 14 August 1915; and his discharge. **Cameron Highlanders 1952-671.**

Telegram sent to all reservists and TA members on the outbreak of WWI, 4 August 1914. **29/90.**

Lt. Col. John C. Miller, Black Watch, six documents, including some dealing with his action of 9 May 1915. **42/73.915.2.**

Pvt. David Smith, 5th and 7th Battalions, Seaforth Highlanders, MS diary of service in France, 1915-18. **72/78.915.1.**

Lt. A. L. Lynden Bell, 1st Battalion, Seaforth Highlanders, diary in Mesopotamia 1916. **72/78.916.1.**

Cpl. George Mutch, MS account of escape from a POW camp in Sennelager, Westphalia, 6-14 November 1917. **75/92.917.1.**

Two letters relating to naval operations off the Belgian coast, 19-20 October 1914. **RN.914.2.**

WRNS, pamphlet 414 'Arrangements', including rates of pay by rank, classification, requisitioning of women, etc. Ts. referring to the engagement of WRNS personnel, 7 November 1918. **WRNS.918.1.**

Ts. entitled 'SS *Brussels*', giving a brief history of the ship and the services of the captain, Charles A. Fryatt, in WWI. **M.Navy.914.1.**

Collection of RAF aerial photographs, and photographs of aircraft, 1914-18. **RAF.918.2.**

Three trench maps of Gallipoli, dated July, October and November 1915. **Gallipoli.915.2.**

Field-Marshal Douglas Haig, copy of his 'Backs to the Wall' order, 11 April 1918, and a signal referring to the cessation of hostilities, 11 November 1918.

Telegram to the British Minister at Berne on the outbreak of WWI, 3 August 1914. **2308.**

Order to all units of the 27th Infantry Brigade, 18 April 1917, received by the 9th Scottish Rifles. **27th Infantry Brigade.9.7.1. 26/90th Regiment.**

Scale of rations for the EEF, 1915-18. **Egyptian Expeditionary Force.915.1.1935-133.**

MS copy of Cease Fire Order to all forces in France, 11 November 1918. **General Order.918.1.**

Field-Marshal Lord Allenby, Order of the Day, 26 September 1918. **Order of the Day.918.1.**

Open letters to British POWs in Germany, November 1918, a left wing appeal to freed POWs. **91972-51.**

'Deutsche Soldaten', propaganda leaflet of the type left in the German trenches after raids, 1917-18, with translation. **Propaganda. 917.1.1959-273.**

H. Peters, 'The Volunteer Force 1914-1920', ts. account of a nascent Home Guard in WWI.

WORLD WAR II

Capt. D. H. Sclater, 208/58 Highland Battery, RA. Collection of letters from North Africa and Italy, 1942-5. **R.A. 912.1.**

Col. R. A. Hay, RE, notebook with material relating to the surrender of German forces in Norway, May 1945. **R.E.922.1.**

Australian Army, instructions for sending mail to POWs and internees in Japanese hands, and other POW desiderata. **Australian Army.945.1. 1946-86.**

Royal Scots Regiment, 1st Battalion war diary in WWII. **5023.1.Library no.qA242.1.**

Royal Scots Regiment, 8th Battalion mobilisation scheme, 1939. **I.V. 5024 Library no.qA242.114.**

Parachute Regiment, 12th Battalion diary, 1944-5, copied from the original in 1969. **Parachute Regiment.944.2.**

Naval message, dated 3 September 1939, ordering warships to commence hostilities at once with Germany. **RN.939.1.**

Correspondence regarding attempts to trace Rolf Nienhoff, the first German pilot to be shot down over Scotland, 1939. **RAF.939.1. 1972-44B.**

Documents taken from German POWs, 1944-5. **German Army.944.1.**

Instructions of the SACSEA to the Japanese forces surrendering in the Singapore area, 3 September 1945, and two Japanese maps of troop concentrations in the area. **Japanese Forces.945.1. 1955-161.**

Photocopy of the Instrument of Surrender of Japanese forces in New Britain, New Guinea, New Ireland, Bougainville, and adjacent islands. Signed aboard HMS *Glory* off Rabaul, 6 September 1945, by the C-in-C Japanese Imperial Southeastern Army, and the GOC, 1st Australian Army. **Japanese Forces.945.2. 1967-61.**

J. Johnston, RAF, notebook kept as a POW in a Japanese camp. **1972-53.**

Lt. J. S. Hume, Ammunition Officer, 8th Battalion, Edinburgh Home Guard. Notebooks, papers and documents. **Edinburgh Home Guard.U.1.**

Devon Record Office, Concord House, South Street, EXETER, Devon EX1 1DX

Devonshire Territorial and Auxiliary Forces Association, minute books, 1907-68, a printed history, army list, standing orders, etc., but no annual reports. **Dep. 1715.**

Devonshire Regiment, papers, 1803-1939. The only WWI and II papers are a special order of the day in 1918 and mobilisation telegrams of 1939. **Dep. 1715 add.**

WORLD WAR I

Branscombe, papers referring to the war effort, 1914-19. **1037 M/LG 4.**

Letters from the front to Northam, 1917-19. **1843 A/PM 1-2.**

WORLD WAR II

Honiton Home Guard, papers of C Company, 1940-5. **Dep. 337 add 1.**

Bideford Home Guard, records, including official history, 1940-6. **R2379A/M 1-12.**
Exeter, ARP spotter's log, 1940-4. **1270.**
Teignmouth UDC, Civil Defence Committee minutes, 1941-4. **R2360A/C 78.**
Bideford Borough, minutes of various war committees, 1939-45. **R2379A/Z28-36.**
County Council records, various emergency committee minutes, etc., 1936-46.

Devonshire Regiment Museum, Wyvern Barracks, EXETER, Devon

Enquiries should be addressed to the Curator.

WORLD WAR I

2nd Battalion, Devonshire Regiment, diary compiled by Lt. Col. A. H. Cope relating to the battle of Bois des Buttes, 27 May 1918, for which the battalion received the Croix de Guerre from the French Government.

East Devon Area Record Office, Castle Street, EXETER, Devon EX4 3PQ

WORLD WAR I

Illuminated address, photographs, Devon Yeomanry and Volunteers and Devonshire Regiment, 1900 and 1914-18.
Exeter Town Clerk's files, 1914-18.

WORLD WAR II

District Council records (East Devon), containing material relating to Civil Defence, ARP and evacuation, 1939-45.
Exeter City, Civil Defence files, 1939-45.
ARP instructions.
Exeter Emergency Information Officer's notes.

Regimental Museum, Seaforth Highlanders,
FORT GEORGE, Inverness

Enquiries should be made to the Curator.

WORLD WAR II

2nd Battalion, Seaforth Highlanders, diary of the campaign in France, May — June 1940, compiled by Lt. Col. J. M. Grant.

County Library, Gillingham Division, High Street,
GILLINGHAM, Kent

Enquiries should be made to the Divisional Librarian.

WORLD WAR I

Box 10 contains a collection of material relating to Maj. James B. McCudden (1895-1918), RFC. McCudden served with Nos 20, 29, 66, 56 and 60 Squadrons in France, July 1916 until his death in action in June 1918. A further collection of materials relating to McCudden is located at the Royal Air Force Museum (see p. 183).

Royal Highland Fusiliers Museum, 518 Sauchiehall Street,
GLASGOW G2 3LW

The Museum holds documentary material pertaining to the Highland Light Infantry, the Royal Scots Fusiliers, the Royal Highland Fusiliers and affiliated regiments. Enquiries should be made to the Curator.

WORLD WAR I

War Diaries
Royal Scots Fusiliers, 1st and 2nd Battalions, 1914-18.
Highland Light Infantry:
1st Battalion, 8 August 1914 — 31 March 1919.
2nd Battalion, 5 August 1914 — 31 March 1919 and August 1919.
1/5th Battalion, 1 July 1915 — 5 May 1919, less December 1917.
1/6th Battalion, 25 May 1915 — 31 March 1919.
1/7th Battalion, 19 May 1915 — 7 May 1919, less December 1917.
9th Battalion, 31 October 1914 — 31 August 1919.

10th Battalion, 11 May 1915 — 15 May 1916.
11th Battalion, 6 May 1915 — 15 May 1916.
10/11th Battalion, 16 May 1916 — 13 June 1919.
12th Battalion, 4 July 1915 — 29 April 1919, less March 1919.
14th Battalion, 3 June 1916 — 30 April 1919.
15th Battalion, 22 November 1915 — 31 October 1919, less February and July 1919.
16th Battalion, 23 November 1915 — 31 August 1919, less January 1919.
17th Battalion, 21 November 1915 — 31 January 1918.
18th Battalion, 31 January 1916 — 28 February 1919.

Other Materials
Highland Light Infantry, Roll of Honour, 1914-18.
Highland Light Infantry Chronicle, 1913-20.
17th Battalion, Highland Light Infantry, record of war service, 1914-18.
5th Battalion, Highland Light Infantry, digest of service, 1914-18.
2nd Battalion, Highland Light Infantry, records, 1902-35.
Royal Scots Fusiliers Magazine, 1914-18.

WORLD WAR II

Royal Scots Fusiliers:
6th Battalion, historical records, 1939-45.
1st Battalion, part I and II orders, 1939.
Highland Light Infantry:
Highland Light Infantry Chronicle, 1939-45.
10th Battalion, daily orders, 2 January — 31 December 1942.
10th Battalion, campaign in Europe, 1944-5.
5th Battalion, skeleton war history, 1939-45.
Roll of Honour, 1939-45.

Strathclyde Regional Archives, P.O. Box 27, City Chambers, GLASGOW G2 1DU

In addition to the material listed below, the Archives contain a large amount of WWII Civil Defence and ARP papers.
TD 366. Documents on the Glasgow Highlanders, 5th Volunteer Battalion, Highland Light Infantry (later the 9th Glasgow Highlanders Battalion, Highland Light Infantry):

Col. Harvie Anderson, rough notes on the history of the Glasgow Highlanders, 1869-1947.

Col. A. H. Menzies, notes on the battalion, 1908-14.

Two histories of the Glasgow Highlanders in WWI.

Rev. Prof. A. J. Gossip, padre of the battalion, notes April 1918, on the fighting of 10-15 April 1918.

'The Western Front', drawings by Muirhead Stone, part II.

Capt. W. D. Maxwell, notes on the operations of the 1st Battalion in France, June 1940.

History of the 1st Battalion, Glasgow Highlanders, 1939-45.

Battalion journal of the 1st Battalion, covering operations in the Low Countries, October 1944 — March 1945.

History of the operations of the 2nd Battalion, June — July 1944 to May 1945, by Col. P. Campbell and his successors, MS and ts. copies.

D-TC 19. Raising of Glasgow Regiments, 1914-15. At the outbreak of war, the City of Glasgow was authorised to raise several battalions and equip these for battle. The material comprises:

1st and 2nd Battalions, Highland Light Infantry, 1914-15, 70 files mainly concerned with recruiting, supplies and organisation.

18th (Service) Battalion, Highland Light Infantry, 1914-15, 26 files mainly concerned with officers, recruiting, supplies and training.

159th (Glasgow) Brigade, Royal Field Artillery, and six companies of RE, 26 files mainly concerned with applications for commissions, appointments of officers, supplies and equipment, and recruiting and billeting.

Glasgow University Archives, The University, GLASGOW G12 8QQ

Enquiries should be made to the University Archivist.

Prof. John Graham Kerr

Professor of Zoology, Glasgow University. Large MSS collection of correspondence, notes, papers and reports referring to war camouflage in both world wars. Kerr claimed partial credit for the development of 'dazzle' and 'biological' camouflage. See *NRA-Scotland 0480* for a detailed listing.

Gloucestershire County Record Office, Shire Hall, GLOUCESTER GL1 2TG

Gloucestershire Territorial and Auxiliary Forces Association, minutes, 1908-63.

Draft history of the Gloster Aircraft Company, with specifications of aircraft and brief details of operations, 1915-65. **D 2147.**

WORLD WAR I

Dursley RDC: National Service Committee, correspondence and circulars, 1917; and registers of arrivals and removals under the National Registration Act of 1915, 1915-19. **DA 26/224/1 and 226/1-2.**
Hucclecote, list of parishioners in the Armed Forces, 1915. **P 183A/PC 4/8**
Names of County Council employees on active service, 1916. **CC/C 1916A.**
Letters from Dyrham parishioners on active service in France, Salonika, the Middle East, HM ships, Ireland, and POW camps, 1914-18. **D1799/C163164.**
Accounts of the Royal Gloucestershire Hussars POW Fund, 1916-18. **D1969/Z3/1,2.**
List of Stowe men killed and press-cuttings. **P317/IN 1/19,MI 2,3.**
Letter from Col. W. F. N. Noel of Stardens, Newent, to F. A. Hyett of Painswick, giving an account of an air raid on Margate, 13 September 1915. **D6/F132.**

WORLD WAR II

B Company, 7th Gloucestershire Battalion, nominal rolls and related papers, 1944. **D 264.**
5th Battalion, Gloucestershire Home Guard, order book and war diary, 1940-4.
Winchomb Invasion Committee war book, 1943-4. **P368a/PC4.**
Can Invasion Committee war book, 1943. **P69a/PC2.**
Identity cards and correspondence of E. C. Pugh, 1940-5. **D2606/2-4.**
ARP warden's report books and papers, 1939-44. **P63 MI 3,4.**
Stonehouse Invasion Committee war book, minutes and circulars, 1941-4, and aerial photograph of bombing targets at Stonehouse, 1941. **P 316a/PC 3/7,8**
Kempsford, war book 1941-4. **P 189A/PC 4/1.**
Thornbury RDC, ARP papers including rosters of duty, officers, incidents, plans, etc. **D 274/E 20.**
War book for the Y group of parishes of the Newent RDC Invasion Committee, 1945. **D410.**
Civil Defence papers, including Administration files, maps, training,

history of ARP in Gloucestershire, blitz, schemes, recruitment, ARP Central Authority minutes, etc.

The records of the rural and urban district councils also contain various material regarding ARP and, to a lesser extent, Civil Defence.

Submarine Museum, HMS Dolphin, *GOSPORT, Hampshire PO12 2AB*

The Museum contains documentary and manuscript material relating to submarines and their development from 1901 to the present. Visits are by prior arrangement only. Enquiries should be made to the Curator.

Local History and Archives, Watt Monument Libraries, 9 Union Street, GREENOCK, Renfrewshire PA16 8JH

WORLD WAR II

Clyde River Patrol, log books successively of the *Mingulary, Kia Ora* and *Avila,* 18 August — 13 December 1941.

Guildford Muniment Room, Castle Arch, GUILDFORD, Surrey GU1 3SX

Enquiries can be directed to the Surrey Record Office.

WORLD WAR I

Papers of the 4th and 5th Earls of Onslow, containing some correspondence referring to various war committees, the TA, etc., *c.* 1910-18.

WORLD WAR II

Guildford Borough Archives, including ARP and Emergency Committee minutes, plans and related material, 1939-45.

Women's Royal Army Corps Museum, Corps Headquarters WRAC, Queen Elizabeth Park, GUILDFORD, Surrey

The Museum covers the service of women with the army from 1917 and contains documentary and manuscript materials relating to the WAAC, QMAAC, ATS and WRAC. Enquiries should be made to the Curator.

Dame Helen Gwynne-Vaughan (1879-1967)
Chief Controller, QMAAC, BEF, France from its formation in February 1917 to September 1918; Commandant, WRAF, September 1918 – December 1919; and Director, ATS, 1939-41. The Museum holds two vols. of diaries covering service with QMAAC in France, 21 March – 3 July 1917, **MC 950, Sub cat D380**; and a package of personal and historical material not to be opened until AD 2100. **MC 1564, Sub cat D564.**

WORLD WAR I

QMAAC Unit, Wimereux, France. Duplicate routine orders issued by Chief Controllers H. Gwynne-Vaughan and L. Davy, 31 July 1917 – 9 December 1919. **MC 54, Sub cat D5.**
Army Council Instructions: No. I069, 1917, referring to general administration and organisation of the WAAC; No. 372, 1918, referring to WAAC uniform, **MC 58, Sub cat D8**; and No. 537, 1917, 'Employment of Women with Armies Abroad'.
General instructions for the employment of women with the British army in France. **MC 76, Sub cat D26.**
Letter of 8 October 1917 from Unit Administrative Officer K. Jordan to Mrs Hubbard, relating to work by her WAAC unit and herself in a hostel in France. **MC 95, Sub cat D45.**
QMAAC, four loose ts. pages headed 'Queen Mary's Auxiliary Army Corps' and giving a list of officers and dates of gazetting. **MC 108, Sub cat D58.**
WAAC, two foolscap printed pages of regulations for the WAAC employed with the British Army in France, 1917. **MC 174, Sub cat D78.**
Orders from HQ, QMAAC, 1918-19. **MC 608, Sub cat D297.**
Miss G. E. G. Watkins, 'Memories of a Hushwaac in France: St. Omer, September 1917 – April 1918 and Paris Plage, April – November 1918'. **MC 946, Sub cat D378.**
QMAAC, 'Service of ex-Forcewoman A. L. Gummersall in France, 1917-1918'. **MC 1939, Sub cat D695.**

QMAAC, 'Experiences during WWI as a WAAC officer', by Mrs O. B. Graham. **MC 1942, Sub cat D698.**

QMAAC, Mrs K. Bottomley, 'Service at Farnborough, Boulogne and Abbeville, 1917-1919'. **MC 1933, Sub cat D688.**

QMAAC, Mrs M. Yelf, 'Service at Tours, Monchy and Cayeux, 1917-1918'. **MC 1934, Sub cat 689.**

QMAAC, A. Kimber, 'Service as a waitress, 1917-1919'. **MC 1936, Sub cat D692.**

QMAAC, Mrs Hill, 'How I became a WAAC, 1917-1918', and 'Sunday in Russia, 1919'. **MC 1937, Sub cat D693.**

QMAAC, Mrs V. Rumbold, 'Home and Overseas with WAAC and QMAAC, 1917-1920'. **MC 1938, Sub cat D694.**

WORLD WAR II

Pamphlet giving conditions of service in the ATS, *c.* 1938. **MC 157, Sub cat D71.**

Ts. rules for NCOs, put out by the OC, B Company, No. 4 ATS, Southern Command, 8 July 1940.

Diary of 102 Group, ATS, BEF, France, 22 March – 17 June 1940, including standing orders by Senior Commander Wagstaff. **MC 1076, Sub cat D407.**

Diary of Chilwell Group, 28 November 1940 – 22 June 1941 and 23 July 1941 – 6 June 1944. **MC 1090, Sub cat D412.**

QMAAC, Miss G. Burgess, 'Reminiscences of a serving woman, 1939-1943'. **MC 1093, Sub cat D414.**

Bound collection of Field-Marshal Montgomery's Personal Messages to the 21st Army Group, Normandy to the Baltic, 6 June 1944 – 8 May 1945. **MC 1482, Sub cat D529.**

ATS documents, March – November 1939. **MC 647, Sub cat D308.**

Folder of ATS letters, 1938-9. **MC 800, Sub cat D335.**

Folder of reports and orders, Tidworth Camp, 1939. **MC 801, Sub cat D336.**

79th (City of London) Company, WRAC/TA, ts. history. **MC 1637, Sub cat D570.**

Record of service of Mrs C. McQuigham during the Casablanca Conference, January 1943. **MC 1704, Sub cat D610.**

Folder of letters of bravery, ATS, 1940-1. **MC 1877, Sub cat D646.**

Miss T. Taylor, 'Service memories of an ATS Driver in the Middle East and Desert Convoy'. **MC 1921, Sub cat D677.**

Miss G. Burgess, 'Memories of ATS service in Cairo, 1942'. **MC 1922, Sub cat D678.**

Lt. Col. M. S. F. Millington, 'Ack Ack in Belgium, 1944-1945'. **MC 1926, Sub cat D682.**
Maj. A. Crofton, 'The ATS with the 8th Army in Italy, 1944-1945'. **MC 1940, Sub cat D696.**
Mrs S. M. Butler, 'Memories of an ATS Subaltern, 1939-1946'. **MC 1941, Sub cat D967.**

Calderdale Central Library, Archives Department, Lister Lane, HALIFAX, West Yorkshire HX1 5LA

WORLD WAR I

Halifax County Borough, War Relief Committee minutes, 1914-21. **HXM:413.**

WORLD WAR II

Halifax County Borough:
ARP Committee minutes, 1936-41. **HXM:217-220.**
Civil Defence Committee minutes, 1941-3. **HXM:221.**
Fire Prevention Committee minutes, 1941-3. **HXM:222.**

Duke of Wellington's Regiment & 4th/7th Dragoon Guards, Calderdale Museums Service, Clay House, Greetland, HALIFAX, West Yorkshire HX4 8AN

There is a collection of original material, consisting of attack and position maps, private letters and diaries, battalion and intelligence reports, and photographs. Enquiries should be made to the Director of the Museums Service.

Dyfed Archives, Pembrokeshire Record Office, The Castle, HAVERFORDWEST, Dyfed

WORLD WARS I AND II

Pembrokeshire Territorial and Auxiliary Army, minute books, 1908-68, and correspondence, 1910-61. **Ref. T.T.A.**

Price and Kelway Collection (Milford), deeds and papers, including 'Pembrokeshire Heavy Brigade Royal Artillery, TA'. **Ref. D/PK.**
ARP Committee and ARP Emergency Committee minutes, 1936-42. **Ref. CC/C/81-83.**
There are also various miscellaneous documents relating to the Pembrokeshire Dockyard.

Hereford Library, Broad Street, HEREFORD HR4 9AU

WORLD WAR I

Herefordshire Regiment Old Comrades Association papers, including 'The Herefordshire Roll of Honour 1914-1919'.
King's Shropshire Light Infantry, book of remembrances, 1914-18.

WORLD WAR II

Home Guard, 3rd Hereford (Hereford City) Battalion, order sheets and duty lists, 1943-4.
Home Guard, 4th (Rural) Battalion, MS notebook relating to liaison, administration, etc.

Herefordshire County Record Office, The Old Barracks, Harold Street, HEREFORD HR1 2QX

Hereford Territorial and Auxiliary Forces Association, minutes, 1908-68. **HCRO G82.**

WORLD WAR II

ARP records, referring to general administration and special topics such as shelters, transport, Civil Defence, fire damage and evacuation. **HCRO G80.**

Herefordshire Light Infantry Museum, TAVR Centre, Harold Street, HEREFORD

The Museum relates to the history of the Herefordshire Regiment. Enquiries should be made to the Honorary Curator.

WORLD WAR I

Rolls of Honour, printed, 1914-19.
EEF, official printed report, 1917-18.
MS extracts from the diaries of Gen. Sir. E. Allenby, 1917-18, containing references to the actions of the 1/1 Herefords.
Letter from H.M. King George V, November 1918.
1914 telegram, 'Mobilize'.
Roll book, A Company, 1/1 Herefords.
MS notes of the history of the Herefordshire Regiment.
Photograph albums.

WORLD WAR II

Final code, Northwest Europe campaign, 1944-5.

Hertfordshire Record Office, County Hall, HERTFORD SG13 8DE

Hertfordshire Territorial and Auxiliary Forces Association. Minute books, 1908-62, and Finance and General Purposes Committee minute books, 1908-67. **Official Accession 108.**

WORLD WAR I

1st Battalion, Hertfordshire Regiment, extracts from war diaries, 1914-19, one vol. **Acc. 1397.**
1st Battalion, Hertfordshire Regiment, notes on its role in WWI compiled by Lt. Col. B. J. Gripper and others, *c.* 1923. **26821.**
1st (Hertfordshire) Volunteer Battalion, Bedfordshire Regiment, scrapbook containing orders, press-cuttings, photographs and reminiscences compiled by Capt. E. G. Crawley, 1906-37. **D/EX 47,Z6.**
Hertfordshire Volunteer Training Corps, Benington and District section, minute book, 1915. **CP101. 29/1.**

Local Recruiting Committee for Tring and District, minute book, 1915-16. **D/EX 120.Z1.**

County of Hertford Central Organising Committee and Local Emergency Committee, reports, 1915, and circulars and letters, 1916-18. **15010-15018.**

List of air raid shelters in Barnet, South Mimms and Shenley, *c.* 1914. **D/P 15. 25/4.**

Barkway Parish, various papers, including some regarding preparations against invasion, 1914-17. **D/P 13. 29/17-19.**

Papers referring to compulsory military service, 1916-18. **15019-15022.**

Album of photographs taken in France, *c.* 1914-18 (in the papers of Col. William Le Hardy). **D/ELh. Z9.**

Album of press-cuttings concerning the sinking of HMS *Pathfinder*, 1914, and other naval matters, 1890-1939. **87585.**

Brig. Sir Edward Beddington, autobiographical memoirs, 1884-1960, including WWI military experiences. **D/EX 205.Fl.**

Capt. Henry Bushby, Royal Defence Corps, war notes and diary, 1916-19. **D/EBu. F1.**

Lt. Col. Arthur Leake, 273 letters to his mother, 1914-18. **86935-87207.** His photograph album is **87584.**

Vice-Admiral Francis Leake, 49 letters to his mother, 1914-17. **87512-87562.**

One bundle of letters to Rev. J. H. Baily of Norton from men on active service, 1915-18. **D/P75. 3/3.**

Halsey family correspondence: Arthur Halsey, RN, 1917-18; Lionel Halsey, RN, 1914-18; Walter Halsey, Egypt, 1917-18; and Reginald Halsey, Middle East, 1914-18. **Accession 1478.**

Letters to Lady Desborough and her daughter Monica, Lady Salmond, including correspondence from military personnel and others in the war. **Accession 1477.**

WORLD WAR II

1st Battalion, Hertfordshire Regiment, war diary, 1939-43, five files. **D/EX47. Z1-5.**

135th (Herts. Yeomanry) Field Regiment, RA (TA), diary during the campaign in Malaya and Singapore, January — February 1942, with a postscript by Lt. Col. P. J. D. Toosey, 1946, duplicated ts. **Library 102c.**

135th (Herts. Yeomany) Field Regiment, RA. Regimental Association of Next-of-kin; newsletters, leaflets, etc., 1942-5. **D/EX210. Z1-3.**

Hertfordshire Territorial and Auxiliary Forces Association, selected papers from its files regarding the Hertfordshire Regiment, 1925-58;

Auxiliary Territorial Service, 1938-9; Hertfordshire Home Guard, 1940-4; Army Cadet Force, 1942-5; and duplicated ts., 'Reminiscences of the Mobile Reserve, 13 Company and E Company, 15th Battalion, Hertfordshire Home Guard', by R. S. Waters. **Official Accession 125.**

Hertfordshire Home Guard, Central Sector, defence schemes of 2nd, 4th and 5th Battalions and Sector HQ papers, 1942-4. **Official Accession 117.**

Hertfordshire Home Guard, 4th Battalion, defence scheme, routine orders and other papers, 1943-4. **Official Accession 109.**

Hertfordshire Home Guard, Weapon Training School, Great Amwell, training course for Home Guard instructors by Capt. C. A. Marques, printed, 3rd ed., 1942. **Official Accession 118.**

Hertfordshire Home Guard, six inch Ordnance Survey map of Little Gaddesden, showing position and range of fire of Home Guard posts at Hudnall Cross, *c.* 1940. **AH2774.**

Hertfordshire County Council, Civil Defence Department: ARP and Home Security circulars, bomb reports and other papers, 1937-50; and copy 'No. 1' of 'County War History', draft ts. history of home defence and ARP activities in Hertfordshire, 1939-45, by Capt. J. E. Slattery. **Official Accession 113.**

'County War History', copy 'No. 2'. **D/EX20. Z3.**

Codicote Invasion Committee papers, *c.* 1940. **D/Z28. Z23.**

Knebworth, papers concerning ARP, 1939-41. **CP55. 7/48.**

Hounslow District Library, Treaty Road, HOUNSLOW, Middlesex TW3 1DR

The Library maintains an index of references to WWI and II in Middlesex, including accounts from the Western Front during the 1st world war. There are various recruiting posters from WWI as well as photographs.

Hove Area Library, Church Road, HOVE, East Sussex BN3 2EG

WORLD WAR I

Mayor and Mayoress of Hove, 1914-18. Two large vols., indexed scrapbooks, mainly of newspaper cuttings, also cartoons, letters, programmes, photographs, and pamphlets of the wartime years and the war effort.

WORLD WAR II

Book of photographs of Sir Andrew Cunningham, Admiral of the Fleet, on the occasion of the conferment of the Honorary Freedom of the Borough of Hove.

Kingston upon Hull Record Office, Guildhall, HULL, North Humberside HU1 2AA

WORLD WAR I

File of correspondence concerning air raids.
Papers of Rose Downs & Thompson Ltd, relating to shell production, 1915-19. **DBR/1914-1936.**

WORLD WAR II

German military map of Yorkshire.
Minutes and files of the Emergency Committee.
Controller's correspondence files dealing with each air raid.
Civilian war dead files, papers and card index.
Service record cards of wardens, messengers, etc.
Casualty lists and analysis.
City Engineer's files relating to shelters, including reports and photographs relating to individual raids.
ARP administrative files.
Returns of damage to property.

County Record Office, Grammar School Walk, HUNTINGDON, Cambridgeshire PE18 6LF

WORLD WAR II

Huntingdon, Civil Defence records, 1939-48.
Peterborough, Civil Defence records, 1939-48.

Borough Archives, Council Office, Oaklands, Stade Street, HYTHE, Kent

WORLD WAR II

C. Humphries, account of Hythe's anti-invasion defences, 1939-45.
'War Time 1939-1945', bound MS vol. of ten chapters on local defence volunteers, evacuation, the Battle of Britain, Home Guard, nuisance raids, air raid wardens, V 1 rockets, etc., with water colour illustrations by Rodney Foster.

Suffolk Record Office, Ipswich Branch, County Hall, IPSWICH, Suffolk IP4 2JB

Suffolk Territorial Army Association, minutes, 1907-68. **IA2:1205.**
Papers relating to various drill halls in Suffolk, *c.* 1909-39. **IA2:1298.**

WORLD WAR I

Civil Defence, ts. notes and maps referring to Civil Defence arrangements in East Anglia, 1918. **HD12:874.**
Lt. Col. William Donnan, letters to his wife, 1914-15, including his views on the war and its development, based mainly on newspaper reports and talks with other officers. **HA228/1/1/1-282.**
Letters regarding the possible German invasion of the East Coast, 1914; handbills concerning lights on the East Suffolk coast, 1914; and a letter from an employee of Lord Cranbook serving in the forces, 1914. **HA43:T501/142.**
Revised instructions for the guidance of the civilian population in the event of enemy landings on the coast, East Suffolk, 1916. **HA43:T501/181.**
Record books of soldiers in Lady Stradbroke's military hospital at Henham, 1914-19. **HA11/A16/10/1-10.**
Letters to Lady Stradbroke from soldiers at the Red Cross Hospital, Henham, 1914-21. **HA11/A16/11.**
Clifford Hosken, papers from an album collected as a journalist relating to WWI, including letters, cuttings, etc. He later became a novelist under the name of Richard Keverne. **HA158:2946.**
Maps, 1937, showing enemy raids, 1914-18. **Acc818/2.**

WORLD WAR II

Suffolk Home Guard records, including battalion papers, company rolls, etc., *c.* 1940-4. **IA1:411**.

Suffolk Home Guard, 7th Battalion, papers, 1940-56. **HD451:4175**.

Photocopies of plans, etc. of German targets, Harwich, Ipswich, Lowestoft, Manningtree and Martlesham, 1940-3. **JA1/41**.

German bomb target briefs and plans relating to the Ipswich area, 1939-42. **HD1:3283**.

ARP records, including committee reports and minutes, 1938-40; maps of Felixstowe and Aldeburgh showing ARP services, 1942 and 1946; circulars and correspondence, 1938-45; handbooks, directions, etc., 1936-46; message forms, 1939-45; record books, 1941-2; and records concerning various ARP centres, 1939-45. **Acc818/1-8**.

Cumbria Record Office, County Hall, KENDAL, Cumbria LA9 4RQ

WORLD WAR I

Dent of Flass (addn.), diary and photographs of Capt. A. E. Dent, 1st King's Royal Rifles in France, 1915.

WORLD WAR II

Capt. D. R. Curwen, papers, including ARP material, 1938-45.

Westmorland County Council: ARP files, including printed circulars, control messages, minute books, registers, correspondence, and evacuation papers, 1935-46.

Surrey Record Office, County Hall, KINGSTON UPON THAMES, Surrey KT1 2DN

Surrey Territorial and Auxiliary Forces Association. Minutes of the Association and committees, deeds and papers, 1907-67.

WORLD WAR II

Minutes of the County Council, various committees, and local authorities in Surrey, containing Civil Defence and ARP records.

Brotherton Library, University of Leeds, LEEDS LS2 9JT

Enquiries should be made to the Sub-librarian.

Prof. A. S. Turberville
Scrapbook of documents, photographs and other material relating to his service as a 2nd lieutenant and later captain in the King's Royal Rifle Corps in France (especially Arras), Belgium and Germany, 1915-19, and with the Leeds Home Guard during WWII. **MS 149/29.**

Lt. W. H. E. Gott
Letters home, written as a POW in Germany, 1917-18. **MS 194/10.**

Archives Department, Leeds Library, Chapeltown Road, Sheepscar, LEEDS LS7 3AP

West Riding Territorial Army Association, minutes, 1908-50.

WORLD WAR I

Leeds Territorials, book of news-cuttings, 1906-15.
Papers relating to the Leeds Rifles, mainly of Col. Henry Bowsfield, 1908-24, including an account of operations at Mount Kemmel, 1918. **Ref. DB.**
Photocopies of several diaries of Leeds soldiers.

WORLD WAR II

Home Guard, 18th Yorkshire West Riding Battalion (Leeds), files and maps, 1941-4.
ARP and Civil Defence records of some local authorities in the Leeds district.

Leicestershire Record Office, 96 New Walk, LEICESTER LE1 6TD

Leicestershire and Rutland Territorial and Auxiliary Forces Association, minute and account books, 1901-67.

WORLD WAR I

1/5 Battalion, Leicestershire Regiment, war diary in France, 1918-19. **DE 101.**

1/4 Battalion, Leicestershire Regiment, orders, trench maps, etc. in France, 1916-18. **DE 1407.**

Leicestershire Regiment, camp and field orders, reconnaissance photographs, etc., 1912-15. **22 D 63.**

Records of war related activities in Leicester and Leicestershire, including minutes of committees referring to POWs, the Volunteer Force, etc., 1914-18. **14 D 35.**

Papers relating to volunteers making sandbags, c. 1914-18. **DE 934.**

Photographs of German POWs at Castle Donington, 1914-18. **DE 381.**

Letters from a soldier to his sister, c. 1914-18. **Misc. 628.**

Letter from a vicar, with the Italian Expeditionary Force, to his parishioners, 1918. **DE 1061/21.**

WORLD WAR II

1/5 Battalion, Leicestershire Regiment, war diary in Norway, 1940. **DE 101.**

Leicester Local Defence Volunteers and Home Guard records, 1940-4. **Misc. 140.**

Leicester Air Raid Shelter map, c. 1939-44. **Misc. 702.**

Leicester Corporation, Special ARP Committee and Emergency Committee minutes, 1939-40. **CM 55/1-2.**

Billesdon RDC, ARP papers, 1938-45. **DE 869/112-120.**

Blaby RDC, Civil Defence and ARP Committee minutes, 1938-45. **DE 1048/89.**

East Sussex County Record Office, Pelham House, St. Andrews Lane, LEWES, East Sussex BN7 1UN

Sussex Territorial Association, records, 1908-68. **D912,917.**

WORLD WAR I

County Council files: emergency acts and circulars; Military Service Bill and Act, 1916-17; and Military Tribunal, list of cases.

Correspondence, circulars and instructions to Col. Edward Frewen concerning defence measures to be taken in Kent and Sussex against invasion, 1911-15. **FRE 886, 4219-4222.**

War letters of Sir Augustus Webster and his son Godfrey. **BAT 4860-73.**

Orders of Lt. Col. Edward Campion to the 2nd Battalion, Seaforth Highlanders at Ypres Salient, as the men experienced their first gas attack. **DAN 487-8.**

WORLD WAR II

County Council, Civil Defence files including reports on bombs, flares and anti-personnel weapons, 1938-48.

County Council committee minute books: ARP, 1935-41; Evacuation, 1939-41; Emergency, 1939-46; and Emergency Feeding Centres, 1941-3.

County Council files: evacuation; war zone courts; war damage; the Home Guard; ARP; war refugees; Civil Defence; National and Military Service, the Armed Forces Act; Emergency Committee; temporary labour camps, POW camps; and miscellaneous including aeroplane spotters, the Air Ministry wireless-station, blackouts, air raid shelters, bombs, etc.

Battle RDC, Emergency Committee minutes, 1939-46, and notifications of death and burials of civilians killed by enemy action and of enemy personnel, 1942.

Lewes Borough: ARP minutes, 1939-40; Civil Defence minutes, 1939-46; and papers concerning action to be taken by local triumvirates in case of enemy invasion, 1941-3.

Newhaven UDC, ARP minutes, 1936-44.

Rye Borough, ARP minutes, 1938-40, and Emergency minutes, 1942-5.

Seaford UDC, ARP minutes, 1939-44.

Home Guard records, 1940-4.

Land Army girl's diary, 1939-40. **D1128.**

Lincolnshire Archives Office, The Castle, LINCOLN LN1 3AB

Lincolnshire Territorial and Auxiliary Forces Association
Minutes, 1908-58.

War diaries: 4th Battalion, Lincolnshire Regiment, 4 August 1914 – 31 December 1915 and 1 October 1939 – August 1944; and Searchlight Garrison, Lincolnshire Regiment, RA, June 1942 – November 1944.

Miscellaneous, file regarding a scheme for a history of the work of county territorial associations during WWI, including correspondence, notes and copies of compilations for Worcestershire and Renfrewshire, 1917-28.

War Office telegrams, August – September 1939.

Officers, Lincolnshire sectors.

Home Guard, Northern Command, duplicated list of officers, corrected to 31 October 1944.

Elwes Collection
This includes some field notebooks, 1916-17, and correspondence concerning WWII service in the Middle East.

Liverpool Record Office & City Libraries, William Brown Street, LIVERPOOL L3 8EW

West Lancashire Territorial and Auxiliary Forces Association, minute books, ledgers and press-cuttings.

359th (4th West Lancashire) Medium Regiment, RA (TA), records, 1859-1959.

WORLD WAR I

The King's Liverpool Regiment, 2nd Volunteer Battalion, records, 1914-20.

Maj. George Higgins, commanding 17th King's Liverpool Regiment, correspondence relating to his death in 1916.

E. G. Williams, King's Liverpool Regiment, pictures and reminiscences of France, 1914-18.

55th (West Lancashire) Division, records, 1914-19.

SS *Henriette Waermann,* night order book of a captured German vessel, 1913-15.

Liverpool Women's War Service Bureau, annual reports, 1914-17, and other items.

Sir Richard Durning Holt (1868-1941)
Correspondence and papers, 1872-1941, including references to the Standing Sub-committee of Supplies in Time of War; the Committee of Imperial Defence, 1911-14, of which Holt was a member; and diaries, 1900-27.

Edward George Villiers Stanley, 17th Earl of Derby (1865-1948)
Director of Recruiting, 1915-16; Under-Secretary of State for War,

1916; Secretary of State for War, 1916-18; and Ambassador in Paris, 1918-20. Papers and correspondence referring to all of these offices.

WORLD WAR II

Liverpool Corporation, ARP and Civil Defence minute books, 1935-44. Miscellaneous items including German invasion maps of Liverpool and press-cuttings referring to the Blitz.

Merseyside County Museum, William Brown Street, LIVERPOOL L3 8EN

WORLD WAR I

Diary of Prof. E. C. Wells, October 1915 − October 1917. As a first year medical student, Wells joined the University OTC in October 1915, moved on to the West Lancashire Brigade as a territorial gunner and went to Bettisfield. He was then transferred to the 3rd West Lancashire Batteries and from there to Shoeburyness and Larkhill. Sent to France in March 1917, Wells described campaign details and life in the diary.

Museum of the King's Regiment (Liverpool)
Photocopies of letters of Lt. Col. J. W. Allen and 2nd Lt. G. W. D. Allen, relating to the 4th Battalion in France, 1915-16.
Correspondence of 2nd Lt. R. D. Jenkins, 1/5th Battalion, in France, 1914-17.
Documents relating to the 17th Battalion in North Russia, 1918-19.
Ts. copies of regimental war diaries, WWI.

Harold Cohen Library, The University of Liverpool, P.O. Box 123, LIVERPOOL L69 3DA

Eleanor Rathbone papers
Files on Czechoslovakian refugees, 1938-9; the All-Party Parliamentary Action Group, 1939-40; refugees and aliens in Britain, 1940-5; deportation of Jews into the USSR, 1943-5; and various wartime activities, 1939-46. **R.P.XIV.2.15-19.**

Llangefni Area Record Office, Shire Hall, LLANGEFNI, Gwynedd

WORLD WAR I

Register of farmers applying for the release of men from the army to work on their land, 1918-19.

WORLD WAR II

Anglesey war weapons and warship week, Committee minutes, 1941-2.
War Service Sub-committee (Finance) minutes, 1940-3.
Civil Defence services and co-ordination of public services in time of war, including maps, plans, etc., 1942.
Account of a British bombing aeroplane which crashed in the sea off Rhosneigr, Isle of Anglesey, ts., 1941.

Army Museums Ogilby Trust, Ministry of Defence (Army), 85 Whitehall, LONDON SW1A 2NP

The Army Museums Ogilby Trust is a private, educational, charitable organisation. It holds a substantial collection of documentary and photographic material relating to the history of dress and uniform for virtually all of the regular and volunteer regiments and corps of the British Army, with occasional material of broader interest mixed in. Some papers of individuals and other documents are also held:

(Henry) Spenser Wilkinson (1853-1937)
Military historian and journalist. The papers consist mainly of a large collection of letters, 1881-1935, to various correspondents. Of particular interest are 72 letters to Field-Marshal Lord Nicholson, 1892-1914; 108 letters to Lord Roberts on military subjects, 1891-1912, 14 letters to Asquith on the conduct of the war, August 1914 — March 1916; and other letters with Lord Kitchener and Field-Marshal Robertson on the war.

Maj. Gen. L. A. E. Price-Davies (1878-1965)
Diaries covering *inter alia* service as a staff and brigade commander in France, 1915-18, and as Battalion Commander, Upper Thames Patrol, Home Guard, 1940-4.

WORLD WARS I AND II

98th Field Company, RE, war diary in France, 1915-18.
Documents relating to the Shanghai Defence Force, 1937.

*London Borough of Barnet, Library Administrative Offices,
Ravensfield House, The Burroughs, Hendon, LONDON
NW4 4BE*

Enquiries should be made to the Borough Librarian.

WORLD WAR II

ARP plans, n.d. **Acc 7363/140.**
First Aid Post, etc., 1939-42. **Acc 7363/141-146.**
Civil Defence ARP, 1939-45, various plans and operations in case of
invasion. **Acc 5494.**
Finchley Borough: particulars of damage and casualties arising from
enemy action, 1939-45; and Civil Defence ARP Finchley log book,
1939-45. **Acc 9215.**
Middlesex Territorial Association: Sailors, soldiers and Air Force
Welfare and Comforts minutes, 1940-1.
Borough of Hendon Welfare and Comforts Organisation for HM Forces:
minutes, 1941-6 **(Acc 4678)**; statement of accounts, 1941-8 **(MS 4679)**;
names and addresses of recipients of parcels, 1940-5 **(Acc 4680)**;
correspondence, 1943-5 **(Acc 4686)**; and miscellaneous papers referring
to POWs **(Acc 4687).**
Ministry of Intelligence Local Committee (Hendon), file of correspon-
dence with the Secretary, 1940-6. **Acc 9215.**
War damage, ARP log book for Hendon, 1940-5. **Acc 9215.**
Map of war damage in the Borough of Hendon, 1942. **7363/134.**

*Battersea District Library, 265 Lavender Hill, LONDON
SW11 1JB*

WORLD WAR II

Home Guard, 28th County of London (Wandsworth) Battalion orders,
June 1940 — December 1944, two vols.
Metropolitan Borough of Wandsworth: air raid damage between June

1944 and March 1945, four vols. of loose leaf folders; and war damage record cards, 1940-5, in alphabetical order of streets.

Beaverbrook Library, 33 St. Bride Street, LONDON EC4A 4AY

The Beaverbrook Library closed in March 1975. The collections of papers held there have been transferred to the House of Lords Record Office (see p. 101).

British Library, Reference Division, Great Russell Street, LONDON WC1B 3DG

The major manuscript repository in Britain outside of the Public Record Office is the Department of Manuscripts of the British Library, which until 1973 was a part of the British Museum. The Library holds some significant deposits of papers for the study of the world wars.

As an introduction to the tools for using the resources of the department, intending researchers should consult T. C. Skeat, *The Catalogues of Manuscript Collections in the British Museum* (London, 1962, rev. ed.). The only two manuscript series to receive additions since 1914 have been the Additional Manuscripts and the Egerton Manuscripts. The Additional Manuscripts were surveyed from **38796** (1914) to **58234** (November 1974) while a similar survey of the Egerton Manuscripts revealed no relevant material. Since both series receive periodic additions, however, the researcher should always consult the indexes and registers in the department.

39257-39258. Impressions of the airship raids over London of 8 September and 13 October 1915, as recorded the following day by boys of the Princeton Street Elementary School, Bedford Row, Holborn.

39928. Printed map with autograph note by Field-Marshal Douglas Haig of the situation in France and Flanders on 25 September 1918, the eve of the breaking of the Cambrai-St. Quentin line.

40730. f. 59. Ts. letter, with autograph corrections, from Theodore Roosevelt to Bertrand Shadwell on how the Allied cause might best be helped, New York, 29 May 1917.

41178. f. 1. Letter of 6 October 1917 from Sir Maurice Hankey, Secretary to the War Cabinet, to Lionel Walter, 2nd Baron Rothschild, asking his opinion on the proposed Balfour Declaration. **f. 3.** Letter of

2 November 1917 from Balfour to Rothschild transmitting the declaration.

42242-42256. Sir William Ashley Papers. Official papers of William (James) Ashley (1860-1927), Professor of Commerce at the University of Birmingham, 1901-25, relating to his public work during WWI. With the official correspondence, white papers, minutes, memoranda and drafts concerning industry, prices, trade and food is a 'Memorandum on the effect on trade and industry of an indemnity to be paid by the enemy at the conclusion of the War', prepared with the assistance of John Maynard Keynes for the Board of Trade. There are other miscellaneous papers concerning reparations.

42510. Scribbling pad of the poet Rupert Brooke, containing notes of military lectures and personal memoranda made while at the Royal Naval Training Division at Blandford, October — December 1914. There are also drafts of war poems, some unpublished.

43697-43701. 'S.M.S. *Wolf*' an unpublished English translation by Walter Farrell of the account by Capt. Karl August Nerger of his ship's cruise in the Indian, Pacific and Atlantic Oceans, 24 November 1916 — 24 February 1918. Included is the translator's introduction, a short biography of the author and considerable supplementary material prepared by the translator. The German edition was published in Berlin in 1918.

45356. Autograph draft of *The Grand Fleet 1914-1916* by Admiral of the Fleet Sir John Jellicoe, preceded by notes on the MS by Admiral Sir Frederic Dreyer who was Jellicoe's Flag Captain at Jutland. The printed version is an expansion of this MS. **Add. MSS 49040** contains Jellicoe's drafts of a three chapter addition to a proposed second edition of *The Grand Fleet.*

45416. Draft text of the special order of the day addressed 'To All Ranks of the British Forces in France' from Field-Marshal Douglas Haig, 11 April 1918. This autograph and signed order became known as the 'backs to the wall message', issued on the third day of the German (Lys) offensive in Flanders.

45715. Various papers concerning the surrender of Leopold III, King of Belgium, to the Germans on 28 May 1940, including much correspondence of William, 6th Duke of Portland, and some of Edward Wood, Foreign Secretary.

45749. Letter of 3 November 1920 from David Lloyd George, Prime Minister, to Alfred B. Raper, MP, concerning the difficulty of meeting his election pledge to bring former Emperor Wilhelm II to trial.

45912-45917. T. E. Lawrence Papers. Miscellaneous books, notes, and papers of Thomas Edward Lawrence (1888-1935), who was with the Arab Bureau, 1914-16, and advisor to King Feisal, 1916-18. Included is his army field service correspondence book relating to the Arabian campaign, 1916-17, and parts of a diary for January-June of 1917. Other correspondence and papers of Lawrence are **45903**, **45904**, **45922**, **45930**, **45983** and **46355**.

45985-46118. The Viscount Gladstone Papers. A selection of the official and private correspondence of Herbert John Gladstone, 1st Viscount Gladstone (1854-1930), who held no office during WWI but corresponded with the main political and military figures of the war. Correspondents include Nicholas I of Montenegro, Balfour, MacDonald, Lloyd George, Churchill, Asquith and Grey. Other Gladstone papers are **46474-46486**.

46281-46345. The Burns Papers. A selection from the official and private correspondence of John Elliott Burns (1858-1943), PC, MP, who resigned his post as President of the Board of Trade in 1914 in opposition to the foreign policy of Asquith and Grey. Correspondents include Asquith, MacDonald, Lloyd George and Churchill. There are also Burns' diaries covering the period of WWI.

46362, ff. 122-126. Foreword for a proposed work on the campaign in the Carpathians during 1914-15 by Gen. Moritz Freiherr von Auffenberg-Komarów, last Austro-Hungarian Minister of War, dated December 1927, in German and possibly a sequel to his *Aus Österreich-Ungarns Teilnahme am Weltkrieg* (1920).

46386-46394. Correspondence of John Alfred Spender (1862-1942), editor of the *Westminster Gazette* and leading liberal journalist. Much correspondence with the major political figures of the time, of whom Spender was an intimate. There are also papers relating to the Cabinet's declaration of war in 1914. Much of the correspondence was used by Spender for his own biography of Asquith.

46766-46775. Austin-Lee Papers. Letters from the years, 1911-31, addressed to Madeleine de Wolff, Lady Austin-Lee, wife of Sir Henry Austin-Lee, Counsellor of the British Embassy in Paris. The collection also contains her diaries written chiefly during the war years.

48203-48208. Correspondence and papers of Walter Shaw Sparrow relating to his *The Fifth Army in March 1918* (1921). Correspondence with F. S. Oliver and Gen. Sir H. Gough, notes and various accounts of the engagement.

48988.M. 'Intensified Air Raids on London', an account of the raids in September 1940 by William Carpenter, Chief Air Warden of Poplar.

48989-49057. The Jellicoe Papers. A selection from the papers of Admiral of the Fleet Sir John Jellicoe (1859-1935). The deposit is arranged as correspondence and papers, 1905-35; literary MSS; and papers relating to the Empire Mission, 1919-20. Some of the correspondence and papers have been published in A. Temple Patterson, ed., *The Jellicoe Papers* (London: Naval Records Society, 2 vols., 1966-8).

49065-49085. Papers and diaries of Senator Basil Van der Vliet of the

Russian Foreign Office. The correspondence covers the period, 1891-1934, and the diaries, 1894-1918.

49374. André Soarès, 'Angleterre', written as a tribute to an ally of France, 1916.

49380.D. Ts. carbon copy of a narrative by Ernest Philip Higgs, of the Shanghai Power Company, concerning his experiences in Shanghai, 1941-5.

49683-49962. Papers of Arthur James Balfour, 1st Earl of Balfour (1848-1930), member of the War Cabinet, 1914; 1st Lord of the Admiralty, 1915; and Foreign Secretary, 1916-19. The papers are divided as royal correspondence and heads of state; correspondence with Prime Ministers, etc.; Cabinet, CID and foreign affairs; papers as Lord President of the Council; correspondence relating to home affairs; family correspondence; general correspondence; letter books; and literary MSS.

50078-50114. Correspondence and papers of Lt. Gen. Sir Edward Hutton (1848-1923). **50086** contains correspondence with Field-Marshal Sir John French, 1900-15, and Field-Marshal Sir Douglas Haig, 1917. **50088** is correspondence with Lt. Gen. Edwin Alderson, 1889-1915. **50089** is correspondence with Lt. Gen. Sir William Riddell Birdwood, 1916-20, and several other officers covering the war years.

50483. Letter from Admiral Sir John Jellicoe to Miss Constance MacMurray relating to the battle of Jutland, 15 December 1932.

50831-50841. Letters and papers of Sir George Sydenham Clarke, Baron Sydenham (1848-1933). Some documents acquired as Secretary of the CID, but mostly correspondence with Sir Valentine Chirol.

50901-50909. Memoranda and correspondence, 1911-28, of Charles Prestwich Scott (1846-1932), editor of the *Manchester Guardian*.

51071-51024. Correspondence and papers of Lord Edgar Cecil, 1st Viscount Cecil of Chelwood (1864-1958), Parliamentary Under-Secretary for Foreign Affairs, 1915-18, Minister of Blockade, 1916-18; and Assistant Secretary of State for Foreign Affairs, 1918-19. Cecil was in charge of the Foreign Office during Balfour's numerous absences and was active in the formation of the League of Nations. There is much official correspondence on foreign affairs, 1915-19; with Lloyd George, 1915-43; Churchill, 1910-52; Balfour, 1906-29; Asquith, 1913-44; Grey, 1914-29; Arthur Chamberlain, 1937-39. **51049** contains memoranda relating to the Dumbarton Oaks proposals and the United Nations.

51252-51254. Papers of Sir Ralph Spencer Paget (1864-1940) diplomatist. Correspondence with Grey, 1906-16; Balfour, 1917-18; Lord Hardinge, 1916-18; and the Foreign Office, 1916-18. Paget was Envoy Extraordinary at Belgrade, 1910-13; Assistant Secretary of State for Foreign Affairs, 1913-15; Chief Commissioner of the Red Cross and St.

John of Jerusalem, 1915-16; and Minister Plenipotentiary to the King of Denmark, 1916-18.

52455-52459. Correspondence and papers of Lt. Col. Sir Archibald Wilson (1884-1940), mainly as Deputy and Acting Civil Commissioner in Baghdad, 1915-24.

52460. The Haig Memorandum, an account of operations on the Western Front, 1916-18, compiled by members of Field-Marshal Douglas Haig's staff, carbon of a ts. copy.

52461-52463. Murray-Robertson Papers. Correspondence between Gen. Sir Archibald Murray, C-in-C Mediterranean and EEF and Gen. Sir William Robertson, CIGS, 1916-18.

52504-52506. Correspondence and papers of Admiral Sir Hugh Evan-Thomas (1862-1928), Second in Command of the First Battle Squadron, 1915-16; Vice-Admiral, 1917; and Admiral, 1920. There are a few family papers but most concern his naval career, 1876-1927.

52537. Letters, mostly copies, written by Capt. Francis H. Mitchell, RN, to his wife and mother during the Dardanelles campaign, 1915-18.

52557-52584. Correspondence and papers of Admiral of the Fleet Andrew Browne Cunningham (1883-1963), C-in-C Mediterranean, 1939-42; and First Sea Lord, 1943-6. Correspondence, diaries, naval telegrams and speeches for the years, 1940-6, as well as the diary of Admiral Sir James Somerville for March — July 1944 and the papers of Admiral Sir Charles Forbes, 1938-40.

52776-52777. Papers of Gen. Sir Horace L. Smith-Dorrien (1858-1930). Statement of his activities in 1914-15, chiefly to refute the account of Sir John French in his book *1914,* and a personal narrative of events between 21 August and 4 October 1914 in support of the preceding statement.

52785-52797. Diaries and papers of Sir Stanley V. Goodall (1883-1965), Director of Naval Construction, 1936-44, and Assistant Controller (Warship Production) at the Admiralty 1942-5.

53738. Seven letters from Admiral Jellicoe, 1920-25, and one letter from Admiral Evan-Thomas, 19 February 1927, to Commander Oswald M. Frewen relating to the battle of Jutland.

53774. Original MS of the war diary of Keith Douglas, published as *From Alamein to Zem Zem* (1946).

54477-54480. Correspondence and papers of Vice Admiral John E. T. Harper (1874-1949) relating to the non-publication of the Official Record of the battle of Jutland. There is a ts. copy of the Harper Record marked with passages to be deleted at the request of the Director of Naval Intelligence and on orders of Lord Beatty; a printed proof copy of the record with amendments; a set of the printed plans; a docket containing copies of internal Admiralty minutes and memoranda dealing with the compilation and publication of the record; and

Harper's own 'Facts dealing with the compilation of the "Official Record of the Battle of Jutland" and The Reason it was not published'. This material was at the Royal United Service Institute until 1968 and has been published in A. Temple Patterson, ed., *The Jellicoe Papers,* vol. II, Appendix.

56093-56098. Notebooks, diaries, correspondence and papers of Admiral of the Fleet Sir Arthur J. Power (1889-1960), commander of HMS *Ark Royal,* 1938-40; 15th Cruiser Squadron, 1942-3; Vice-Admiral, Malta. 1943-4; and C-in-C East Indies, 1945.

56379-56402. Diaries and some papers, 1937-46, of Sir Oliver Harvey, 1st Baron Harvey of Tasburgh (1893-1968). The papers mainly relate to his position as principal private secretary to Anthony Eden and Viscount Halifax, Secretaries of State for Foreign Affairs. The papers have been partly published as John Harvey, ed., *The Diplomatic Diaries of Oliver Harvey 1937-1940* (1970).

British Library of Political and Economic Science, London School of Economics, Houghton Street, LONDON WC2A 2AE

The Library holds a number of collections of private papers and some miscellaneous manuscripts and documentary material. There is no published catalogue. Access may generally be obtained on application to the librarian.

PRIVATE PAPERS

Beveridge Papers
Personal and family papers of William Henry Beveridge, 1st Baron Beveridge (1879-1963). Beveridge was Assistant General Secretary, Ministry of Munitions, 1915-16, and Second Secretary, Ministry of Food, 1916-18. The papers are divided into general categories of which the following have interest:

WWI: work at the Ministry of Munitions, 1915-16; the Man-power Distribution Board, 1916-18; Reconstruction papers, 1914-21; Ministry of Food, 1916-19; and papers relating to the peace negotiations.

Politics, correspondence relating to and reporting on the Dumbarton Oaks Committee proposals on peace, 1945.

Other interests and activities, various material on the Dumbarton Oaks proposals, 1944, and the Crimea Conference, 1945.

Visits abroad, United States and Canada, 1943.

Courtney Papers
MS correspondence, journals, and miscellaneous papers of Leonard Henry Courtney, 1st Baron Courtney of Penwith (1832-1918). Although not in office during WWI, Courtney was a strong critic of British diplomacy prior to and during the war. Some of his papers relate to WWI.

Hugh Dalton Papers
Papers of (Edward) Hugh (John Neale) Dalton, Baron Dalton (1887-1962), Minister of Economic Warfare, 1940-2, and President of the Board of Trade, 1942-5. His papers contain diaries from 1916 to 1960 with occasional short gaps while his subject files, dating from 1926, contain many documents and notes on rearmament and defence; the war, 1939-40; the Ministry of Economic Warfare, 1940-1; the SOE, May 1942; and the Prime Minister's personal minutes, 1942-5.

Warren Fisher Papers
Papers of Sir (Norman Fenwick) Warren Fisher (1879-1948). Fisher was Permanent Secretary to the Treasury from 1919 to 1939. In the late 1930s he headed many inter-departmental committees concerned with the preparations for war. The papers cover the period, 1926-39, and include the following items of interest: report to the Prime Minister on Air Defence, 1938; comparison of the strengths of the British and German Air Forces, 1938; Report on Czechoslovakia, 1938; other papers relating to Czechoslovakia and Munich, 1938; note on incompetence in the Air Ministry; note for Sir Horace Wilson for the Prime Minister on British air weakness, 1939; letter to Wilson on *inter alia* the incompetence of the Foreign Office and the Armed Forces, 1939.

Passfield Papers
Private papers of Sidney James Webb, Baron Passfield of Passfield Corner (1859-1947), and Beatrice Potter Webb (1858-1943). The collection contains Beatrice's diary, correspondence of both Webbs, and various papers arising from their public activities which may have some relevance.

Webster Papers
Papers of Sir Charles Kingsley Webster (1886-1961), Stevenson Professor of International History at the London School of Economics, 1932-53. Webster was Special Adviser to the Foreign Office on United Nations affairs, 1944-6. He was with the British delegation at Dumbarton Oaks and San Francisco 1944-5, and served on the Preparatory Commission and UN General Assembly in London, 1945-6. Many of his papers relate to his work at the UN while others concern

his own academic work. There are, for example, the papers relating to *The Strategic Air Offensive against Germany, 1939-1945,* published in 1961 with Noble Frankland.

Wise Papers

The papers of Sir Fredric Wise (1871-1928) cover the period, 1913-57, but for the most part are post-WWI. There is some material about Germany and British government finances, as well as an envelope containing a map of the Western Front, and pamphlets about naval actions. There is also material relating to the Volunteer Training Corps of which Wise was president, including lectures, notes and sketch maps used for addressing the troops, and other miscellaneous corps papers.

MISCELLANEOUS MATERIAL

R. (Coll.) Misc. 20 M151. European War, 1914-18, 18 vols. of press-cuttings relating to financial and commercial questions.

R. (Coll.) Misc. 76 S1922. *Nachrichten für die Truppe,* 25 April 1944 — 1 May 1945, with gaps, a daily newspaper dropped by the Allies on or behind the German Western Front.

R. (Coll.) Misc. 80 M115. The Polish question during and after the war, a two vol. collection of printed and ts. memoranda and other documents in German, Polish and French, 1915-21.

R. (Coll.) Misc. 81 M116. Max Weber, *Der verschärfte U-Boot–Krieg* (1916) 16 pp.

R. (Coll.) Misc. 82 M117. Wolfgang Kapp, MS, mimeographed and ts. confidential memoranda, in German, on German policy, 1916.

R. (Coll.) Misc. 83 M118. Germany's Ukrainian policy and interests, a collection of printed and mimeographed material in German and Russian, 1914-18.

R. (Coll.) Misc. 84 M119. Discussion of Germany's war aims and peace terms, a four vol. collection of printed, mimeographed and MS material in German, 1914-18.

R. (Coll.) Misc. 86 M125. Food and fodder questions in Germany, a collection of reports and leaflets, Berlin, 1915-21.

R. (Coll.) Misc. 87 M126. German economic problems, 1914-18, a collection of reports and articles. Berlin, 1914-18.

R. (Coll.) Misc. 104 M165. German war finance, propaganda, 1914-18, 37 parts in one.

R. (Coll.) Misc. 111 M175. Press censorship in Germany, 1914-18, a collection of printed, mimeographed and MS material, 1914-18.

R. (Coll.) Misc. 112 M174. German occupation of Belgium, 1916-18, a collection of reports and leaflets.

R. (Coll.) Misc. 137 M206. Germany, Kriegsministerium, Kriegs-Rohstoff-Abteilung, Bewirtschaftung von kriegswichtigen Stoffen, 1914-18: a collection of printed and ts. material, Berlin, 1914-18.

R. (Coll.) Misc. 144 M210. William Henry Beveridge, papers collected during his tenure as Assistant General Secretary of the Ministry of Munitions, 1915-16.

R. (Coll.) Misc. 148 M220. Great Britain in war time, November 1940 – May 1941, 51 boxes of newspaper cuttings and mimeographed material on social conditions, collected by the Ministry of Information.

R. (Coll.) Misc. 149 M221. Two vols. of material relating to the German war loans, 1914-18.

R. (Coll.) Misc. 159 M232. United Kingdom, Ministry of Food, Statistical Branch, one vol. of material relating to food conditions and food control in foreign countries, 1917-19.

R. (Coll.) Misc. 233 M338. Rudolf Rocker, Alexandra Palace Internment Camp, a study of the life of the prisoners by one of them, 1918.

R. (Coll.) Misc. 254 M378. Jewish Central Information Office, *Documents on Nazi Rule*, issues 1-89, London, 1945-6.

R. (Coll.) Misc. 255 186908. Bulgaria, Natsionalniia Komitet na Otechestvenia Front, pamphlets, newspapers and miscellaneous papers relating to the Fatherland Front and Bulgarian national culture, Sofia, 1944-5.

R. (Coll.) Misc. 255(4) 186908. D. Bratanov, *Borbata sreshtu fashizma.* Suiuz na Sotsialisticheskata Mladezh v Bulgariia, Sotsialisticheskata Biblioteka, No. 4, Sofia, 1944.

R. (Coll.) Misc. 255(6) 186908. Dimo Kazasov, *Political Bulgaria between 1913-1944,* Sofia, 1945.

R. (Coll.) Misc. 255(9) 186908. Stefan Karakostov *Kultura i fashizm: belezhki, statii, reportazhi i dokumenti ot antifashistkata borba,* Sofia, 1945.

R. (Coll.) Misc. 272 M402. Freya Moltke and Marion York (compilers), *Der Nachlass von Kreisau: unveröffentlichte Entwürfe zum 20 Juli 1944,* photocopy of transcript.

R. (Coll.) Misc. 294 M457. Hungary, 1919-46, a collection of anonymous memoranda on public finance, foreign relations and economic conditions, mimeographed in Hungarian, Budapest, 1946.

R. (Coll.) Misc. 356 M643. World War, 1939-45, a collection of newspaper cuttings relating to continental trade, December 1939 – March 1940.

INTERNATIONAL MILITARY TRIBUNAL

The Library contains an incomplete set of the proceedings of the International Military Tribunal of the Far East, 1945-8.

Guildhall Library, Basinghall Street, LONDON EC2

Lloyd's of London (Insurance)
War casualty books, 1914-22, incomplete. Details of ships lost or damaged by wartime activities, including captured German vessels and cargoes from various ships detained in British ports, 5 August 1914 – 16 June 1922. **MS. 14,934; MS. 14,935** is indexes, 1917-22.

City of London Territorial and Auxiliary Forces Association
Records of the City of London Territorial and Auxiliary Forces Association, including *inter alia* committee minute books, 1908-28; General Policy Committee minute books, 1928-68; and Recruiting Committee minute books, 1908-38. The remaining records are administrative in nature. **MS. 12,606-626.**

London Rifle Brigade
MS. 9386-9410 are the archives of the London Rifle Brigade. The records are administrative in nature, consisting of accounts, ledgers, subscription list, etc., except for **9400** which is the Brigade war diary, 1914-19.

No. 1282 City of London Squadron: Air Training Corps
Civilian Committee minute book, 1941-7, and other administrative papers including a scrapbook of press-cuttings and photographs referring to the Corps, 1941-6. **MS. 14,387-390.**

Inns of Court and City of London Yeomanry
MS. 14,490-524 are the archives of the Inns of Court and City of London Yeomanry, 1803-1939. There is little material for WWI. The majority relates to routine administrative matters, including the General Committee minute books, 1910-19; daily orders, 1914-19, of the Inns of Court OTC; attestation books, 1908-18, of the Inns of Court Rifle Volunteers; various muster rolls, registers of members, committee records, orderly room registers, and battalion orders, March 1916 – November 1918 of the 2nd Battalion, County of London Volunteer Regiment.

Haringey Libraries, Museums & Arts Department, Bruce Castle, Lordship Lane, LONDON N17 8NU

WORLD WAR I

Robert Craigmyle Morrison, 1st Baron Morrison of Tottenham (1881-

1953). He joined the army as a private and served in France, 1915-19. Diary pencilled in a notebook covering March 1916 – November 1918.

WORLD WAR II

Tottenham ARP Committee minutes, January 1939 – October 1946. Tottenham Civil Defence Committee minutes, September 1939 – October 1946, one box of loose stencilled sheets.
Tottenham ARP Control Room personnel strengths (location not stated), September – December 1939, MS vol.
List of air raid incidents in Tottenham, giving time, type of bomb, location, casualties and damage, August – December 1940, 30 foolscap ts. sheets. List of air raid incidents in Tottenham as above, December 1940 – June 1941, including an account of rocket incidents after July 1944, 12 ts. quarto sheets.
List of air raid incidents in Tottenham as above, January 1942 – July 1944, seven ts. foolscap sheets.
Notice of a motion to be considered at a meeting of Tottenham Borough Council on 18 July 1944 urging the systematic bombing of German towns and villages in retaliation for the indiscriminate use of long range rockets.
Diary of air raid incidents in Tottenham, August 1940 – December 1940, including note by WD assessor of war damage, 1947, foolscap notebook, 60 pp., MS.
Diary of air raid incidents in Tottenham as above, January 1942 – July 1944.
Incident map, showing location of all bomb incidents in Tottenham during the course of the war, approximately 67 inches x 85 inches (OS map 1938 ed., scale 1:2500).
Wood Green Civil Defence Committee, index of wartime bomb incidents in Wood Green, refering to an unlocated map.
Hornsey Civil Defence Committee, register of wartime bomb incidents arranged by streets.
A large collection of official photographs of war damage within the former boroughs of Hornsey, Tottenham and Wood Green.

House of Commons. See *House of Lords Record Office.*

House of Lords Record Office, Westminster, LONDON SW1A 0PW

The House of Lords Record Office is the general archive of Parliament.

Practically all original Parliamentary papers from 1497 that have been officially preserved are given over to this library and archive. Housed in the Palace of Westminster, it contains the records of both Houses of Parliament, all documents presented to or purchased by either House, and the papers accumulated in the various parliamentary and non-parliamentary offices of the Palace.

The Record Office Search Room makes nearly all these materials available to researchers, who should first consult Maurice F. Bond, *Guide to the Records of Parliament* (London, HMSO, 1971). This work describes the classes of records, their development and their use. Intending researchers should first write to the Clerk of the Records concerning the specific nature of their research and if possible the particular documents which they wish to consult.

The library of the House of Commons is private and intended solely for the use of Members of Parliament.

The House of Lords Record Office also has a section of *Historical Collections* which contains miscellaneous manuscript material and deposits of political papers, often unrelated to parliamentary matters, The *Historical Collections* section became the recipient of the greater part of the contents of the Beaverbrook Library when that institution closed in March 1975. The collection of papers transferred from the Beaverbrook Library are described in K. V. Wheeler, *A Guide to the Political Papers, 1874-1970, deposited by the First Beaverbrook Foundation* (House of Lords Record Office Memorandum No. 54, 1975). The following is a brief survey of the relevant papers in the *Historical Collections* section.

128. *Samuel Papers 1883-1962*

Papers of Herbert Louis Samuel, Viscount Samuel (1870-1963). Postmaster General and Chancellor of the Duchy of Lancaster, 1915-16; Home Secretary, 1916; Leader of the Liberal Party in the House of Lords, 1944-55. The collection consists of general political papers, 1888-1962; family letters of political interest, 1881-1938; and subject files, 1890-1962. The subject files include Cabinet notes and papers; accounts of visits to the front in 1915 and 1917; correspondence with Admiral Lord Fisher, 1917; the British Special Commission to Belgium, 1919; evacuation and Civil Defence, 1938-40; blockade, 1940, etc. This collection is described in House of Lords Record Office Memorandum No. 35 (1966). **129** is personal and literary papers of Herbert Samuel, including his papers referring to Israel, and is described in House of Lords Record Office Memorandum No. 41 (1969). It contains little referring to either of the world wars.

141. *Stansgate Papers*
Papers of William Wedgwood Benn, 1st Viscount Stansgate (1877-1960). Service with the RNAS and RFC in WWI; Vice-President of the Allied Control Commission for Italy, 1943-4; Secretary of State for Air, 1945-6. There are no papers specifically related to the Allied Control Commission and few referring to his tenure as Secretary of State for Air. The collection contains various files on war and aviation, 1916-c. 1939, and many files referring to WWII in various parts of the world such as North Africa, Ethiopia, the Balkans, France and Germany.

158. *Harris Papers*
Papers of Sir Percy Alfred Harris (1876-1952). Chief Whip of the Parliamentary Liberal Party, 1935-45; Deputy Leader, 1940-5; and Chairman of the House of Commons All Party Panel, 1940-5. The collection consists of diaries, correspondence, literary papers, press-cuttings, photographs, etc.

The following collections are from the Beaverbrook Library:

184. *Beaverbrook Papers 1903-64*
Papers of Sir William Maxwell Aitken, 1st Baron Beaverbrook (1879-1964). Chancellor of the Duchy of Lancaster and Minister of Information, 1918; member of the War Cabinet and Minister for Aircraft Production, 1940-1; Minister of State, 1941; Minister of Supply, 1941-2; Minister of War Production, February 1942; and Lord Privy Seal, September 1943 – July 1945. The papers are divided into twelve series, **A-L**. Of particular interest for the present purpose is **Series D**: WWII, comprising 88 boxes of papers emanating from his various ministries, semi-official papers including Cabinet papers and extracts, general alphabetical correspondence files, and general subject files not relating specifically to a ministry. The papers are rich in material relating to Canadian, American and Russian relations, aircraft statistics, oil supplies and raw materials, relations with other ministries, Cabinet war committees, War Cabinet minutes, correspondence with ambassadors and diplomats, etc.
Series E: WWI, comprising 19 boxes, contains far less material directly related to the war than does **Series D** to WWII. There is, however, some interesting and significant information in the Ministry of Information and Duchy of Lancaster files. Also of interest is **Series C**: special correspondence, 1911-64, comprising 55 boxes of correspondence with most of the leading political and literary figures of the time and covering a wide range of topics. The remaining series are peripheral to the present concern.

185. *Blumenfeld Papers 1891-1948*
Papers of Ralph David Blumenfeld (1864-1948). Editor of the *Daily Express*, 1904-32. The papers are divided into personal correspondence, political correspondence, and wartime and military correspondence. The political correspondence contains letters from a wide range of political and public figures and has some reference to the outbreak of war in 1914. Wartime and military correspondence relates to WWI and to military, air and naval affairs in general. There are significant runs of letters from Admiral Lord Beresford, the 19th Earl of Derby and Sir Samuel Hoare.

187. *Davidson Papers 1911-61*
Papers of John Colin Campbell Davidson, 1st Viscount Davidson (1889-1970). Davidson served as secretary to a number of ministers, including Andrew Bonar Law, 1913-20. During WWII he was Honorary Advisor on Commercial Relations and Controller of Production at the Ministry of Information. There are three boxes of papers referring to Viscount Harcourt at the Colonial Office, 1913-15, and 15 from Bonar Law's tenure there. The collection includes much material on Australia and conscription, the Dardanelles campaign, the war in Africa, and manpower and recruiting in the Dominions. There are many in-letters, addressed mainly to Bonar Law and also four boxes on the Commercial Relations Division at the Ministry of Information, dealing with trade matters in wartime, 1940-1.

188. *Donald Papers 1885-1933*
Papers of Sir Robert Donald (1860-1933). Editor of the *News Chronicle*, 1902-18. **Folder 4**, 1908-17, contains nearly 30 letters, mostly from Admiral Lord Fisher but a few to him, dealing with the conduct of WWI, relations between the army and navy, the Dardanelles campaign, and Fisher's opinion of various figures, including Lloyd George, Churchill and Balfour. **Folder 5**, 1912-17, contains copies of various memoranda and papers Fisher sent to the Prime Minister and Churchill about the state of the navy and its part in the war, a copy of Churchill's evidence before the Dardanelles Commission, and a few copies of Fisher's correspondence with Lloyd George and others on the same subject.

189. *Hannon Papers 1874-1963*
Papers of Sir Patrick Joseph Henry Hannon (1874-1963). General Secretary of the Naval League, 1911-18; member of the National Service League Council, 1911-15; and MP, 1921-50. There are some papers referring to his association with the Navy League and various parliamentary papers concerning a number of WWII committees such as

the war policy group, the post-war policy sub-committee, and the British-American Parliamentary Group.

191. *Bonar Law Papers 1881-1923*
Papers of Andrew Bonar Law (1858-1923). Leader of the Conservative Party, 1911-21; Secretary of State for Colonial Affairs, 1915-16; Chancellor of the Exchequer, 1916-18; member of the War Cabinet, 1916-19; Prime Minister, 1922-3. The main interest here is first with Bonar Law as head of the Colonial Office, where he was engaged in relations with the colonies during the war and the conduct of the war in general, and second as Chancellor of the Exchequer where he was nearly a second Prime Minister. He also became an important influence in the peace negotiations.

192. *Lloyd George Papers 1882-1945*
Papers of David Lloyd George, 1st Earl Lloyd George of Dwyfor (1863-1945). Chancellor of the Exchequer, 1908-15; Minister of Munitions, 1915-16; Secretary of State for War, June — December 1916; and Prime Minister, 1916-22. The papers are divided into **Series A-I** and are the largest collection of a British Prime Minister's papers in existence. **Series C** contains his papers as Chancellor of the Exchequer and a fair amount on the conduct of the war, peace moves and foreign affairs generally. **Series D** is papers as Minister of Munitions and is much more concerned with the war effort and related matters. **Series E** as Secretary of State for War is only three boxes, two of which contain semi-official and Cabinet papers while the other is correspondence between Lloyd George, the War Office, British representatives abroad, and foreign governments. His tenure as Prime Minister is covered by **Series F** which contains *inter alia* nearly all the War Cabinet minutes to 1919, minutes of the Imperial Conferences of 1917 and 1921, and of the Peace Conference and subsequent international conferences. Many of these papers are not available at the Public Record Office.

195. *Stevenson Papers 1912-49*
Papers of Frances Stevenson, later Countess Lloyd George (1888-1972). Confidential secretary and mistress of David Lloyd George. The collection consists of letters and a diary which throw light on the personality and relationships of Lloyd George, as he confided his private hopes, fears and opinions about events and people to Frances. The diary has been edited by A. J. P. Taylor as *Lloyd George: A diary by Frances Stevenson* (London, 1971) while the letters have appeared under the same editorship as *My Darling Pussy, The Letters of Lloyd George and Frances Stevenson* (London, 1975).

196. *Strachey Papers 1885-1927*
Papers of John St. Loe Strachey (1860-1927), editor of the *Spectator,* 1898-1925. Strachey corresponded with a wide variety of people on many topics, some of which are of a military nature. There is correspondence referring to army tactics in WWI, the relative military strengths of Britain and Germany just before the war, and very interesting memoranda of Strachey's visits to the front during the conflict.

197. *Wargrave Papers 1904-36*
Papers of Edward Alfred Goulding, 1st Baron Wargrave (1862-1936). Goulding never attained high office but was a close business associate of Lord Beaverbrook. His correspondence includes runs of letters on political events from various public figures. There is a lively series of letters from Admiral Lord Fisher on the navy and his opinion of Churchill and Lloyd George.

199. *Balfour Papers 1939-44*
Papers of Harold Harington Balfour, Baron Balfour of Inchrye (b. 1897). Parliamentary Under-Secretary of State for Air, 1938-44, and Minister Resident in West Africa, 1944-5. Balfour accompanied Lord Beaverbrook on the supply mission to Moscow in October 1941. There is his contemporary account of the mission, subsequently published as *Moscow Diary 1941.* Balfour wrote several other narratives: 'An Account of some post-Moscow Government events', which deals with supplies to Russia and Smuts' view of post-war development; 'Dunkirk Days — Battle of Britain: as seen from the desk of the Under-Secretary of State for Air'; 'The Battle of Training: an account of the birth of the Commonwealth Air Training Plan'; and 'History of Boeing Boat Purchases', incorporating some of Beaverbrook's correspondence and notes from Churchill. There are a few letters of little interest.

200. *Melville Papers 1915*
Lady Sarah Melville was secretary to Andrew Bonar Law, 1907-16. When Bonar Law joined the Cabinet in 1915, she noted down anything she felt to be important, such as his comments after a Cabinet meeting, remarks on letters received, and his feelings on the conduct of the war, especially the Dardanelles campaign. 46 sheets.

Department of Documents, Imperial War Museum, Lambeth Road, LONDON SE1 6HZ

The Imperial War Museum illustrates and records all aspects of the two world wars and other military operations involving Britain and the Commonwealth since August 1914. The Department of Documents is a repository for documentary records of all types relating to warfare in the 20th century. It also collects and disseminates information on the documentary holdings of European and American archives and research institutes. Access to some collections is governed by special restrictions. Enquiries should be made to the Keeper of the Department of Documents.

The collections fall into two broad categories: foreign material, consisting largely of captured German records transferred to the Museum by various government departments; and a substantial collection of the private papers of individuals.

FOREIGN MATERIAL

Records of the Reich Ministry of Armaments and War Production

This Ministry was headed by Albert Speer from 1942 to 1945 and the collection consists of microfilm copies of Speer's ministerial papers covering the various aspects of armament planning, development and production both during and prior to WWII. Included within this same collection are copies of the minutes of the Central Planning Committee and the records of the Planungsamt and Rohstoffamt, together with papers from the Reichswirtschaftsministerium, dealing largely with matters of taxation and commerce, 1934-45.

The series also contains some papers of organisations either subsidiary to or related to Speer's ministry, such as the Organisation Todt and military commands in German occupied countries. The final part of the collection is formed by the records of many major German companies such as Messerschmitt and I. G. Farben, mainly covering the years, 1939-45.

Records from the Reich Air Ministry

This collection of papers of Field-Marshal Erhard Milch, State Secretary for Air and Generalluftzeugmeister (Gfm), mainly covers the period, 1939-45. The papers are made up of microfilm copies of 71 vols. of files containing details on aircraft, air defence, research and development, production and procurement, and are organised as follows: vols. 1-11, Jägerstab conference, 1944; vol. 12, Rüstungsstab conferences, August 1944 — January 1945; vols. 13-29, Gfm conferences under the chairmanship of Milch, March 1942 — June 1944; vols. 30-33, conferences between Göring and Milch and the Reichsministerium für Rüstung und Kriegsproduktion, August 1943 — May 1944; vols. 34-41, Reich Air Ministry development conferences, July 1942 — March 1944; vols. 42-45, conferences on flak and night fighter development, supply conferences and conferences with German General Staff, 1939-44; vols. 46-48, Central Planning Committee conferences, June 1942 – November 1943; vols. 49-61, miscellaneous conferences, reports and correspondence, 1934-44; vols. 62-65, conferences with Göring, 1936-44; and vols. 66-71, miscellaneous reports and correspondence, 1942-3.

Enemy Documents Section (primarily photocopies)
Campaign Files-West, 1939-40, containing France, Belgium, Netherlands and Luxembourg.
Campaign Files-West, 1940-5, containing the Dieppe Raid, military administration, defence measures, Rommel's command, Normandy invasion, and the defence of northwest Germany and the Netherlands: reports, war diaries, unit orders, maps, etc.
There are also Campaign Files for: Norway, 1940-5; Operation Sea Lion, 1940-1; Eastern (Poland and Russia); Balkans and Crete; North Africa, 1941-3; and Italy and Sicily, 1943-5.
Operational Plans, 1938-45. OKW and OKH, files of the WFSt., OKH/Op. Abt. 1 and 2, including Czech and Austrian invasions.
German Intelligence documents, including Fremde Heere West und Ost; Abwehr and OKW/Ausland and WFSt./Ic.
German High Command Files, 1920-45, concerning the structure and organisation of the Reichswehrministerium, Reichskriegsministerium, OKW and OKH. The collection contains files for 1933-9 and WWII, including war diaries of OKW and OKH, Führer directives, conferences, etc. There are also fragmentary papers of individuals: Halder, Jodl, Goebbels, Greiner, Deyhle, Lahoussen and Warlimont.
Military, Economic and Armaments documents, 1920-45, comprising economic regulations, economic organisation for war, armaments production, economic intelligence reports on Britain and the USA, armaments statistics, and material relating to the war economy.
General Military Organisation and Statistical files: OKH/Org. Abteilung Chefsachen, files, 1940-5; OKH/Org. Abteilung, war diaries and appendices, 1941-5; OKH and OKW, strengths and casualty files, 1931-45; Order of Battle files, 1936-45; and Army Personnel Office files, 1933-45.
Files on special subjects: weapons documents mostly relating to rocketry and the V 2; SS and Waffen SS documents such as unit diaries, morale and strength reports, relations with police in occupied countries, lists of concentration camps with numbers of guards and prisoners; fragments of Himmler's diaries; papers relating to the capitulation period; various documents relating to Adolf Hitler; the Führer HQ war diary, August 1939 – July 1942; and the diary of Martin Bormann as secretary to Hitler, 1941-3.

War crimes files comprising documents and statements relating to executions, extermination of Jews, concentration camps, etc., and miscellaneous files.
Non-military files, miscellaneous policy and diplomatic documents, material relating to the NSDAP, and correspondence of Dr Todt.

Channel Islands Occupations Records
Microfilms of a selection of the files of the German administration of the Channel Islands during WWII. The original and complete collection is held by the Channel Islands authorities.

Ministry of Technology Collection
German technical documents on armaments and aircraft research, particularly German aircraft handbooks of WWII.

Peenemünde Archives
Microfilms of the records of the German rocket research and development centre at Peenemünde.

German Intelligence Collection
Maps and books of photographs showing details of the location of strategic points in Great Britain, prepared by German Intelligence before WWII.

Allied Intelligence Files
Original copies of most of the reports of the Combined Intelligence Objectives Sub-committee, the British Intelligence Objectives Sub-committee, the Field Intelligence Agency (Technical), and other intelligence evaluation teams.

Italian Ministry of War Production
The Italian material consists mainly of the records of the Italian Ministry of War Production, 1940-3.

Records of the International Military Tribunal: Nuremberg
Material relating to the Nuremberg trials, 14 November 1945 – 10 October 1946, has been transferred from the Public Record Office, where it was formerly **F.O. 645**. The records mainly consist of American, British, French and Russian trial briefs, prosecution document books, prosecution exhibits, defence briefs and final speeches, and trial transcripts.

Records of the American Military Tribunals: Nuremberg
Formerly **F.O. 646** in the Public Record Office, this is an almost

comprehensive record of the 12 trials held at Nuremberg by US authorities, 21 November 1946 — 13 February 1948. The cases tried were Medical, Field-Marshal Milch, Justice, Pohl, Flick, I. G. Farben, Hostages, Rasse und Siedlungshauptamt, Einsatzgruppen, Krupp, Ministers, and High Command. The material comprises mainly trial transcripts and defence and prosecution document books.

Miscellaneous Trials: Europe
Formerly **F.O.** 647 in the Public Record Office, these records consist of: five bound vols. of daily transcripts in the trial of Field-Marshal Albert Kesselring held in Venice, February — May 1947; copies of documents relating to the Roechling trial held at Rastatt, 1948-9; and judgement rendered in the von Falkenhausen trial in Brussels, 1951.

International Military Tribunal: Far East
These documents, formerly **F.O.** 648 in the Public Record Office, cover the proceedings of the trials of Japanese war criminals held in Tokyo, April 1946 — December 1948. The material consists of daily transcripts, prosecution and defence summations, court exhibits, charges against the defendants, narrative summaries of the proceedings, miscellaneous legal documents, and judgements and opinions. Included in the same section are daily transcripts of the trials of Hiroshi Tamura and Soemu Toyoda. 1948-9.

PRIVATE PAPERS AND MEMOIRS

The Museum is receiving steady accessions to its collection of private papers and memoirs, now numbering in the thousands. The following listing contains the papers of high ranking officers and officials, and a selection of the more important or more interesting papers of middle and lower level personnel. It is not all original material, some is on microfilm and some photocopied.

Field-Marshal Lord Alanbrooke (1883-1963)
Copies of some twenty personal letters, containing a few useful comments on the fall of France, 1940-6.

Maj. Gen. S. C. M. Archibald (1890-1973)
Memoirs, 1909-50. Archibald served with the RFA at Le Cateau, Aubers Ridge, the first and second battles of Ypres, Loos, Somme, Messines and Nieuport. There is much description of tactics and trench warfare. In WWII he commanded the 11th Anti-aircraft Division, 1941-3, and then served as adviser to Canada on anti-aircraft defence.

Commander A. H. Ashworth
Diaries covering his service as a midshipman in the cruiser *Cornwall,*
August 1914 – March 1915, and the battleship *Warspite,* March
1915 – December 1916, including accounts of the battles of the
Falkland Islands and Jutland.

Kemal Ataturk (1881-1938)
Ts. memoirs of the Anafartalar battles on the Gallipoli Peninsula.

Vice-Admiral Harold Tom Baillie-Grohman (b. 1888)
Two volumes of autobiography, the first of which gives an account of
his career to 1922 in destroyers and minesweepers. The second covers
service as Flag Officer, Schleswig-Holstein, 1945-6.

1st Baron Balfour of Inchrye
Diary of the Anglo-American Mission to Moscow, 21 September – 10
October 1941. Led by Lord Beaverbrook and Averill Harriman, the
mission negotiated the supply of war material to the Soviet Union.

Maj. C. J. Ball
Records of the 29th Division Association, with special reference to
Gallipoli, and papers regarding his service with the Allied Control
Commission in Germany in the early 1920s.

Robin Band
Ts. account of his experience at the fall of Singapore and as a POW in
Burma working on the Burma-Siam Railway.

Air Vice-Marshal G. G. Banting (1898-1973)
Various papers concerning his air force career, mainly WWII.

Gen. Sir Evelyn Barker (b. 1894)
Two folders of operation orders and records pertaining to the 49th
(West Riding) Division in France, June – November 1944.

Maj. R. E. S. Barrington (b. 1877)
Two MS vols. of letters in dairy form, written during his service as a
squadron commander with the 13th Battalion (Scottish Horse Yeomanry), Black Watch Regiment, in Gallipoli and Egypt, 1915-18.

Maj. Gen. Donald Roland Edwin Rowan Bateman (1901-1969)
Official papers and post-war correspondence referring to service in
North Africa and at Cassino in WWII.

Col. W. A. Bickford
Account of the British mission to Czechoslovakia in 1938 to observe the enforcement of the Munich agreement. Bickford was sent to the area around Pilsen. The collection also contains miscellaneous papers relating to his subsequent service in Burma.

Air Vice-Marshal Christopher Neil Hope Bilney (b. 1898)
Memoirs and log book of service in the RNAS as a seaplane pilot with the Eastern Mediterranean Fleet in 1918, and in the British occupation force on the Caspian Sea, 1919.

Field-Marshal Lord Birdwood
Series of letters written by Sir William Riddell Birdwood (1865-1951), GOC Australia New Zealand Army Corps, 1914-18, covering his command of the Anzac Corps at Gallipoli and in France, 1915-17.

Maj. Gen. H. L. Birks (b. 1897)
Correspondence with Sir Basil Liddell-Hart and Maj. Gen. Sir Percy Hobart on tank warfare, 1916-45.

R. D. Blumenfeld
Letter from David Lloyd George on the war, 25 October 1915 and another letter from Gen. Sir Julian Byng, 19 April 1918. Blumenfeld was editor of the *Daily Express*, 1904-32.

Capt. A. V. Board
Diary of service with the Machine Gun Corps on the Western Front in early 1916, including recapture of the 'Bluff'.

Col. John Herbert Boraston (1885-1969)
Papers relating to the operations of the Eighth Division in France, including a war diary to December 1915, and service with GHQ in 1918. He subsequently served as Personal Secretary to Haig, with whom there is correspondence, 1919-20.

Lt. Gen. Sir Roger Bower (b. 1903)
Official briefs, reports, statistics, maps and related papers concerning his service in Operation MARKET, Holland, 17 September — 9 October 1944; Operation DOOMSDAY, Norway, 10 May — 25 August 1945; and operations in the Holga area of Palestine, November 1945.

Brig. Gen. Roland Boys Bradford (1892-1917)
Biography by Col. Thompson. Bradford served with the 2nd Durham Light Infantry, 18th Brigade, 6th Division. Aged 25, the youngest

general in the British Army, he was killed at Cambrai on 30 November 1917.

Air Vice-Marshal Sir (William) Sefton Brancker (1877-1930)
Miscellaneous ts. and MS reports on the early organisation, supply and recruitment of the RFC, 1914-17.

Maj. Gen. William Throsby Bridges (1861-1915)
Diary from 1 January to 23 April 1915 of the commander of the Australian Division which took part in the first landings at Anzac Cove, Gallipoli, recording weather, meetings, inspections, training and administrative work.

Squadron Leader Brooke
Ts. report on 'The Theory, Command and Control of Long Range Penetration Forces', used in Burma, 1944.

Brig. Ian Bruce
Ts. account by the commanding officer of the 1st Battalion, Gold Coast Regiment, setting out in detail its role in the East Africa campaign, 1940-1.

Admiral Sir Harold Burrough (b. 1888)
Papers relating to service at Jutland and in WWII. Burrough was gunnery officer in HMS *Southampton* at Jutland; Assistant Chief of Naval Staff, 1939-40; Commander, Cruiser Squadron, 1940-2; Commander, Naval Forces, Algiers, 1942; Flag Officer Commanding, Gibraltar and Mediterranean Approaches, 1943-5; and British Naval C-in-C, Germany, 1945-6.

Brig. C. G. Buttenshaw
'Blade Force War Diary', MS diary of an attempt to seize Tunis in 1942 by a *coup de main,* with maps and photographs.

Vice-Admiral C. Caslon
Ts. 'Recollections of the Battle of Jutland', clear and detailed account by the starboard six inch gun control officer in the battleship *Malaya* of the 5th Battle Squadron.

Robert Catalan alias Robert de l'Eure
Vol. of reconstructed transcripts of radio cable messages between Allied forces and the French Resistance during the battle of Normandy, June — August 1944.

Wing Commander Thomas Reginald Cave-Browne-Cave (1895-1969)
Important collection of papers concerning aeronautics, 1914-30, with special reference to the development of the airship.

Vice-Admiral Sir Peter Cazalet (b. 1899)
Letters, charts, notes and reports, 1940-57, referring to his service as captain of HMS *Durban,* 1941-2; commander of the 23rd Destroyer Flotilla, 1944-5; and Commodore for Administration, Mediterranean Fleet, 1945-6.

Group Capt. (Geoffrey) Leonard Cheshire (b. 1917)
Flying log books, 1939-45, and report records of 617 Squadron, February — May 1944.

Field-Marshal Lord Chetwode
Official memoranda, battle orders, some official and semi-official correspondence, and a few personal letters of Field-Marshal Sir Philip Walhouse Chetwode, 1st Baron Chetwode (1869-1950) referring to his service as commander of the Desert Column, EEF, December 1916 — October 1918. Chetwode also commanded the 20th Corps in the advance on Jerusalem in 1917.

Maj. Gen. Sir Campbell Clarke
Papers referring to his service at the War Office as Director of Artillery, 1939-42, and Director-General of Artillery, 1942-5. They are very useful on anti-tank measures.

Group Capt. C. Clarkson
Copy of a report on the interrogation of Galland, 1945, and general notes on German fighter tactics in WWII.

Capt. Reginald Colby
Extensive collection of papers of a British propaganda officer in Madagascar, 1942-3. His work was aimed at justifying the British occupation and the arrival of the Free French Government.

Lt. Col. Edwin Berkeley Cook (1869-1914)
Diary, letters and other papers relating to his command of the Composite Regiment of the Household Regiment in France, August — October 1914.

Lt. Col. G. H. Cooke
Extensive collection of letters relating to his service in East Africa and India during WWI. Also papers relating to petrol supplies for the British forces in North Africa, 1942-4.

Brig. Gen. Edmund W. Costello (1873-1949)
Two albums of documents, photographs, newspaper cuttings and maps relating to service as a staff officer in Mesopotamia with the 12th, 7th and 15th Indian Divisions, 1915-18, and as Commander, 12th Indian Infantry Brigade, 1918-19.

Gen. Sir John Cowans
Letters, press-cuttings and photographs of Gen. Sir John Stevens Cowans (1862-1921), Quartermaster-General of the Forces, 1912-19.

Admiral Sir John Crace (1887-1968)
Journals, logs and diaries kept as Rear Admiral commanding the Australian Squadron, 1939-42. The collection also includes accounts of the battles of the Coral Sea, River Plate, and Cape Matapan.

Lt. Col. E. B. B. Creagh
Letters and a diary relating to service with the RFA on the Western Front, 1914-18. and with GHQ, Egypt, 1939-45.

Sir Herbert Creedy (1878-1973)
Private Secretary to successive Secretaries of State at the War Office. The papers comprise a few useful letters and many miscellaneous cuttings and papers relating to service as private secretary to Lord Kitchener, Secretary of State for War, 1914-16.

Air Commodore George Bentley Dacre (1891-1962)
Photocopy of a 71 pp. ts. diary kept while he was a Turkish POW after capture at Gallipoli in 1915.

Maj. Gen. Guy Payan Dawnay (1878-1952)
Served as Chief of Staff to Gen. Hamilton in the Dardanelles; to Gen. Allenby in Egypt, Palestine and with the EEF, 1916-17; and to Gen. Haig in France, 1918. The papers comprise official and private MSS, letters, documents, maps, and reports concerning the Dardanelles, 1915; Egypt and Palestine, 1916-17; France, 1918; and miscellaneous documents from WWII, as well as literary works.

Rear Admiral Sir Oswald Dawson (1882-1950)
There is a MS autobiography covering the years 1882-1919. From 1912 to 1917 Dawson served in the battleship *Thunderer* and from 1917 to 1918 in the battleship *Orion*. There is also Dawson's diary for 10 January 1944 — 2 April 1945 as a Commodore in charge of Mercantile Convoys.

Admiral Sir Dudley de Chair (1864-1958)
Naval Secretary to the 1st Lord of the Admiralty, 1912-14; Commander of the 10th Cruiser Squadron (Northern Blockade), 1914-16; Naval Adviser to the Foreign Office on blockade affairs, 1916-17; Commander of the 3rd Battle Squadron, 1917-18; Admiral commanding Coastguard and Reserve, 1918-21; and President of the Inter-Allied Commission for the destruction of enemy warships, 1921-23. He also served as naval adviser for Balfour's mission to the United States, 1917. The collection comprises his war service diary, a ts. draft of his autobiography, 1874-1930, papers relating to the command of the 10th Cruiser Squadron, miscellaneous papers on the blockade, and various other miscellaneous, naval and private papers and correspondence.

Brig. H. K. Dimoline
Official papers, photographs and a scrapbook concerning his service in the RA with the 4th and 7th Indian Divisions in North Africa and Burma. There are also a few pieces from his tenure as Chief Commandant, Malayan Police Volunteer Reserve, 1949-57.

Capt. G. Donald
Flying log books covering service in Britain, in the aircraft carriers *Vindex* and *Engadine,* 1915-17, and in the Eastern Mediterranean with No. 2 Wing, RNAS, 1917-18.

Lord Douglas of Kirtleside
William Sholto Douglas (1893-1969). Commanded Nos. 43 and 84 Fighter Squadrons, 1917-18; Assistant Chief of Air Staff, 1938-40; Deputy Chief of Air Staff, 1940; AOC in Chief Fighter Command, 1940-2, Middle East Command, 1943-4, and Coastal Command, 1944-5; and AC-in-C, British Air Forces of Occupation in Germany, 1945-6. The papers comprise his official service papers, 1922-68; a record of WWI experiences by Squadron Leader W. S. Douglas; notes and despatches on the Leros operation, Operation OVERLORD, and Coastal Command operations. There is also correspondence relating to *Years of Combat* (1963).

Lt. Gen. Sir Robert Drew
Copy of a report of the 1st (British) Airborne Division, RAMC, 20 June 1945, entitled 'Reports by Medical Officers of 1 A/B Division on Operation MARKET and their subsequent experiences, 17 September 1948 — 8 May 1945'.

Admiral P. W. Dumas
Diaries from 1903 to 1918, including those as Naval Attaché in Berlin, 1906-8.

Vice-Admiral J. W. Durnford
Unpublished autobiography and papers covering his career, 1904-48. Durnford served in the cruisers *Argyll* and *Shannon* in WWI; commanded *P39* in the Portsmouth Escort Flotilla on cross-Channel duties, 1918; commanded the cruiser *Suffolk* in Home waters, 1939-40; served on the Commonwealth of Australia Naval Board, 1940-2; and was Flag Captain in the battleship *Resolution*, 1943, and Director of Naval Training. There is naval correspondence, 1924-49; personal correspondence, 1926-63; and miscellaneous naval papers.

Maj. Gen. G. G. A. Egerton
His diary as GOC, Sicily, 1915-16, and many notebooks concerning his tenure as Inspector General of Infantry Training in Britain, 1916-17.

Vice-Admiral W. de M. Egerton
Two diaries kept as a Commodore of Trans-Atlantic Convoys, July — November 1942.

Capt. J. Ellerton
Various reports of proceedings, of which the most interesting are those concerned with Operation PEDESTAL, the last convoy from Britain to Malta to come under heavy attack, August 1942.

Lance Cpl. W. N. Elliott
Diaries and memoirs of his service with the East Lancashire Regiment in Arakan and Burma, 1944-5.

Maj. Gen. Sir Richard Ewart (1864-1925)
Autobiography with special reference to his service in France, 1914-15, and as Deputy Adjutant and Quartermaster-General in East Africa, 1915-18. Also his diary as President of the Commission for the Repatriation of POWs, 1919-20.

Vice-Admiral Sir Alistair Ewing
Diary kept as 1st lieutenant in the destroyer *Imogen*, 26 August 1939 — 8 May 1940, during the Norwegian campaign and convoy work, with maps of the ship's movements.

Sir Roy Fedden
Papers containing extensive material relating to many aspects of his long connection with British aircraft development. Included are schedules and detailed drawings of a number of his engine designs such as the Jupiter, Hercules, Taurus and Centaurus.

Capt. T. H. Findlay
Journal by an officer of the transport *Myrmidon,* concerning a relief mission to the retreating Serbian army in Albania, December 1915 — January 1916. There is a good description of the condition of the Austrians and Serbs in Albania.

Maj. J. Finnerty
Ts. memoir of 329 pp. describing the retreat in Burma, 1942, with reference to his capture and life as a POW in the Far East.

Lt. Col. B. J. H. Fitzgerald
Letters and a diary kept during his appointment as Private Secretary to Gen. Sir John French.

Maj. Gen. W. A. K. Fraser
Two diaries covering his service in the cavalry on the Western Front, 1914-18, and with the South Persia Rifles, 1918-22.

Gen. Sir James Gammell
Letters from Gallipoli and the Near East, 1915-18; report on mechanised operations in Egypt, 1917; and papers referring to army training, 1940-3. There are also papers regarding his tenure as representative of the British Chiefs of Staff with the Soviet Union and head of the British Military Mission to Moscow in 1945.

J. R. Gardiner
Diary of the trek across the Chaukkan Pass from Burma to India, May — June 1942.

Commander L. Gardner
Diaries and letters covering service as a midshipman in HMS *Cornwall* and HMS *Warspite,* 1914-16, and as Flag Lieutenant to the C-in-C, Mediterranean, 1917-19.

Air Vice-Marshal W. C. C. Gell
Papers relating to his service with the Royal Warwickshire Regiment, 1914-35, including command of the 1/5 Brigade in France during WWI. The collection also contains papers and photographs relating to his service career and command of the United Kingdom Balloon Barrage, 1939-45.

Maj. the Lord Glyn
A large collection of letters relating to the entire service record of Sir Ralph George Campbell Glyn, 1st Bt. (1885-1960). The most important letters concern the mission of Arthur Paget to Russia and Serbia in the

spring of 1915 and Glyn's view of the Dardenelles campaign during the autumn of 1915.

Lt. Col. R. B. Goodden
An important collection of letters, diaries and papers concerning his service in the British Adriatic Mission and as a liaison officer with the Serbian Army, 1915-18. There are also papers referring to service as a military attaché in Eastern Europe and the Baltic States in the 1920s.

Admiral J. H. Godfrey
Naval memoirs covering his service from 1903 to 1946. During WWI he was involved in naval operations off Gallipoli, 1915, and in the Mediterranean, 1917-18. Most interest concerns a lengthy discussion of his posts as Director of Naval Intelligence, 1939-42, and Flag Officer Commanding, Indian Navy, 1943-6.

Gen. Sir William Godfrey
Official documents relating to naval aspects of the Dardanelles campaign in WWI, covering convoy orders, the landings and the evacuation.

Air Commodore P. R. C. Groves
File of letters and documents concerning service in the Air Ministry and with the British delegation to the Paris Peace Conference, 1918-20.

Gen. Sir (James) Aylmer Lowthorpe Haldane
His 'Shorncliffe Diary' as Commander of the 10th Infantry Brigade, 1912 – August 1914.

Gen. Franz Halder
Six bound cyclostyled vols. of a transcript of his diary as Chief of Staff to the German Army, August 1939 – September 1942.

Maj. Lord Hampton
Diary of D Squadron of the Worcestershire Yeomanry concerning the conquest of Palestine, Syria and Jordan after the arrival of Allenby in June 1917. The diary describes the campaign in great detail from June 1917 to 1919. Sir Herbert Stuart Pakington, Lord Hampton, was a major in the Worcestershire Yeomanry.

Admiral Sir Cecil Harcourt (1892-1959)
Two photograph albums covering his service as Captain of HMS *Duke of York*, 1941-2, and as C-in-C and head of military administration in Hong Kong, 1945-6.

Lt. F. Hawkings
Diary from 10 March 1914 to 18 March 1919. Hawkings served with
the Queen Victoria's Rifles, 9th Battalion, County of London Regiment, Territorial Force. The diary is a gripping and immediate account
of trench warfare and records the first and second battles of Ypres and
the advance to Cambrai in 1918.

Admiral Sir Geoffrey Hawkins
Journal from 17 March 1913 to 10 May 1915 as a midshipman in the
cruiser *Natal* on patrol duties in the North Sea and off the Norwegian
coast.

Brig. V. F. S. Hawkins
Ts. diary entitled 'Operations of the 5th Infantry Brigade, 2nd Division
in Assam, 30 March — 12 May 1944, with special reference to the
Battle of Kohima', 88 pp. and maps.

Maj. Gen. Patrick Hagert Henderson (1876-1968)
Collection of albums, notes, official papers and diaries of his service in
the RAMC from 1900. Henderson served with the Embarkation Staff at
Southampton, 1914; the 7th Division in France, 1914-15; the 28th
Division in Egypt and Macedonia, 1915-17; and the 27th Division in
Macedonia, South Russia and Trans-Caspia, 1917-19.

Vice-Admiral Harold Hickling
Autobiographical and naval writings, maps, diagrams, and papers
relating to the battles of Coronel and the Falkland Islands (during
which he was a lieutenant in the *Glasgow*) 1914-64. Papers relating to
command of the cruiser *Glasgow,* 1940-1, and to Mulberry Harbours,
1943-6. Hickling was a member of the 1942 Admiralty mission to
Washington and on the staff of Admiral Sir Bertram Ramsey in
planning the construction of the Mulberry artificial harbours for the
invasion of Normandy. In 1944 he was naval officer in charge of
Mulberry B at Arromanches, Normandy.

Capt. T. J. N. Hilken
Journal as commander of HMAS *Sydney,* 13 January 1939 — 13
December 1940; captain of the escort carrier *Emperor* in the Home
Fleet, including participation in Operation TUNGSTEN against the
Tirpitz, and Operation DRAGOON in the invasion of Southern France,
5 September 1943 — January 1945; and Naval Officer in Charge,
Penang, Malaya, where he accepted the Japanese surrender and served
as Military Governor, 10 August — 26 September 1945. There are also

various papers relating to Operation JURIST in Penang, August — September 1945.

Admiral Sir Deric Holland-Martin
Records of his service as commander of the destroyer *Nubian* in the Mediterranean, 1943.

Air Chief Marshal Sir Leslie Hollinghurst
Mainly official and semi-official records of the airborne operations in Arnhem and Operations TRANSFIGURE, AMHERST and KEYSTONE, 1944-5. For the main Hollinghurst papers, see the Royal Air Force Museum (p. 183).

Gen. Lord Horne
Maps, a few letters, and operation orders of Gen. Henry Sinclair Horne, Baron Horne of Stirkoke (1861-1929), covering his command of the 1st Army in France, 1916-19.

Rear Admiral H. Horniman
Autobiography of naval service, 1887-1925, including service in the battlecruiser *Inflexible* from November 1912 to April 1915. The *Inflexible* took part in the battle of the Falkland Islands in 1914.

Maj. General Harold Arthur Hounsell (1897-1970)
Voluminous records of service in the RA, with special reference to his command of Anti-aircraft Forces in Tunisia, Italy and the United Kingdom, 1942-51, and many low level official documents. There is also private correspondence, 1940-9, mostly post-war.

Air Commodore T. E. B. Howe
Photographs kept by Howe and Squadron Leader W. R. Dyke Acland of early naval aviation; miscellaneous documents concerning naval aviation, 1915-39; and miscellaneous papers on the Empire Air Training Scheme, 1940-4.

Vice-Admiral J. Hughes-Hallett
Mainly official papers, 1940-63, relating to his service in Combined Operations from 1941 to 1943. He was Naval Force Commander in the Dieppe raid, August 1942. There is also correspondence referring to the Mulberry Harbours.

Lt. Gen. N. M. S. Irwin
Papers relating to the Dakar operation, 1940, and the Arakan campaign, 1943, by the general in command of each. There are reports, notes, orders, and letters, including some from Wavell and Mountbatten.

Brig. Gen. J. L. Jack
Four ts. vols. with photographs, cuttings and sketches, covering service on the Western Front as a captain in the Scottish Rifles; commanding officer of the 2nd West Yorkshires; and 28th Brigade Commander, 1914-19. This was used as source material by John Terraine for *General Jack's Diary* (1964).

Lt. Gen. Sir Hugh Jeudwine
Papers regarding command of the 55th Division on the Western Front, 1916-18.

Maj. Gen. R. F. Johnstone
Questionnaire prepared for a conference between the British and Japanese commanders in Burma, held at the HQ of the British Burma Command, 12 February 1946.

Mrs G. A. Jones
Semi-official diary kept as Deputy Controller, WAAC, responsible for the Expeditionary Force canteens in France, 1918-19.

Lt. Gen. Sir Henry Karslake
Important short report, published only in edited form, on operations south of the Somme, May — June 1940, with special reference to the lines of communication.

Sir Gilbert Laithwaite
An account with six appendices of the experiences of a 2nd lieutenant in the 4th Battalion, 20th Lancashire Fusiliers, 52nd Brigade, 17th Division during the German offensive of March — April 1918 in the Havrincourt Salient. For papers relating to Laithwaite's later career, see the India Office (p. 134).

Gen. Sir Gerald Lathbury
Copy of the diary he kept as a temporary brigadier in the Oxfordshire and Buckinghamshire Light Infantry at Arnhem, 17 September — 23 October 1944. For the original diary, see the Airborne Forces Museum. (p. 5).

Maj. Gen. J. C. Latter
Account of experiences as Adjutant to 2/5 Battalion, Lancashire Fusiliers in France, 25 September — 28 October 1917, and subsequent service as a staff officer in Italy.

Maj. G. Lett
Account of the resistance movement in the Apuania area of Italy, 1943-5.

Maj. Gen. Harold Victor Lewis (1887-1945)
Large collection of letters covering his service with the 10th Baluch Regiment, Indian Corps in France, October 1914 – September 1915, and in East Africa, January 1916 – December 1917. There are also later papers covering army service in India to 1939.

Maj. Gen. D. L. Lloyd-Owen
A large collection of material covering the entire history of the Long Range Desert Group in North Africa, the Aegean, Italy and the Balkans in WWII, including Lloyd-Owen's own diary and items collected from former members of the group.

Maj. Gen. Lord Loch
Papers of Edward Douglas Loch, Baron Loch (1873-1942) as a senior staff officer at GHQ, France, 1914-17, and as 110th Brigade Commander, July 1917 – January 1918.

Air Marshal Sir Harold Lydford
Most papers pertain to his tenure as AOC British Forces in Aden, 1945-8, but there are also extracts from despatches of Air Command, Southeast Asia, concerning the RAF regiment protecting advanced airfields during the Allied advance of 1943-5. These papers are subject to the 30-year Rule.

Maj. Gen. Lewis Owen Lyne (1879-1970)
The records include his unpublished autobiography. The MS has specific reference to his command of the 169th Infantry Brigade in the United Kingdom, Iraq, North Africa and Italy, 1942-4; command of the 59th Staffordshire, 50th Northumbrian and 7th Armoured Divisions in Northwest Europe, 1944-5; and his tenure as Military Governor of the British zone of Berlin, 1945-8.

Lt. K. C. Macardle
Diary of his service with the 17th Battalion, Manchester Regiment, on the Western Front, 1916. He was killed at the Somme in July of that year.

Maj. Gen. A. I. MacDougall
WWI diaries of a staff officer with the 5th Royal Irish Lancers and 6th Corps, and Brigade Major of the 64th Infantry Brigade, 1914-18.

Lt. Col. G. S. McKellar
Records of the OC, 1st Anti-aircraft Brigade Workshop, RAOC, during the British retreat across Belgium and France and the evacuation at Dunkirk in May 1940.

Lt. Gen. Sir Kenneth McLean
Copy No. 43 of War Cabinet (Chiefs of Staff Committee) Paper, 'Operation OVERLORD', 31 July 1943, issued to McLean as 'Brigadier, Plans' of COSSAC.

Gen. Sir Gordon MacMillan of MacMillan
Files relating to MacMillan's service and various commands: Brigade Commander, 55th West Lancashire Division in the United Kingdom, 1940-1; BGS, 9th Corps, North Africa; BGS to General Anderson commanding the 1st Army; command of the 152nd Infantry Brigade, 51st (Highland) Division in the invasion of Sicily, 1943; command of the 15th (Scottish) Division in the invasion of Normandy, 1944; command of the 49th (West Riding) Division at Nijmegen Island, 1944-5; and command of the 51st (Highland) Division at the German surrender, 1945. There is also a despatch concerning the British occupation of Palestine, 1947-8.

Lt. Col. G. Maitland-Edwards
Copy of an account of a journey to the Russian front and a tour of inspection of the battlefields during the 1917 offensive by Lt. Gen. Sir Charles Barter, British military representative to Russian HQ in the field, and his Italian and Rumanian counterparts, General Romei and Coanda. Maitland-Edwards was a staff officer to Barter.

Lt. Col. P. M. Marjoribanks-Egerton
Various documents and exhibits relating to the British court martial of Field-Marshal Albert Kesselring for war crimes in connection with the shootings of partisans and civilians in Italy during WWII. Marjoribanks-Egerton was a member of the court.

Lt. Gen. Sir Giffard Martel
The collection includes plans, photographs and reports referring to his experimental work on the development of mechanized warfare after WWI. There are also correspondence files and articles referring to British defence policies during and after WWII.

Maj. Gen. J. S. S. Martin
Diary written by Martin as a captain during the siege of Kut, December 1915 — April 1916.

Lt. Gen. Sir Noel Mason-Macfarlane
WWI diaries and notes of service in Mesopotamia and France. WWII papers relating to his posts as Director of Military Intelligence with the BEF, 1940; Governor of Gibraltar, 1942-4; and Chief Commissioner of the Allied Control Commission in Italy, 1944. Included are his diaries for 1943, 1944 and 1946, and correspondence with the Italian leaders, Badoglio and Sforza. There are no papers relating to the British Military Mission to Moscow in 1941-2, of which he was head.

Gen. Sir (Frederick) Ivor Maxse (1862-1958)
71 files of official and private notes, documents, photographs and published works concerning his career, 1909-19. Maxse was Commander of the 1st Guards Brigade at Mons, the Marne and the Aisne in 1914; 18th Division Commander, 1915-1916; Lt. Gen. commanding the 18th Corps, 1917; and Inspector-General of Training in France, 1918.

Milford Haven Collection
Naval papers of the 1st, 2nd and 3rd Marquesses of Milford Haven, 1854-1940. The papers consist of letters, reports, despatches, and midshipman's journals for Louis Alexander Mountbatten, 1st Marquess of Milford Haven (1854-1921), George Louis Victor Henry Sergius Mountbatten, 2nd Marquess (1892-1938), and David Michael Mountbatten, 3rd Marquess (1919-70). The 1st Marquess was 1st Sea Lord, 1912-14, and Admiral of the Fleet, 1921, while the 2nd Marquess served in the battle cruiser fleet and was present at the battles of Heligoland, the Dogger Bank and Jutland. The 3rd Marquess served in HMS *London,* 1937; HMS *Kandahar,* 1939-41; and HMS *Bramham,* 1942. The collection is held on microfilm and can only be consulted with the permission of the Broadlands Archives Trust, Broadlands, Romsey, Hampshire.

Rear Admiral Hugh Miller
Papers, 1898-1935, including diaries, 1910-12 and 1914-15, and a ts. autobiography covering the period 1880-1919. Miller was secretary to Admiral of the Fleet Sir Rosslyn Wemyss for most of the period, 1908-18.

Brig. L. R. Mizen
Records, mostly official, of service with 2/12 Frontier Force Regiment, Indian Army, in the Burma campaign, 1943-5.

Admiral Sir Vaughan Morgan
Diaries as Flag Lieutenant to Admiral Jellicoe during the Empire Mission, 1919-20; Papers relating to Dunkirk, 1940; and a few post-war papers. Morgan was Director of Signals at the Admiralty, 1943-5.

Gen. Sir William Morgan
Five short essays by Morgan on Alanbrooke; Alexander; operations in Belgium and France, 10 May — 3 June 1940; operations in Belgium and France, 25-28 May 1940; and the withdrawal to Dunkirk and evacuation.

Brig. A. F. S. Napier
Diary of service with the RFA in France, 1914-15, and diaries as military adviser to the Minister of Supply, 1940-5.

Brig. Gen. J. H. H. Nation
Various pieces from WWI, including a minute from Haig to the Adjutant-General on the best date for opening the Somme offensive, 1916.

Gen. Sir Cameron Nicholson
Diary with 'O' Battery, Rocket Troop in March 1918, dealing with the withdrawal of the 5th Army; other short WWI personal accounts; Nicholson's description of Operation SICKLEFORCE in Norway, April — May 1940; and the official report by Gen. Sir Bernard Paget on Operation SICKLEFORCE 25 April — 1 May 1940.

Brig. Gen. C. L. Norman
Diaries, 1914-18, and some letters.

Maj. Gen. Sir Edward Northey
Northey commanded the Nyasaland and North Eastern Rhodesia Frontier Force, December 1915 — May 1918. The collection includes a complete run of the Force's war diary for that period.

Operation Neptune
Photocopies of seven American reports on the invasion of Normandy.

Admiral Sir William O'Brien
Brief account of an attempt to disrupt German river traffic in the spring of 1940 by floating delayed action mines down the Rhine River.

Maj. Gen. Sir Archibald Paris (1861-1937)
Twenty MS letters, March 1915 — July 1916, dealing with the Gallipoli

campaign and the role of the Royal Naval Division. Paris was commander of the Royal Naval Division, 1914-17.

Vice-Admiral Sir John Parker
Ts. acccount, by a watch-keeping lieutenant in the destroyer *Hero,* of the second attack on Narvik, 13 April 1940.

J. R. Parsons
Copies of letters to his family by Parsons from Russia, 1915-17, as assistant to the naval mission of Rear-Admiral R. F. Phillimore, and other miscellaneous papers relating to the mission.

Admiral Sir (William) Edward Parry (1893-1972)
Large collection of diaries and letters covering his entire career from 1905, with particular reference to the battle of the River Plate where he commanded HMS *Achilles.* Parry served as a lieutenant in various ships during WWI; assumed command of HMS *Achilles,* 1939; became 1st Naval Member of the New Zealand Naval Board, 1940-2; commanded HMS *Renown,* 1943; was naval commander of Force L in the invasion of France, 1944; and Deputy Head of the Naval Division, Control Commission for Germany, 1945-6.

Admiral Sir Henry Pelly
Papers, 1901-20, mainly relating to his command of the battle cruiser *Tiger,* 1914-16.

Lt. Gen. A. E. Percival (1887-1966)
Papers relating to his entire career, especially useful for the Malayan campaign, 1940-2, and papers and correspondence relating to the *Official History of the War.* Percival was BGS 1st Corps, BEF, 1939-40; GOC 43rd (Wessex) Division, 1940; Assistant CIGS, War Office, 1940; GOC 44th (Home Counties) Division, 1940-1; GOC Malaya, 1941-2; and a POW, 1942-5.

Admiral Sir Richard Phillimore (1864-1940)
Commander of the battle cruiser *Inflexible* at the battle of the Falkland Islands, 1914, and the bombardment of the Dardanelles, 1915; Principal Beach Master at the Gallipoli landing, 1915; attached to Imperial Russian HQ, 1915-16; and commander of the 1st Battle Cruiser Squadron, 1916-18. The collection includes papers relating to his career particularly the Russian assignment.

Gen. Sir William Platt
One bound vol. entitled 'The Campaign against Italian East Africa

1940-1941'. Platt commanded the British and Allied forces operating from the Sudan.

Admiral Sir Manley Power

Papers, 1942-70, including naval operations orders and MS notes for Operation TORCH, 1942, and MS minutes on Operation HUSKY, 1943, with notes by Power, Admiral Sir Andrew Cunningham and others.

Rawlinson Collection: 4th Army Papers

Large collection of war diaries, operations orders and instructions, fortnightly and daily intelligence summaries, corps narratives, and corps operations orders of the 4th Army in France from 5 February 1916 to 11 November 1918. Also maps relating to the battle of the Somme, the Somme front, the Belgian coast, Ypres front, Amiens front, the final offensive and post-armistice positions.

Gen. L. A. Rayski

Personal reminiscences explaining the failure of the Polish Air Force in 1939, and miscellaneous letters, papers and notes. Rayski was C-in-C of the Polish Air Force, 1926-39, and Deputy Chief of Army Administration, 1939-43.

Maj. W. R. Read

Very complete diaries covering his service as a pilot on the Western Front with 3 Squadron, 1914; 5 Squadron, 1915-16; 45 Squadron, 1916; and 216 Squadron, 1918. The collection also contains his unpublished autobiography and photograph albums.

Maj. Gen. D. W. Reid (1897-1970)

His papers consisting of autobiographical and miscellaneous Indian Army papers, including service in Mesopotamia during WWI, 1897-1937; East African and North African campaign papers as commander of the 29th Indian Infantry Brigade, 1940-2; Italian campaign papers as commander of the 10th Indian Division, 1944-6; and post-war papers, photographs and publications.

Maj. Gen. Henry Hampton Rich

Memoirs from the Mesopotamian campaign to the siege of Kut; recollections of experiences as a POW in Turkey, 1916-18; and copies of answers to a questionnaire, circulated to survivors of the siege in 1970, requesting an assessment of Maj. Gen. Sir Charles Townshend, commanding officer at Kut.

Vice-Admiral Sir Maxwell Richmond
Reports, articles, a few letters and addresses, mostly pertaining to his
service in destroyers during WWII.

Gen. Sir Thomas Riddell-Webster
Five files of demi-official papers covering service as Lt. Gen. in charge
of administration in the Middle East, 1941-2, and as Quartermaster-
General, 1942-6.

Vice-Admiral Sir Ballin Robertshaw
Brief autobiography, diary of the 1939 staff mission to the Soviet
Union, and other miscellaneous papers. Robertshaw commanded HMS
Wallace, 1940; served at the Admiralty, 1941; was on the staff of the
C-in-C Mediterranean, 1942-3; witnessed the Normandy invasion, 1944;
and commanded HMS *Cleopatra,* 1944-6.

Maj. P. L. Rome
Account, by a subaltern in the Durham Light Infantry, of the battle of
Kohima, April 1944.

Field-Marshal Erwin Rommel
Three bound vols. of photocopies of the MS for Rommel's book,
Infanterie Grieft an, an expansion of his 1914-18 diary with tactical
notes added; and five albums of photographs taken by Rommel in
France, 1940, and North Africa, 1941-2.

Brig. G. R. P. Roupell
Account of his service with the 1st Battalion, East Surrey Regiment,
14th Infantry Brigade in France, 1914-17. There is also a 143 pp. ts.
account of his WWII career as GSO 1, 44th Home Counties Division,
1939; commander of the 36th Infantry Brigade, 12th Division, 1939;
retreat with the BEF, 1940; and escape to Spain, 1941.

Vice-Admiral E. G. N. Rushbrooke
Papers, 1911-68, comprising miscellaneous documents and certificates
from WWI and notes on naval operations in the Western Mediterranean
and South Atlantic during WWII. There is also correspondence with
Donald McLachlan referring to his *Room 39: A Study in Naval
Intelligence (1968).*

Lt. W. B. St. Leger
Diaries of a subaltern, 2nd Battalion, Coldstream Guards, covering in
great detail his service on the Western Front, 1916-18.

Air Commodore Charles Rumney Samson (1883-1931)
Papers comprising his personal file, reminiscences from WWI, certifi-
cates and appointments, pilot's log books, reports, early aviation
papers, and information relating to the official history, *War in the Air.*
Samson served in Belgium, France, the Dardanelles, Egypt and the Red
Sea.

Gauleiter Fritz Sauckel
Miscellaneous papers, 1898-1944, as Minister of Labour Supply.

Vice-Admiral Sir Guy Sayer
Official reports relating to naval operations in the Southwestern
Approaches and the English Channel, 1942-3, and the assaults on
Malaya and Sumatra, September — October 1945. Sayer was concerned
with Operation ZIPPER and was Naval Officer in Charge, Port Dickson.
There is material in the reports on the occupation of Brittany.

Vice-Admiral A. C. Scott
Diary from 20 October 1914 to 31 December 1916. Scott was captain
of the light cruiser *Blonde,* attached to the 4th Battle Cruiser Squadron,
1914-16. In 1916 he became captain of the light cruiser *Dublin,* which
saw action at the Dogger Bank and Jutland.

Vice-Admiral B. B. Schofield
Two midshipman's logs kept while serving in the battle cruiser
Indomitable, 1913-15.

Sir Geoffrey Shakespeare
Personal correspondence, July 1940 — November 1944, containing
inter alia material concerning the defection of Rudolf Hess and the
Mediterranean blockade. Shakespeare was Parliamentary and Financial
Secretary to the Admiralty, 1937-40; Parliamentary Secretary to the
Department of Overseas Trade, 1940; and Parliamentary Under-
Secretary of State, Dominions Office, 1940-2.

Capt. C. E. R. Sherrington
Papers mainly concerned with his post as Secretary of the Railway
Research Service in WWII. They show the role of the Service in the
planning of the strategic bombing offensive against Germany and
occupied Europe.

J. Simons
Two books by Prof. Bernard on French and European resistance,
1939-45, and a 188 pp. account of the history of the Milices

Patriotiques of Schaerbeek, with extracts from the diaries of J. Dustin, a member of this Belgian resistance group, 1940-4. Also included are German passes and official stamps, presumably forged, and an account and three copies of the fake edition of *Le Soir* published on 9 November 1943 by the French Resistance.

Air Commodore F. A. Skoulding

Collection of WWI reports, including notes taken by Corp. F. A. Skoulding for Gen. Trenchard, 3 May 1916; also two vols. entitled 'The Dissolution of the Luftwaffe' by Air Marshal Sir Philip Wigglesworth, 1945-6. Some of this collection is still restricted under the 30-year Rule.

Gen. Sir Horace Smith-Dorrien

28 letters, 16 June – 13 November 1920, between Smith-Dorrien and the official historian, Maj. A. F. Becke, concerning the battle of Le Cateau, 22-29 August 1914, and including transcripts of official records.

Gen. Sir Reginald Stephens

Lectures, narratives, diaries, MSS, official orders, relating to service on the Western Front, 1914-18. Stephens commanded the 5th Division from 1 April 1916 to the end of the war.

R. J. Stopford

A few papers relating to his service with the Friends Ambulance Unit and the RASC, 1914-19; and records concerning the Runciman Mission to Czechoslovakia, 1938, and the administration of the Czech Refugee Trust Fund, 1938-9.

Lt. Gen. Sir William Stratton

Papers relating to Operation BUMPER held in the United Kingdom as an anti-invasion exercise, September – October 1941, and similarly *Victor*, 22-25 January 1941. There is also a training memorandum on infantry and tank co-operation.

Brig. H. C. T. Stronge

Memorandum on the morale and state of preparedness for war of the Czech Army, September 1938. Stronge was British Military Attaché in Czechoslovakia, November 1936 – December 1938.

Maj. A. E. Sturdy

Some of Gen. Ironside's original handwritten despatches on the North Russian campaign, 1918-19; copy of the GHQ war diary, North Russian

Expeditionary Force, 1918-19; and letters and miscellaneous notes on the Russian campaign. Related material can be found in the papers of Lt. Col. A. G. Burn and Capt. W. V. Rendel.

Maj. Gen. W. T. Swan
Detailed diaries and approximately 900 letters home, covering his appointments as Assistant Director of Medical Services, BEF, August 1914 – July 1915; Deputy Director of Medical Services, 7th Corps, BEF, July 1915 – January 1918; and Director of Medical Services, BEF, January – September 1918.

Maj. Gen. Sir Gilbert Szlumper
Diary, 25 August 1939 – 2 November 1945, recording his career in various government positions dealing with transport during WWII. The collection also includes a diary of a visit to South Africa, November 1944 – April 1945, and miscellaneous reports and papers, 1916-68.

Vice-Admiral A. G. Talbot
Collection of papers relating to his service as Director of Anti-Submarine Warfare at the Admiralty, 1939-40.

Wing Commander N. Tangye
Ts. diary kept while serving as RAF Liaison Officer on the personal staff of the Commanding General, US Strategic Air Force (Europe), July – October 1944. The diary deals with Anglo-American relations and army-air force relations of both the British and American sides.

Maj. Gen. Sir Nigel Tapp
Seventeen accounts by officers of the 7th Field Regiment, RA, of the first two days of the invasion of Normandy, 1944.

Lord Thomson of Cardington
Diary, 1918-21 of Christopher Birdwood, Baron Thomson of Cardington (1875-1930), as Brig. Gen. attached to the staff of the Supreme War Council at Versailles. He was then sent to Mudros as the bearer of the terms of the British armistice to the Turks. The diary mainly records the progress of the peace negotiations.

Gen. Sir Andrew Thorne
Papers collected for an article on the action at Gheluvelt, 29-30 October 1914, and published in *The Household Brigade Magazine,* Summer 1932.

Air Vice-Marshal H. K. Thorold
Miscellaneous collection of papers relating to service with the West
African Reinforcement Route, 1940-2.

Lt. Gen. Sir Francis Tuker
Tuker was Director of Military Training, GHQ, India, 1940-1; commander of the 34th Indian Division, 1941, and the 4th Indian Division,
1942-4; GOC, Ceylon, 1945; and commander of the 4th Indian Corps,
1945. The papers cover his entire military career.

Maj. Gen. Sir Stanley von Donop
Von Donop was Master of Ordnance in 1914 only to be removed from
office by Lloyd George. There is one file box containing three binders
of press-cuttings and one file of official Ministry of Munitions papers,
1913-16.

Maj. Gen. G. P. Walsh
Official papers referring to the 10th Corps in North Africa, 1942; 30th
Corps in Sicily, 1943; 8th Army operations in Italy, 1944; and Burma,
1944-5. Walsh was Chief of Staff of the 8th Army, 1944, and ALFSEA,
1945.

Prof. C. K. Webster
At the outbreak of war in 1939, Prof. Webster of the London School of
Economics and D. W. Brogan became responsible, under the auspices of
Chatham House, for writing on the trend of opinion in the United
States. The Foreign Research and Press subsequently grew from this
activity. The papers consist of correspondence between Webster and
various departments of the British government, the BBC, the Far East
Committee, the United States, etc. For the main corpus of Webster's
papers, see the British Library of Political and Economic Science
(p. 96).

Admiral Sir William Whitworth
Whitworth was Vice-Admiral commanding the Battle Cruiser Squadron,
1939-41; Second Sea Lord, 1941-4; and C-in-C, Rosyth, 1944-6. His
papers mainly relate to the Norwegian campaign, 1940, but also contain
a series of letters from Admiral A. B. Cunningham, 1941-3.

J. Williams
Two interesting accounts of his service with the Chindits in Burma,
1944.

Admiral of the Fleet Sir Algernon Willis
Memoirs covering his service as Chief of Staff to the C-in-C,
Mediterranean, 1939-41; C-in-C, South Atlantic, 1941-2; Second in
Command, Eastern Fleet, 1942-3; Flag Officer, Force H, 1943; C-in-C
Levant, 1943; and Second Sea Lord and Chief of Naval Personnel,
1944-5.

Field-Marshal Sir Henry Wilson (1864-1922)
Papers of service as Sub-chief of the General Staff under the French,
1914; Chief Liaison Officer with French HQ, 1915; commander of 4th
Corps, 1915; head of a mission to Russia, 1916-17; head of Eastern
Command in the United Kingdom, 1917; British representative to
Supreme War Council, 1917; and CIGS, 1918-22. This important
collection consists of his diaries, 1893-1922, and correspondence,
1917-22.

India Office Library and India Office Records, 197 Blackfriars Road, LONDON SE1 8NG

The India Office Library and the India Office Records are part of the
Foreign and Commonwealth Office. Access is generally unrestricted
within the limits of the Public Records Act of 1967 and subsequent
directives. Private collections accumulated during the tenure of an
official appointment are also subject to the statutory rule governing
access to official records. Reader's tickets may be obtained by members
of the Foreign and Commonwealth Office, members of the Diplomatic
Corps accredited in London, and those recommended by a person of
recognized position.
For the India Office Library see S. C. Sutton, *A Guide to the India
Office Library* (London, HMSO, 1967) while for the India Office
Records see J. C. Lancaster, 'The India Office Records', *Archives,* IX,
no. 43 (April 1970).

INDIA OFFICE RECORDS: EUROPEAN MANUSCRIPTS

Arnold Collection: **MSS.Eur.F.145**
Papers of Sir Frederick Blackmore Arnold (1906-68), Secretary to the
Government of Burma, Reconstruction Department, 1942-4, and to the
Commerce and Supply Department, 1946-7. Closed.

Bailey Collection: **MSS.Eur.D.658**
Papers, 1918-40, of Lt. Col. Frederick Marshman Bailey (1882-1967).
They mainly concern Bailey's mission to Tashkent in 1918 and the role

played by Sir George Macartney. Bailey also served with the IEF in Flanders and Gallipoli, 1915, and as a Political Officer in Mesopotamia and Persia, 1917-18. **MSS.Eur.C.162** is 'Major Bailey's Russian Diary 1918-1920' which formed the basis of his *Mission to Tashkent* (London, 1946).

Baird Collection: MSS.Eur.B.239
MSS copies of letters, August 1914 – October 1918, of 2nd Lt. R. D. Baird who served with the Rifle Brigade in France, August – December 1914; ADC-HQ, 2nd Cavalry Division, BEF, August 1915 – December 1916; ADC, East Force, EEF, Palestine, December 1916 – July 1917; 2/24th London Regiment, Palestine, July – October 1917; and ADC-HQ, 20th Corps, EEF, Palestine, January – October 1918.

Bethmann-Hollweg
Letter to Mir Usman Ali Khan Bahadur Fath Jang, Nizam of Hyderabad, from Theobald von Bethmann-Hollweg (1856-1921), German Chancellor, 1909-17, during WWI. **MSS.Eur.E.247.**
Specimen of letters in German and Hindi from Bethmann-Hollweg to the Indian Princes during WWI. **MSS.Eur.E.204.**
Specimens of letters written in German, Hindi and Urdu from Bethmann-Hollweg to the Indian Princes during WWI. Also letters from Mahendra Pratap to the Indian Princes. **MSS.Eur.E.209.**
Letter in German and Hindi from Bethmann-Hollweg to the Maharajah of Jammu and Kashmir, with an English translation.**Photo.Eur.33.**
History of letters addressed by Herr von Bethmann-Hollweg, German Chancellor, to various Indian princes during the Great War, n.d. **MSS.Eur.D.790.**

Birdwood Collection: MSS.Eur.D.686
Semi-official and private papers, 1888-1917, of Field-Marshal Sir William Riddell Birdwood, 1st Baron Birdwood of Anzac and Totnes (1865-1951). GOC, Australia New Zealand Army Corps, 1914-18, and Australian Imperial Force, 1915-20. The bulk of the collection is private and semi-official papers of Field-Marshal Earl Kitchener, 1888-1909, whom Birdwood served as military secretary, 1900-2. The Birdwood papers contain little, mainly some letters from Kitchener commenting on affairs in England, Egypt and India, 1911-14, and copies of telegrams between Birdwood, the Secretary of State for the Colonies, the War Office and the Governor General of Australia on the individual role of Anzac.

Brabourne Collection: MSS.Eur.F.97
Papers of Michael Herbert Rudolph Knatchbull, 5th Baron Brabourne

(1895-1939) as Governor of Bombay, 1933-7; Governor of Bengal, 1937-9; and Acting Viceroy and Governor General, 1938. The collection contains a few packets of secret military papers for 1939.

Brayne Collection: MSS.Eur.F.152

Letters, papers and diaries, 1900-52, of Frank Lugard Brayne (1882-1952). Diaries, correspondence and notes of Brayne as Deputy Chief Political Officer in Aleppo, 1917-19. Also correspondence while serving with the EEF, April 1918 — January 1919. Other miscellaneous notes and papers relating to WWI and the Indian Army. There is much correspondence of Brayne as Brigadier and Adviser on Indian Affairs, Welfare General's Branch, General Staff, India concerning post-war planning and resettlement of Indian servicemen during WWII. The collection also contains correspondence and notes of Brayne as Inspector of Amenities for Indian Troops, Iraq Force, and in the Far East during WWII.

Richard Gardiner Casey: Photo.Eur.48

Xerox copies of personal diaries of Richard Gardiner Casey, Baron Casey (b. 1890), as Governor of Bengal, 1944-6. Closed.

Chartered Bank of India: MSS.Eur.D.750

Ts. account, dated 14 July 1942, of the evacuation of Rangoon by the Chartered Bank of India in February 1942.

Chelmsford Collection: MSS.Eur.E.264

Papers of Frederic John Napier Thesiger, 1st Viscount Chelmsford (1868-1933) as Viceroy of India, 1916-21. In addition to the usual correspondence and despatches with the Secretary of State for India, there are many files relating to Persia and WWI.

Chin Hills Battalion: MSS.Eur.E.250

MS history of the Chin Hills Battalion (Military Police), 1894-1949. **MSS.Eur.E.230** is an extract of the foregoing, entitled 'Official (Manuscript) History of the Chin Hills Battalion in Burma, 1942-1945'.

Curzon Collection: MSS.Eur.F.111

Correspondence and papers of George Nathaniel Curzon, 1st Marquess Curzon of Kedleston (1859-1925). The collection has three sections: from leaving Oxford to his appointment as Viceroy of India, 1882-98; as Viceroy and Governor General, 1899-1905; and papers about India collected by Lord Curzon after his term as Viceroy, printed vols. The following vols. have some pertinence to WWI: **104-105** and **419**, papers relating to Indian Army administration, 1899-1920; **442**, Cabinet papers and notes by Curzon on commissions for Indians in the army, 1916-18; and **443**, miscellaneous Cabinet papers and notes on India, especially army and military equipment, 1916-23. **MSS.Eur.F.112/138-154** comprises printed War Cabinet papers, 9 December 1916 – 27 October 1919, and printed War Committee and War Cabinet (Allied Conference) papers, 1915-18.

Dorman-Smith Collection: **MSS.Eur.E.215**
Papers of Sir Reginald Hugh Dorman-Smith (b. 1899) as Governor of Burma, 1941-6. **Photo.Eur.11** consists of secret telegrams, 8 December 1914 – 3 May 1942, from Dorman-Smith to the Rt. Hon. L. S. Amery, Secretary of State for India and Burma. The originals are in the Imperial War Museum (see p. 106).

Dunlop Smith Collection: **MSS.Eur.F.166**
Letters and papers, 1855-1921, of Lt. Col. Sir James Robert Dunlop Smith (1858-1921), Political ADC to the Secretary of State for India, 1910-21.

Erskine Collection: **MSS.Eur.D.596**
Papers of John Francis Ashley Erskine, Lord Erskine (1895-1953) as Governor of Madras, 1934-40. There is some material relating to the outbreak of WWII and the Government of India.

Ghadr Party
Catalogue of hostile oriental propaganda pamphlets (old edition); abstracts of pamphlets in oriental languages, 1914-18; translations of the *Ghadr*, 1915-17; and two copies of a catalogue of hostile oriental propaganda pamphlets, new series, July 1919. **MSS.Eur.E.288.**
United States of America vs. Franz Bopp and others, reporter's transcript of the trial of the Ghadr Party conspirators in California, 20 November 1917 – 23 April 1918. **MSS.Eur.C.138.**

Grant Collection: **MSS.Eur.D.660**
Letters and papers of Sir (Alfred) Hamilton Grant (1872-1937) as Foreign Secretary to the Government of India, 1914-19. A few of the letters deal with various aspects of the war, the Arab Revolt against Turkey, and army matters. There is also some correspondence with Balfour on Turkish peace terms.

Haig Collection: **MSS.Eur.F.115**
Papers of Sir Harry Graham Haig (1881-1956) as Governor of the United Provinces, 1934-9, containing some material relating to the reaction of the Indian Government to the outbreak of war, 1938-9.

Hallett Collection: **MSS.Eur.E.251**
Papers of Sir Maurice Garnier Hallett (1883-1969), Governor of Bihar, 1937-9, and Governor of the United Provinces, 1939-45. The papers cover the period 1907-47, and contain material on various aspects of WWII.

Howell Collection: **MSS.Eur.D.681**
Papers and correspondence of Sir Evelyn Berkeley Howell (1877-1971). Howell was Censor of the Indian Mails IEF, in France, 1914-16, and served in the administration of Mesopotamia, 1916-21. The papers cover the years 1877-1965, and include his weekly reports as Censor and lengthy extracts of Indian letters as illustrations. There is also some material pertaining to Mesopotamia, 1918.

Hume Collection: **MSS.Eur.D.724**
Weekly letters, 1927-47, of Andrew Parke Hume (1904-65) to his parents, and personal diaries, 1927-47. Hume served as Deputy Secretary, Department of Supply, 1941; Deputy Controller-General of the Food Department, Government of India, 1943; and Joint Secretary, Munitions Production, Department of Supply, 1943-6.

India, Pakistan and Burma Association Collection: **MSS.Eur.E.158**
Papers, 1941-72, of a trade association formed in 1942 to promote British trade with these countries.

Indian Army Regimental Histories: **MSS.Eur.C.142**
Regimental histories of the Indian Army. The bibliography was submitted in part requirement for the University of London Diploma in Librarianship by M. A. Myers, May 1957.

Indian National Army: **MSS.Eur.A.73**
Unpublished printed pamphlets, *c.* 1943, issued by the Indian National Army, including a list of 'Do's and don'ts for officers and men of the Indian National Army' and a series of platoon lectures on subjects connected with the Indian independence movement.

Indian Police Collection: **MSS.Eur.F.161**
Papers illustrating the history of the Indian Police used by Sir Percival Griffiths for his *To Guard My People: The History of the Indian Police* (1971).

Indian Soldiers' Fund: **MSS.Eur.F.120**
Minutes, reports, accounts, correspondence, etc., 1914-19, of the

Indian Soldiers' Fund, established to maintain a hospital and provide comforts, etc. for the Indian troops in WWI.

Keyes Collection: MSS.Eur.F.131

Letters, papers and despatches, 1904-39, of Brig. Gen. Sir Terence Humphrey Keyes (1877-1939). Keyes was attached to the Russian Army in Romania in 1917; on special duty in Russia, 1917-18; and attached to the General Staff, South Russia and Army of the Black Sea, 1919. Relevant papers concern Keyes' role in charge of the Mekran Mission, 1916, and in the British Military Mission to South Russia, 1917-20. See also MSS.Eur.B.228, 'Account of the Bahrain Islands' and two letters from Keyes in 1914 as political agent in Bahrain.

Col. Robert Welland Knox: MSS.Eur.D.756

Two official files concerning Col. Robert Welland Knox (1873-*c*. 1950) of the Indian Medical Service, 1897-1923, referring to his service record, 1897-1923; and official war diary, January 1916 — June 1919, of the 121st Indian Field Ambulance Unit, of which Knox was commander in Mesopotamia.

Laithwaite Collection: MSS.Eur.F.138

Papers, 1912-71, of Sir (John) Gilbert Laithwaite (b. 1894), Private Secretary to the Viceroy of India, 1936-43. The collection includes correspondence and papers relating to Burma, 1942-9. Closed.

Linlithgow Collection: MSS.Eur.F.125

Papers of Victor Alexander John Hope, 2nd Marquess of Linlithgow (1887-1952) as Viceroy and Governor General of India, 1936-43. There are 180 vols. covering these years. Principal correspondents are the Marquess of Zetland, L. S. Amery, R. N. Reid, L. R. Lumley, F. V. Wylie, Lord Erskine, J. G. Laithwaite, Viscount Templewood, H.M. The King Emperor, and various governors of Indian provinces.

Meston Collection: MSS.Eur.F.136

Papers, 1906-36, of James Scorgie Meston, 1st Baron Meston (1865-1943), Lieutenant Governor of the United Provinces of Agra and Oudh, 1912-18. He assisted the Secretary of State in representing India at the Imperial War Cabinet and Conference of 1917.

Monro Collection: MSS.Eur.D.783

Letters, papers, newspaper cuttings, scrapbooks and photographs, 1900-46, of Gen. Sir Charles (Carmichael) Monro (1860-1929), C-in-C India, 1916-20. The correspondence is mainly concerned with the general military situation in 1917. The collection also includes *Ten*

Chapters, 1942-1945 (1945) by Field-Marshal Viscount Montgomery of Alamein with a covering note by 'H.V.' dated 27 August 1946.

Montagu Collection: **MSS.Eur.D.523**
Correspondence, 1917-22, relating to Indian affairs of Edwin (Samuel) Montagu (1879-1924), Secretary of State for India, 1917-22. The collection does not include any material relating to his tenure as Minister of Munitions and member of the War Committee, 1914-16. See also **MSS.Eur.D.591**, 'Life of the Hon. Edwin Samuel Montagu' by Sir David Waley, two vols. ts.

Sir Hubert Rance Collection: **MSS.Eur.F.169**
Memoirs and papers of Sir Hubert Rance as Governor of Burma, 1946-8. The collection includes one file marked 'Dorman-Smith's file', dated 1945-6, and dealing with the Burmese leader, Aung San. Closed.

Reading (Private) Collection: **MSS.Eur.F.118**
Personal and semi-official papers, 1898-1936, of Rufus Daniel Isaacs, 1st Marquess of Reading (1860-1935). President of the Anglo-French Loan Mission to the USA, 1915; Special Envoy to the USA, 1917; and Special Ambassador and High Commissioner to the USA, 1918. The correspondence is alphabetical but there are also files of correspondence with E. S. Montagu, D. Lloyd George, members of the Royal Family, Lord Mottistone, H. Samuel, Lord Birkenhead, J. Simon and others. The semi-official papers include Cabinet documents, 1913-15; War Cabinet documents, 1916-19; and papers relating to the USA Mission, 1917-19.

Records of the 3rd (Duke of Connaught's Own) Battalion, Seventh Rajput Regiment: **MSS.Eur.F.159**
Eight vols. of biographical and historical material relating to the European and Indian officers of the regiment.

Reid Collection: **MSS.Eur.E.278**
Papers, 1918-1963, of Sir Robert Niel Reid (1883-1964). Acting Governor of Bengal, June – October 1938 and February – June 1939; Governor of Assam, 1937-42; and China Relations Officer, Calcutta, 1942-3.

Col. Harry Ross: **MSS.Eur.B.235**
Six vols. of memoirs covering his entire career in the Indian Army, 1892-1929. **Vol. 3** covers Ross as second in command of the 105th Mahratta Light Infantry, 1914-16; in Mesopotamia as commander of

the 2nd Battalion, 103rd Mahratta Light Infantry, 1916; and service in India, 1916-18.

Royal Indian Navy Coastal Forces: **Photo.Eur.91**
Ts. account of the Royal Indian Navy Coastal Forces, 1942-5, by Lieutenant Commander Thomas H. L. Macdonald, RINVR, Staff Officer, Coastal Reserve.

Wilfrid W. Russell: **MSS.Eur.D.621**
His diaries from 1935 to 1956. Russell served in the Indian Air Force, 1940-2.

Capt. J. C. Thornton: **MSS.Eur.D.791**
Programmes and other ephemera, 1917-18, concerning his service in the RA, India and Mesopotamia.

Vernon Collection: **MSS.Eur.D.744**
Lt. Col. Herbert Bowater Vernon, military papers, 1916-57, relating to the history and WWI record of the 27th Punjab Battalion.

Vickers-Armstrong Ltd: **MSS.Eur.D.749**
File of correspondence, March 1941 — July 1942, between the Woking Mosque Trust and Messrs. Vickers-Armstrong Ltd, concerning the latter's request to extend their premises for wartime aircraft production and build on ground belonging to the Mosque.

Walton Collection: **MSS.Eur.D.545**
Private correspondence on official matters, 1905-42, of Sir John Charles Walton (1885-1957). Assistant Under-Secretary of State for India, 1936, and Deputy Under-Secretary of State for Burma, 1942-6.

Whyte Collection: **MSS.Eur.D.761**
Eight vols. of diaries of Sir (Alexander) Frederick Whyte (1883-1970). The first three vols., October 1917 — June 1919, are primarily a political commentary on the last year of WWI and subsequent peace negotiations, based on his experience as Liberal MP for Perth, 1910-18; a lieutenant in the RNVR, 1914-17; and special correspondent for the *Daily News* at the Paris Peace Conference. The last two vols. cover June — October 1934 and describe a visit to China, Japan, Korea and Manchuria as an independent political observer, including interviews with Chiang Kai-shek, Koki Hirota and Mamoru Shigemitsu.

Zetland Collection: **MSS.Eur.D.609**
Correspondence and papers of Lawrence John Lumley Dundas, 2nd

Marquess of Zetland (1876-1961). Governor of Bengal, 1917-22; Secretary of State for India, 1935-50; and Secretary of State for Burma, 1937-40. The collection includes Bengal diaries, 1917-19; correspondence, 1917-20, with Montagu, Austen Chamberlain, King George V and others; correspondence with Linlithgow, 1936-40; correspondence and papers relating to India and Burma, 1937-40; and Cabinet papers of Zetland and L. S. Amery, 1939-40.

INDIA OFFICE RECORDS: ADMINISTRATIVE

Aden: Residency Records: R/20
Records of the Political Residency and Chief Commissionership, 1839-1937. The collection contains some files relating to WWI, especially war files, 1906-36.
Records of the Secretariat, from 1937, including Ordinary, 1937-9; WWII: Ordinary; and WWII: Confidential.

Burma Office: M
The general files, 1937-48, include monthly intelligence reports, defence matters, communications and transport, intelligence from occupied Burma, administration in Burma during active operations and afterwards, etc. There are also subject files such as the Burma Road, Dr Ba Maw, a report on the Wingate Expedition of 1943, etc.

Military Department: L/MIL
Many relevant series, including:
Lists of papers referred to the Military Committee of the Council of India, 1885-1923.
Secret and confidential telegrams to and from India, 1914-37.
Military and marine letters and despatches from India, 1880-1930.
Secret military despatches from India, 1906-35.
Military Department correspondence, 1882-1948.
Entry in the Service: officer recruitment and related, to 1921.
Personal files: Indian Army records of service, promotions, etc., to 1947.
Military Department: Library, containing confidential and official prints and published material such as *Indian Army List, Orders and Instructions*, to 1947; *Burma Army List, Orders and Instructions*, 1937-44; *Royal Air Force Orders (India)*, 1920-1946; and Orders of Battle, training manuals, etc.
Military miscellaneous series, containing many items on WWI relating to movements of Indian troops and intelligence matters; papers of a military and political nature on Mesopotamia, 1914-22; reports of the

Indian Censor of Mails in France with lengthy extracts of letters, 1914-18; and administrative matters such as hospital, personnel, etc. There are only two items for WWII: a list of Italian prisoners in India, 1942; and a document regarding Far East relief requirements, 1944.

Persian Gulf Territories: Residency Records: **R/IS**
The records for Bushire, Bahrain, Muscat and Trucial Oman contain some material on naval and air stations and communications for the period of both wars. Kuwait was part of the area administered by the IEF in WWI but most of the papers of the Political Agency in Kuwait for 1914-18 are lacking. There is some WWII material covering various aspects of the British presence in and relations with Iraq, including general despatches from Baghdad, 1941-4, and the Iraqi coup d'état, 1941.

Political and Secret Department: **L/P&S**
The records of this department are the main source in London for the study of the Indian Princely States, frontier questions, administration of areas outside the sub-continent and foreign relations. In terms of the two world wars, the more interesting series are:
Political and Secret subject files, 1902-31, containing much material on WWI such as Persia, diaries, 1914-18; Persia, German affairs, 1914-16; and the Anglo-Japanese Alliance, 1911-21. There are also numerous files on the 'German War' in various contexts: Arabia, the Arab Revolt, Afghanistan, Egypt, Persia, native chiefs, Mesopotamia, Iraq, Turkey, German agents in China and Siam, etc. Such WWII material as exists is mainly located in **L/P&S/12**.
Political and Secret files, 1912-30.
Political (External) Department, files and collections, 1931-50.
Political (Internal) Department, files and collections, 1931-50.
Memoranda: reports, memoranda and printed material. There are many items for WWI pertaining to Persia, Arabia, the Arab Revolt, Turkey and Mesopotamia such as 'The War: proposed employment of Japanese troops in Mesopotamia, 13 December 1917'; 'Arabia: Arab Revolt. Memorandum on British commitments to King Hussein, 25 October 1918'; 'Turkey: The intellectual and political forces at present predominant in the Ottoman Empire, including notes on German agents and their misdeeds, and Turkish intrigues among Indian Muhammedans. Memorandum prepared at the request of the Prime Minister', 1916. There are only a few documents from WWII, most of which pertain to oil concessions.
Library, containing many books, printed reports, unpublished notes, journals, background reports and India Office memoranda. There are various items relating to the two world wars.

Revenue and Statistics Department: **L/E**
The papers of this department, 1880-1921, concern *inter alia* the effect of WWI on trade. The records of the Economic and Overseas Department, 1924-46, deal with economic aspects of WWII.

War Staff Department: **L/WS**
The War Staff was formed in 1939 within the Military Department of the India Office and became responsible for the administrative detail of the 'war' subjects, while routine military matters continued to be handled by the normal Military Department staff. The War Staff was divided into three sections: General, Intelligence and Supply. The relevant series of records are:
War Staff 'WS' Series files, 1921-50, covering various aspects of the war effort in India and relating to India.
Other War Staff files, 1940-51 but mostly 1944 and 1945, covering a variety of subjects, e.g. 'Planning Operation ZIPPER', 'Operation SEXTANT', morale reports, India Command and SEAC, 1943-4.
Registers and indexes of War Staff files, 1939-49.

Institute of Contemporary History and Wiener Library, 4 Devonshire Street, LONDON W1N 2BH

The Institute and Library is a leading resource for the study of Nazism, Fascism, the history of Germany since 1914, and the history of the Middle East in the 20th century. There is little manuscript material but the Library does hold the following items of relevance to WWII:
Some 40,000 documents, published and unpublished, relating to the International Military Tribunal trials in Nuremberg, 1945-9, with a partial index.
Documentation of the trial of Karl Adolf Eichmann (1906-62) in Israel, May — October 1961. Eichmann was head of the Jewish Department of the SS.
Press Archive, *ca.* 2,000,000 cuttings, mainly from British and German newspapers relating *inter alia* to the history of Germany, Nazism and the persecution of Jews since 1933.

Islington Central Library, Reference Division, 68 Holloway Road, LONDON N7 8JN

WORLD WAR I

Mayor of Le Havre, France, letter to BEF units, May 1919.

Metropolitan Borough of Islington, minutes of proceedings of the Recruiting Committee and Islington Battalion Committee, 1915-16.

WORLD WAR II

23 MS diaries covering the war period, 1939-45, of a former civilian resident of Highbury.

Ten items and correspondence relating to HMS *Quail*, 1944-5, between Councillor A. W. Wynn, then Mayor of Islington, and Lieutenant Commander R. L. Jenks, plus a telegram signed by Sir John Anderson. The destroyer was 'adopted' by the former Metropolitan Borough of Islington.

HANSAK Fire-Watchers' Patrol Book, WWII, a record book of Highbury, Aberdeen Park, Northolme, Sotheby, Ardilaun and Kelross Roads.

Lambeth Public Libraries, Archives Department, Minet Library, 52 Knatchbull Road, LONDON SE5 9QY

CIVIL DEFENCE RECORDS: **Acc. No. F51089**

Minutes of ARP Committee and Civil Defence Emergency Committee: correspondence, miscellaneous files, petty cash book.

Incident files with card index and index to war damage cases, 30 vols.

Training leaflets and cerberus exercises files.

Personnel index: fire guards, shelter wardens, etc.

Allocation, casualty service, clothing stock and recruit index.

Personal scrapbooks and photographs.

FIRST SURREY RIFLES ASSOCIATION: **Class IV/36**

Battalion orders, news sheets, annual files, officers' mess accounts, minute books and registers, visitors books, day orders, programmes of reunion dinners, etc., 1859-1962.

Personal collections including photograph albums of WWI, diary for 1914, battalion magazines and several general photographs of battle areas and servicemen.

Leyton Library, High Road, Leyton, LONDON E10 5QH

WORLD WAR II

Town Clerk's Department: files referring to Civil Defence and ARP matters with a large scale incident map. They are as yet unsorted but mainly consist of correspondence.

Liddell Hart Centre for Military Archives, The Library, King's College London, Strand, LONDON WC2R 2LS

The Liddell Hart Centre for Military Archives serves as a depository for private papers bearing on military affairs in the 20th century. Intending researchers must initially make application in writing to the Librarian stating the purpose of their research and the papers they wish to consult. Although listed below, certain papers may not be available for consultation.

Gen. Sir Ronald Forbes Adam (b. 1885)
Memoranda relating to his service as Adjutant-General to the Forces, 1941-6.

Field-Marshal Alanbrooke
Field-Marshal Alan Francis Brooke, 1st Viscount Alanbrooke (1883-1963). Various staff and field commands relating to artillery in WWI; GOC-in-C Anti-aircraft Command, 1939; GOC-in-C Southern Command, 1939-40; Commander of 2nd Army Corps in France, 1939-40; C-in-C, Home Forces, 1940-1; and CIGS, 1941-6. Papers covering his career. Closed.

Maj. Gen. Sir George (Grey) Aston (1861-1938)
Commandant, Royal Military Academy, 1914-17; employed in secretariat of the War Cabinet, 1918-19. Papers covering his career including WWI. The collection also contains diaries, articles and writings on various topics, and correspondence with Lord Grey and others.

Brig. Gen. Colin Robert Ballard (1868-1941)
Letters, mainly to his family, referring to service in WWI, commanding 1st Norfolk Regiment and 7th, 95th and 14th Infantry Brigades in France and Flanders.

Maj. Thomas Balston (1883-1967)
Papers and photographs referring to service as a lieutenant with the 12th Gloucestershire Regiment; Staff Captain with the 95th Infantry

Brigade in the UK, 1914-15; and DAAG in France with the 3rd Division, 1917-18, 3rd Corps, 1918-19.

Maj. Gen. N. W. Barnardiston (1858-1919)

Papers relating to the Anglo-Japanese capture of Tsingtao, 1914, and diaries and papers concerning command of the 39th Division in Britain and France, 1915-19.

Gen. Sir William Bartholomew (1877-1962)

Director of Military Operations and Intelligence, 1931-43; Chief of General Staff, India, 1934-7; and GOC-in-C, Northern Command, 1937-40. The papers are mostly correspondence with Dill, Chetwode and others in the 1920s and 1930s.

Brig. Gen. Sir Edward Beddington (1884-1966)

Copy of duplicated memoirs titled 'My Life', 1960, containing an account of his service as staff officer to Gen. Lord Gough of Vimy in WWI. Beddington served on the War Office General Staff and as Deputy Director of Military Intelligence during WWII.

Lt. Col. Sir Reginald Benson (1889-1968)

Papers as liaison officer with Group des Armées du Nord and the Grand Quartier Général in France, 1916-19, including French and British casualty and strength figures, intelligence summaries, operational planning, and correspondence between the commanders-in-chief.

Victor Bonham-Carter

Notes for his biography of Field-Marshal Sir William Robertson, *Soldier True* (1965) with a ts. and corrected proof; notes and transcript dealing with the period when Robertson was CIGS, for two programmes in the BBC TV series, 'The Great War'.

Maj. Gen. Viscount Bridgeman

Robert Clive Bridgeman, 2nd Viscount Bridgeman (b. 1896). Papers mainly referring to the BEF in France and Belgium, 1939-40, including Lord Gort's despatch with maps and comments thereon. Other papers concern the 1928 Staff College study of the 1915 Italian campaign; armoured support for infantry in the 7th Infantry Brigade, 1933-4; and papers by Maj. Gen. G. M. Lindsay.

Lt. Gen. Sir Charles Broad (b. 1882)

His papers have been destroyed but a letter to the Librarian contains an account of incidents in his career. There are also copies of letters exchanged with R. Alastair Rickard, historian, describing the situation with tanks in the 1920s and 1930s and why only adequate tanks were available in 1940.

Air Chief Marshal Sir Robert Brooke-Popham (1878-1953)
Files referring to air defence in Great Britain, and Brooke-Popham's service as Inspector-General of the RAF, 1935; AOC British Forces, Iraq, 1928-30; C-in-C RAF, Middle East, 1936-7; in the Empire Air Training Scheme, 1939-40; C-in-C, Far East, 1940-1; and in the ATC, 1942-7.

Maj. Gen. Sir Thompson Capper (1863-1915)
Papers referring to the Indian Staff College, 1908-11; lecture about the effect of aircraft on war, 1913; surrender of the German High Seas Fleet, 1918; and some papers of his brother, Maj. Gen. Sir John Capper (1861-1955).

Lt. Gen. Laurence Carr (1886-1954)
Letters to his wife from service in France, 1915-19; India, 1920-6; and Palestine, 1936-7.

Brig. H. V. S. Charrington (1886-1965)
Papers referring to service with the 12th Lancers in France and Flanders, 1914-18; his book *Where Cavalry Stands Today* (1927); command of 1st Armoured Brigade in Greece, 1941; and his subsequent report on the earlier operations in Eritrea and Abyssinia, 1941.

Maj. Gen. Arthur Reginald Chater (b. 1896)
Papers and photographs referring to Somaliland Camel Corps and the military command of the colony, 1937-40.

Brig. F. A. S. Clarke (1892-1972)
Copy of his unpublished ts. 'Memoirs of a professional soldier in peace and war' by 'Muskateer', describing service from 1915-47 in Gallipoli, Palestine, India, Ireland, The Saar, France, West Africa, Algiers and Italy, and his command of Essex Sub-District, 1945-7. The collection also contains copies of articles by him in service and other journals.

Lt. Gen. Sir (George) Sidney Clive (1874-1959)
Letter book and personal diaries, 1914-19, including period as head of the British Mission at French GHQ, 1915-18.

Capt. R. H. Covernton
Ts. of 'Fifty Odd Years of Memoirs' covering his career, 1893-1945,

including service with RE Signals during WWI in South and Southwest Africa, France and Britain, and life in the Channel Islands under German occupation during WWII.

Col. Sir Henry Darlington (1877-1959)

Ts. of his *Letters from Helles* (London, 1936), and orders, letters and messages relating to 2nd Battalion, Northamptonshire Regiment and 5th Battalion, Manchester Regiment in Egypt and Gallipoli.

Maj. Gen. Francis H. N. Davidson (1892-1973)

Series of narratives relating to the Allied Military Mission to Moscow, 1939; service with 1st Corps, BEF, 1939-40; and as Director of Military Intelligence, 1940-4. There is also his map as CCRA, 1st Corps, for the advance to the River Dyle and subsequent withdrawal, and maps prepared to show Queen Mary the progress of the war.

Maj. Gen. Sir Francis W. de Guingand (b. 1900)

Miscellaneous papers, mainly 1942-5, covering work as Chief of Staff to the Eighth Army and 21st Army Group.

Gen. Sir Miles Dempsey (1896-1969)

Complete set of Second Army Planning Intelligence summaries and Second Army Intelligence summaries, 1944-5.

Maj. Gen. William Alfred Dimoline (1897-1965)

Papers covering his career, 1914-62: service with the East Surrey Regiment, 1914-19, in France; with Royal Signals from 1920; in the Abyssinian and Madagascar campaigns during WWII; command of 11th (East African) Division in Burma; and GOC East Africa, 1946-8.

Brig. Gen. Sir James Edward Edmonds (1861-1956)

GSO, 4th Division, 1911-14; Deputy Engineer in Chief, BEF, 1918; officer in charge of Military Branch, Historical Section, CID, now Cabinet Office, 1919-49. Miscellaneous papers concerning his military career and position as Cabinet Office official historian of WWI.

Maj. Gen. J. F. C. Fuller (1878-1966)

Two vols. on the battle of Cambrai; two vols. on tank strategy and tactics, 1916-18; and five vols. on tank corps operations, compiled at his request immediately after the Armistice, 1918. Copy of the *Tragedy of Europe*, 1940-6, five vols. a day-by-day commentary on WWII by F. Neilson. Correspondence of Fuller and Mitzakis with 26 naval and military leaders of WWII on the offensive value of CDL tanks. Letters to his parents, 1892-1922 and pocket diaries for 1900-2, 1909 and

1918-63 (mainly engagements). Correspondence with his American publisher, 1961-5. The main collection of Fuller's papers is at Rutgers University, New Brunswick, New Jersey, USA.

Lt. Gen. Sir Humfrey M. Gale (1890-1971)
Papers and diaries referring to service as Deputy Chief of Staff and Chief Administrative Officer at SHAEF, 1942-5.

Capt. Gerard Garvin (1896-1916)
Garvin was the son of J. L. Garvin, editor of *The Observer,* and was killed at the Somme in July 1916. Trench diary, notebooks, and letters to and from his family.

Gen. Sir Alfred Reade Godwin-Austen (1889-1963)
Papers relating to his appointment to command in Somaliland just before the evacuation of August 1940, including a letter from the Governor replying to Godwin-Austen's request that he leave the colony.

Maj. Gen. Sir John Winthrop Hackett (b. 1910)
Photographs, ts. essays and related papers about Arnhem, collected by Theodore A. Boeree, a retired officer of the Dutch Army who witnessed the parachute drops and did considerable research after WWII.

Gen. Sir Ian Hamilton (1853-1947)
GOC-in-C, Mediterranean and Inspector-General of Overseas Forces, 1910-15; Commander of Mediterranean Expeditionary Force, 1915. Papers covering his entire career, especially strong on Gallipoli, and many private papers after 1916.

Brig. Gen. Philip Howell (1877-1916)
Papers referring to cavalry organisation and tactics before 1914, the 4th Hussars in Flanders, and the defence of Salonika, 1915-16.

Gen. Lord Ismay
Gen. Hastings Lionel Ismay, 1st Baron Ismay of Wormington (1887-1965). Service in Somaliland, 1914-20; Secretary of the CID, 1938-40; Chief of Staff to the Minister of Defence, 1940-5; and Deputy Secretary (Military) to the War Cabinet, 1940-5. Papers relating to his entire career.

Admiral F. W. Kennedy (1862-1939)
Papers as captain of HMS *Indomitable,* 1912-16, mainly an account of the part played by his ship in the pursuit of the *Goeben* and the *Breslau*

in August 1914. Other papers concerning the bombardment of the forts at the entrance to the Dardanelles in November 1914, the sinking of the *Blücher* in January 1915, and HMS *Indomitable* at Jutland, 1916.

Lt. Gen. Sir Launcelot Kiggell (1862-1954)
Director of Home Defence, War Office, 1914-15; Chief of General Staff to the British Armies in France, 1915-18. Correspondence with Sir William Robertson and Sir Henry Wilson, when each was CIGS; correspondence with General Haig, 1909-18; demi-official correspondence as Chief of General Staff to Haig in France, 1916-17; and notes on the Chantilly Conference, 1916.

Maj. Gen. S. W. Kirby (1895-1968)
Papers related to his book *Singapore: the Chain of Disaster* (1971). Closed.

Capt. G. H. Lever (1892-1973)
Papers and photographs referring to service as a wireless operator in German West Africa, 1914-15, and with the British Military Mission in South Russia, 1919-20.

Maj. Gen. Sir Richard Lewis (1895-1965)
Papers mainly concerning his work at AFHQ, 1942-4, and as Deputy Director-General for Finance and Administration, European Regional Office, UNRRA, 1945.

Capt. Sir Basil Liddell Hart (1895-1970)
Military historian and theorist. Correspondence, memoranda, lectures and other papers on military matters, with papers of Maj. Gen. Sir Percy Hobart, Maj. Gen. G. M. Lindsay and Chester Wilmot. A large and highly significant collection relating to warfare in general, tank warfare, and the two world wars. It remains for the present at Medmenham, Bucks.

Lt. Gen. Sir Wilfrid Lindsell (1884-1973)
Memoranda and notes accumulated as Quartermaster-General of the BEF, 1939-40, especially with reference to the withdrawal to Dunkirk; notes on the maintenance of the 8th Army and RAF support from El Alamein to Tunisia, 1943; memoranda, correspondence and lectures, mainly on India as a base for operations in the Far East, 1944-5; post-war lectures and newspaper articles on war administration and the Suez Canal question.

Col. Roderick Macleod
Annotated ts. of letters received from Field-Marshal William Ironside, 1931-9, and a copy of Macleod's unpublished account as an artillery officer in WWI.

Lt. Gen. Sir William Marshall (1865-1939)
Letters to his brother, 1915-19, as commander of the 87th Brigade of the 29th Division at Gallipoli; of the 42nd, 29th, and 53rd Divisions in the above campaign; of the 27th Division at Salonika; and as GOC-in-C, Mesopotamia Expeditionary Force.

Maj. Gen. Sir Frederick (Barton) Maurice (1871-1951)
Correspondence and papers, including those relating to the 'Maurice Case' and the debate in the Commons over his letter to *The Times* in May 1918.

Gen. Sir Frank Walter Messervy (b. 1893)
Miscellaneous publications and narratives produced by units of the Ministry of Information and the Indian War Department, referring to operations of SEAC and the Central Mediterranean Force in WWII; and War Office manuals, concerning warfare in non-industrialised areas, written by Messervy. For his main papers, see the National Army Museum (p. 156).

Brig. Gen. John Montagu
Brig. Gen. John Walter Edward Douglas-Scott-Montagu, 2nd Baron Montagu of Beaulieu (1866-1929). Adviser on Mechanical Transport Services to the Government of India, 1915-19. Correspondence, speeches and memoranda referring to air policy in WWI, and photographs and notes on India and mechanical transport, 1915-19.

Field-Marshal Sir Archibald (Armar) Montgomery-Massingberd
(1871-1947)
Papers covering his career, 1891-1944, including an unpublished autobiography. Service as GSO 2, 4th Division in France; Chief of Staff to 4th Corps under Rawlinson; and Chief of Staff to 4th Army under Rawlinson from 1916.

Gen. Sir Richard O'Connor (b. 1889)
Commander of Western Desert Corps, captured in Libya and escaped in December 1943. Copy of his unpublished account of attempted escapes from Italy, April 1941 — April 1943.

Maj. Gen. Sir (William) Ronald Campbell Penney (1896-1964)
Brigade Major, Shanghai, 1931-3; Signal Officer in Chief, Middle East, 1941-3; Chief Signal Officer, 18th and 15th Army Groups, North Africa, Sicily and Italy, 1943; command of 1st Division in Italy, 1944; and Director of Intelligence, HQ SACSEA, 1945. Papers referring to Shanghai, 1932; Middle East, North Africa and Sicily, 1941-3; Anzio, 1944; and SEAC, 1945.

Maj. Gen. Sir William Platt (b. 1885)
Bound copy of lectures on his campaign against Italian East Africa, 1940-1, delivered at the University of Cambridge in 1951.

Gen. Sir Harold (English) Pyman (1908-71)
Service in the Western Desert, including command of 3rd Royal Tank Regiment, 1941-3; Brigadier General Staff, Home Forces, 1943-4; Brigadier General Staff, 30th Corps for Normandy invasion, 1944; Chief of Staff, 2nd Army, 1944-5; and Chief of General Staff, ALFSEA, 1945-6; Papers covering his career.

Field-Marshal Sir William Robertson (1860-1933)
Quartermaster-General, BEF, 1914; Chief of General Staff, BEF, 1915; CIGS, 1915-18; and GOC-in-C Eastern Command, 1918. Papers covering his military career from 1898, including personal and semi-official correspondence as CIGS, 1916-18.

Brig. Harold Sandilands (1876-1961)
Correspondence, 1945-60, with Field-Marshal Sir Cyril Deverell (1874-1947) and others regarding Deverell's removal as CIGS in 1937.

Brig. Ivan Simson (1890-1971)
Ts. of his book *Singapore: Too Little Too Late* (1972), concerning the Malayan campaign, 1941-2, as seen by him as Chief Engineer.

Maj. Gen. Sir Edward (Louis) Spears (1886-1974))
Head of the British Military Mission to Paris, 1917-20. WWI papers. Closed.

Lt. Col. Sir Albert Stern (1878-1966)
Papers relating to the development of the armoured fighting vehicle during the world wars.

Maj. Gen. Sir Andrew Stuart (1861-1936)
Notebooks and diaries as Director of Works, British Armies in France, 1914-19.

Maj. Gen. Sir Ernest (Dunlop) Swinton (1868-1951)
Papers referring to his libel action with H. G. Wells; copies of his inaugural lecture as Chichele Professor of Military History at Oxford University, and other publications.

C. A. Vlieland
Ts. of 'Disaster in the Far East 1941-1942', an unpublished account based on his experiences as Secretary for Defence in Malaya.

Field-Marshal Erich von Manstein (1887-1973)
Papers relating to his trial for war crimes in 1949.

Capt. G. C. Wynne (1889-1964)
Military papers dealing mainly with WWII, including a letter by Lt. Gen. Kenneth Anderson, May 1943, rebutting criticisms of his command of the 1st Army in North Africa.

Sir Hubert Young (1889-1964)
Photocopies of papers on operations in the Hejaz, 1917-18. For the originals and copies of other papers relating to his service in the Middle East, see the Middle East Centre, St. Antony's College, Oxford (p. 254).

MISCELLANEOUS COLLECTIONS

MISC. I. *Capt. F. O. Miksche*
Copy made at the Ministry of Aircraft Production in 1944 of an unsigned article on Miksche's book *Is Bombing Decisive?* (1943).

MISC. III. The Rt. Hon. Leopold Amery's correspondence with Sir Basil Liddell Hart, 1954-7, and several Army League pamphlets and reports, 1955-66.

MISC. IV. *Lt. Garth Smithies Taylor (1896-1916)*
Copies of letters and photograph to his family, 1914-16, during service with the 2nd Sherwood Foresters at Ypres and the Somme.

MISC. V. *Lieutenant Commander Patrick Dalzel Job (b. 1913)*
MSS and photograph referring to service in WWII, including running special motor torpedo boats in Norway.

Archives and Local History Department, The Manor House, Old Road, Lee, LONDON SE13

WORLD WAR I

S. Godley, letter, dated 1920, describing the occasion on which he won a VC at Mons. **A70/15.**
Testimonial from the residents of Hither Green to T. H. Fielding in appreciation of his work during air raids, 1919. **A73/16.**

WORLD WAR II

Lower Ardgowan Road fire spotters: log books, correspondence, official notices and circulars, 1941-5. **A62/2.**
Warden's Post B21, Lewisham, journal in 23 vols., 1940-5. **A62/14.**
Fire Lee (A10 Section) fire watchers record book and map of the section, 1941-2. **A66/11.**
Lewisham Civil Defence files, control incidents, 1940-5. Access is restricted, and they are only available with written permission from the Town Clerk and Chief Executive Officer.
Album of goodwill from the women of Moscow to the women of Lewisham, *c.* 1942. **A67/1.**

Marylebone Library, Marylebone Road, LONDON NW1

The Marylebone Library holds the archives of the former boroughs of Paddington and St. Marylebone.

WORLD WARS I AND II

Paddington: local tribunal records, 1916-18; ARP minutes, 1938-45; Local ATC branch records, 1939-54; war damage alphabetical card index; and Emergency Committee minutes, 1940-5.
St. Marylebone: local tribunal records, 1915-18; Emergency Committee minutes, 1940-5; ARP records, 1939-45; war damage papers arranged alphabetically; and 'History of the St. Marylebone ARP Unit', written by one of the officers, with miscellaneous related papers, 1940-5.

Ministry of Defence, Air Historical Branch, Queen Anne's Chambers, 3 Dean Farrer Street, LONDON SW1H 9JX

The Air Historical Branch is concerned principally with the collection, collation, indexing and cataloguing of primary source papers and records from all units of the RAF and branches of the Air Force Department. Records handled by the Branch are not generally available but may, under certain specific conditions, be made available to approved researchers under the 30-year Rule. The Branch also produces occasional historical studies for departmental use, a few of which are published by HMSO, such as *Operational Research in the Royal Air Force* (1963).

Ministry of Defence Library (Central and Army), Old War Office Building, Whitehall, LONDON SW1

The Library serves as a reference service for the Ministry of Defence and holds no primary source material. It does have a large collection of Ministry of Defence printed documents and publications, some of which are unobtainable elsewhere.

National Army Museum, Royal Hospital Road, LONDON SW3 4HT

The National Army Museum covers the history of the British Army to 1914, that of the Indian Army to 1947, and the histories of other Commonwealth armies up to independence. The library of the Museum contains a large collection of books and journals related to these subjects, army publications and pamphlets, and a substantial collection of prints, drawings and photographs. A full range of regimental histories, campaign histories and army lists is available on open shelf in the Reading Room. Application for a reader's ticket should be made to the Director.

WORLD WAR I

5201-33. Field-Marshal Henry Seymour Rawlinson, Baron Rawlinson of Trent (1864-1925). Journals, diaries, sketch-books, photograph albums and other papers. Lord Rawlinson commanded the 4th Division, 7th Division and 3rd Cavalry Division in Belgium, 1914; 4th Corps, 1914-16; 4th Army, 1916-18; became British Military Representative on the Allied Supreme War Council, February 1918; and commanded the 5th Army from March 1918.

5310-48. 2nd Royal Munster Fusiliers war diary, 13 August 1914 – January 1915.

5312-33. 2nd Cavalry Division, ts. 'Summary of Information', 1914.

5511-16. Documents relating to the Royal Irish Regiment and Gen. J. Burton Forster, 1914-18.

5602-390. Gen. Sir Charles Anderson, commanding Meerut Division, operations order for attack on Neuve Chapelle, 9 March 1915.

5603-11. Lt. Col. Henry Francis Jourdain (1872-1968) of the Connaught Rangers, five diaries kept on service in Gallipoli, August – September 1915; Salonika, 1915; and Serbia and Bulgaria, 1916.

5603-12. Lt. Col. Henry Francis Jourdain, Connaught Rangers, eleven diaries kept on service in France and Flanders, 1917.

5603-50. Capt. N. P. Clarke and Lt. H. D. O'Hara, Royal Dublin Fusiliers, two letters from Gallipoli, 1915.

5706-36. Capt. M. C. C. Harrison, 2nd Battalion, Royal Irish Regiment, account of the first battle of Ypres, 1914.

5707-26. Two plans of trenches.

5903-34. Newspapers: *BEF Times,* December 1916 and March 1917; *Kemmel Times,* July 1916; and *Somme Times,* July 1916.

5904-130. Note on the Indian Army Corps to 20 November 1914; a message from Chetwode to Swift; and a German order relating to 'troop comforts'.

5905-41. Gen. Sir Ian Hamilton, farewell message on relinquishing command in Gallipoli, October 1915.

5910-237. Book of maps and orders relating to the Mesopotamia campaign.

6001-75-76. Capt. N. R. Wilkinson, Coldstream Guards: three notebooks; a diary for 1915; and a bundle of intelligence reports and other documents collected by him.

6012-80. Propaganda leaflet in German headed 'By Balloon'.

6012-221. East Africa, Somaliland Camel Corps order book, 10 January 1914 – 17 September 1917.

6012-234. Miscellaneous documents relating to the Kut campaign, including five communiqués from Maj. Gen. Charles Townshend.

6012-275. Trench map of the Armentières area.

6012-282. Maps depicting the war in Russia and the Balkans, 1915.

6012-288. Copy of the Special Order of the Day, 4 December 1915, signed by Maj. Gen. Charles Townshend with Parade State.

6012-299. Ts. copies of various despatches by Maj. Gen. Charles Townshend from Kut.

6021-291. Narrative and data concerning the Volunteer Artillery Battery at Kut, commanded by A. J. Anderson.

6012-337. W. G. Bagot Chester: personal war diary from 12 August 1914 in India to 4 December 1914 in France; and 19 October 1916 in Southampton to 1 December 1917 in Palestine and Egypt.

6012-352. Operations orders and plans covering withdrawal from Gallipoli, 13-16 December 1916.

6012-353. Ts. copy of a letter from a Turkish officer to his wife containing adverse intelligence about the state of the Turkish forces in the Gallipoli area.

6012-398. Two pages of MS diary, 30 April − 4 July 1916, describing the trek from Kut to Kastamuni by 2nd Lt. A. R. Ubsdell, 66th Punjabis.

6012-399. Notebook containing MS copy of a communiqué from Maj. Gen. Charles Townshend to his troops at Kut, 26 January 1916.

6012-400. Three diaries of 2nd Lt. A. R. Ubsdell, 15 February 1915 until just before the siege of Kut.

6108-55. 29th Division, ts. orders for the advance into Germany after the Armistice, 1918.

6111-135. 3rd Corps Operations Order No. 33 and 14th Division Operations Order No. 27, both for an assault across the Tigris, 22 February 1917; and 39th Brigade operations orders for supporting activities, 22 February 1917.

6111-146. Letter from Wiley West of the North Irish Horse to Capt. Henley, written shortly before West was killed on the Western Front and received a posthumous VC.

6112-637. Two envelopes of papers relating to the Artists Rifles in France and North Russia.

6112-661. 99th Deccan Infantry, letters from Lt. Col. F. D. Davidson referring to the regiment's service in East Africa, 1914-17.

6208-52. Divisional command ordering cease fire, 11 November 1918.

6302-61. Packet of letters from Murmansk from Trevor Barlow to his mother, 1918-19.

6307-50. Field-Marshal Lord Auchinleck, four sketch maps made as a captain during operations against the Turks in Mesopotamia, 1916.

6308-14. MS memoirs of Col. J. J. Grove regarding service on the Western Front.

6308-21-1. Map of St. Quentin, 1916.

6308-52. Letter relating to the use of dum dum bullets by the Germans, n.d.

6308-54-10-18. Training diagrams of various types of grenades.

6308-69. Sir John Ponsonby, documents and maps referring to his command of the Guards Brigade and the 40th Division on the Western Front, 1917-18.

6308-126-24. Letter of congratulations to the Allied armies from Marshal Ferdinand Foch, 1918.

6308-126-23. Facsimile of Field-Marshal Earl Kitchener's letter asking for 300,000 recruits, 16 May 1915.

6308-126-28. Jan Smuts, printed copy of a speech, 'The Coming Victory', given on 4 October 1917.

6308-126-30A. General Routine Orders, Adjutant-General's Branch No. 369, Field-Marshal Haig's last orders in France, 1919.

6308-134. Special Order of the Day, 10 January 1919, with exchange of courtesies between Field-Marshal Douglas Haig and Marshal Henri Pétain.

6309-28-4. Col. W. L. Malcolm, 31st Punjabis, documents, including a telegram on the outbreak of war.

6309-621. Maps: 2nd Army Motor Transport Circuits, northeast France; France, Lens area; Belgium, Tournai area; Belgium and France, Ypres area; and northwest Europe, Mons area.

6309-624. Message from 179th Brigade to 1st Battalion, 19th Punjabis, giving the situation during the Turkish retreat, September 1918.

6312-32. Field service notebook compiled during the Cameroons campaign by Col. C. H. B. Weston, West Africa Regiment.

6312-54. Royal Dublin Fusiliers, MS signal 'Mobilize' received by the 2nd Battalion, 5.00 pm on 4 August 1914.

6312-248. Orders of the day by Field-Marshal Douglas Haig, April – September 1918, and map of Arras overprinted '3rd Army'.

6312-259. West Africa Expeditionary Force, Cameroons: nominal roll of Europeans, October 1915, printed.

6404-74. Mesopotamia, field service notebook with reconnaissance reports submitted by Lt. V. Hodson of the 10th Lancers, 1917.

6405-86. Dardanelles, photocopy of a 'Report on the Dardanelles Landing' by David French, April 1915.

6406-1. Special Order of the Day by Maj. Gen. T. A. Cubitt, commanding the 38th Regiment, Welsh Division, 7 September 1918, in appreciation of the regiment's valour.

6407-62. Printed instructions from the Central Training Camp, Etaples, including the duties of company commander and company sergeant major in trench warfare; and handout sheet, in German and English, protesting against the French use of coloured troops during the occupation.

6407-92. Maps: German order of battle at the commencement of the Armistice, November 1918; battle positions at Favreuil; and positions near Courtrai, marked Maj. A. S. Wright.

6409-22. London District School of Instructions, Chelsea Barracks: two notebooks of Capt. E. Harborow, City of London Volunteer Regiment, for two courses, 15 April – 10 May 1918.

6409-57. Mesopotamia, military map of the area around Kut showing defensive positions, with notes in red pencil, 1916.

6409-64. Printed proclamation by the GOC in Mesopotamia to the people of Iraq on the occasion of the successful conclusion of hostilities against the Turkish armies, 2 November 1918. Another copy **7503-59.**

6411-16. Map of operations of the 37th Division, 21 August − 5 November 1918; map of an area of the front line showing the location of pill boxes, hedges, etc. around Bucquoy; map of the front near Bucquoy; and C. Company, 37th Battalion, Machine Gun Corps, four pages of field instructions referring to the attack at Bucquoy, 1918.

6508-5. Ts. memoir 'The Thin Khaki Line', by Sgt. A. T. Matthews concerning the Royal Irish Regiment.

6509-28. Trench maps, Western Front.

6510-143. Maj. Gen. Sir Clement Milward (1877-1951), commanding King's Own Light Yorkshire Infantry. Diaries of Mons to Ypres, 1914; Gallipoli, Greece and Suvla Bay landings, 1915; France 1916-17; and Mesopotamia, 1917-18.

6510-196. Letters of Lt. Hugh Farrar Northcote, Indian Army from Mesopotamia, where he was killed in April 1916.

6602-37. Col. C. O. R. Mosse, documents: censored letters of Indian troops in Mesopotamia; MS 'India in the War', n.d.; and 5/6 Rajputana Rifles, MS diary, 1914-15.

6602-63. Lahore Division, field standing orders, 14 October 1914.

6602-68. Archangel Expedition, two letters, an account and a map, 1918-19.

6607-15. Capt. A. H. B. Brooks, 18th Lancers: diary, 1 January − 14 October 1914, covering *inter alia* a surveying expedition on the Turko-Persian border and the Russian troop build-up on the Turkish border.

6612-38. Letter of 29 July 1914 from A. H. A. 10 Downing Street, Whitehall, to the CIGS stating that the Cabinet had determined the warning telegram for the 'precautionary stage' should be issued that afternoon.

6702-74. Documents relating to the 76th Punjabis: MS notebooks covering the history of the regiment, 1776-1918; 25 MS pages of notes and extracts relating to the regiment's history; and MS diary of Capt. S. van B. Laing regarding manoeuvres, 1908-14, and the war service of the regiment.

6702-73. Mesopotamia, operations orders of the 27th Punjabis, 1 February 1918.

6702-91-1-25. Maj. Gen. Sir Charles John Mellis (1862-1936). Service in Egypt and Mesopotamia where he was captured at Kut in 1916, spending the remainder of the war as a POW. Of most interest are MS letters and notes referring to the Kut campaign.

6707-10. Maj. Gen. Sir James Marshal Stewart (1861-1943). Division Commander, East Africa Expeditionary Force, 1914-16, and Commander, Aden Field Force, 1916-20. Documents regarding Stewart and the East African campaign, including correspondence with Gen. Jan Smuts concerning Stewart's dismissal. There is also an official report on the operations of 1st Division, 5-16 March 1916.

6707-12. Ts. copy of 'Standing Orders in the Trenches' issued to section officers of the 230th Machine Gun Company, South of Gaza, 6 September 1917.

6707-44. Mesopotamia, ts. copy of a letter, 31 March 1916, from Capt. C. D. Noyes, 2nd Rajput Light Infantry, to Col. F. A. Smith commanding Secunderabad Infantry Brigade, describing action against the Turks near Kut.

6709-16. Mesopotamia, letters and journals of W. C. Spackman, Indian Medical Service, attached to the 48th Pioneers, mostly concerning the Mesopotamia campaign, the siege of Kut and his experiences as a POW, 1914-18.

6709-33. Operations of the 5th Cavalry Division in Palestine during the advance to Aleppo, September — October 1918.

6709-72. Allied propaganda leaflet dropped on German soldiers showing, in map form, the Allied advances from 8 August to 8 September 1918.

6710-18. Printed extract from *The Nineteenth Century Magazine,* giving an eye-witness account of the operations of the 10th Indian Division at Cambrai, 1917, 16 pp.

6803-4. Lt. Col. R. J. Marker, Coldstream Guards, ADC to Lords Curzon and Kitchener, and Military Secretary to Lord Kitchener, 1881-1914. Letters and notes referring to his death on the Western Front, November 1914; letters from Capt. B. C. Lousada, York and Lancaster Regiment, describing *inter alia* service on the Western Front; and an extract from the diary of Lt. V. E. C. Dashwood, Royal Sussex Regiment, describing events leading to the death in action of Lt. E. A. Lousada, October — November 1914.

6803-59. H. R. Wade, 'October 1918 in Mesopotamia', 10 pp. ts., and map dealing with the operations which ended in the surrender of Ismail Hakki Bey's army on the Tigris.

6806-21. Maj. E. B. Hawkins, King's African Rifles. Documents including copy letters and reports as commander of E Company, December 1914 — December 1915; MS notes for war diary, July 1916; ts. copy of a report from Capt. H. Rayne, Senior Military Officer, Turkana, 20 May 1917, describing an action against Abyssinian tribesmen; and ts. memorandum, in German, from Von Lettow, 23 July 1917.

6807-244. Part of a MS notebook containing a description of the death of Lt. Col. G. K. Ansell commanding 5th Dragoon Guards, September 1914.

6910-3. Greece: eight articles by Lt. Col. H. B. Holt from the *Cork Weekly Examiner,* 31 July — 18 September 1969, regarding service with 6th and 7th Battalions, South Cork Militia in Greece, 1916.

7001-2. Saddler Sgt.-Maj. Denis Willison, Northamptonshire Yeomanry, diary in France, 3 August 1914 — 17 March 1915.

7004-5. Gallipoli, five printed maps issued by the War Office, 1908, and a trench diagram, 1915.

7004-30. Chiffons de papier, Proclami Tedeschi nel Belgio e nella Francia, 1914-16. Original French texts and Italian translations, printed in Milan, with an introduction by Ian Malcolm, MP, 1917.

7005-17. Maj. Gen. Edward Douglas Loch, Baron Loch (1873-1942), Grenadier Guards. Papers relating to his military career but only four photographic items relate to WWI.

7011-10-13. Capt. C. R. Rawlinson, 2nd Battalion, Royal Munster Fusiliers: twelve MS pp. from field notebooks giving an account of action near Etreux, 27 August 1914.

7011-17. Sir Alexander Anderson (1879-1965), a major in the Volunteer Artillery Battery, Kut, and POW in Turkey. Papers relating to the siege of Kut, plans of Kut, and the experiences of the troops after the surrender.

7201-41-4. R. S. Waters, ts. dairy referring to the 40th Pathans from their landing in France to the battle of Ypres, 1915, and personal documents, 1900-15.

7203-41. G. Uloth, 7th Light Cavalry, bound vol. of letters to his mother, November 1915 — February 1920, describing operations in East Persia and Persian Baluchistan, 1915-18, and against the Bolsheviks in Russian Turkestan, January 1918 — May 1919.

7208-14. Documents concerning the Egypt and Palestine campaigns, 1918-19, including the 'Special Order of the Day' announcing the demobilization of the EEF, January 1919.

7208-55. Royal Irish Regiment, two albums of press-cuttings and other documents, 1914-18.

7301-55. Brig. Gen. Ernest Joseph MacFarlane Wood (1867-1939), 97th Deccan Infantry: notebook with biographical details, and diaries for 1916-17. Wood served in Mesopotamia, 1916-18.

7303-13. Col. Jarvie Webb Wilson. Bound album of records of service as a temporary officer, East Surrey Regiment, 1914-19, and regular service with the 15th Punjab Regiment, 1919-41. Letters, telegrams and extracts from orders.

7305-14. 291st (4th London) Field Regiment, RA, TA, documents illustrating the training and active service of the regiment from 1860 to 1961.

7306-67. Lt. Gen. Eric de Burgh (1881-1948). Ts. autobiography including account of his active service on the Western Front.

7402-29. Letter from Mary Frances Maxwell to her sister giving a vivid impression of a military hospital, Boulogne, 18 March 1915, 20 pp. MS.

7402-30. Brig. Gen. Lawrence Lockhart Maxwell (1868-1954). Letters and papers referring to service, 1894-1918. Maxwell served on the Western Front, 1915-17, and in Egypt and Palestine, 1918.

7402-31. Francis A. Maxwell (1871-1917). Extracts and transcripts of letters, 1916-17. He commanded the 12th Battalion, Middlesex Regiment and later the 27th Infantry Brigade, 9th (Scottish) Division.

7402-32. 42 copies and original letters of Col. David Maxwell, some regarding service with the 2nd South Lancashire Regiment.

7402-34. Lt. Col. Eustace Maxwell (1878-1916). 36 MS letters, some relating to service during WWI with several regiments and giving a description of life and warfare in the trenches.

7402-153. Maps published by the Geographical Section, General Staff, for the use of British troops in France and Belgium, each with a glossary of French topographical terms on the reverse: Ypres, 1916; Lille, 1916; and Neuve Chapelle, 1916.

7403-29-48 to 144. Harry Hopwood, CQMS, 6th Battalion, Manchester Regiment, 81 MS and ts. letters to his family while on service in Egypt, October 1914 — June 1915; Gallipoli, June — September 1915; Egypt, 1916; and France, March 1917 — November 1918.

7403-79. Maj. E. C. Staples, photocopies of 13 letters covering service with the 4th Rajputs until the disaster at Ahwaz, and later with the 11th Rajputs in Persia, February — September 1915.

7405-57. Official and confidential war diary of Temp. Maj. H. L. Templar, as commander of 599 Company, ASC (Heavy Repairs Depot), 14 February 1916 — 30 June 1917 in East Africa.

7407-93. Mesopotamia, photocopy of ts. version of the diary of Maj. P. C. Saunders, Indian Supply and Transport Corps, covering November — December 1914, March 1915, April — May 1915 and April — July 1916. The diary relates the surrender of Kut and the march of the prisoners to Kastamuni via Baghdad.

7407-126. Papers of Maj. A. F. Harper, 84th Punjabis in Mesopotamia, 1916-18, including diary for 1916; memoranda and orders issued as commander of the Machine Gun Company, 28th Brigade, 1916; map of the area around Baghdad; and personal papers.

7407-138. Diary of Maj. George Swinley, 14th Sikhs, until 5 May 1915, covering service in Egypt and the Gallipoli landings.

7408-63. Ts. copy of the diary of Sgt. William Barron, 4th Battalion, Northamptonshire Regiment, 1915-19, describing conditions on the Gallipoli front, evacuation to Egypt and battalion life at the Suez Canal.

7408-79. Mesopotamia, papers of Lt. R. B. Woakes, 2nd QVO Sappers and Miners, consisting of diary, December 1916 — March 1917; account of the advance of 14th Division to Baghdad with maps and plans of fortifications; and certificates.

7408-82. Lt. Col. J. McConville, memoirs and certificates, 1896-1946. Service with Royal Irish Rifles, 1896-1915; commissioned into King's Liverpool Regiment, 1915; and taken prisoner at Kut, 1916.

7412-82. Miscellaneous papers referring to 41st Dogras: printed memorandum by the Adjutant-General of India on the treatment of Indian officers and men by British officers, 1913, and regimental orders for mobilisation, 9 August 1914.

7503-21. Westminster (later Berkshire and Westminster) Dragoons; regimental papers, 1901-1967, containing orders, diaries and other material including service in Palestine during WWI.

WORLD WAR II

5407-34. Original telegram announcing the outbreak of war, received at HQ, Calcutta Presidency, from General Staff, Simla, dated 17.45 hrs on 3 September 1939.

5903-113. Changi Camp, Singapore: 'P.O.W.C. Echo' produced by officers of Coke's Rifles, *c.* 1945. See also **6005-34**, 'P.O.W.C. Echo', mimeographed newspapers produced at Changi Camp, Singapore, 1942, and **6301-63**, bound vol. of ts. 'P.O.W.C. Echo'.

5903-136. Messages, sketches and notes from the battle of Keren, February — March 1940.

5911-161-3. Burma, memoir of the evacuation of Rangoon.

5912-161. 'A Rough Account of the Evacuation of the Women's Auxiliary Service (Burma) from Rangoon', n.d., anon.; 'Evacuation from Rangoon of the Women's Auxiliary Service (Burma)', n.d., anon.; and 'A Wasbie in Burma', a letter from Miss W. S. B. Clayton to her uncle, 1944 (reprinted from *The Log,* March/April 1945).

6005-291. Eritrea: 10th Indian Infantry Brigade, Operations Order No. 6 of 16 January 1941, and Operations Order No. 11 of 25 January 1941; notes on the advance into Eritrea by Lt. Col. G. S. R. Webb, Brigade Major, 10th Indian Infantry Brigade; and war diary for the battle of Keren.

6012-250. German propaganda leaflet aimed at Americans.

6012-286. German propaganda documents dropped on the 3rd Gurkha Rifles in Italy, and other related papers.

6012-351. Eritrea, complimentary messages on the advance of the 52nd Division from Keren to Asmara, 1940.

6111-47. Imphal, division orders for the 9th Indian Infantry Brigade, 18 June 1944 and for the 5th Indian Division, 19 June 1944.

6111-181. 325 Anti-aircraft Company, RE Searchlight Battery, RA: war diary, August 1939 – May 1941.

6305-49. Documents of W. R. P. Ridgeway, private secretary to Field-Marshal Lord Auchinleck, referring to Narvik, 1940, and India, 1941-7.

6305-155. Rajputana Rifles, 1st Battalion, original MS and two ts. copies of operational orders for attack on Halfaya Pass, 16 June 1940.

6308-12. Burma: 'The 28th Japanese Army', Southeast Asia Translation and Interrogation Centre Publication No. 243, 1 October 1946; operations of the 33rd Indian Corps in Burma, four vols.; 'Account of the history of the Japanese 33rd Army', Southeast Asia Translation and Interrogation Centre Publication No. 244, 3 October 1946; account of the operations of the 17th Indian Division, from 8 May 1945 to the Japanese surrender; war history of the 64th Indian Infantry Brigade; and map of Burma showing the main artillery locations, 16 July 1945, and main routes taken by the retreating Japanese forces.

6309-93. Propaganda leaflets and printed messages from the C-in-C North Africa, Sicily and Italy, 1942-5.

6311-51. Map of the route of the 79th Armoured Division in the Normandy landings, 1944.

6311-141-2. German propaganda leaflet, 'Hitler's Last Appeal to Reason', 19 July 1940.

6312-29. Lt. Gen. P. N. O'Connor commanding 13th Corps, photocopy of a ts. account of the Libyan campaign, 1941, and his capture and removal to Sulmona POW camp in Italy.

6409-52. Documents relating to the Courtney and Mann families: letters of Henry G. Courtney, March – September 1940, covering service with the Ambulance Car Company, BEF; 'A letter from Macedonia', ts. account of WWI experiences with the Royal Garrison Artillery, anon, but probably by Courtney; MS diary of Henry Courtney in France, 8 March – 10 April 1915; and map of Struma, Macedonia, WWI.

6410-38. Combined Inter-Service Historical Section, Simla, notes on British officers in the Indian Army during WWII.

6411-47. Imphal: scrapbook kept by Col. Brecher regarding the 3/9 Jat Regiment, April 1944; 9th Indian Infantry Brigade, divisional orders relating to Imphal and Kohima road, 18 June 1944; and 5th Indian Division, divisional orders relating to Imphal and Kohima Road, 19 June 1944.

6505-55. Correspondence between Lord Auchinleck and Brig. Gen. G. N. Molesworth, Director of Military Operations and Intelligence, India: variety of subjects including Auchinleck's views on the Chindits, 1943; Pacific war, weapons, officer training, etc, 1944; lack of supplies in India, welfare of forces, Auchinleck's fight for equal pay for Indian

Army and regular army officers, 1944. Restricted until the death of each correspondent.

6509-14. Ts. and MS diaries of various personnel in the 5th Battalion, 2nd Punjab Regiment, during the Malayan campaign, 1941-2.

6510-143. Maj. Gen. Sir Clement Milward (1877-1951). Diaries relating to service with the Northumberland Home Guard, 1940-2.

6510-197. Various official proclamations and orders relating to France, 1940, and northwest Europe, 1944-5.

6605-25. 5th Mahratta Light Infantry in North Africa at Sollum-Matruh; account of the battle of Keren, February — March 1940; and recruiting information, published by the Poona Recruiting Office, 1942.

6702-74. Ts. and MS documents relating to the history of the 3rd Battalion, 1st Punjabis in WWII.

6710-5. Maj. Gen. H. Williams, 'A Brief Account of the Divisional Engineers, 1st Armoured Division, 1939-1940', ts., 1951.

7203-33-2,3. Lt. Col. J. E. B. Barton, 13th Frontier Force Rifles: correspondence, cuttings and other documents relating to Maj. Gen. Orde Wingate and the campaigns in East Africa, 1940-1, and the Chindits in Burma, 1943-5.

7302-44. Documents of Maj. E. H. Cooke, Burma Rifles: 'The Story of the Burma Rifles' by Maj. C. M. Enriquez, ts., 1948; 'Personal diary of events in Burma leading to the withdrawal of the Burma Army to India with an account of our journey through the Hu Kong Valley, May — June 1942' by Maj. Cooke; 'The Burma Campaign', printed pamphlet based on a lecture by T. L. Hughes, 1943; and 'Tribute to Burma Rifles, Part Played in Wingate Expedition', printed sheet.

7304-1-12. Jungle Warfare School, Shimoga, programme for jungle training course, c. 1944, 42 pp. ts.

7305-14. 291st (4th London) Field Regiment, RA, TA, regimental documents illustrating training and active service from 1860 to 1961, with special reference to 1939-45.

7306-121. Ts. notes and sketch maps regarding service of the 2nd Battalion, The Baluch Regiment, in the Malayan campaign, 1941-2.

7308-47. Singapore Volunteer Corps, details of POWs and roll of honour of the Singapore RA.

7309-2. Documents compiled by Brig. G. C. Ballentine, commanding the 44th Infantry Brigade, in connection with the compilation of the *Official History of the War against Japan.*

7311-68. *Fauji Akhbar: Indian Forces Weekly*, a few copies from March — May 1943.

7403-114 Fol. 7. Three maps of Malaya used by Combined Operations, including a road map originally printed in 1937, and two large scale plans of Singapore showing defence installations and the details of the town.

7407-115. Photocopy of 43 pp. printed booklet, *Royal Deccan Horse, Accounts of Operations in Burma, January to May 1945.*

7408-82. Lt. Col. J. McConville, memoirs including service as Regional Officer, London Civil Defence Area, 1942-6.

7409-77. Gen. Sir Frank Walter Messervy (b. 1893). Two bound vols. and one folder of press-cuttings relating to his career, 1940-6. Messervy commanded Gazelle Force, Sudan and Eritrea, 1940-1; 9th Indian Infantry Brigade at Keren, 1940; 4th Indian Division in the Western Desert and Cyrenaica, 1942; 7th Armoured Division in the Western Desert, 1942; was Deputy Chief of General Staff, Middle East Force, 1942; 43rd Indian Armoured Division, 1942-3; GHQ, India Command, 1943; 7th Indian Division in Arakan and Kohima, 1944; 4th Corps in Burma, 1944-5; and GOC-in-C, Malaya, 1945-6.

7409-78 Fol. 7. Gen. Sir Frank Messervy: printed orders issued on disbandment of the 'Anti-Japanese Army', Force 136, 1 December 1945; to the 4th Indian Division before an unspecified battle, n.d.; to the 4th Indian Division in North Africa, 24 December 1941, outlining its successes to date; on relinquishing command of the 4th Indian Division, 1 January 1942; and on relinquishing the post of GOC-in-C, Malaya, 4 October 1946.

7412-30. Col. J. L. Maxwell, five bound MS notebooks containing his journal, 1926-50, referring to service with the Sudan Defence Force in Abyssinia and the Western Desert, and later with the Royal Scots Fusiliers in Italy and Germany.

7502-35. Local Defence Volunteers, No. 5 Platoon, Porthpean Section, St. Austell, Cornwall, standing orders nos. 1-70, June — August 1940.

7503-21. Westminster (later Berkshire and Westminster) Dragoons: regimental papers, including service in Burma and Normandy, and records of men passing through 102 Officer Cadet Training Unit, 1939-42.

MF 9/2. Documents submitted in connection with ordnance, by the surrendering Japanese army in Burma.

National Maritime Museum, Romney Road, LONDON SE10 9NF

The National Maritime Museum is the only major naval museum in Britain and holds significant collections of technical material, manuscripts and documents, photographs and paintings,

DRAUGHT ROOM

Perhaps the largest technical archive in Britain, the Draught Room is a depository under the Public Records Act, receiving certain Admiralty documents as these are declassified by the Public Record Office. The most important part of the collection, **Adm. 138** is Ships' Covers, 1870 to (currently) 1937, comprising memoranda, letters, and notes on the design, construction and subsequent alterations of individual ships. This is a highly significant series for the historian. There is a more detailed discussion of the nature of Ships' Covers in D. J. Lyon, 'Documentary Sources for the Archaeological Diver — Ships' Plans at the National Maritime Museum", *International Journal of Nautical Archaeology,* 1974. **Adm. 168** is Contracts and **Adm. 170** Specifications, but neither has any real value to the historian. The Draught Room also contains a complete set of plans for virtually every vessel (including converted merchant ships) sailing with the Royal Navy since 1800.

In addition there is a collection of miscellaneous technical documents stemming mainly from the Department of Naval Construction. A good collection of plans of WWI German warships is also held, as are the records of a number of shipbuildings firms, such as Thorneycroft, and those of Vickers Armstrong regarding naval guns. An appointment is necessary.

MANUSCRIPT COLLECTION

The Reading Room contains a large collection of MS and documentary material. Application for a reader's ticket should be made to the Director of the Museum.

Mario Arlotto
Account of the escape of the *Goeben* and *Breslau* near the Morea Peninsula, August 1914.

Capt. Sir Ion Hamilton Benn (1863-1961)
Naval papers, mainly WWI operations on the Belgian coast.

Capt. H. T. A. Bosanquet (1871-1959)
Naval papers and papers on air navigation, 1880-1953. Bosanquet served on the Admiralty War Staff (Trade Division), 1914-15; was attached to the RNAS and RAF, 1915-18; and served on the Admiralty War Staff, 1939-45.

Vice-Admiral Francis Clifton Brown (1874-1963)
Captain of HMS *Skirmisher* 1914; saw action in the Dardanelles; became Rear Admiral in the Royal Hellenic Navy, 1918; and was head of the Naval Mission to Greece, 1917-19. Most of the papers are pre-1914 but there are official memoranda and correspondence, 1914-18, and papers relating to his period as Naval Attaché in Greece, 1918-21.

Vice-Admiral Sir Harold A. Brown (1878-1968)
Personal papers, 1894-1959. Brown was Director General of Munitions Production, Ministry of Supply, 1936-9; Controller General of Munitions Production, Ministry of Supply, 1939-41; Senior Supply Officer and Chairman of the Armament Development Board, 1942-6.

Admiral of the Fleet Alfred Ernle Montacute Chatfield, Baron Chatfield (1873-1967)
Flag Captain to Admiral Sir David Beatty during WWI, first in HMS *Lion* and then as Fleet Gunnery Officer in HMS *Queen Elizabeth*; 1st Sea Lord 1933-8; Chairman of the India Defence Committee, 1938-9; Minister for the Co-ordination of Defence with a seat in the War Cabinet, 1939 until his resignation in 1940. The papers consist of autobiographic MS on early life; command in the Atlantic and Mediterranean, 1929-33; 1st Sea Lord, 1933-8; papers regarding the India Defence Committee, 1938-9; Minister for Co-ordination of Defence, 1939-40, papers relating to duties and functions of the Ministry, Anglo-American relations, sinking of the *Royal Oak* at Scapa Flow in 1939, general correspondence, and speeches; Civil Defence; and miscellaneous correspondence and papers referring to the battle of Jutland.

Admiral Sir Walter Henry Cowan (1871-1956)
Captain's order book, HMS *Zealandia*, 1914; track chart of the battle of Jutland, where Cowan commanded HMS *Princess Royal;* track chart of the action of 17 November 1917; three rolls of reproductions of photographic aerial diagrams concerning the sinking of the *Hood* and *Bismarck,* 1941; and photographic albums and pamphlets.

De Vitre Papers.
Transcripts of letters from the Rev. John Durham Denis de Vitre to his mother, written while serving as a chaplain in HMS *Canopus* in the Dardanelles, 1915.

Admiral Sir Barry Edward Domville (1878-1971)
Assistant Secretary to CID, 1912-14; command of various ships during

WWI; and various command and staff appointments during WWII. Diaries, 1894-1969, complete for both wars, and ts. autobiography 'From Admiral to Cabin Boy'.

Admiral Sir Alexander Ludovic Duff (1862-1933)
Director of Mobilisation Division of Admiralty War Staff, 1911-14; Rear Admiral, 4th Battle Squadron, 1914-17; Director of the Anti-submarine Division, 1917; and Assistant Chief of Naval Staff, 1918-19. Correspondence with Lord Jellicoe, 1916-33; Duff's MS notes on the dismissal of Jellicoe with copies of internal Admiralty correspondence; correspondence with Admiral Bethell, 1917-18; miscellaneous letters, 1917-37; Admiralty and Ministry of Shipping papers, 1918; note on Duff's services; four letters between Lord Jellicoe and Lady Duff, 1934; various papers relating to convoy work, 1917-18; private diary as Second in Command, 4th Battle Squadron, Grand Fleet, in HMS *Emperor of India,* 22 October 1914 − 26 November 1916; and diary of the American Mission, September − October 1918.

Lieutenant Commander J. B. Edmundsen
Journal aboard HMS *Repulse,* HMS *Arrow* and HMS *Nelson,* 1940-1.

Capt. A. J. Enstone
Papers regarding RAF and RNAS, 1914-18.

Sir Eustace Tennyson d'Eyncourt (1868-1951)
Director of Naval Construction, 1912-23; Vice-President of the Tank Board, 1918; and member of the Advisory Commission for Aeronautics during WWI. Papers.

Admiral Sir William Wordsworth Fisher (1875-1937)
Commanded HMS *St. Vincent* at the battle of Jutland and was Director of the Anti-submarine Division, 1917-18. Fisher's scheme for an offensive into the Heligoland Bight, 30 December 1914; his scheme to counter destroyer attacks, 13 March 1916; anti-submarine proposals, 5 December 1916; plan for an attack on the Elbe estuary, n.d.; J. J. Thomson's plan for an attack on the Weser, n.d.; report on the rate of destruction of enemy submarines, 4 June 1918, and other anti-submarine papers; notes for a lecture on the anti-submarine offensive; papers on tactics, naval policy and shipbuilding; and post-war papers.

Capt. R. V. Penrose Fitzgerald
Rough copy of an account of the search for the *Dresden* after the battle of the Falkland Islands, 1914.

Capt. Gordon Colquhoun Fraser (1866-1952)
Fraser served as Captain, Defensive Mining in the Torpedo and Mining Division of the Admiralty during WWI. The papers comprise a few letters of 1918 relating to minelaying and an annotated copy of J. S. Cowie, *Mines, Minelayers and Minelaying* (1949).

Admiral Sir Sydney Robert Fremantle (1867-1958)
Fremantle served in the Dardanelles, 1915; commanded the 9th Cruiser Squadron, 1916; the 2nd Cruiser Squadron, 1917; the Aegean Squadron, 1917-18; and was DCNS, 1918-19. The papers comprise memoranda on the war in the Aegean, 1916-17; important minutes, DCNS, January 1918 – April 1919; other papers of the DCNS, 1918-19, dealing with the concluding phases of the war, surrender of the German Fleet, the Holland Channel ports, selected papers initiated by the DCNS, etc.; and collected essays, lectures and articles, 1904-19.

Admiral Sir Cyril (Thomas Moulden) Fuller (1874-1942)
Fuller was Senior Naval Officer with the Togoland and Cameroons Expeditionary Forces, 1914-16. Papers relating to the campaign in Togoland and the Cameroons, 1914-17.

Grand Fleet
Diaries of the Grand Fleet, 26 July 1914 – 31 December 1918, and war diaries, 4 August – 30 December 1914, 19 vols. presented by Admiral Sir Charles Madden.

Sir (William) Graham Greene (1857-1950)
Permanent Secretary of the Admiralty, 1911-17, and Secretary to the Ministry of Munitions, 1917-20. Letters, extracts, notes and memoranda of departmental administration, containing Sea Lords' minutes and comments on their powers, 1915; Controller's Department, various correspondence and memoranda, 1916-17; Munitions, 1915-18, including a number of letters and notes to Lloyd George and Churchill; Dardanelles campaign and Commission, 1915-16, containing printed reports; General Review of the Naval Situation, 24 March 1917 (secret, printed); papers regarding Greene's invention to capture Zeppelins, 1915; other papers regarding the *Lusitania*, declaration of war, submarine peril, and the convoy system; and articles and correspondence on the lives of admirals and statesmen, including Balfour, Carson, etc.

Admiral Sir Frederick Tower Hamilton (1856-1917)
Second Sea Lord, 1914-16. Journals, 1870-1916, including those kept as Second Sea Lord, October 1915 – June 1916; loose papers, service

records and official letters, including memoranda on official subjects and original letters received, 1914-17; private letters, 1880-1917; and official papers, 1914-16, including printed secret and confidential papers received as Second Sea Lord, Admiralty Board memoranda on the Air Service and Air war, secret and confidential Admiralty intelligence reports, papers connected with Admiralty Board meetings, secret correspondence on policy matters (including minutes on the resignation of Fisher) and some letters from Jellicoe and Churchill.

Admiral Sir Louis Henry Keppel Hamilton (1890-1957)
Service in the Cameroons during WWI and Flag Officer Commanding, Malta, 1943-5. Journals for 1908-11, 1914-18, 1920-1, 1924-5, 1927-8, 1932, 1945-8, 1950, including service aboard HMS *Cumberland*, 1914-15; HMS *Lagos*, 1915, on Cameroons expedition, English Channel and North Sea; and HMS *Taurus*, 1917-18, on coastal work and Channel patrols. Loose official ships' papers, including service documents and appointments; journal and memoranda referring to the Cameroons, 1914-15; letters of proceedings, signals and orders, 1939-47; and photographs, speeches and notebooks. Loose letters consisting of letters from naval officers, 1915-21; flag promotion letters, 1941; letters from friends, 1906-19, letters written by himself, 1906-19; letters written during the Cameroons campaign, 1914-15; letters to his family, 1906-19; and other letters written and received, 1902-56.

Commander C. B. Hampshire (?1875-1963)
Loose papers containing nine plans and specifications of 'Land platforms for Naval Guns', 9 July 1915; chart of the Dardanelles and other papers; and plans and orders for the Dardanelles attack, at which Hampshire was present.

Admiral J. E. T. Harper
Xerox account of the battle of Jutland.

Dr Charles Brehmer Heald (1882-1974)
Temporary surgeon, RN, 1914-15; Lt. Col. RAF; and Principal Medical Officer, RAF, in the Middle East. Journal kept aboard the hospital ship SS *Roehill*, 18 August – 18 October 1914, at Scapa Flow and on North Sea patrol; private journals kept as temporary surgeon on HMS *Conqueror*, 2nd Battle Squadron, 24 November 1914 – April 1915; letters from family, 18 August 1914 – 18 February 1915; short memorandum, 'Medical arrangement for action', n.d.; short memorandum, 'The medical care of lines of communication at the commencement of the war', n.d.; 'Reminiscences of a Gerant' by Heald; and army book with copies of letters and personal accounts.

Vice-Admiral William Hannam Henderson (1845-1930)
Editor of the *Naval Review* from 1913. Some possible interest contained in correspondence with A. T. Mahan, Julian Corbett, Lloyd George, and Lord Milner. There is also a collection of newspaper cuttings and articles on naval subjects, especially naval aviation.

Admiral Sir John Jellicoe, 1st Earl Jellicoe
Letters to E. E. Bradford, 1914-17; letter to Walter Runciman, President of the Board of Trade, 1916; and letter to Jellicoe from Grand Admiral von Tirpitz, 31 January 1914.

Admiral Sir (Thomas Henry) Martyn Jerram (1858-1933)
Jerram commanded the China Station, 1913-15, where he had to deal with Count von Spee's Squadron, reduce the German colonies, and protect British shipping. He then commanded the 2nd Battle Squadron, 1915-16, leading the line at Jutland. Commissions, certificates and other service documents; papers relating to the China Station, 1912-15; letters to his brother, Charles Jerram, 1902-16; and papers relating to service in the Grand Fleet, 1916-17, including Jutland reports and despatches and letters from Jellicoe, Keyes and Field.

Sir (William Archibald) Howard Kelly (1873-1952)
Draft memoirs covering his career to 1933, including service as naval attaché in Paris, 1911-14, command of HMS *Gloucester* and the chase of the *Goeben*, 1914; service records comprising full accounts of the command of the *Gloucester,* as Commodore of the British Adriatic Force, 1917-19, and as British representative in Turkey, 1940-4; and press-cuttings and articles, 1926-49.

Admiral of the Fleet Sir John Donald Kelly (1871-1936)
One file each on his command of the Light Cruiser *Dublin,* including the chase of the *Goeben* and the Dardanelles campaign, 1914-16; HMS *Weymouth,* North Sea and Atlantic, 1916-17; and HMS *Princess Royal* in the 1st Battle Cruiser Squadron, 1918-19.

Commander O. C. G. Leveson-Gower
His diary for 1914 and letters to his family with references to the Dardanelles campaign.

Admiral of the Fleet Sir William Henry May (1849-1930)
White Paper on the International Situation, 1914; first report of and correspondence relating to the Dardanelles Commission, 1917; final report of the Dardanelles Commission, December 1917; report of the Mesopotamia Commission, 1917; and papers on Admiralty policy,

1903-19, referring to the building programme, reconstruction policy and reorganization.

Sir Archibald Berkeley Milne (1855-1938)
C-in-C Mediterranean, 1912-14. Signal log, 2 August — 17 August 1914; telegrams received from the Admiralty, 27 July — 19 August 1914; diary of events, 27 July — 17 August 1914; four bundles of official correspondence, papers and accounts regarding the *Goeben*, August 1914; personal letters, 1914-33; and press-cuttings.

Sub-Lt. Charles W. Murray (1894-1945)
Officer in the RNVR. Notebooks compiled as base intelligence at Stornaway, 1914-18, containing much information on German submarine warfare; list of Allied ships, with identity numbers of German submarines taking part in the action, 1914-18; history of the death or surrender of German submarines, classes U, UB and UC, in numerical order, 1914-18; MS notebook on warfare at sea, mainly concerning submarines; list of ships sunk and by which submarine if known.

Admiral of the Fleet Sir Gerard Henry Uctred Noel (1845-1918)
Diaries in letter form, 1880-1918, and small collection of letters from his son, Francis Noel, Flying Officer in the RFC, to his wife, during the early years of WWI.

Admiral David Thomas Norris (1875-1937)
Commodore in Command, Persian Gulf and British Naval Forces on the Caspian Sea, 1918-19. Papers regarding HMS *Arlanza*, mined in the White Sea, 1915; papers as Flag Captain, East Indies and Gulf, November 1916 — April 1917; 'In and out letters before leaving Baghdad', June — August 1918; 'Caspian Letters of Proceedings once Despatches', 1918-19; 'Letters of Proceedings, Caspian 1918'; 'Dunster-force and Oddments', 1918-19 comprising signals and intelligence reports; 'In signals at Baku', 29 July — 8 October 1918; 'Out signals at Baku', 31 July — 9 October 1918; and photograph album, 1912-26.

Admiral of the Fleet Sir Henry Francis Oliver (1865-1965)
Director of Intelligence, Admiralty War Staff 1913-14; Chief of Admiralty War Staff, 1914-17; Admiralty Reorganisation and DCNS, 1917; and Rear Admiral commanding 1st Battle Cruiser Squadron, 1918. Service documents; memoirs and biographical material; papers concerning visit to Antwerp, October 1914; papers regarding visit to Dardanelles, 1915-16; other papers, 1914-18; and general papers, 1914-65.

Capt. Richard Oliver-Belassis
Précis notes of Damage Control course, 1943, and ship's standing orders and routines, 1926-43, including some of HMS *Eagle* which he commanded from 1937 to 1939.

Capt. A. T. G. Peachey
Papers relating to the battle of Jutland, 1916; signals and other papers regarding surrender of the High Seas Fleet, 1918; war signal logs, 1939-42; and signals, reports and other papers concerning command of HMS *Delhi* in North Africa, Sicily, Salerno and Anzio, 1942-4.

Admiral Robert Stewart Phipps Hornby (1866-1956)
C-in-C North American and West Indian Station, 1914-15. His general memoranda on naval topics: gunnery, torpedoes, education and the Admiralty Reconstruction Committee, 1914-19; rough notes on the North American and West Indian Station, including a journal of proceedings, 1914-15, and a diary for part of 1915; signal log comprising messages sent and received 1914-15; papers regarding his invention of a gas propelled torpedo, 1916-36; memoranda composed during WWI on naval projects, mainly torpedoes and the wireless; and the anti-Zeppelin net barrage.

Sir James Porter (1851-1935)
Medical Director of the Navy, 1908-13. Correspondence as Medical Director, 1908-13; wartime service in the Dardanelles, 1915-16; letters and signals from Gallipoli, August — November 1915; letters arranging transport and hospital trains, 1914-17; and the Ministry of National Service, 1917-19.

Admiral Sir Henry Daniel Pridham-Wippell (1885-1952)
Second in Command, Mediterranean Fleet, 1940, and Flag Officer Commanding, Dover, 1942-5. Mediterranean operations, 1940-1, comprising operations orders, signals and letters of proceedings; papers concerning Operation DEMON, the evacuation of Greece, April 1941; report of the Board of Enquiry into the attack on Alexandria Harbour, December 1941, with evidence and appendices; 'Mediterranean Fleet Narratives' by Lieutenant Commander Stitt; and war diaries of the Dover Command, 1940-4.

Capt. Theobald John Claud Purcell-Buret
Papers, 1939-52, including diaries as a commander of troopships, 1939-42.

Admiral Herbert W. Richmond (1871-1946)
Assistant Director of Operations, 1913-15; liaison officer with the Italian Fleet, 1915; commander of HMS *Commonwealth, Conqueror* and *Erin* in the Grand Fleet, 1916-17; and Director of Staff Duties and Training, 1918. Private diaries, 1886-1920; diaries of Lady Richmond, 1914-15; common place books relating to various war and military administration subjects; family and general correspondence, alphabetically arranged; miscellaneous papers; war college lectures; and various war memoranda, February 1914 — September 1915.

Admiral Sir William George Tennant (1890-1963)
Chief Staff Officer to 1st Sea Lord, 1939-41; sent to Dunkirk to assist with evacuation, 1940; command of HMS *Repulse,* and then of cruiser force in the Eastern Fleet, 1940-3; responsible for Mulberry Harbours in planning for Operation OVERLORD 1943; and Flag Officer, Levant and Eastern Mediterranean, 1944-6. Papers refer to Dunkirk, HMS *Repulse,* Eastern Fleet, Madagascar, Normandy, and general strategy.

Admiral Sir Bertram Sackville Thesiger (1875-1966)
Command of the light cruiser *Inconstant,* 1914-16; the battle cruiser *Inflexible* at Jutland, 1916; HMS *Calypso,* 1917-19, in the North Sea; and Commander of Convoys and Flag Officer in Charge, Falmouth, during WWII. His journals, 1914-44; and ts. memoirs..

Commander Gerald William Vivian (1869-1921)
Command of Naval Flying Base Ship *Hermes,* 1913-14, and other ships subsequently. Papers referring to HMS *Sirius,* 1914, and HMS *Patia,* 1914-15; Air Department reports, 1915-16, duties and organisation; official correspondence, 1916-18; Air Department memoranda, 1916-18; papers concerning HMS *Liverpool,* 1916-17, and HMS *Roxburgh,* 1918; and correspondence, 1913-21.

Arnold White (1848-1925)
Journalist and lecturer specialising in naval affairs. Correspondence with the leading naval figures of the time, 1900-22.

Capt. William Bourchier Sherard Wrey (1865-1926)
Portion of wartime diary as Principal Naval Transport Officer at Southampton, 1914-18, and related miscellaneous papers. There is also a diary of a visit to France in 1918.

MISCELLANEOUS

HMS *Highflyer,* 2nd class cruiser, log for 1914-18.

Signal message from the Prime Minister to Rear Admiral P. L. Vian after the battle of Sirte, 1942.

German wireless messages during the battle of Jutland, 1916, collected by Admiral Hipper's flag lieutenant.

Diary of a German rating on the *Altmark*, 1939-40..

Details of the administration of the naval arsenal at Kiel by the occupying forces, 1945.

Casswell collection of narratives relating to the evacuation of Dunkirk.

Copies of 94 W/T messages between Admiral Sir David Beatty and Admiral Franz von Hipper, December 1918.

Naval Library, Ministry of Defence (Navy), Empress State Building, Lillie Road, Fulham, LONDON SW6 1TR

Barley — Waters MSS

A large collection of valuable papers and other material referring to trade defence in WWI, collected by Commander F. Barley and Lt. Gen. D. Waters.

Rear Admiral Roger M. Bellairs (1884-1959)

War Staff Officer to the C-in-C Grand Fleet, 1916-19. Papers regarding the Grand Fleet, 1917-18.

Capt. Thomas E. Crease (1875-1942)

Material regarding his service as Naval Secretary to Admiral Sir John Fisher during the latter's appointments as 1st Sea Lord and President of the Board of Invention and Research during WWI.

Rear Admiral Sir Edward Evans-Lombe (1901-74)

Papers concerning service as Naval Assistant to the 3rd Sea Lord, 1939-42; Commander of HMS *Glasgow*, 1942-3; Director of the Gunnery Division at the Admiralty, 1943-4; and Chief of Staff, Eastern Fleet, 1944, and Pacific Fleet, 1944-6.

Admiral John H. Godfrey (1888-1971)

Naval Staff College lectures concerning Jutland, and supplementary papers referring to service in the Mediterranean, 1917-18.

Admiral of the Fleet Sir Henry Jackson (1855-1929)

Papers as 1st Sea Lord, 1915-16.

Local History Department, Newington District Library,
155/157 Walworth Road, LONDON SE17 1RS

WORLD WAR II

Bermondsey Borough Council: incident register, 1940-4.
Camberwell Borough Council: ARP Committee papers, 1939; ARP
Committee, abstract ledger No. 1, 1940; and incident register, 1940-5.
Southwark Borough Council: air raid incident message forms, 1940-5;
incident register, 1940-3; occurrences reports, 1940-5; reports of air
raid damage, 1940-2; and street index of air raid incidents, 1940-4.

Public Record Office, Chancery Lane, LONDON WC2A 1LR

As the official depository of the separate archives of the various
departments of the British government and central courts of law, the
Public Record Office has custody of literally millions of documents.
Here are to be found the records of the Royal Navy, Army and Air
Force, the Foreign Office, the several War Cabinets, and the various
ministries and departments, all of which make the Public Record Office
the main repository of material in Britain for the study of the two
world wars.
To gain access to the PRO, intending researchers must complete an
application form to secure a reader's ticket, valid for five years. British
subjects must have the recommendation on p. 2 of the form made and
signed by a person of recognized position. Applicants not of British
nationality can submit a letter from their embassy or high commissioner's office. Tickets are issued at the enquiries desk in Chancery
Lane from Mondays to Fridays or by post.
Departmental records normally become open to inspection 30 years
after their creation but since January 1972 the more important classes
relating to WWII have been opened. The Lord Chancellor may prescribe
a longer or shorter period for whole classes or for particular items.
Notices in the Search Rooms summarise the exceptions.
Considerable time can be saved initially if the researcher is already
somewhat familiar with the nature of the records and the system for
their use. The official *Guide to the Contents of the Public Record
Office* (London, HMSO, 1963-8, 3 vols.) is the necessary starting point.
Vol. 1 deals with the records of the Chancery, the Exchequer and other
courts of law. Vol. 2 covers the records of the State Paper Office and
public departments, while vol. 3 refers to records transferred between

1960 and 1966. Loose-leaf supplements outlining more recent acquisitions are kept in the Search Rooms. Other general works on the PRO are Hilary Jenkinson, *Guide to the Public Records — Introductory* (London, 1949) and V. H. Galbraith, *An Introduction to the Use of the Public Records* (London, 1952).

The records in the PRO are divided into major divisions called 'groups' which usually, but not always, correspond to the administrative departments from which the records emanated. Groups are designated by an abbreviation, such as **Adm.** for *Admiralty,* **W.O.** for *War Office,* etc. Within each record group are 'classes' of materials such as in-letters, out-letters, committee minutes, etc., which are designated by a number. Thus **Adm. 50** represents the class **Admirals' Journals** in the record group *Admiralty.* The next division after classes is 'pieces' which normally represent a given volume, bundle or box. The piece number is set off from the group and class designations by an oblique stroke, e.g. **Adm. 50/47.** Each volume has an index to the subject matter of its contents and the first volume of a series is also provided with a glossary of technical terms. In addition, the PRO publishes a series of finding aids called *Lists and Indexes* which give listings of the classes within groups and are most useful.

A series of handbooks for the researcher is published by HMSO. Indispensible for present purposes is *The Second World War: A Guide to Documents in the Public Record Office* (1972), which was prepared to coincide with the opening of the WWII records. The Colonial Office is covered by *The Records of the Colonial and Dominions Office* (1964) and *List of Colonial Office Confidential Print to 1916* (1965). Four handbooks deal with the Cabinet: *List of Cabinet Papers, 1880-1914* (1964); *List of Cabinet Papers, 1915 and 1916* (1966); *The Records of the Cabinet Office to 1922* (1966); and *The Cabinet Office to 1945* (forthcoming). Excluding WWII, the Foreign Office is treated in *The Records of the Foreign Office 1782-1939* (1969). Of broader reference are *Classes of Departmental Papers for 1906-1939* (1966) and *Records of Interest to Social Scientists 1919 to 1939: Introduction* (1971). Each handbook contains a discussion of the functional administrative sources of the records, essential for their intelligent use, and a listing of classes.

The material in the PRO is too vast to attempt a summary of classes relevant to the world wars, but the records of a few ministries and departments contain a 'private papers' class, in which the papers stemming from the tenure of office or career of an individual are gathered. This is especially true for the Foreign Office **(F.O. 800).** There is also a class within the Public Record Office Group **(PRO 30)** for the deposited papers of individuals. The following is a summary listing of many relevant private office and deposited papers.

Field-Marshal Sir Alan Francis Brooke, 1st Viscount Alanbrooke (1883-1963)
Correspondence as CIGS, 1941-6, to the Prime Minister and others. **W.O. 216.**

Field-Marshal Sir Harold Alexander, 1st Earl Alexander of Tunis (1891-1969)
Official and semi-official correspondence, mainly as Supreme Allied Commander, Mediterranean, 1944-5. **W.O. 214/1-69.**

Sir Alan Garnett Anderson (1877-1952)
Chairman of the Royal Commission on Wheat Supplies, 1916, and Controller of the Admiralty, 1917-18. Papers, 1916-18. **PRO 30/68.**

Arthur James Balfour, 1st Earl of Balfour (1848-1930)
Secretary of State for Foreign Affairs, 1916-19, and Lord President of the Council, 1919-22. Papers, 1916-22. **F.O. 800/191-204.**

Evelyn Baring, 1st Earl of Cromer (1841-1917)
Papers, 1872-1929, including speeches, general correspondence and copies of articles written, 1914-17. **F.O. 633.**

Francis Leveson Bertie, 1st Viscount Bertie of Thame (1844-1919)
British Ambassador in Paris, 1905-18. Papers, 1896-1918. **F.O. 800/151-186.**

James Bryce, Viscount Bryce of Dechmont (1838-1922)
British Ambassador to the United States, 1907-13. Correspondence, 1904-21. **F.O. 800/331-335.**

Sir C. L. Bullock (b. 1891)
Air Staff, Air Ministry, 1917-18. Papers, 1917-18. **AIR 19/84-85, 108.**

Sir Alexander Cadogan (1884-1968)
Ambassador Extraordinary, 1935; Deputy Under-Secretary of State for Foreign Affairs, 1936-8; and Permanent Under-Secretary of State for Foreign Affairs, 1938-46. Miscellaneous correspondence, 1934 – August 1939. **F.O. 800/293-294.**

(Edgar Algernon) Robert Cecil, Viscount Cecil of Chelwood (1864-1958)
Parliamentary Under-Secretary of State for Foreign Affairs, 1915-18; Minister of Blockade, 1916-18; and Assistant Secretary of State for Foreign Affairs, 1918-19. Papers, 1915-18. **F.O. 800/187-190.**

George Nathaniel Curzon, Marquess Curzon of Kedleston (1859-1925)
Correspondence as Secretary of State for Foreign Affairs, October 1919
— January 1923. **F.O. 800/146-150.**

Sir James Drummond, 16th Earl of Perth (1876-1951)
Foreign Secretary, 1915-19. Correspondence, 1915-18. **F.O. 800/329,
383-5.**

Sir Edward Grey, Viscount Grey of Fallodon (1862-1933)
Secretary of State for Foreign Affairs, 1905-16. Papers, 1918-29, but
mainly 1918-19. **F.O. 800/209-14.**

Sir Nevile Henderson (1882-1942)
Ambassador to Germany, 1937-9. Correspondence, 1924-41. **F.O.
800/264-71.**

Sir Hugh Hugessen (1886-1971)
Ambassador to China, 1936-7. Private office correspondence, 1936-8.
F.O. 800/297.

Rufus Daniel Isaacs, 1st Marquess of Reading (1860-1935)
Special Ambassador and High Commissioner to the United States,
1918. Papers, 1918-29, but mostly 1918-19. **F.O. 800/209-214.**

Archibald Clark Kerr, Baron Inverchapel (1882-1951)
British Ambassador to Iraq, 1935-8; Ambassador to China, 1938-42;
Ambassador to the USSR, 1942-6; and special British envoy to Java,
1946. Miscellaneous correspondence, 1935-49. **F.O. 800/298-303.**

*Horatio Herbert Kitchener, 1st Earl Kitchener of Khartoum
(1850-1916)*
Papers originating in his office as Secretary of State for War, February
1914 — October 1916. **W.O. 159/12-22.** Papers about his life and
career, deposited by his great nephew. **PRO 30/57.**

*Field-Marshal Frederick Rudolph Lambart, 10th Earl of Cavan
(1865-1946)*
Commanded the Guards Division in Flanders, 1915; the 14th Corps in
France, 1916-17; and all British troops in Italy, 1917-18. Private
papers, 1916-19. **W.O. 79/66-71.**

Sir Walter Langley (1855-1918)
Assistant Under-Secretary at the Foreign Office, 1907-18. Correspondence, 1886-1918. **F.O. 800/29-31.**

Lt. Gen. Sir George MacDonogh (1865-1942)
Director of Military Intelligence, 1916-18. Papers, 1916-18. **W.O. 106/1510-17.**

Brig. Gen. Sir Osborne Mance
Director of Railways, Light Railways and Roads during WWI and communications expert in the British delegation to the Paris Peace Conference. Papers regarding both offices. **PRO 30/66.**

Alfred Milner, 1st Viscount Milner (1854-1925)
Member of the War Cabinet, 1916-18, and Secretary of State for War, 1918-19. Papers, 1915-20. **PRO 30/30.**

Gen. Sir Archibald James Murray (1860-1945)
Inspector of Infantry, 1912-14; Deputy CIGS, 1914-15; and CIGS from 1915. Papers relating to France, Belgium, Gallipoli and Egypt, August 1914 — December 1915. **W.O. 79/62-65.**

Sir Arthur Nicholson
Permanent Under-Secretary of State for Foreign Affairs, 1910-16. Miscellaneous correspondence, 1889-1916. **F.O. 800/336.**

Maj. Guy W. Nightingale
Service with the 29th Division at Gallipoli, 1915; on the Western Front to the end of the war; and with the North Russian Expeditionary Force, 1919. Letters to his family, 1910-26, and diary for 1915. There are also 20 letters from Capt. T. W. Filgate, Royal Munster Fusiliers, at the Western Front in 1915. **PRO 30/71.**

Air Chief Marshal Sir Wilfrid Rhodes (1888-1953)
Chief Executive, Ministry of Aircraft Production, 1942-5. 42 files in **AVIA 10** (unregistered papers series).

Walter Runciman, Viscount Runciman of Doxford (1870-1949)
Lord President of the Council, 1938-9. Papers referring to his mission to Czechoslovakia, 1938. **F.O. 800/304-308.**

Thomas Henry Sanderson, 1st Baron Sanderson of Armthorpe (1841-1923)
Permanent Under-Secretary of State for Foreign Affairs, 1894-1906. Papers, 1860-1922. **F.O. 800/1.**

Sir Orme Sargent (b. 1884)
Counsellor, Foreign Office, 1926-33; Assistant Under-Secretary,

Foreign Office, 1933-9; and Deputy Under-Secretary, Foreign Office, 1939-46. Correspondence; 1926-48. **F.O. 800/276-279.**

Count Alfred von Schlieffen (1833-1913)
Chief of the German General Staff, 1892-1906, and architect of the German strategy at the outset of WWI. Papers, 1905-12. **Cabinet 20.**

Archibald Henry MacDonald Sinclair, 1st Viscount Thurso (1890-1970)
Secretary of State for Air, 1940-5. Papers, 1940-6. **AIR 19/73-557.**

Sir Francis Hyde Villiers (1852-1925)
Envoy Extraordinary and Minister Plenipotentiary to Belgium, 1911-19. Correspondence, 1897-1919. **F.O. 800/22-33.**

Edward Frederick Lindley Wood, 1st Earl of Halifax (1881-1959)
Lord President of the Council, 1937-8, and Secretary of State for Foreign Affairs, 1938 — December 1940. Miscellaneous correspondence, August 1937 — December 1940. **F.O. 800/309-328.**

Sir (Howard) Kingsley Wood (1881-1943)
Secretary of State for Air, 1938-40. Papers, 1938-40. **AIR 19/25-72, 556, 558-559, 570.**

Royal Air Force Museum, Aerodrome Road, Hendon, LONDON NW9 5LL

The Royal Air Force Museum was formally opened in 1972 and includes the Department of Aviation Records and Library. The Library is concerned with the literature of aviation history and aerospace developments, and holds a large and growing collection of Air publications, periodicals, official government, military and RAF publications. The Aviation Records Department includes an Archives Collection and a Documents Collection, comprising material pertaining to civil and military aviation history.

ARCHIVES COLLECTION

Air Marshal Sir Richard Atcherley (1904-70)
Air Staff Officer to the Inspector General, HQ Training Command, 1938-9; OC, 219 Night Fighter Squadron, 1939-40; service at Narvik, Norway, 1940; OC 54 Night Fighter Officer Training Unit, Church Fenton, 1941; various UK sector commands, 1941-2; AOC, 211 Group, Desert Air Force, 1943; Air Support Training HQ, AEAF, 1944; and

Commander, Central Fighter Establishment, 1945. Unlisted papers, 1923-67. **AC 73/6.**

Group Capt. Douglas Bader (b. 1910)
Fighter pilot; Commander of the first RAF Canadian (242) Fighter Squadron, 1940; and POW, 1941-5. Unlisted papers, 1939-70. **AC 72/6.**

Air Commodore David Bonham-Carter (1901-74)
Service with the Royal Canadian Air Force, 1940-3 and No. 5 (Bomber) Group, 1943-5. Unlisted papers, 1885-1971. **AC 74/13 and AC 75/6.**

Commander Frederick Boothby (1881-1940)
Airplane and balloon pilot, 1914; mission to Somaliland to report on feasibility of air operations against Mullah, 1914-15; commanded RNAS armoured cars and then Barrow Airship Station, 1915; Howden, 1916-17; and Experimental Airship Station, Pulham St. Mary, 1918-19. Papers, 1909-25. **AC 70/1.**

Air Chief Marshal Sir John Nelson Boothman (1901-57)
Unlisted papers, 1922-42. **AC 72/14.**

Air Chief Marshal Sir Norman Howard Bottomley (1891-1970)
Service in Europe with the East Warwickshire Regiment, 1914-15; RFC in France, 1915-18; Senior Air Staff Officer, HQ Bomber Command, 1938-40; commanded a bomber group, 1940-1; Assistant Chief of Air Staff (Operations), 1942-3; and Deputy Chief of Air Staff, 1943-5. Papers, 1915-61. **AC 71/2 and AC 71/8.**

Air Commodore H. G. Bowen
Unlisted papers, 1912-64. **AC 73/19.**

Air Vice-Marshal Sir Willett Bowen-Buscarlet (1898-1967)
Unlisted papers, 1916-63. **AC 75/12.**

Marshal of the Royal Air Force Sir Dermot (Alexander) Boyle (b. 1904)
Unlisted papers, 1974. **AC 74/19.**

John Theodore Cuthbert Moore-Brabazon, 1st Baron Brabazon of Tara (1884-1964)
Pioneer aviator; responsible for the RFC Photographic Section and the development of aerial photography in WWI; Minister of Transport,

1940-1; and Minister of Aircraft Production, 1941-2. Papers, 1906-64, covering his periods in office and various aspects of avitation. **AC 71/3.**

Air Commodore H. R. Busteed (1887-1965)
Unlisted papers, 1912-64. **AC 73/16, 17.**

Group Capt. G. I. Carmichael
Unlisted papers, 1912-64. **AC 72/22** and **AC 73/3.**

Group Capt. Stuart Douglas Culley (1896-1975)
Service in the RNAS with the Grand Fleet and Sea Patrol, 1917-18; Syrian campaign, 1941; Inspector of the Royal Iraqi Air Force, British Military Mission to Iraq, 1937-40; OC, RAF Palestine and Transjordan, 1940-1; Air Ministry, 1941-2; North Africa and Italy, 1943-4; and India, 1945. Unlisted papers, 1918-74. **AC 74/11, AC 74/233** and **AC 75/17.**

Air Vice-Marshal Sir Alexander Paul Davidson (1894-1971)
Service with the RFC and RAF, 1914-18; staff officer to the Inspector-General of the RAF, 1938; Air Attaché Poland, Lithuania, Latvia and Estonia, 1939-40; Bomber Command, 1940-1; HQ Levant, 1942; HQ Middle East, 1942-3; AOA Malta, 1943; AOA Coastal Air Force, 1943-4; and AOC Iraq and Persia, 1944-5. Unlisted papers, 1916-54. **AC 71/25.**

Group Capt. E. C. Dearth
Papers, 1918-68. Of some interest are files of papers referring to impressed civilian aircraft, unit administration and lapping honing of Pegasus cylinders, 1940. There are also several files of what appear to be unit operations papers, 1940-2. **AC 73/40.**

Air Commodore C. W. Dicken
Unlisted papers, 1925-46. **AC 75/13.**

Air Chief Marshal Hugh Dowding, 1st Baron of Bently Priory (1882-1970)
AOC-in-C, Fighter Command, 1936-40, and special duty for the Minister of Aircraft Production in the United States, 1940-1. Papers, 1929-65, including AOC-in-C personal file, 1937-42; letters and papers regarding the battle of Britain, 1942-65; file concerning his American duty, 21 November 1940 – 21 June 1941; and copies of reports on night interception trials, Kenley and Tangmere sectors, September – November 1940. **AC 71/17.**

Air Chief Marshal Sir Douglas Evill (1892-1971)
Service in WWI, head of the RAF delegation to Washington, 1942; and Vice-Chief of the Air Staff and Additional Member of the Air Council, 1943-6. Papers, 1910-69, including his sea log as a midshipman and sub-lieutenant, 1905-14; flying log books, 1914-67; diaries as military representative on the Supreme War Council, 1939-40; war diaries, 1939-40; various files referring to the air defence of France, 1940, and Egypt, 1941-2; WWII correspondence; and other personal papers. **AC 74/8.**

Air Vice-Marshal Sir Edward Hedley Fielden (b. 1903)
Unlisted papers, 1930-45. **AC 73/12.**

Lt. Commander A. Goodfellow (1897-1969)
Service with the RFC in WWI and the RNVR(A) during WWII. Papers, 1915-45, including his diary for November 1939 — July 1942, and flying log books, 1917-41. **AC 74/16** and **AC 75/10.**

Hardinge Goulburn Giffard, 2nd Earl of Halsbury (1880-1943)
Service as a major with the RFC and RAF in WWI. Papers, 1915-28, including two boxes of war papers, 1916-18; 28 files of Air Staff papers by Lord Tiverton, 1928; references to bombing, 1916-18; file relating to Lord Tiverton's system for dropping bombs, 1917; and other miscellaneous papers and press-cuttings. **AC 73/2, 9.**

Handley Page Records 1909-71
Company records, and correspondence and papers of the Managing Director's Office, mainly relating to the period of Sir Frederick Handley Page (1885-1962), founder and first Managing Director. The records include a fair amount of WWII material. **AC 70/10, AC 73/7, 38** and **AC 75/1.**

Lt. Gen. Sir David Henderson (1862-1921)
Director General of Military Aeronautics, 1913-18. Papers including four folders of correspondence as Director General of Military Aeronautics, June 1916 — February 1918; draft chapters of his biography; papers referring to the amalgamation of the RFC and RNAS, 1916-18; two folders of personal letters, 1905-14; a few papers of Lady Henderson; and *c.* 70 letters from his son Ian regarding service in France in the trenches and then with the RFC. **AC 71/4, 12, 73/33** and **74/2.**

Air Chief Marshal Sir Roderick Maxwell Hill (1894-1954)
Service with No. 60 Squadron, RFC, in France, 1916-17; commanded

Experimental Flying Department, Royal Aircraft Establishment, 1917-23; Director of Technical Development, Air Ministry and Ministry of Aircraft Production, 1938-40; Director General of Research and Development, Ministry of Aircraft Production, 1940-1; Controller of Technical Services, British Air Commission in Washington, 1941-2; Commandant, RAF Staff College, 1942-3; AOC No. 12 (Fighter) Group 1943; Commander of Air Defence, Great Britain, 1943-4; AOC-in-C Fighter Command, 1944-5. Unlisted papers, 1917-52. **AC 72/18.**

Air Chief Marshal Sir Leslie (Norman) Hollinghurst (1895-1971)
Service with the RFC, 1916-18; Air Ministry staff, 1939; Director of Organisation, 1940; Director General of Organisation, RAF, 1941-3; AOC No. 38 Group, 1943-4; and Air Marshal commanding Base Air Forces, Southeast Asia, 1944-5. Papers, 1915-71, including a few letters, 1916-17; ts. histories of Nos. 20 and 84 Squadrons; Review of Air Transport Operations on the Burma Front, up to June 1944; some correspondence and papers regarding visit to Canada for the air conference, 1942; a few letters concerning command of No. 38 Group; letter of 17 August 1945 from Air Marshal C. A. Bourchier referring to the situation in Burma; other miscellaneous papers. **AC 73/23.**

Group Capt. George Bayard Hynes (1887-1938)
Service with the RFC in France, 1914-20. Unlisted papers, 1909-1931. **AC 74/24.**

Air Chief Marshal Sir Philip Bennet Joubert de la Ferté (1887-1965)
Service with the RFC in France, 1914-15; Egypt, 1916-17; Italy, 1917-18; AOC RAF, India, 1937-9; Assistant Chief of Air Staff, 1941; OC-in-C, Coastal Command, 1941-3; and Deputy Chief of Staff for Information and Civil Affairs, SEAC, 1943-5. **AC 71/14:** boxes 7 and 8 contain Air Intelligence notes, 14th Wing, RAF, Italy, 1918 and other miscellaneous papers. **AC 74/21, 22** and **AC 73/1** contain as yet unlisted papers.

Air Chief Marshal Sir Trafford Leigh Leigh-Mallory (1892-1944)
AOC No. 12 Fighter Group, 1937-40, and No. 11 Fighter Group, 1940-2; AOC-in-C Fighter Command, 1942; Air C-in-C, Allied Expeditionary Air Forces, 1943-4; and command of No. 8 Squadron, RFC, 1916-18. Papers, 1912-69, including personal papers, 1917-46; letters and telegrams of congratulations on his DSO and to No. 8 Squadron; 'Copies of Reports on Wing Engagements (No. 12 Group) September 1940', file; correspondence book concerning No. 8 Squadron, 1916-17; envelope containing correspondence recovered from the air crash in which he died; and papers relating to German aeroplane

artillery signals (sent to OC Wireless, No. 8 Squadron). **AC 71/24** and **AC 74/17.**

Group Capt. G. E. Livock
Reports, notebooks, log books and diaries, 1918-31. The only WWI item is 'Pilot's reports on Special Long Recon Flights Yarmouth—Heligoland Bight', 1918. **AC 71/23.**

Maj. James B. McCudden (1895-1918)
Fighter pilot and ace; service with Nos. 20, 29, 66, 56, and 60 Squadrons, RFC, in France, July 1916 — June 1918. **AC 72/4,** 15 letters to his wife, December 1914 — February 1918; **AC 72/5,** letters to his family and other correspondence, 1914-18; and **AC 73/8,** his flying log book, 22 February 1916 — 26 February 1918. For other McCudden material, see also **DC 71/50.**

Lt. Col. Cecil L'Estrange Malone (1890-1965)
Service with RNAS, 1914-18: command of HMS *Ben-my Chree,* 1915-16, and service in the Dardanelles campaign; command of East Indies and Egypt Seaplane Squadron, 1916-18; Plans Division, Admiralty, 1918; 1st Air Attaché British Embassy in Paris, 1918; and Air Representative, Supreme War Council, Versailles, 1918. Unlisted papers, 1909-24. **AC 71/18** and **74/18.**

Air Vice-Marshal Sir Paul (Copeland) Maltby (1892-1971)
Service in France with the Royal Welch Fusiliers, 1914-15; transferred to the RFC, 1915, and served in France and Britain to the end of the war; AOC 24th (Training) Group, 1938-40; 71st (AC) Group, 1941-1; AOC RAF Java, 1942; and POW, 1942-5. Papers, 1914-62, including diaries, October 1914-16; bundle of letters from Nos. 15 and 16 Squadrons, 1916-17; American diary, August — October 1941; family letters, 1940-5; notebooks kept as a POW; list of personnel in the POW camp, 1942-6; file 'Malaya Operations 1941-2'; file, 'POW papers 1942-5'; various files and reports on air operations and operations generally in Malaya and the Netherlands East Indies, 1941-2. **AC 73/15, 24.**

Marshal of the Royal Air Force Cyril Louis Norton Newall, 1st Baron Newall of Clifton upon Dunsmoor (1886-1963)
Service with the RFC from 1914 and with the RAF from 1918; Chief of Air Staff and Senior Member of the Air Council, 1937-40; and Governor General and C-in-C of New Zealand, 1941-6. Unlisted papers, 1918-56. **Ac 71/10** and **72/8.**

Air Vice-Marshal Sir Anthony L. Paxton (d. 1966)
Unlisted papers, 1930-50. **AC 72/27.**

Air Chief Marshal Sir Richard Peirse (1892-1970)
Deputy Chief of Air Staff, 1937-40; member of the Air Council, 1939;
Vice-Chief of Air Staff, 1940; AOC-in-C Bomber Command, 1940-2;
AOC-in-C India, 1942-3; and Allied Air C-in-C, Southeast Asia, 1943-4.
Unlisted papers, 1913-65. **AC 71/13.**

Air Marshal Sir Walter (Philip George) Pretty (1909-75)
Unlisted papers, 1928-56. **AC 75/24, 25.**

Air Commodore A. J. Rankin (1896-1974)
Unlisted papers, 1918-68. **AC 74/4, 10.**

Wing Commander A. R. M. Rickards (1898-1937)
Personal papers, 1917-36. **AC 70/8.**

Air Chief Marshal Sir James Robb (1895-1968)
Service with the Northumberland Fusiliers and the RFC in WWI;
Commandant, Central Flying School, 1936-40; AOC No. 2 Bomber
Group, 1940; AOC No. 15 Coastal Group, 1941; Deputy Chief of
Combined Operations, 1942; AOC RAF, North Africa, 1943-4; and
Chief of Staff (Air) to Eisenhower, 1944-5. Unlisted papers, 1916-63.
AC 71/9 and **AC 74/25.**

Marshal of the Royal Air Force Sir John Maitland Salmond
(1881-1968)
Director General of Military Aeronautics and member of the Army
Council, 1917; Commandant of the RFC and RAF in the Field,
1918-19; Director of Armament Production, Ministry of Aircraft
Production, WWII; and Director General, Flying Control and Air Sea
Rescue, Air Ministry, WWII. Papers, 1914-43, and unlisted, including
papers referring to awards and decorations. Various correspondence.
AC 71/20 and **AC 73/14.**

Air Marshal Sir Robert Saundby (1896-1971)
Service with the Royal Warwickshire Regiment, 1914; transferred to
the RFC, 1915 and served in France and Flanders, 1916-17; Director of
Operational Requirements, Air Ministry, 1938-9; Assistant Chief of Air
Staff, 1940; and Bomber Command, 1941-5. Papers, 1914-71, including
an envelope with letters to his parents, 1914-18. There are also many
files of lectures and related papers on air warfare, tactics, strategy, etc.
AC 72/12.

Marshal of the Royal Air Force Sir John Slessor (b. 1897)
Service with the RFC in France and Egypt, 1915-18; Air Representative, Anglo-French conversations, 1939, and Anglo-American Staff
conversations, 1941; Assistant Chief of Air Staff, Casablanca Conference, 1942-3; AOC-in-C Coastal Command, 1943; and C-in-C RAF
Middle East and Mediterranean, 1944-5. Papers. AC 75/28.

Air Commodore Sydney W. Smith (1889-1971)
Unlisted papers, 1913-70. AC 72/7, 32 and 74/14.

Air Marshal Sir Ralph Sorley (1898-1974)
Assistant Chief of Air Staff (Technical Requirements), 1941; Controller
of Research and Development, Ministry of Aircraft Production, 1943-5;
and member of the Air Council. Papers, 1920-69. AC 72/19.

Sowrey Papers
AC 70/3, 5 and 74/1 are papers and photographs relating to Air
Commodore John Sowrey (1892-1967), Group Capt. Frederick Sowrey
(1893-1968), and Air Commodore William Sowrey (1894-1968). Most
of the material appears to relate to WWI but there is also some material
concerning East Africa, where William Sowrey was AOC during the
Abyssinian campaign, 1940-2.

Rear Admiral Sir Murray Sueter (1872-1960)
Director of the Air Department at the Admiralty, 1912-15; member of
the Advisory Committee on Aeronautics, 1908-17; Superintendent of
Aircraft Production, 1915-17; and commander of RNAS units in South
Italy, 1917-18. Unlisted papers, 1913-19. AC 74/12.

Supermarine Records 1916-65.
Over 1,700 items, mainly drawings of various aeroplanes with some
technical reports. There are a few aeroplanes from WWI and many from
WWII. AC 70/4.

Maj. Gen. Sir Frederick Hugh Sykes (1877-1954)
Commander of the RFC Military Wing, 1912-14; commander of the
RFC in France, 1914-15; commander of the RNAS in the Eastern
Mediterranean, 1915-16; Deputy Director of the War Office, 1917;
General Staff, Supreme War Council at Versailles, 1917-18; Chief of Air
Staff, 1918-19; and Chief of the British Air Section at the Paris Peace
Conference. Unlisted reports, correspondence and papers, 1904-19 AC
73/35.

Marshal of the Royal Air Force Arthur William Tedder, 1st Baron
Tedder of Glenguin (1890-1967)
Service with the RFC in France, 1915-17, and Egypt, 1918-19; Director
General of Research and Development, Air Ministry, 1938-40; Deputy
AOC-in-C Middle East, 1940-41; AOC-in-C Middle East, 1941-3; Air
C-in-C Mediterranean Air Command, 1943; and Deputy Supreme
Commander under Eisenhower, 1943-5. AC 71/22 is his notebook from
the RFC School of Instruction at Reading, 1916, and staff college
lectures, while AC 72/26, 73/34 and 73/5 are unlisted papers, 1923-44.

Marshal of the Royal Air Force Hugh Montague Trenchard, 1st
Viscount of Wolfeton (1873-1956)
Assistant commander, Central Flying School, 1913-14; GOC, RFC in
the Field, 1915-17; and Chief of Air Staff, 1918-29. Papers, 1891-1951.
AC 71/19 and 72/11.

Air Chief Commandant Dame Katherine Watson-Watt (1899-1971)
Director of the Women's Auxiliary Air Force, 1939-43, and missions to
North America and the Middle East, 1943-4. Unlisted papers, 1939-70
AC 72/17.

Group Capt. Frederick Winterbotham (b. 1897)
Service with the Air Staff and Foreign Office, 1929-45, and Chief of
Air Intelligence, WWII. Unlisted papers, 1934-43. AC 72/23.

DOCUMENTS COLLECTION

In addition to the items listed below, the Documents Collection also
includes various flying log books of pilots in both wars, several sets of
course notes from WWI training installations, and a number of
collections of WWII propaganda leaflets, mostly in French and German.
DC 70/4 Letter of 14 July 1917 from Lt. Indralal Roy to his sister
from the British Flying School, Vendôme, France.
DC 70/12 Letters from an RNAS officer in France to his mother,
August — October 1915.
DC 70/19 Ts. copy of 'And the Woodpecker said . . .' by Squadron
Leader V. K. Jacobs relating his experiences in SEAC, 1941-4.
DC 70/22 Nine POW newspapers, 1943-4, mostly from Stalag IV B.
DC 71/1 Navigation log of a raid from Honington to the Black Forest
which attempted to set fire to the forest, May 1940.
DC 71/8 4. Night photographic reports of the Dusseldorf and Bremen
raids, 1942.

11. Duplicated notes on bombing operations and damage to private property caused by flying, 1916.

13. Handwritten notes on 'Aerial bombs, high explosives and incendiary mixtures used in the filling of bombs', 1916.

32. Japanese propaganda leaflets intended for Indian troops in Malaya, 1942.

57. AC 22 Second Annual (draft) Report by the Air Committee on the Progress of the RFC, 13 May 1914.

71. Ts. copy of the Singapore surrender agreement between the Japanese and SACSEA, 4 September 1945.

73-82. Files of official American test reports on various planes and their equipment and some files of 'Aircraft Technical Notes', 1917-18.

87-95. Reports, diagrams and photographs of captured German WWI aircraft: Fokker E III, Fokker D.7, Fokker Triplane, DFW Two Seater, LVG Two Seaters, Zeppelin biplanes, Siemens-Schuckert, Zeppelin 'Giant', engine of the Zeppelin L.44, French notes on the Zeppelin L.49 and L.Z.77, Albatross a/c, Brandenburg a/c, Albatross single seat scouts, Giant and R planes, Pfalz Scouts, Roland a/c, Rex Scout a/c, and Giant a/c.

101. HQ Allied Expeditionary Air Force, War Room Instruction No. 1, 29 August 1944.

104. File containing tracings of preliminary plots of precision bombing by RAF No. 3 Group, 1 May 1944 − 25 February 1945.

118-124. ts. of *Enemy Coast Ahead* (1946) by Wing Commander Guy Gibson, 1944.

172. Copy of a combat report by Lt. Gordon and Lt. Gauld regarding an aerial fight at Kemmel and Dickebusch with a German LVG two seater, 2 August 1918.

176. MS account (by G. W. Mapplebeck?) of a forced landing behind German lines and life on the run, 10-20 March 1915.

This collection also includes various engineers' and Bomber Command log books from WWII and intelligence log books, 1944-5.

DC 71/18 Unofficial log book/diary, recording the Mesopotamian campaign and the fall of Kut, 1913-18.

DC 71/30 Auxiliary Air Force, Balloon Command, No. 911/23 Squadron, standing orders and diary, 1943-4.

DC 71/32 Photocopy of ts. account by a Belgian civilian of the early landings of the 2nd TAF Typhoons at Brussels/Melsbroek, 1944.

DC 71/38 Report with photographs of artillery shoots conducted with airplane spotting, October 1916 and May 1917, and translation of a German document entitled 'Salvage of Aeroplanes', addressed to front line units, June 1918.

DC 71/46 Photocopies of the flying log books of 2nd Lt. W. S. Douglas,

May 1915 — August 1916, subsequently 1st Baron Douglas of Kirtleside and Marshal of the RAF.

DC 71/50 Four MS vols. entitled 'Five Years in the Royal Flying Corps' by Capt. James B. McCudden, WWI fighter pilot and ace. For other McCudden papers, see **AC 73/8** and **AC 72/4, 5**.

DC 72/2 Lt. James Caldwell, RAF. Personal papers and correspondence, including correspondence with his father, 1917-18, and correspondence relating to his death in action, 1918.

DC 72/10 Ts. copy of a diary kept by Cpl. Ernest Palmer as a POW in the Netherlands East Indies, 19 February 1942 — 10 May 1943.

DC 72/20 Air Marshal Patrick Playfair, ts. unpublished autobiography, 'An Airman's Day'.

DC 72/30 Letter of 9 March 1941 from the Ministry of Aircraft Production to H. Eveleigh regarding his aerial mines proposal.

DC 73/2 Photocopies of No. 5 Squadron records, including ts. copy of a personal diary of 2nd Lt. L. A. Strange, 'With No. 5 Squadron in France 1914-18'; final reports, March — May 1943; patrol reports, October 1942 — February 1943; preliminary reports, March — May 1943; and files relating to the history of the squadron.

DC 73/3 Tables showing the numbers of German and Italian submarines destroyed by Allied action, 1939-45, and table of hours flown by Coastal Command from Gibraltar, Agadir and Morocco, September 1941 — May 1944, with results.

DC 73/11 Photocopies of files referring to the history of 42 Squadron in WWI and II.

DC 73/19 File containing printed papers dealing with qualifications, pay, organisation and service requirements in the RNAS and RFC, and their amalgamation as the RAF, 1917-18.

DC 73/24 Order of battle for 221 Group in Burma, listing wings, squadrons and locations, 18 May 1945.

DC 73/27 Miscellaneous documents regarding 655 Squadron during the Italian campaign, and notes on A and B flights for the squadron history, December 1943 — May 1945.

DC 73/30 Air Chief Marshal Sir Theodore McEvoy. Ts. of 'The Development of Air Fighting', covering WWI to post-WWII, with various appendices on firepower, performance, rules for combat, etc.

DC 73/31 Documents relating to Mr J. G. Gordon, including the diary of 52 Squadron, 16 November 1916 — 10 November 1918.

DC 73/32 Four diaries of POWs describing their capture in Malaya and imprisonment at Harokoe, off New Guinea, 1942-5.

DC 73/38 Book of photographs and reports recording the reconnaissance activities of 52 Squadron, June 1918 — January 1919, compiled by E. E. Crowe.

DC 73/48 Ts. copy of a diary kept by Cpl. Candy, from the beginning of the siege of Kut to his death as a POW, subsequently continued by an unknown person, 2 October 1915 — 16 September 1916.

DC 73/65 10th Balloon Company, RAF, No. 45 Balloon Section, summary of artillery, intelligence and work done, 4 June 1918; and Capt. E. L. Post, recommendations for 'Fighting in the Air', 28 February 1917.

DC 73/66 Diary of 2nd Lt. L. Morris, observation pilot, 11 Squadron, 18 May — 31 July 1916, and letter of 25 November 1916 from a fellow pilot, describing Morris' death in action.

DC 73/76 Ts. diary for Lt. W. R. Read of the first RFC contingent in France, 12 August — 1 November 1914.

DC 73/82 Six combat reports by A. Ball, 15-25 September 1916.

DC 73/86 RNAS studies giving the details of layout, installations and bridges with vertical photographs of the port of Ostend, 1 December 1916; Bruges Harbour, 1 February 1917; and the port of Zeebrugge, 1 January 1917.

DC 73/90 Photocopies of confidential reports on air operations, 1939-45:

1. Burma, January — September 1945.
2. RAF operations in the Western Desert and Eastern Mediterranean, 18 November 1941 — 19 May 1942; air operations in East Africa, 10 February — 5 April 1941; and 'Salek Mastiff' in mid-Java, 10 September — 15 December 1945.
3. Operations by the Northwest African TAF in the capture of Sicily, n.d., and air operations in Crete, 17 April — 21 May 1941.
4. Operations AMHERST and KEYSTONE, Holland, 7 July 1945; Operation DOOMSDAY, Norway, 14 June 1945; Operation VARSITY, Rhine, 20 May 1945; Operation MARKET, Holland, 1 January 1945; and Operation NEPTUNE, France, 1944.

DC 73/100 Correspondence relating to C. R. Gurl's early service with the RNAS and RAF, including bomb trials on surplus ships, 25 August 1917 — 29 May 1924.

DC 73/104 F. L. Bruns, unpublished MS regarding his RFC and RAF career as a mechanic, n.d., with personal documents and reminiscences.

DC 73/122 Maj. Douglas Jones. Ts. copy and photocopy of MS, original notes on liaison work during WWI, n.d.

DC 73/124 Account of a reconnaissance flight to Constantinople in 1918, and photocopy of a letter from the Germans at Chanak reporting the fate of missing British airmen in the Dardanelles area, 5 February 1918.

DC 73/129 Lt. Col. C. F. Lee's diary, entitled 'Aeroplane and Seaplane Officer on British Mission to USA to advise on Aviation Matters', 16 December 1917 — 21 April 1918.

DC 73/139 Copy of translations of Luftwaffe conferences held by

Reichsmarschall Hermann Goering at Karinhall and OKW HQ in 1940.
DC 74/5 Letters from German POWs in British camps, 24 December 1916 — 20 May 1917.
DC 74/29 Scrapbook of photocopied articles and photographs regarding Czech airmen and squadrons in the RAF, 1940-5.
DC 74/39 Missing Research and Enquiry Service, correspondence and files referring to the fate of downed British airmen, 1945-7.
DC 74/69 Book compiled by H. T. Haugh at RAF Tregantle Fort, Plymouth, with notes on covering, rigging and aircraft structure, and details of the Bristol Scout, O.H. 6, D.H.4, Nieuport two seater, J.N.4, and Camel, *c.* 1918.
DC 74/81 Photocopy of a letter of 5 June 1942 from Sgt. E. A. Manson at RAF Lichfield to J. Manson, describing raids on Cologne and Essen.
DC 74/84 Documents and correspondence related to Sgt. J. Gilvary, including his Air Force diary, 1 January — 13 August 1943.
DC 74/89 Three reports on air combat in the Havrincourt area, 27 December 1917; Staden and Hooglede area, 17 June 1918; and an unspecified area, 20 April 1918.
DC 74/102 Air Chief Marshal Sir Arthur Longmore (1885-1970). Service in France, Italy and at Jutland during WWI; AOC-in-C, Training Command, 1939; member of the British Air Mission to Australia and New Zealand, 1939; AOC-in-C RAF, Middle East, 1940-1; and retired, 1942. Copies of documents, 1911-70, including autobiographies 'My Early Days 1885-1910' and 'RN and RAF 1911-1945', letters, despatches and miscellaneous material covering both wars. There are several WWI letters from Winston Churchill.
DC 74/127 Diaries of Wing Commander R. E. Wilson of the barrage balloon unit 1940-4. There is also an album of press-cuttings, messages and orders relating to 939, 940 and 941 Squadrons of the Balloon Command, 1940-8.
DC 74/135 Capt. F. Williams. Diary as a two seater pilot with 66 and 55 Squadrons, 5 April 1917 — 24 September 1918; diary with 55 Squadron, 9 January — 5 September 1918; his log book; movement orders of 55 Squadron; and ts. of his book, *With the Rollo Fours,* n.d.
DC 74/144 Photocopies of nine translations of German eyewitness reports on flooding, resulting from a raid on Mölme Dam, 1945.
DC 74/154 Short histories of some 100 RAF squadrons, usually from 1914-15 to 1937-8.
DC 74/166 Guide to German language leaflets dropped by the Allies in Europe during WWII, 31 July 1945.
DC 74/169 Photocopy of part of an unidentified guide to Allied leaflets, 1941-5; Belgian, Channel Islands, Czech, Danish, Dutch, French, Italian, Luxembourg, Norwegian, Slovak, Polish, and the German 'T' series.

DC 74/179 Letter of 1 February 1916 from the Ministry of Munitions to A. Mullins concerning his suggestion of trailing bombs for aircraft.

DC 74/180 Notebook compiled by LAC R. S. E. Bronson on bomb disposal work in WWII with much technical information on bombs and their disposal, and his diary, 16 January 1943 — 7 August 1945.

DC 74/193 Photocopy of entries, 1-9 November 1918, from Lord Wakefield of Kendal's log book relating to the landing of Sopwith Pup 9944 on the deck of HMS *Vindictive,* 1 November 1918.

The Library and Muniment Room, Royal Army Medical College, Millbank, LONDON SW1

The Library of the Royal Army Medical College contains a collection of manuscript material pertaining to the Royal Army Medical Corps and aspects of military medicine. A printed catalogue is available. Permission to use the library must be obtained by writing to the Commandant of the Royal Army Medical College.

WORLD WAR I

38. Miscellaneous documents relating to the 2nd Lowland Field Ambulance in the Dardanelles and Middle East.

242. War diary kept by Lt. Gen. Sir Neil Cantlie as Deputy Assistant Director of Medical Services with the 6th Division on the Somme, September — October 1916. See also **465.**

248. Documents relating to Col. Thomas B. Beach (1866-1941), including his WWI diaries as Assistant Director of Medical Services in Alexandria, Egypt.

364. Papers, 1914-18, of Lt. Gen. Sir Matthew Fell (1872-1959). **949** is documents relating to service with the RAF, 1918-21.

365. WWI papers of Sir Anthony Bowlby, Advisory Consulting Surgeon to HM Forces in France, edited and annotated by Sir G. Gordon-Taylor.

384. Diaries of service with 72 Field Ambulance, 1915-19, by Lt. Col. W. J. Webster.

421. Diary of G. H. Swindell while serving with 77 Field Ambulance, 25th Division, on the Western Front.

453. Diary of Col. J. R. Lynch, mainly recording experience as a POW in Germany during the early part of the war.

465. Papers relating to the army service of Lt. Gen. Sir Neil Cantlie (b. 1892), who served with the Royal Army Medical Corps, 6th Division and 9th Corps in France and Flanders.

466. Papers relating to the army service of Maj. Gen. Sir Ernest Cowell

(1886-1971), who served as Surgical Specialist with the BEF, 1915-18 and OC, No. 1 Casualty Clearing Station, 1918-19.

488. Three letters by a German POW, 1917.

493. Henry Harris, MS account of 89 Field Ambulance, TA, mainly relating to Gallipoli.

518. Maj. H. G. Trayer, Notes on Serbian Barrel, 1915.

523. Maj. Gen. Sir William Donovan (1850-1934), Director of Medical Services Embarkation, 1914-19. Personal documents, cuttings and photographs covering service in Africa, India and in WWI.

524. Maj. Gen. Robert Eric Barnsley (1886-1968). Collection of papers and photographs covering service in WWI and II. Barnsley served with the RAMC in France, 1915; with the Salonika Force, 1915-18; with the Army of the Black Sea, 1918-21; as director of Medical Services, East Africa Force, 1940-1; and as Director of Medical Services, Southern Command, 1941-7.

535a. Lt. Col. T. E. Gibbon, letter describing his experiences as a Battalion Medical Officer in the King's Own Scottish Borderers at Mons, 1914.

542. Maj. J. P. Silver, papers and photographs relating to 17 Field Ambulance.

543. Col. W. W. C. Beveridge, diaries as Assistant Director of Medical Services, Sanitation.

588. Maj. Gen. Robert J. Blackham, bound vol. of reports on the second battles of Marne and Aisne, 1918.

602. Maj. Gen. Robert J. Blackham, sketch plans of advanced dressing stations on the Western Front, 1916-17.

603. Maj. Gen. Robert J. Blackham, sketch plans of advanced dressing stations in France and Italy.

699. Cpl. C. Chamberlain, diary while with 9 Field Ambulance, 1914.

728. War diaries of 26 General Hospital and 2/3 HC Field Ambulance, 1915-16.

739. Capt. H. W. Kaye, very complete diary of a medical officer in France, September 1914 — August 1916.

780. Map showing route followed by 16 Field Ambulance, 6th Division, in the advance to the Aisne, 1918.

964. F. E. Morley, miscellaneous papers, including his Gallipoli diary.

968. J. Q. Evans, diary while with 29 Field Ambulance.

1002. A. Atkinson, history of 2/3 City of London Field Ambulance.

1004. Pvt. A. Horrocks, almost complete diary while with 1 East Lancashire Field Ambulance, 1914-18.

1012. Maj. A. P. Hatt, personal papers referring to service with 38 Field Ambulance.

1101. Capt. H. Upcott, diary relating to casualty clearing stations in France and Italy.

WORLD WAR II

122. Brig. L. R. S. MacFarlane, notes on the treatment of amoebic dysentery among Allied POWs in Thailand, 1943-4.

273. Japanese POW documents.

304. Treatment of war wound shock, MRC War Memo No. I, 1940.

335. S. Mussett, Japanese POW documents.

405. Lt. Col. Francis S. Irvine, Commandant and Director of Studies, Royal Army Medical College. War diary of the College, 1939-45.

408. Personal papers of Maj. Gen. Sir Percy S. Tomlinson (1884-1951) as Director of Medical Services with the 21st Army Group in the Middle East, September 1943 — November 1944.

439. POW papers of Brig. J. Taylor in Changi Camp, Singapore, 1942-5.

465. Papers relating to the army service of Lt. Gen. Sir Neil Cantlie (b. 1892) as Assistant Director of Medical Services with the 46th Division; Deputy Director of Medical Services with the 5th Corps in North Africa and Italy; and Deputy Director of Medical Services with Eastern Command in India.

466. Papers relating to the army service of Maj. Gen. Sir Ernest M. Cowell (1886-1971) as Assistant Director of Medical Services with the 44th (Home Counties) Division, 1939-40; Deputy Director of Medical Services with 3rd Corps in France, 1940, and 2nd Corps, 1940-2; Director of Medical Services for Allied Forces, North Africa, 1942; Deputy Director of Medical Services, Allied Forces, Northwest Europe, 1944; and Primary Medical Officer of the Allied Control Commission in Germany.

478. Col. E. Scott's diaries while commanding medical units in Norway, Sudan, North Africa, Italy and Greece, 1940-5.

487. Pvt. J. Tancred, an account of a private in the Royal Pioneer Corps who died from exhaustion as a stretcher bearer at Monte Cassino, 4-5 December 1943.

495. Brig. C. Donald, 'With the Eighth Army in the Field', an account of foward surgery in the Western Desert, May — June 1944.

496. Lt. Col. W. G. Harvey, reports on Japanese POW camps, 1944-5.

648. Maj. D. T. Richardson, tour notes of visits as Director of Health to India, 1944-5.

651. Dr H. D. Chalke, notes and hygiene records while Assistant Director of Army Health, Allied army in Italy.

695. Red Devils 224 Field Ambulance in Normandy, 1944.

696. Market Garden: The Story of the RAMC of the 1st Airborne Division, 1944-5.

712. Col. E. Neild, with Pegasus in India (153 Gurkha Battalion).

732. Lt. Col. R. A. Andrews, history of 217 Field Ambulance, June 1940 — February 1941.

779. Brig. F. A. R. Stammes, reports as Consultant-Surgeon to the Allied armies in Italy, 1944-5.

789. Lt. Col. J. M. Scott, history of 128 (Wessex) Field Ambulance in Northwest Europe, 1944-5.

814. Col. K. Bush, Medical Services, 2nd Division in Burma, 1944.

815. Col. W. J. Officer, Medical Services, 2nd Division in Burma, 1944-5.

816. Col. W. J. Officer, medical report on the Special Force (Chindits), 1943-4.

840. Col. W. J. Irwin, an account of the 'Alexander Outrage' (Singapore 1942), with source material.

944. Col. J. R. MacDonald, a doctor goes to war.

982. Various anonymous accounts of life in Japanese POW camps in Malaya.

1016. Brig. L. R. S. MacFarland, four medical reports on Japanese POW camps.

1042. Dr C. Lendon, Diseases among POWs in Japanese hands.

The Mytchett Collection, especially box files **801/12** and **801/13**, contains various WWI and II miscellaneous papers, including unit papers and histories of field ambulances.

The Library, Royal Artillery Institution, Old Royal Military Academy, LONDON SE18 4JJ

The Library of the Royal Artillery Institution contains a large collection of manuscript and documentary material, a substantial collection of official artillery publications, a large collection of books and other printed matter relating to artillery, and some photographs and drawings. Associated with the Institution are the Museum of the Royal Regiment of Artillery and the Artillery Museum. An appointment is necessary.

MANUSCRIPT COLLECTION

Brig. Gen. Austin Thomas Anderson (d. 1949). Diary of the 1914-18 War, three vols. MS and ts. Anderson served in France from 1914 and was Commander, RA, 62nd Division from 1916. **B2/712a.**

Brig. Edgar Carnegie Anstey (1882-1958), papers. Anstey served with the RA in WWI; was Passive Air Defence Officer, London District, 1938-40; special employment, Southern Command, 1940; member of the Historical Section, Cabinet Office, 1940-2; and military correspondent, 1942-5.

Anti-aircraft Command: history of AA Command, vol. 2, n.d. and ts., copy no. 3, official. **C3/53.**

Maj. R. A. Archer-Houblon, 'I Troop, Royal Horse Artillery, in the war against Germany 1914-18', ts. 1926. **C3/10.**

Maj. A. F. Becke, 'Mon journal pendant la guerre 1914-15', MS with maps. **L/238.**

Capt. A. F. Becke, 'The European War 1914-19', vol. I. **MS 81.**

Capt. W. H. Bloor, war diary with the RFA in WWI. **B5/461.**

Capt. J. A. Brymer, record of the 33rd Field Regiment, RA, 6 June 1944 — May 1945, ts. **C1/7.**

Lt. Col. Alfred H. Burne (1886-1959), papers. Burne served with Q Battery, Royal Horse Artillery, in Europe during WWI and was Commandant, 121 Officer Cadet Training Unit, 1939-42.

Lt. Col. S. M. Cleeve, 'Big guns in the field', ts., maps and illustrations. **Ms G3f/57.**

Lt. Col. S. M. Cleeve, 'History of super-heavies', 1914-41, ts. **G3f/57a.**

Lt. Col. H. M. Dawson, 'Memoirs of the Great War', ts., 1932. **B2/775i.**

81st Company, Royal Garrison Artillery (later 38th Howitzer Battery), historical records, MS, 1855-1922. **C3/49a.**

Operational record of 11th Army Group and ALFSEA, November 1943 — August 1945, ts. and maps, n.d. **B5/221.**

Lt. Col. G. W. P. Fennell, History of 5th Field Regiment, RA, 1939-45. **C3/36.** Another photostat copy, **C1/314.**

42nd Field Battery, diary for 1943-5. **C3/55a.**

45th Field Battery, history and diary, one vol. ts. and photographs. **C3/50a.**

Gen. Sir Webb Gillman (1870-1933). One box of papers. Gillman was an officer on the General Staff, War Office, 1912-14; on the General Staff of the BEF, 1915; and Chief of General Staff, 1917-19.

Maj. B. A. Goldstein, OC, 154 Siege Battery, Royal Garrison Artillery. War diary, 1916-18, three vols. MS. **MS 103.**

Maj. M. N. T. Gubbins, diary entitled 'Day to day life on the Western Front 1914-18'. **Lower Cupboard 06.**

Maj. C. B. A. Hire, 'Rock Armament 1704-1958', ts., 1958. **Ms 116.**

Brig. R. Hudson, papers relating to WWII.

Brig. Gen. A. H. Hussey, war diary, 1914-18, two vols. Hussey was Commander, RA, 5th Division.

Field-Marshal William Edmund Ironside (1880-1959). Letters concerning WWI and North Russia to Col. R. Macleod. Ironside was a staff officer in France with the 6th Division, 1914; with the 4th Canadian Division, 1916; and commander of the 99th Infantry Brigade of the 2nd Division, seeing action at Vimy Ridge, Passchendaele and the Somme. He then commanded the Allied forces in North Russia, 1918-19. **MS 124.** For Ironside's diaries, 1920-22, see **B5/903.**

Ernest Jones, compiler, 'History of 211 Royal Artillery Training Regiment 1939-48', ts. C1/316.

Maj. J. P. Kaestlin, 'Presidential Gunners — History of the Indian Artillery', ts., 1959. M/Ms 998.

Maj. J. N. Kennedy, 'Australian Corps Heavy Artillery, operations from 8 August — 18 September 1918', two ts. vols. with maps. MS 119.

Maj. Gen. John Mather Kirkman (1898-1964) papers, Kirkman served with the RA in France and Belgium, 1917-18, Deputy Director of Military Intelligence, War Office, 1942; and BGS, Southern Command, 1944, and Greece, 1945.

Lt. Col. L. H. Landon, papers relating to WWII.

Brig. H. B. Latham, notes on super-heavy artillery 1939-45, ts. and MS, 1960. G3f/56a.

Maj. Gen. Alexander Anderson McHardy (1868-1958), papers. McHardy served with the RA in Europe during WWI and as ARP Sub-controller in WWII.

Col. R. Macleod, 'Field-Marshal Ironside's story as told to me and from notes he left behind', ts.

Gen. Sir (E.C.) Robert Mansergh (1900-70). One trunk of papers. See MD 490 for service details and obituaries. Mansergh served during WWII in Eritrea, Abyssinia, the Western Desert, Libya, the Middle East, Persia, the Iraq Force, Arakan, Assam, Burma and the liberation of Singapore. He commanded the 11th (East African) Division, 1945; 5th Indian Division, 1945; and was C-in-C Allied Forces in the Netherlands East Indies, 1946.

Brig. B. G. Mason, one box of papers relating to WWII.

Brig. Eric Edward Mockler-Ferryman (b. 1896). He served with the Royal Horse Artillery, 1914, and the 37th Division Artillery in France and Flanders, 1915-19. In WWII, he saw service with Intelligence and SOE. One box of papers; WWI diary B2/462C; memoirs D2/131C; and 'Last Four Weeks of the Great War', ts., MD 455.

Maj. J. L. Mowbray (1875-1916), ts. diary as RA Brigade Major in France, August 1914 — January 1915. Ms 916.

R. H. Newman's diary, 'Guns, Guts and Gunners'. Diary Cupboard E Library.

123 Heavy Battery, Royal Garrison Artillery, Horse Bock (?), commenced 1st October 1915 at Brandloek, Flanders, MS and photographs. C3/24.

Photographs, sketches and drawings of ordnance, 1889-1915. G3d/53/6.

Maj. D. Packard, papers relating to WWII.

Maj. Gen. Hetman Jack Parham (b. 1895). MS diary referring to Northwest Europe, 1944. Ms 110.

Maj. P. H. Pilditch, 'War diary of an artillery officer 1914-18', ts., n.d. B2/775R.

Sgt. J. G. Pooley, Royal Garrison Artillery. 'A Soldiers' Tale of the Great War', ts. MS 123.

Maj. S. W. H. Rawlins, 'History of the development of the British artillery in France 1914-1918', ts. B2/761c.

Lt. E. J. M. Robertson, war diary, August 1914 — March 1915. Service with the 70th RFA in France and Belgium, including the Aisne, Mons and Flanders. B2/464A.

Brig. C. W. Row, letters, pamphlets, and documents regarding WWII, mainly relating to coast artillery and coast defence at Dover, 1939-45.

Gen. H. Rowan-Robinson, 'Guns in the Great War', MS 80.

2nd Field Battery, RA, Digest of Service 1716-1936, including MS and ts. documents, letters, etc. relating to the history of the battery.

6th Anti-aircraft Division, war diary for 1939-42, three vols. ts. and one vol. maps. C3/54.

Capt. J. B. Sopper, 'History of the 21st Mountain Battery, Indian Artillery, in the Malayan campaign, December 1941 — February 1942', ts. C1/311/26.

A. E. Strange, 'History of the Riding Establishment, Royal Artillery, 1803-1932', ts., 1932. M/Ms 1050.

A. E. Strange, 'Short history of the 37th Siege Battery, Royal Artillery, 1915-1919', ts., 1932. C1/719.

J. M. A. Tamplin, 'Surrey Rifle Volunteers: A century of volunteer and traditional service, 1859-1959', ts., 1959. C1/310/20.

Record of artillery defences, Tobruk, April — November 1941, ts, and maps, compiled in the field. C1/315.

Maj. Gen. Sir (Henry) Hugh Tudor (1871-1965). 'Diary of the War 1914-1918', ts., 1959. Tudor commanded the RA, 9th (Scottish) Division, and then in 1918 the 9th Division. B2/775j.

2/1st Hampshire Battery, RFA, records. C3/41.

Lt. Gen. Sir Herbert C.C. Uniacke (1866-1934). One trunk of unlisted papers. Uniacke served as Chief Instructor, Royal Horse Artillery and RFA, 1913-14; commanded a brigade of Royal Horse Artillery in France, 1914; GOC, RA, 3rd and 5th Corps and then the 5th Army; and Deputy Inspector of Training, British Armies in France and Flanders, 1914-18.

Maj. Gen. H. C. C. Uniacke, 'Some episodes during Battle — Fighting on the Western Front, World War I', ts., n.d. M/Ms/1000. Published in *Journal of the Royal Artillery,* 1918-20.

Maj. Victor Walrond, 'Diary of the Great War 1914-1919', ts., two vols. D2/194b.

Col. William Warren Robinson (1882-1969), papers regarding WWI. He served with the RA. Brig. Alec Warren Greenhaw Wildey, Gunner in charge of the Singapore Anti-aircraft Command. Papers relating to the Command during WWII.

Brig. John Peter Alexander Wildey, RASC, 'Ack-ack of Malaya', MS. **Ms 02/265.**

Lt. Col. J. L. Willis, diaries of WWII service.

Lt. J. P. Wills, diaries of service with the RA in WWI. **CFC 124 Diary Cupboard.**

MILITARY DOCUMENTS

7. Lt. Col. Moberly, notes on the history of the 19th Siege Battery in France, 1915-16. Ts., n.d., with an album of photographs..

8. Changes in designation of Royal Garrison Artillery companies nos. 1-34, 1902-51. Revised from Lt. Col. Leslie's pamphlet by J. Squire.

9. Papers on WWI artillery subjects, including instructions, memoranda, maps, etc., France, 1917.

69. Sketch map of the battle of Sidi Nsir, 26 February 1943.

86. Capt. J. E. C. Oliver, 302 Battery, RFA. Account of the surrender of Jerusalem, 9 July 1919, ts.

89. 2nd Lt. A. E. Robinson, 29 Battery, 42nd Brigade. Account of service in the 3rd Division in France and Belgium, 1917-18, entitled 'This Suitcase Accompanied . . . '

118. Rev. E. Q. Snook, Chaplain to 36 Light Anti-aircraft Regiment, RA, in Burma. Diary at Rangoon, 29 April – 15 May 1945.

141. Brig. Philip S. Myburgh (1893-1963), four files of papers relating to Tobruk and Burma.

163. German magazine *Jugend,* no. 28 (1916), nos. 14, 21, and 33 (1917).

184. Maj. Gen. Sir John Headlam. Reports on the Artillery Mission to the USA, 1917, three vols. ts., and the final report on the Mission's work, ts., 1919.

184a. Maj. Gen. Sir John Headlam, report on a visit to Russian Front, 1917, ts.

188a. Maps, plans, ts. accounts and reports relating to WWII by Brig. H. J. Parham.

188b. Operations of the 1st Germany Army and the German defeat at Tunis, April – May 1943; RA, Second Army notes, reports and plans concerning the Normandy landing, June 1944; and early letters and reports of Brig. Parham, September – December 1942.

207. Mechanical Transport, Field Artillery and Heavy Batteries, file of correspondence relating to WWI, 1917, and letters of Gen. Beckett, 1916-17.

211. 19th Corps, RA war diary for 1918 and other documents.

214. 5th Battery, 45th Brigade, RFA, citation of action fought on 27 May 1918, signed by Field-Marshal Montgomery.

216. Flak towers in Germany, description and illustrations, ts., 1946, with photographs.

218. Maj. A. F. Becke, MSS and ts. referring to the RA in Italy, 1917-18, and Mesopotamia, 1914-18.

224. Brig. H. B. Latham, 'Destruction of Zeppelin 15, an early success', ts., 1950.

226. 155th Field Battery, RA, at Sidi Nsir, Tunisia. Newspaper cuttings of the battle, 26 February 1943.

230. Panorama of a portion of the German front line about two miles south of Ploegsteert, drawn by Lt. Roberts while serving with Battery 189, RFA, 41st Division, summer 1916.

233. Capt. W. B. Mackie, diary of service with the RFA in France, 4 August 1914 — November 1918, ten vols.

243. Brig. H. B. Latham, 84th Battery, RFA at Kemmel Hill, 25 April 1915, related correspondence. Published in the *Journal of the Royal Artillery,* 1953.

247. Maj. Gen. J. C. Dalton, MS 'Reminiscences of Royal Artillery Officers', 1930.

250. 'Two appreciations of Lt. Gen. Sir Edward A. Fanshawe' by Lt. Gen. Eric de Burgh and Maj. W. H. Skrine, MS, 1950.

258. Capt. P. G. E. Warburton, extracts from diaries during service with the 37th Battery, RFA, 5th Division, Western Front, 1916-18.

259. Maj. Gen. Machida, report of the siege of Tsingtao, 23 August — November 1914, ts., n.d.

259a. Anonymous diary of a German soldier during the siege of Tsingtao, July — November 1914, MS translation.

268. Lt. Col. R. A. G. Nicholson, war diary with 115 Field Regiment, RA, 1944-5.

272. El Alamein, 23 October — 4 November 1942. Official order of Battle of the 8th Army, ts., two copies.

278. Lt. C. J. Titchener, 'History of 7th Army Group, Royal Artillery, 14 April — 2 May 1945, in Italy', ts.

285. 1st Air Landing Anti-tank Battery, RA, Exercise FUSTIAN, July 1943, official ts.

287. Tabulated foreign equipments, n.d., official ts., 1945.

288. Maj. C. P. F. Pierret, four notebooks on foreign equipments, MS, *c.* 1940.

301. El Alamein, 30 Corps operations orders.

307. Personal messages from the Army Commander, 8th Army, intended to be read out to the troops, Christmas 1942 — 11 August 1944, signed 'B. L. Montgomery'; *8th Army News* for 19 December 1942, 18 January and 7 April 1943; and other notices to troops.

319. 22nd Division Operations Target, Piton des Mitrailleuse, September 1916.

335. Lt. Gen. Sir Lawrence Parsons, 'The Natal Campaign, 1943-1944', ts.

336. 'German pre-rifled long range high explosive shells, 1943-1944', ts.

344. Brig. C. Max Vallentin, mimeographed official report of the escape of an officer of the 5th Indian Division on 11 September 1943 in Italy, with maps and a photograph.

345. Gallipoli, maps and photographs, 1915.

346. German code handbook, 1917-18.

352. Air photographs of Ypres, WWI.

357. Maj. A. F. Becke, 'The Marne 1914', ts.

364. Sir Lawrence Bragg's personal account of sound ranging in WWI, ts.

394. Summary of the war diary of the 59th Field Battery, RA, attached to 255th Tank Brigade, concerning the capture of Meiktila in Burma, December 1944 – March 1945, ts.

399. Original copy of survey, 129 (Lowland) Field Regiment during campaign in Burma, WWII; gunner support for second Chindit expedition, 1944; and sketch map of Tiddim Road and accompanying letter.

400. Capt. H. P. Burnyeat, account of the battle of Nery, 1 September 1914, diary of Lt. Col. H. B. Dresser and letters relating to the Western Front, WWI.

400a. Maj. I. O. D. Preston, account of the assault on Meiktila, with maps, and the 59th Field Battery in the Burma campaign, WWII.

406. Brig. H. J. Parham, 'The Normandy Landings, 6 June 1944', ts.

407. Col. J. W. Renny-Tailowr, letters from Mesopotamia, WWI.

414. Col. R. Macleod, two letters relating to the battle of Le Cateau, August 1914.

415. Short history of the 1st Air Landing Light Regiment, RA, 1941-5.

419. Employment of 100 Heavy Anti-aircraft Regiment, Sicily and Salerno landings, secret, copy no. 15, from Maj. Gen. F. LeJeune.

420. History of the 12th Army against the Japanese, 28 May – September 1945.

425. Lt. Gen. Sir Edmund Schreiber, 'The Great War', ts., 1914.

430. Maj. Gen. A. A. Goschen, memoirs of WWI.

432. Maj. A. C. Fergusson, commanding 21st (Kohat) Mountain Battery, account of Gallipoli, 1915.

434. 'Sir John French's Despatches: Official Records of The Great Battles of Mons, the Marne and the Aisne', printed with maps. *Ibid,* second series, 'Official Story of the Battle around Ypres, Armentières, etc. and the defence of Antwerp', with maps.

436. Le Cateau, August 1914, correspondence between Bdr. G. H. Cutts and Lt. W. K. Morrison of the RAMC.

440. 1st Hong Kong Indian Regiment, RA. War diary, 1940-1, with

appendices and reports relating to the imprisonment of the regiment and a list of members joining the Indian National Army.

455. Brig. E. E. Mockler-Ferryman, 'Last Four Weeks of the Great War', ts.

482. Enemy artillery equipment captured in the Middle East and North Africa, WWII.

485. RA, Second Army, Operational Instruction No. 2, 1944.

486. Artillery lessons from the campaign in Italy, 1943-5.

488. Brig. S. Mead, notes on heavy artillery, 1914-18.

489. 24th Indian Mountain Regiment, RA, war diary, 1944.

491. H. Thuiller, six articles on the Mesopotamia campaign and meeting with the Czarist Cossack column, 1916-20, with three articles on other aspects of the war.

497. Brig. G. E. W. Franklyn, 'From Deepcut to France', mobilisation of the 25th Brigade, RFA, August 1914.

504. 110th Brigade, RFA, ts. report on action at Vaulx-Vraucourt, 22 March 1918.

507. Maj. H. W. Newcombe, war diary of service on the Western Front with Batteries 47, 56, and 60 of the 44th Brigade, RFA, 1914-18.

509. 18th Division, various battle and fire plan maps, 1914-18.

520. 21st Anti-tank Regiment, Copies of the newspaper, *Twenty One*, 1945-6.

525. Col. R. Macleod, story of the 4th Army, ts.

528. K. M. Goddard, two ts. accounts of the battle of Keren, March 1941.

532. 2nd Lt. J. R. S. Roper of Chestnut Troop, war diary for 1918.

538. 22/56 Field Battery, history during battle of Flanders, 14 May — 3 June 1940.

552. Private letters from WWI written to the Misses Hughes.

573. Royal Sussex Regiment, 7th (Service) Battalion, history during WWI.

577. 1st Division, intelligence summary of the fall of Lampedusa, Italy, WWII.

587. The Rifle Brigade, diary of campaigns in the Sudan, Africa, Egypt, China, Malta and Gibraltar, 1896-1918.

596. H. E. Danks, diary of 52nd Heavy Anti-aircraft Regiment, 1939-45, and other notebooks.

601. W. J. Kemp, 'The laying out of lines of fire at Neuve Chapelle, WWI', ts.

603. 82nd (West African) Division, RA in the Arakan campaign, December 1944 — May 1945.

Royal College of Physicians, 11 St. Andrew's Place, Regent's Park, LONDON NW1 4LE

WORLD WAR II

US Military Intelligence Report on Adolf Hitler as seen by his doctors, 29 November 1945.
D. E. Bedford and Sir J. Parkinson, notes on the medical history of Sir Winston Churchill, restricted access.
Dr G. H. Rossdale, notes on the medical history of Sir Anthony Eden, 1928-53, restricted access.

Royal Commonwealth Society, 18 Northumberland Avenue, LONDON WC2N 5AP

The Society maintains a library of some 400,000 books, pamphlets, official reports, periodicals, manuscripts, photographs, drawings and maps. Students who are not members of the society may gain admittance by application to the librarian. The following entries are drawn from Donald H. Simpson, ed., *The Manuscript Catalogue of the Library of the Royal Commonwealth Society* (London, Mansell, 1975).

Royal Colonial Institute
'The Empire at War Files' comprise 21 files, one book and an envelope of cuttings relating to the preparation and publication of Sir Charles Lucas, ed., *The Empire At War* (Oxford, five vols., 1921-6). There is correspondence with the Admiralty, War Office, and Colonial Office as well as with various parts of the Empire.

Sir William Lamond Allardyce
Allardyce was Governor of the Falkland Islands, 1904-15. His scrapbooks contain some cuttings relating to the battle of the Falkland Islands in 1914.

Sir Walter Buchanan-Smith
Buchanan-Smith worked in the Colonial Service in Nigeria, 1909-35. There are approximately 230 letters to his family, some of which probably relate to WWI. In addition, there is a 32-page carbon copy of a ts. diary relating to the East African campaign, 1916-17. Some 200 photographic prints relating to campaigns in East and West Africa, 1914-18, are included in a photographic album.

Souvenirs of Palestine Campaign
Folder of seven miscellaneous printed, MS, ts. and photographic items relating to the Palestine campaign, 1916-19.

Diana Hartley: Indian Nursing Collection
Hartley was Secretary of the Trained Nurses Association of India, 1935-44. Reports, articles, and photographs of her work in India, including WWII material.

British Association of Malaysia
The Association was founded in 1960 to collect personal records ranging from contemporary diaries and letters to retrospectively compiled accounts. The collection contains the following items of interest:

R. K. Walker, eyewitness account of the sinking of the Russian cruiser *Zemchug* by the German raider *Emden* at Penang, 1915.

A. M. Thompson, accounts of the sinking of the *Zemchug,* the destruction of the *Emden,* the Singapore Mutiny, and other wartime experiences.

A. H. Dickenson, W. Lowther Kemp and M. B. Shelley, personal experiences during the Singapore Mutiny of 1915.

Memorandum on the political situation in Malaya immediately preceding the outbreak of WWII, 1942.

Memorandum on organization in Malaya, September 1939 — February 1942, concerned with political intelligence and security.

Malayan Communist Party proclamation of 7 November 1945.

British Military Administration, Malaya: notifications, notices, etc., October 1945 — February 1946, relating to the Kedah-Perlis-Kroh region.

W. D. Brown, the bombing and evacuation of Klang.

H. R. Oppenheim, diary of the escape of a party of Federated Malay States volunteers, 15 February 1942, and the diary of Maj. Gen. Gordon Bennett, GOC Australian Forces in Malaya.

M. C. Hay, another version of the above escape.

S. J. Nias, escape from Malaya in February 1942 by a Federated Malay States volunteer.

Sir Shenton Thomas, Malaya's war effort by the governor of the Straits Settlements.

Various: the experiences of 21 men serving in various capacities in different parts of the country, from the outbreak of WWII to surrender.

J. D. Hill, notes on the first few days of the Japanese attack on Kedah.

Guy Hutchinson, the Johore Volunteer Engineers at war.

Anonymous diary of the fall of Singapore.

'My diary 1942', diary of a Japanese civilian in Kuala Lumpur during the occupation.

A. P. Ross, 'Escape from Singapore', extract from the diary of a Malayan government official, February 1942.

Muriel Reilly, war diary kept in Singapore, 8 December 1941 — 13 February 1942.

D. S. Ainger, diary of a POW in Singapore.

W. F. N. Churchill, 'To those who laughed', one man's record of the Civilian Internment Camp, Singapore, 1942-5.

J. C. Coutts-Milne, recollections of a POW in Changi.

Anonymous impression of Changi Civilian Internment Camp.

C. E. Collinge and others, report on the internment of civilians by the Japanese, February 1942 — August 1945.

N. R. Jarrett, miscellaneous records kept as camp quartermaster, Civilian Internment Camp.

John Weekly, documents and records concerning the Civilian Internment Camp, Singapore.

A. A. Duncan-Wallace, diary of a civilian internee in Singapore.

There are other civilian recollections of the internment camps, as well as the *Nominal Roll of the Singapore Civilian Internee Camp* and *List of POW and Internees* collected by the Australian Malaysian Research Bureau.

Frederick William Hugh Migeod
Migeod served in the Colonial Service from 1900 to 1919. His papers include 'Manifold books, Togoland Operations', August — December 1914.

East African Carrier Corps Papers
Material collected by H. B. Thomas, including 'Standing Orders and Regulations . . . for the forces in British East Africa and Uganda 1915', with ts. and MS amendments; Military Labour Bureau handbook, 1916(?); miscellaneous memoranda, orders and signals; anddiary of H. B. Thomas, 14-17 April 1917. Thomas was a captain in the Carrier Corps.

Lucy Langridge
Her papers contain a letter of 16 July 1915 from Kenya, concerning wartime events.

Northern Rhodesia Production Committee
Northern Rhodesia statistics of war munitions, with an introductory note by A. Royden Harrison, Chairman of the committee, 22 June 1944. The introduction sketches the activities of the committee,

1941-4, while the remainder of the material comprises statistics and a list of personnel.

Maj. Frederic J. Newnham
Falkland Islands defence papers. Newnham commanded the Falkland Islands Defence Force from 1915. The papers contain his own history of the force, list of members from 1914-19, miscellaneous reports, and the Falkland Islands' publication of Vice-Admiral Sturdee's despatch of 19 December 1914, concerning the battle of the Falkland Islands.

Horace M. Moore-Jones
During WWI, Moore-Jones served as a sapper in the New Zealand Engineers and then as a war artist. The library contains two original paintings made during the occupation of Anzac Cove, Gallipoli, 1915.

The Royal Regiment of Fusiliers, City of London Headquarters, H.M. Tower of London, LONDON EC3N 4AB

Application should be made to the Commandant of the regiment for permission to use the regimental archives.

WORLD WAR I

Royal Fusiliers war diaries:
1st Battalion, October 1914 — May 1919.
2nd Battalion, January 1915 — April 1919.
3rd Battalion, December 1914 — April 1919.
4th Battalion, August 1914 — April 1919.
7th Battalion, July 1916 — December 1918.
8th Battalion, May 1915 — February 1918.
9th Battalion, May 1915 — June 1919.
10th Battalion, July 1915 — March 1919.
11th Battalion, July 1915 — April 1919.
12th Battalion, August 1915 — February 1918.
13th Battalion, July 1915 — March 1919.
17th Battalion, November 1915 — April 1919.
18th Battalion, November 1915 — April 1919.
19th Battalion, November 1915 — April 1919.
20th Battalion, November 1915 — April 1919.
21st Battalion, November 1915 — April 1919.
22nd Battalion, November 1915 — January 1920.
23rd Battalion, November 1915 — January 1920.

24th Battalion, November 1915 — March 1919.
25th Battalion, March 1915 — March 1919.
26th Battalion, March 1915 — March 1919.
32nd Battalion, May 1916 — February 1919.
38th Battalion, May 1916 — February 1919.
39th Battalion, May 1916 — February 1919.
40th Battalion, May 1916 — February 1919.
City of London Regiment war diaries:
1/1 Battalion, March 1915 — May 1916.
1/1 Battalion, August 1914 — May 1919.
2/2 Battalion, January 1917 — February 1919.
1/3 Battalion, August 1914 — August 1917.
1/4 Battalion, January 1915 — May 1919.
2/4 Battalion, January 1917 — June 1918.
3rd Battalion, February 1915 — November 1918.
Battalion orders:
City of London Regiment, 1st Reserve Battalion, 1917-18.
City of London Regiment, 4/2 Reserve Battalion, 1916.
Miscellaneous:
1st Battalion, digest of service, 1919-39.
2nd Battalion, digest of service, 1914-39.
Composition of HQ, British Armies in France, 1918.
GHQ, France, 1918-19. Small printed booklet containing statistics of guns, prisoners, expenditure of ammunition, motor transport and airplanes, 1918-19 (only six copies printed).
Order of Battle, British Armies in France, 1918.
20th Battalion, *Pow Wow Magazine,* 1914-16.
Royal Fusiliers Battalion recognition patches, 1914-18.
13th Battalion Operations Order No. 36, 13 April 1916.
City of London Regiment, evacuation orders, Suvla, Gallipoli, 18 December 1915.
Royal Fusiliers, three vols. of press-cuttings.
Regimental histories and personal diaries:
H. C. O'Neil, 'Fusiliers in the Great War', MS.
Frederick Longman, 4th Battalion, Royal Fusiliers, journal in France with a few letters from the front, 26 July — 17 October 1914.
The Rev. Noel Mellish, Hon. Chaplain to the Royal Fusiliers, untitled narrative of experiences in France, 1916-18, 103 pp., ts., n.d.

WORLD WAR II

Royal Fusiliers war diaries:
9th Battalion, September 1939 — December 1945.

2nd Battalion, December 1944.

City of London Regiment war diaries:

1st Battalion, September 1939 — November 1940; May — October 1941; August 1942 — December 1943; January — April 1944; and January — December 1945.

Royal Fusiliers Infantry Training Centre, Hounslow, war diary, 1939-40.

Miscellaneous:

Casualties on Service, all battalions, 1940-5.

Casualties on Service, all battalions, 1944-6.

1st Battalion, intelligence log in Italy, October 1944 — July 1945.

Royal Fusiliers, 12th Battalion, photograph album, 1940.

Capt. W. Jones, New Zealand Division, ts. account of the battle of Tuma West, Sidi Barrani, December 1940.

Regimental histories:

'Always a Fusilier', six MS and ts. vols. containing the war history of the Royal Fusiliers, 1939-45. *A Short History of the 6th City of London (Silvertown) Battalion, Home Guard, May 1940 — May 1944*, pamphlet.

Royal United Services Institute for Defence Studies, Whitehall, LONDON SW1

The manuscript holdings of the Institute have been transferred to various repositories, primarily the National Army Museum and the National Maritime Museum. The Institute still maintains its library of books and journals.

School of Oriental and African Studies, Malet Street, LONDON WC1

WORLD WARS I AND II

MS. English 257247. Papers of Sir Henry Mortimer Durand (1850-1924). **19 1.** notes on the 18th Hussars for his book *The Eighteenth Hussars in the Great War* (1921), and **17 e.** correspondence with *The Times* for its 'History of the Mesopotamia Campaign'.

MS. English 145982. Eleven folders of MS and ts. notes and drafts, letters, memoranda, speeches, broadcasts, press releases and a few press-cuttings of Barbara Whittingham Jones, journalist and broadcaster specializing on Southeast Asia. The bulk of the material relates to Indonesia in 1945-6, but there is one folder on Thailand in WWII.

Science Museum, Library, Exhibition Road, LONDON SW7

Pearson Papers
Papers of Sir Weetman Dickinson Pearson, 1st Viscount Cowdray (1856-1927). The collection includes some papers relating to his tenure as President of the Air Board, January — November 1917.

Archives Department, Shepherds Bush Library, Uxbridge Road, LONDON W12 8LJ

WORLD WAR II

Civil Defence records of the Metropolitan Boroughs of Fulham and Hammersmith during WWII.

Archives Department, Shoreditch District Library, Pitfield Street, LONDON N1 6EX

WORLD WAR II

London Borough of Hackney, WWII Civil Defence records.

21st Special Air Service Regiment (Artists) Museum, B Block, Duke of York's Headquarters, King's Road, LONDON SW3

The Museum contains runs of the *Artists Rifles Gazette*, the *Artists Rifles Chronicle*, and *Mars and Minerva*. There is also the Artists Rifles Record of Service and Roll of Honour 1914-19; personal documents of members, and the memoirs of Cpt. C. J. Blomfield 'Once an Artist Always an Artist', and Col. Mays, 'Memoirs of the Artists Rifles'. Enquiries should be made to the Secretary, Artists Rifles Association.

Stratford Reference Library, Water Lane, LONDON E15 3NJ

WORLD WAR II

WWII records for the London Borough of Newham, comprising the former County Boroughs of East Ham and West Ham. Unless otherwise stated, the material indicated is common to both.

Minutes and reports of councils and committees.

Lists of incidents and casualties.

File of the local weekly newspaper.

War damage photographs, an extensive collection for West Ham.

Some log books of warden posts in West Ham.

Files regarding building repairs and requisitioned properties in West Ham.

Accounts of individual local services compiled with a view to producing histories of the boroughs during the War, neither published. There are similar contributions from some major firms for West Ham.

Local History Department, London Borough of Camden, Swiss Cottage Library, 88 Avenue Road, LONDON NW3 3HA

WORLD WAR I

138th Battery, Royal Garrison Artillery, Photographs.

WORLD WAR II

St. Pancras ARP papers, three boxes, mainly correspondence; and Hampstead ARP records, incomplete.

Tower Hamlets Libraries Department, Central Library, Bancroft Road, LONDON E1 4DQ

WORLD WAR II

Bethnal Green ARP: air raid damage records, 1940-5 (incident reports, wardens reports, and messages and action taken).

Poplar ARP: air raid messages, 1940; correspondence, 1942-4; and committee reports.

Aircraft log books: Mitchell II (FV. 998) of Squadron 180, 27 April — 20 June 1944; Tempest V (EJ. 775) of Squadron 274, 19 January — 25 February 1943; and Mitchell II (FL. 685) of Squadron 180, 8 February — 28 March 1943.

Manuscripts and Rare Books Room, The Library, University College London, Gower Street, LONDON WC1

Readers from outside University College should write to the Librarian for permission to consult the particular collection or items in which they are interested. The card catalogues of the manuscript collections were surveyed to reveal the following items:

Family letters of Arnold Sandwith Ward (1876-1950). Ward was Special Correspondent for *The Times,* 1899-1902 in Egypt, the Sudan and India, and became MP for West Hertfordshire in 1910. He served as a lieutenant in the West Hertfordshire Yeomanry in Egypt and Cyprus, 1914 and 1915. His papers contain some wartime letters from Egypt and Cyprus. **MS. ADD. 202.**
Papers of Dr Moses Gaster (1856-1939), who was a founder and President of the English Zionist Federation. It was at his house in London that talks were initiated between prominent Zionists and Sir Mark Sykes on behalf of the Foreign Office, which led to the Balfour Declaration of November 1917. The papers cover the period, 1874-1939, and include correspondence, notes, MSS, photographs, diaries, and other personal material. There is, for example, correspondence with Chaim Weizmann.

University of London Library, Senate House, Malet Street, LONDON WC1.

The manuscript holdings of the University of London Library are described in Joan Gibbs and Paul Kelly, 'Manuscripts and archives in the University of London Library', *Archives,* XI, 51 (Spring 1974). There is a printed *Catalogue of the Manuscripts and Autograph Letters in the University Library* (1921) and *Supplement* (1930). Typescript catalogues cover the collection to the present. A survey of all these catalogues produced the following items:

Manuscripts
MS. 800. Papers of Emile Cammaerts (1876-1953), Professor of Belgian Studies at the University of London, 1931-47. He was deeply involved in Belgian politics and Anglo-Belgian relations. There is material relating to both world wars and, in particular, his deep involvement in the public defence of King Leopold III from May 1940 to the abdication crisis of 1950. Papers relating directly to Leopold are restricted until after his death. The papers are divided into personal papers and correspondence, 1897-1967; Belgian politics and affairs, 1906-53;

literary papers, 1906-53; University of London, 1931-51; and religion, 1927-53.

MS. 813. 'Notes for H.R.H. The Prince of Wales' Visit 1925' by Sir Reginald Tower, Minister Plenipotentiary to Argentina and Paraguay, 1910-19. The notes include 'Argentina's position in the world today with reference to the war and her relations to neighbouring countries', 'Brief retrospect on Argentine politics and Argentina's attitude during the war', and 'Persons who had enemy connections or sympathies in varying degree during the war'.

MS. 817, Diaries of Lt. Col. Alfred Claude Bromhead (1876-1963), who was seconded for special service to the Russian armies, February 1916 — January 1917, and again, April — September 1917. The diaries give a daily detailed account of events, encounters and conversations during these periods. Bromhead's function was the showing of propaganda films to the Russian forces. His work took him to the Finnish, Baltic, Ukrainian, Caucasian and Turkish, and Rumanian fronts. There is also a ts. carbon copy of the diaries, with an introduction by Maj. J. Bromhead. A copy of this last is also in the Imperial War Museum (see p. 106).

Microfilms of Manuscript Material

MIC. 124. Auswärtiges Amt: German Foreign Office documents at Whaddon Hall, Bucks., relating to Italy, 1867-1920, reproduced on 25 reels of microfilm. See American Historical Association, Committee for the Study of War Documents, *A Catalogue of files and microfilms of the German Foreign Ministry Archives, 1867-1920* (Oxford 1959).

MIC. 166. US National Archives: WWII collection of seized enemy records. Material relating to the German campaign in the Balkans and the offensive against the USSR, containing HQ of the German Armed Forces High Command; HQ of the German Army High Command; German Field Commands: Armies; and German Field Commands: Panzer Armies.

Archives Department, Victoria Library, 160 Buckingham Palace Road, LONDON SW1W 9UD

The Victoria Library contains the pre-1965 archives of the former City of Westminster.

WORLD WAR II

Emergency Committee minutes, 1939-45.
Civil Defence records, 1939-45, including a map of incidents in the city,

1940-5; incidents reports, 1940-5; and ten albums of bomb damage photographs. Unlisted.

'The War in Westminster: a summary report of the City Council's Civil Defence and related services, compiled by the City Librarian on the instructions of the Emergency Committee', May 1945, 16 pp.

Walthamstow Museum of Local History, Old Vestry House, Vestry Road, Walthamstow, LONDON E17 9NH

Enquiries should be made to the Curator

WORLD WAR I

Volunteer Training Corps, Walthamstow, Hoe Street Company, minutes, 1915-19.

Essex Volunteer Regiment, Walthamstow Battalion, Hoe Street Company, accounts, etc., 1916-19.

WORLD WAR II

Walthamstow Borough Council, papers regarding war damage repairs, 1943-5.

Walthamstow, Chingford and Leyton Civil Defence papers, (?)1939-64, unsorted.

Plan of Lebus Factory, Ferry Lane, Walthamstow, showing underground shelters.

Kent County Archives Office, County Hall, MAIDSTONE, Kent ME14 1XQ

Chevining Papers

This collection includes papers of James Richard Stanhope, 7th Earl Stanhope and 13th Earl of Chesterfield (1880-1967). Parliamentary Secretary to the War Office, 1918-19; 1st Lord of the Admiralty, 1938-9; and Lord President of the Council, 1939-40.

Minutes of the Kent Territorial and Auxiliary Forces Association and committees, 1908-68. **MD/TA.**

Queen's Own Royal West Kent Regiment, records, 1847-1966. The material covers both wars, including war diaries for ten battalions in WWI and a ts. copy of the diary of Gen. Charles Townshend at Kut,

1915-16. **WKR.** Virtually all of the documentary material relating to the regiment is now in the Archives Office but a small amount remains at the Regimental Museum in support of its exhibits. The Museum is located at the Maidstone Museums and Art Gallery, St. Faith's Street, Maidstone.

WORLD WAR I

Amherst MSS, containing *inter alia* a description of life in the trenches, 1915-17, by Hugh Amherst, 4th Earl Amherst (1856-1927).
Papers of the clerk of the County Council acting in other capacities during WWI.
West Kent Appeal Tribunal under the Military Services Acts, 1916-18.
Local Emergency Committee, correspondence. **C/A2/6.**
Emergency labour scheme for London defences. **C/A2/8.**
Recruitment, correspondence and other papers. **C/A2/13-14.**
National Service, correspondence. **C/A2/15.**

WORLD WAR II

Proceedings of the County Council, special report, 'The County Administration in the War 1939-1945'.
County Council minutes: ARP, 1936-9; Kent Emergency, Southeastern Civil Defence Region, 1939-47.
Civil Defence Division, various documents including daily incident maps, war diaries, photographs of bomb damage, incident reports, etc.

John Rylands University Library of Manchester, Deansgate, MANCHESTER M3 3EH

Field-Marshal Sir Claude John Eyre Auchinleck (b. 1884)

GOC-in-C Norway 1940; GOC Southern Command, 1940; C-in-C India, 1941 and 1943-7; C-in-C Middle East, 1941-2; and War Member, Viceroy's Executive Council (India), 1943-6. There are only a few papers before 1940, the majority being copies of official papers and notes concerning all of his commands.

Manchester Public Libraries, Archives Department, Central Library, MANCHESTER M2 5PD

MANCHESTER REGIMENT COLLECTION

These records, which were formerly in the regimental museum at Ladysmith Barracks, Ashton-under-Lyne, include the following relevant material:

Regimental diaries, records of events and index of stations, two vols, 1758-1945.

Historical records, comprising digests of services, 1758-1939, and official war diaries, 1900-50.

Operation orders and reports, 1899-1954.

Histories, including officially published accounts, personal diaries and contributions by members of the regiment.

Various other administrative categories, such as commissions, warrants, attestations, accounts, organisation and training, etc.

WORLD WAR I

Papers of 2nd Lt. W. J. Pegge, 1/6 Rifle Battalion, King's Liverpool Regiment, including two nominal rolls and foot books, 1918 and n.d.; two field message books, 1917-18; and several notebooks on training and trench maps. M198.

Transcripts of letters from Walter Dixon Scott about life in the army. Scott was killed in the Dardanelles, October 1915. MISC/391.

Letters referring to a bomb dropping near the British Museum, 1915. L1/58/3/454, 457.

Letters concerning ten Zeppelins passing over Dover and the possibility of closing the Public Record Office, 1916. L1/58/3/55.

Letters to Mrs M. G. Fawcett from members of the International Women's Suffrage Alliance, containing references to the war's effect on the movement, the attitude of the United States to WWI and the efforts of the international peace movement. M50/2/22/16-276.

WORLD WAR II

Manchester Information Committee, minutes and correspondence, 1940-5. M77.

Simon Archives, private papers of Sir Ernest Darwin Simon, 1st Baron Simon of Wythenshawe (1879-1960), comprising a large collection of files and notebooks reflecting his many public interests. Papers relating to the Ministry of Information, 1939, are **M11/14/26, 27**, and **M11/16/19**. Special application for consultation is required.

Derbyshire Record Office, County Offices, MATLOCK, Derbyshire DE4 3AG

Derby Territorial and Auxiliary Forces Association: minutes. 1907-68; annual reports and accounts, 1924-67; and County Cadet meeting minutes, 1942-68. **D.530 R/—**.

WORLD WAR I

Lord Lieutenant's circular letter on defence, 1914, and papers concerning local presentations to Bdr. C. F. Stone VC, MM and Lance Cpl. Meakin MM, 1918. **D302 Z/08**.
Report of Belper Committee for helping Belgian refugees, 1915. **D302 Z/0Z8**.
Xerox copy of field service card sent by Charles Swift, despatch rider in the Royal Corps of Signals, 1915. **D437 Z/Z1**.
Unlisted correspondence and papers on the territorial service of Col. Herbert Brooke-Taylor, *c.* 1908-22, including recruitment for WWI and County records of war service. **D.504 M/—**.
Gunner J. B. Titterton, letters from the Western Front commenting on conditions in the trenches, recruits, the superior calibre of regular army men of all ranks, poor French civilian morale resulting from lack of food, the final German rout, and open country beyond the Hindenburg Line, 1917-19. **D.557B/—** and **849 Z/—**.
Ruhleben Internment Camp, school prospectus, 1917. **D.881 M/Z1**.
Capt. W. K. S. Haslam, Dp Battery, 232nd Brigade, RAF BEF France, war diary for 6 July 1916 — 24 April 1917. The collection also contains MS trench sector plans for Ronsart to 31 August 1916, Mouchy au Bois (*c.* 18 July 1916), La Brazelle Farm, Pigeon and Biez Woods taken by 46th Division, 5 March 1917, and part printed Trench Map 57D NE Douchy les Ayette corrected to 7 September 1916 with field artillery manuals and hectograph instruction booklet on the use of No. 1 Director. **D.1079 M/—** unlisted.
William Valentine Ball, ts. memoirs including his arrivals in Buenos Aires on 4 October 1913, reports of pre-war fighting between French and Germans in city Cafés, his return with a party of British to join the army just before the outbreak of war, and his posting with 1/4 Queens

Own Royal West Kent Regiment, then to India. Ended as OC No. 43
Brigade Supply Troop, Risalpur, 1921.
Annual statement of accounts of the temporary Isolation Hospital at
Tideswell, showing its use as temporary accommodation for Belgian
refugees, 1915. **D.1494 A/PZ3.**

WORLD WAR II

German propaganda leaflet on the V1, 1944. **D.545 Z/Z1.**
Photographs of a Handley Page Halifax Mark III and crew, with an
escape phrase book and Eisenhower circular letter, 1944. **D.826M/−.**
Sherwood Foresters, miscellaneous papers, late 19-20th century,
including Maj. Gen. H. Murray, 6th British Armoured Division, General
Order of the Day, Udine, 5 May 1945. **D828Z/−.**
Pvt. Harry Iremonger, Japanese notebook giving dates of capture at
Barling, 30 December 1941; subsequent moves including railway work
in Thailand and Japan, 1941-5; patriotic and other verses relating to his
capture and imprisonment; addresses; and three cards home from No. 2
POW Camp, Thailand. **Temporary deposit.**

The Air Photograph Library, Department of Geography,
University of Keele, Keele, NEWCASTLE, Staffordshire
ST5 5BG

The University of Keele is custodian for the Ministry of Defence and
the Public Record Office of a unique library of 7,500,000 photographic
prints. The major part of the collection is 5,500,000 prints representing
a major section of the Library of the Allied Central Interpretation Unit,
RAF Medmenham, accumulated between November 1939 and May
1945. The collection covers Western Europe but does not include any
country now a member of the Warsaw Pact or any neutral country in
WWII. There is no cover for the United Kingdom held at Keele.
In addition to the Western European collection, there are 3,295 boxes
of small scale survey photographs of former British colonial territories
in Asia and Africa, which constitute the Reserve Library of the
Directorate of Overseas Surveys.
Enquiries should be addressed to the Keeper of Aerial Photography and
should contain the name of an identifiable feature, the latitude and
logitude from Greenwich of the site required to the nearest minute, and
a map extract or tracing from a published map showing the precise area
required. If the date of an incident is significant, a range of acceptable
dates should be added.

XVth/XIXth The King's Royal Hussars, Home Headquarters, Fenham Barracks, NEWCASTLE UPON TYNE NE2 4NP

The regimental museums of the XVth/XIXth The King's Royal Hussars and the Northumberland Hussars are housed in the John George Joicey Museum, City Road, Newcastle upon Tyne, but most of the documentary and manuscript material relating to both regiments is held at Home Headquarters, XVth/XIXth The King's Royal Hussars. Enquiries should be made to the Curator at Home Headquarters.

WORLD WAR I

XVth/XIXth The King's Royal Hussars:
Sgt. D. Brunton, 19th QAOR Hussars, 'Diary of the Great War'.
Lt. F. E. de Groot, 15th The King's Royal Hussars, eyewitness account of the first time tanks were used at the battle of the Somme, 26 September 1916.
Lt. F. E. de Groot's original list of a digging party, taken from a field message book, 17 September 1916.
Lt. F. E. de Groot, officer's advance book No. 321.
Letter of 2 October 1916 from 1st Cavalry Division to 9th Cavalry Brigade referring to work by digging party at No. 4.
14th Reserve Cavalry Regiment, regimental orders issued by Col. F. K. G. Aylmer, 26 June 1915 — 31 December 1915 and 1 January — 4 April 1916.
Northumberland Hussars:
Lt. I. A. Patterson, personal letters to his mother and sister from Belgium and France, 1914-18.
Letters from the POW camp at Kaustigall by Pillau, East Prussia.
Extract of regimental order, 10 November 1914, visit by Sir John French to congratulate the regiment on being the TA regiment in action.
C Squadron diary kept by Sgt. Maj. Halliday, October — November 1914.

WORLD WAR II

XVth/XIXth The King's Royal Hussars:
Campaign diary, Northwest Europe, 1944-5.

Northumberland Record Office, Melton Park, North Gosforth, NEWCASTLE UPON TYNE NE3 5QX

Northumberland Territorial and Auxiliary Forces Association, records, 1908-64.

WORLD WAR I

Recruiting pamphlets, 1914-18. **ZAN M13/E23.**
Jasper Ridley, letters home while on service with the BEF in France, 1914-15. **ZRI 26/17.**
Capt. J. C. Spence, RAMC, photocopy of his diary, 1915-16. **NRO 1010.**

WORLD WAR II

4th Northumberland (Hexham) Home Guard, papers and photographs relating to F Company, 1940-4, and G Company, 1939-45.
County Civil Defence administrative files, 1937-45.
Blyth Civil Defence and ARP records, 1938-68.

Tyne and Wear Archives Department, County Record Office, 7 Saville Place, NEWCASTLE UPON TYNE NE1 8DQ

WORLD WAR I

Minutes of the Naval and Military Hostel, 1914-18.
Bundle of forms relating to the local tribunal under the Military Services Act, 1916, with comments of the military representative.
File of objections by Britons, 1915-16.
Certificate A of RFC, 1916, with letter from a POW at Holzminden, Hanover to his parents, 1917.

WORLD WAR II

Watch (ARP) Committee minutes, Newcastle, February 1938 — September 1941.
ARP files, Sunderland.
Lord Mayor's Emergency Committee minutes, Newcastle, 1939-40.
Emergency (Civil Defence) Committee minutes, Newcastle, 1941-63.

Newcastle upon Tyne University Library, Queen Victoria Road, NEWCASTLE UPON TYNE NE1 7RU

Runciman Papers
Walter Runciman, 1st Viscount Runciman of Doxford (1870-1949).

President of the Board of Trade, 1914-16, and Lord President of the
Council, 1938-9. The collection contains many Cabinet papers, WWI
documents, reports, much correspondence, and papers referring to his
mission to Czechoslovakia, 1938. See *NRA 13873* for a detailed listing.

Trevelyan Papers
Sir Charles Philips Trevelyan, 3rd Baron Trevelyan of Wallington
(1870-1958). MP and Parliamentary Secretary to the Board of
Education, 1908-14, resigning on the outbreak of war to take a leading
role in the Union of Democratic Control. The collection contains many
notes for speeches; Parliamentary papers relating to the war; letters and
papers concerning the formation of the Union of Democratic Control
and its activities, 1914-26; letters referring to his expulsion from the
Labour Party over the Cripps memorandum of 1939; and a MS
notebook and letters from Russia, 1939. See *NRA 12238* for a detailed
listing.

North Riding County Record Office, County Hall, NORTHALLERTON, North Yorkshire DL7 8SG

North Yorkshire Territorial and Auxiliary Forces Association, records,
1908-67. **NG/TA.**

North Riding of Yorkshire County Council Records.
Finance and General Purposes Committee, ARP Sub-committee,
minutes, 1936-41.
Emergency Committee for Civil Defence, minutes, 1939-41.
Emergency Committee, minutes, 1939-46.
NRCC Social Services Committee files relating to emergency feeding
and rest centres, emergency hospital schemes, etc, 1939-47.

District Council Records
Aysgarth RDC: ARP Committee minutes, 1938-43; ten ARP correspon-
dence files, 1939-45; and two Invasion Committee correspondence files,
1942-44.
A number of the RDC and UDC records in the custody of the Record
Office contain files on ARP, Civil Defence, billeting and evacuation.

Gisborough (Chaloner) Archive
Letters of condolence when Tim Chaloner was missing, 1916.
ZFM 321B.
Letters, mainly to and from Tim Chaloner as a POW, 1916-19.
ZFM 321C.

Extracts from letters written in France by Maj. C. L. A. Ward-Jackson, bound ts., 1915-18. **ZFM 321F.**
WWII letters and papers. **ZFM 323.**

Marquess of Zetland Archive
ZNK X10. The archive may contain some WWII letters of the 2nd Marquess and does contain the following Parliamentary papers relating to WWI:
Official reports of Commons debates for 27 July 1914, extract only, and 3-6 August 1914.
Diplomatic correspondence concerning WWI, published by the French Government and presented to Parliament, December 1914, HMSO.
Identical text of the above correspondence, published by *The Times* as 'The French Yellow Book'.
Correspondence relating to the 'European Crisis', British diplomatic documents, presented to Parliament, August 1914, HMSO.
Report of a select sub-committee of the CID on the 'Insurance of British Shipping in time of War', dated 30 April 1914 and printed at the Foreign Office, 2 August 1914.
Despatch for the British Ambassador at Berlin concerning the rupture of diplomatic relations with the German Government, presented to Parliament, August 1914, HMSO.
Printed answers to Parliamentary questions on the Belgian Neutrality Treaty, 5 August 1914.
Vote of £100 million credit for naval and military operations arising out of the war, 5 August 1914.
Supplementary estimate for additional naval officers and men, 5 August 1914.
Supplementary estimate for additional soldiers, 5 August 1914.
Currency and Bank Notes Bill, 6 August 1914.
Despatch from the British Ambassador at Vienna referring to the rupture of diplomatic relations with the Austro-Hungarian Government, presented to Parliament, September 1914.
Correspondence regarding the naval and military assistance granted to the British Government by her Overseas Dominions, presented to Parliament, September 1914.
Correspondence relating to gifts of foodstuffs and other supplies to the British Government from her Overseas Dominions and Colonies, presented to Parliament, September 1914.
Despatches from the British Ambassador at Berlin relating to an official German organisation for influencing the press of other countries, presented to Parliament, September 1914.
Documents respecting the negotiations preceding the war, published by the Russian Government and presented to Parliament, October 1914.

Diplomatic correspondence concerning the war, published by the Belgian Government and presented to Parliament, October 1914.

Correspondence regarding events leading to the rupture of relations with Turkey, presented to Parliament, November 1914.

Financial Statement, 1914-15, with rates of income tax and super tax, 18 November 1914.

Printed answers to Parliamentary questions on naval casualties, 25 November 1914.

Correspondence regarding gifts from the British Overseas Dominions and Colonies, presented to Parliament, December 1914.

Despatch from the British Ambassador at Constantinople summarising events leading up to the rupture of relations with Turkey and the reply presented to Parliament, December 1914,

Despatch from the British Ambassador at Petrograd enclosing a memorandum on the subject of the temperance measures adopted in Russia since the outbreak of war, presented to Parliament, January 1915.

Austrian and German papers found in possession of Mr James F. J. Archibald, Falmouth, 30 August 1915.

MISCELLANEOUS

Newspaper cutting about the killing of Belgian priests.

Newspaper cuttings from *The Times* about Bethmann Hollweg's attempted justification of his "scrap of paper" remark, 26-27 January 1915.

Reprint of Will Irwin's account in the *Daily Mail,* of the battle of Ypres.

Eight sheets of MS notes for speeches.

Northamptonshire Record Office, Delapré Abbey,
NORTHAMPTON NN4 9AW

WORLD WAR II

RDC: ARP, Civil Defence, Fire Brigade and food control files, 1939-45.

County Council: ARP, evacuation hostels and Civil Defence records, 1935-62.

Territorial Forces Association: Northamptonshire minutes, 1908-50; Huntingdonshire minutes, 1922-50; and joint minutes, 1951-68.

Northampton Home Guard, 12th Battalion: records, 1940-7; muster roll, 1945; and photograph album, 1941-4.

*Norfolk Record Office, Central Library, NORWICH
NR2 1NJ*

Norfolk Territorial and Auxiliary Forces Association, minutes and
other papers, 1908-68.

WORLD WAR I

Invasion emergency papers, Ingham area, 1914-18.
Appeal for lower bread consumption, 1917 (East Barsham parish
records).
Invasion instructions, 1917 (Fersfield parish records).
War diary of F. Dunham of the Cyclists' Battalion, 25th London
Regiment on the Western Front, 1916-18, published as *The Long Carry*
(1970).
Suffolk POW's Aid Committee subscription book, WWI (Carlton
Colville parish records).

WORLD WAR II

North Walsham, Home Guard papers, 1943-4.
Norwich Corporation, ARP files, 1939-45.
Norwich and Great Yarmouth, Xerox copies of details of air raids,
1939-45.
Great Yarmouth Borough Archives: Town Clerk's Department, files and
papers concerning war damage, ARP, etc., 1940-57; and Civil Defence
records, including control logs, air raid reports and casualty returns,
1939-47.
Norfolk County Council: ARP Committee files, 1938-45; and Civil
Defence war diary, 1939-45. **C/AR1/1-35.**
Blakeney Invasion Committee papers, 1940-2. **NRS 26886, 171 x 5.**
ARP and Civil Defence papers, 1939-45 (Burgh St. Margaret and
Swaffham parish records).
Papers relating to evacuation, 1939-45 (Winfarthing parish records).
Forces welfare fund papers, 1939-45 (Swaffham parish records).

*The Royal Norfolk Regiment Museum, Britannia Barracks,
NORWICH NOR 02R*

Application to use the records should be made to the Regimental
Secretary.

WORLD WAR I

War diaries, 1914-18, of the 1st, 2nd, 1/4th, 1/5th, 7th (S), 8th (S), 9th (S) and 12th (S) Battalions.

Miscellaneous papers relating to the 1st, 2nd, 4th and 5th Battalions.

Standing orders, 10th Battalion, 1915.

War casualties, MS and official records of officers and soldiers.

Roll of POWs, Kut-el-Amara.

Regimental Roll of officers, 1882-1927.

Roll of officers of 4th Battalion, 1860-1920.

Roll of officers holding regular commissions, 1685-1921.

Collection of newspaper cuttings relating to the history of the Norfolk Regiment, 1857-1930.

Battle honours, WWI and Afghan War of 1919.

Inspection reports and parade states, 1914-18.

Digest of services, 1st Battalion, 1909-39.

Digest of services, 2nd Battalion, 1857-1939.

Reports of courts-martial, 1st Battalion, 1905-7, not open to the public.

Miscellaneous papers and collection of newspapers relating to volunteers, 1914-18.

Col. P. V. P. Stone, personal papers, including maps and field notes.

Lt. Col. F. C. Lodge, diary and personal papers.

Maj. F. DeW. Harman, diaries and miscellaneous papers.

Capt. Dunn, service documents and miscellaneous papers.

Lt. J. B. Young, miscellaneous papers.

Capt. J. McQueen, personal papers and correspondence.

WORLD WAR II

War diary, 2nd Battalion, 10-28 May 1940 and 1945-6.

Recommendations for decorations, 1st and 2nd Battalions.

Nominal Roll of 4th, 5th and 6th Battalions, Malaya, 1942-5.

Register of deaths and graves of POWs, Malaya, 1942-5.

Battle honours, 1939-45.

Papers, documents and correspondence relating to the massacre of A Company, 2nd Battalion at Le Paradis, 1940.

Casualties, 1939-45, official record of officers and soldiers.

Correspondence and miscellaneous papers concerning the provision of comforts for POWs.

Norfolk Home Guard, MS history.

Lt. Col. G. P. S. de Wilton, diaries.

Miscellaneous papers concerning the escape from captivity of Lt. F. Fitch.

Maj. Gen. E. C. Hayes, diary describing the Japanese surrender to China.

Lt. Col. J. E. Knight, collection of personal papers and documents regarding the Malayan campaign and POW camp.

Nottingham City Archives Office, The Guildhall, NOTTINGHAM NG1 4BT

The Archives Office is shortly to be amalgamated with the Nottingham-shire Record Office.

WORLD WAR I

War diaries of Pvt. Joseph Albert Bodill, driver in Army Service Corps Motor Transport on the Western Front, 3 January 1917 — 1 March 1918 and 22 March — 31 December 1918. **M24, 251.**

Copy of a war diary on the Western Front, kept by the commanding officer of the 5th Battalion, Sherwood Foresters, together with operation orders, reports of some engagements and maps, 1914-19, compiled by L. W. de Grave as ts. record for the Battalion in 1931. **M24, 258.**

Charles Edward Coulthard, vol. of reminiscences, including his service in the RAMC in Egypt and Palestine, 1915-19, compiled *c*. 1963 and restricted until 2001. **M24, 531.**

Dame Laura Knight, letters to her husband Harold describing the Nuremberg trials, at which she was official artist, with some sketches of defendants, 1946. **M24, 067.**

Two letters of . . . Hickling, one from Longmoor camp, Hampshire, and the other from France to his daughter Vera, describing army life, 1917. **M19, 835-6.**

Incomplete letter from (?)E. H. Cupitt to Annie and Frank, describing an air raid on Nottingham, 1915. **M12, 625.**

WORLD WAR II

Nottingham Air Raid Wardens' papers, including minutes of commanders' meetings, notes and correspondence regarding training and enrolment, and reports of bombs dropped, 1938-45. **ARP/1-22.**

ARP papers from the City Engineer's Department, including claim forms for damages sustained during bombings.

Nottinghamshire Record Office, County House,
High Pavement, NOTTINGHAM NG1 1HR

Territorial and Auxiliary Forces Association of the County of
Nottingham: minute books, 1908-69; register of the National Reserve,
1911-14; and various committee minute books.

WORLD WAR I

Letter of 18 March 1918 from Percy Forrest referring to army life in
France. **DD.446/5.**
Queries for local emergency committees, administrative arrangements
for evacuation of population and other emergency measures in case of
invasion, issued by the Nottingham Chief Constable, 6 November 1917.
DD.371/1.
'Instructions for the Guidance of the Civil population in the Event of a
landing by the Enemy in this County', printed government circular,
c. 1917. **DD.371/3.**
'Emergency Measures in the Event of a Hostile Landing', revised
instructions for emergency committees, *c.* 1917. **DD.371/4.**
Map of Nottinghamshire, showing routes for refugees from Lincolnshire
and roads to be reserved for military use in the event of invasion,
c. 1917. **DD.371/6.**
W. Hunt, three diaries covering his entire war service in France, 19
December 1916 — 12 December 1917 and 22 March — 7 December
1918, including three maps of war areas with fronts marked, Picardy
and Ypres areas, *c.* 1917-18. **DD.299/1-6.**

WORLD WAR II

Official war pamphlets, leaflets and notices containing advice and
instructions, issued by the British Government and Nottingham
Corporation, with a German propaganda leaflet dropped in England,
c. August 1940. **DDTS addit. 14/6/1-46.**
Nottinghamshire Civil Defence:
War diaries, June 1940 — May 1945. **CD 1/1-3.**
Files relating to the Minister of Home Security, 1940-5. **CD 1/4-5.**
Civil and military combined defence correspondence, 1942. **CD 2/2.**
Home Guard sector defence schemes, 1940-4. **CD 2/4.**
Files referring to exercises 'Progressive' and 'Lea', 1943. **CD 2/5-6.**
County Invasion Committee correspondence, 1942. **CD 3/1.**
There are many more items relating to invasion defence planning,

co-ordination with the RAF, liaison, emergency measures, incident returns and files concerning specific local authorities.

Sherwood Foresters Regimental Museum, The Castle, NOTTINGHAM

The Museum holds an uncatalogued collection of war diaries, manuscripts, maps and photographs. Enquiries should be made to the Curator.

University of Nottingham Library, University Park, NOTTINGHAM NG7 2RD

Drury-Lowe MSS
Packet of photographs taken at the Front, 1915, and other military papers immediately after the war, 1919. **Dr N 32-34.**
Correspondence relating to No. 1 Platoon, Spondon Home Guard, 1941. **Dr N 35.**

Middleton MSS
Letters, 1913-15, of Lt. Francis G. G. Willoughby, 9th Battalion, Rifle Brigade, killed at Flanders on 9 August 1915. **Mi 4 F 157-169.**
Letters, 1900-16, of Commander Henry E. D. H. Willoughby RN, killed at the battle of Jutland in 1916. **Mi 4 F 170-190.**
Letters of Maj. Michael P. G. Willoughby, later 11th Lord Middleton, concerning the Mesopotamia campaign, 1915-16 and 1918-19. **Mi 4 F 192-558.**

Cowley MSS
Maj. George Evelyn Cowley, small group of letters sent to his father while on active service, 1915-18, and letters about him, 1919. **Co C 19-25.**

Miscellaneous MSS
The German occupation of Lille, 1914-18, one portfolio and letters and enclosures. **Acc. 96 + 327.**
German propaganda leaflet, 1940. **Acc. 130.**
Willoughby R. Norman Deposit: two vols printed, *The Grenadier Guards in the War of 1939-1945* (Aldershot, 1949); and one photocopy of *Destruction of the German Armies in Western Europe,* 6 June 1944 — 9 May 1945, HQ 12th Army Group, restricted. **Acc. 295.**

OXFORD

As one of the most famous university towns of England, Oxford with its many colleges and the Bodleian Library has much to offer the student of modern British history. Although lacking a central modern repository for private collections such as Cambridge possesses in Churchill College, Oxford has two extensive and unique modern archives in Rhodes House and the Middle East Centre of St. Antony's College. The Bodleian Library contains important collections as well as much lower level material. As with Cambridge, however, many of the Oxford college libraries have no modern holdings relevant to the two world wars. For a discussion of and guide to the libraries of Oxford, see Paul Morgan, *Oxford Libraries outside the Bodleian* (Oxford, Bodleian Library, 1973).

Department of Western Manuscripts, Bodleian Library, OXFORD OX1 3BG

The Bodleian Library houses an extensive collection of western manuscripts. There is a printed catalogue to 1915, while the accessions of succeeding years are catalogued in typescript with a card index. Lists can be found in the *Bodleian Quarterly Record* (later the *Bodleian Library Record*) and the annual reports of the Library. Intending researchers should write initally stating their interests and requesting an application for a reader's ticket.

Christopher Addison
Christopher Addison, 1st Viscount Addison (1869-1951). Parliamentary Secretary to the Ministry of Munitions, 1915-16, and Minister of Munitions, 1916 — July 1917. 136 box files mostly relating to his work at the Ministry of Munitions, and his diary, June 1914 — February 1919, subsequently published as *Four and a Half Years* (1934). The collection is uncatalogued at present although a rough list is available. **Ref. Addison Papers.**

Herbert Henry Asquith
Herbert Henry Asquith, 1st Earl of Oxford and Asquith (1852-1928). Prime Minister, 1908-16, and Secretary of State for War, March — August 1914. Letters, memoranda and pamphlets covering most aspects of his administration. **Ref. MSS. Asquith 1-152. MS.Eng.hist.g.24** is his engagement diary for 1915.

James Bryce
James Bryce, Viscount Bryce (1838-1922). British Ambassador to the United States, 1907-13. Papers and correspondence covering his career and life, partly catalogued. **Ref. Bryce Papers.**

L. B. Cholmondely
Correspondence of the Rev. Lionel B. Cholmondely, Chaplain to the British Embassy in Tokyo, 1914-20. Many of the letters are from participants in the war and some of Cholmondely's contain comment on Japanese attitudes and reactions. **MS.Eng.lett.d.99.**

Andrew Clark
'Echoes of the Great War in an Essex Village', written and compiled by the Rev. Andrew Clark of Chelmsford, Essex. 92 vols. of daily impressions, including letters and other material. **MSS.Eng.hist.c.88-177c.** The collection also contains 65 vols. of news-cuttings, collected and annotated by Clark under the title 'English Words in Wartime', 1914-19. **MSS.Eng.misc.e.265-329.**

Harry Crookshank
Harry Frederick Comfort Crookshank, Viscount Crookshank (1893-1961). Financial Secretary to the Treasury, 1939-43, and Postmaster General, 1942-5. Mostly notes for speeches and press-cuttings, with his diary for July 1934 – October 1951. **MS.Eng.hist.b.223** and **c.596-606.**

Lionel George Curtis (1872-1955)
Fellow of All Souls College, Oxford. There are many publications on international affairs. The papers are in the process of being catalogued.

Sir Willoughby Hyett Dickinson
Papers relating to the League of Nations Movement in Britain, 1914-44. **MS.Eng.hist.c.402-407.**

Sir Charles Patrick Duff (1889-1972)
Diary with notes of an officer in the Gallipoli campaign, 19 March 1915 – 28 March 1916. **Dep.d.142-144.**

H. A. L. Fisher (1865-1940)
Papers of this historian including a large collection of letters from many politicians and statesmen. **Box 3/1** contains a packet labelled 'Army commissions for Indians 1916'; **box 9/1**, 'Wartime visits to France'; **box 11a.**, miscellaneous printed papers on the war; and **box 24**, miscellaneous notes on conversations with David Lloyd George.

R. W. M. Gibbs
Diary with daily comment and many news-cuttings on the war, 1914-20. **MS.Eng.misc.c.159-197.**

Strickland Gibson
Notes on musketry training, November — December 1916, at the Eastern Command School of Musketry, Hythe. **MS.Eng.misc.e.87.**

Martin Gilbert
Uncatalogued material: photocopy of the autobiography of Margo Asquith, 1914-15; photocopy of the diary of Field-Marshal Sir Henry Wilson, Russia, 1917; and Dunlop-Smith's original diary, Paris Peace Conference, 1919.

Sir Edward Grey
Sir Edward Grey, 1st Viscount Grey of Fallodon (1862-1933). 101 letters to Sir Henry Newbolt, 1900-32. **MS.Eng.lett.d.316.** Letters to Louise Creighton, wife of Bishop Mandell Creighton, 1911-31. **MS.Eng.lett.e.73/2.**

Sir Edward Grigg
Sir Edward William Macleay Grigg, 1st Baron Altrincham (1879-1955). Parliamentary Secretary to the Ministry of Information, 1939-40; Financial Secretary to the War Office, 1940; Joint Under-Secretary to the War Office, 1940-2; and Minister Resident in the Middle East, 1944-5. There is little relating to his official career. **MSS. Film 999-1013.**

Ernest Morris Hains
Letters of Acting Cpl. Ernest Morris Hains, 7th Indian Division Signal Company, EEF, to his wife, 1916-19, with a few postcards and photographs, a printed letter of thanks from Gen. E. H. H. Allenby, 26 September 1918, and a demobilisation chit, 29 March 1919. **MS.Eng.lett.d.266.**

Lewis Harcourt
Lewis Harcourt, 1st Viscount Harcourt (1863-1922). Secretary of State for the Colonies, 1910-15; Acting President of the Board of Trade, 1915-16; and deep involvement in the negotiations with Germany, 1911-14. The collection contains many Cabinet papers referring to the war, and other papers concerning the administration of and military operations involving the colonies. **Ref. Harcourt Papers.**

Alfred Harmsworth
Alfred Charles William Harmsworth, 1st Viscount Harmsworth (1864-1922). Chairman of the British War Mission to the United States, 1917; Chairman of the British Mission to the United States, 1917-18; and Director of Propaganda in Enemy Countries, 1918. Ts. copies in chronological order of bulletins to the *Daily Mail*, 1916-20. **MS.Eng.hist.d.303-305.**

(William) Denis Johnston (b. 1901)
BBC war correspondent in the Middle East, Italy, France and Germany, 1942-5. Dionysia, war memoirs, revised and published as *Nine Rivers from Jordan* (1953). **MS.Eng.misc.d.314-316.**

T. E. Lawrence
Transcripts of letters from T. E. Lawrence, W. G. Lawrence and F. H. Lawrence mainly to their mother, 1905-34, published by M. R. Lawrence as *The Home Letters of T. E. Lawrence and his Brothers* (1954). **MS.Eng.lett.c.146-147.** Other Lawrence papers held by the Library are not available until AD 2000.

J. L. Lemberger
Army slang, 1914-18, collected by J. L. Lemberger and published in the *Bodleian Quarterly Record*, II (1917-19), 123-5 and 152-4. **MS.Eng.misc.d.93.**

Sir Donald Maclean (1864-1932)
Uncatalogued papers, 1906-19, relating mainly to general party politics and his chairmanship of the Liberal Party, 1919-21. **Dep.a.49-50, c.465-471, 473, and e.171.**

Sir James MacPherson
Sir James Ian MacPherson, 1st Baron Strathcarron (1880-1937). Parliamentary Secretary to the Under-Secretary of State for War, 1914-16, Under-Secretary of State for War and member of the Army Council, 1916-19. There are few relevant papers. **MS.Eng.hist.c.490-492, d.309.**

Sir Frederick Marquis
Sir Frederick James Marquis, 1st Earl of Woolton (1883-1964). Minister of Food, 1940-3, and Minister of Reconstruction, 1943-5. Uncatalogued papers, not available at present. **Ref. Woolton Papers.**

John Masefield (1878-1967)
Autograph and carbon copies of his preface to *The Battle of the*

Somme (1919) with ts. transcripts of autograph reports, **MS.Eng.d.624**; his copy of the Ordnance Survey map of the Somme area, December 1916, used and marked during his researches for *The Battle of the Somme*, **MS.Eng.misc.e.670**; his pocket book for 1917 containing drafts of poems, addresses and notes on the battle of the Somme, **MS.Eng.misc.g.77**; and ten letters to his wife and children from France, February — June 1917, **MS.Eng.lett.d.310, ff. 200-214.**

Sir Alfred Milner
Sir Alfred Milner, Viscount Milner (1854-1925). Member of the War Cabinet, 1916-18, and Secretary of State for War, 1918-19. **107-151** are papers concerning WWI. **Ref. Milner Papers.** Other Milner papers are **MS.Eng.hist.c.686-709, d.362, and e.305-307.**

Walter Monckton
Walter Turner Monckton, 1st Viscount Monckton of Brenchley (1891-1965). Director-General of the Press and Censorship Bureau, 1939-40; Deputy Under-Secretary of State for Foreign Affairs, 1940; Director-General of British Propaganda and Information Services in Cairo, 1941-2; and Solicitor General and delegate on the Allied Reparation Commission in Moscow, 1945. Papers relating to the Ministry of Information, Cairo, and other wartime assignments. **Ref. Monckton Papers.**

Monmouthshire Regiment
3rd Battalion war diary, 1914-16. **MS.Eng.hist.f.9-10.**

(George) Gilbert Murray (1866-1957)
Regius Professor of Greek, University of Oxford, 1908-36; Chairman, League of Nations Union, 1923-38; and author of various publications from 1915 referring to British foreign policy and international affairs. These as yet uncatalogued papers contain many letters concerned with both world wars, particularly a large number from and about conscientious objectors in WWI.

Edward Jonah Nathan
Papers of Edward Jonah Nathan of the Chinese Engineering and Mining Company, including references to his activities during the Japanese occupation of North China, 1939-45; three diaries kept during the occupation, 1941-3; and Col. Peter D. MacFeats' notes and maps for bombing targets in occupied North China, especially the mining areas, 1942. **MS.Eng.hist.c.450-451.**

Sir Matthew Nathan (1862-1939)
Papers, 1876-1939, including diaries for 1914-18 and papers concerning London defences, 1916. Nathan was Under-Secretary to the Lord Lieutenant of Ireland, 1914-16; employed on London defences, 1916; and Secretary to the Ministry of Pensions, 1916-19. **Ref. MSS. Nathan 1-671.**

A. G. S. Norris
'Arcadia to Hiroshima', ts. 1949. **MSS.Eng.misc.d.313.**

William Waldegrave Palmer
William Waldegrave Palmer, 2nd Earl of Selborne (1859-1942). President of the Board of Agriculture, 1915-16. Papers including correspondence with the King, Prime Minister and Cabinet ministers, Cabinet business, sketches of fellow Cabinet members and three vols. of reminiscences. **Ref. Selborne Papers.**

James Paterson
Letters of James Paterson of the London Scottish Regiment to his wife from Belgium, 1914; France, 1914-17; and Italy, 1917. **MS.Eng.hist.c.320.**

Hilda M. Pickard
Account of her escape from Germany after the war began in August 1914, with some drawings and photographs inserted. **MS.Eng. misc.d.790.**

Sir Ernest Pollock
Sir Ernest Murray Pollock, 1st Viscount Hanworth (1861-1936). Controller of the Foreign Trade Department, 1917-19. Some papers referring to his activities at the Paris Peace Conference and one bundle concerning the German war trials of 1921-2. **Ref. Pollock Papers.**

Ewart Rink
Three documents concerning the death of Ewart Rink, a Dutch underground worker, in Auschwitz Concentration Camp, 1942. **MS. Germ.c.14, fols. 43-46.**

Sir Horace Rumbold (1869-1941)
Chargé d'Affaires in Berlin, 1913-14; at the Foreign Office, 1914-16; and British Minister to Switzerland, 1916-19. Uncatalogued papers.

(?)Shand
Autograph album of a conscientious objector named Shand in the

Wakefield Work Centre, 1918, containing some detailed experiences of fellow detainees, 1916-18. **MS.Eng.hist.g.21.**

Selina Bridgeman Shuttleworth
Approximately 300 letters collected by Selina Bridgeman Shuttleworth, widow of Lawrence Ughtred Kay-Shuttleworth, killed in WWI. Her two sons, Richard Ughtred Paul, 2nd Baron, and Ronald Orlando Lawrence, 3rd Baron, were killed in 1940 and 1942 respectively. The uncatalogued letters are from her husband and sons, and from the sons to each other.

Stalag Luft IV
Prospectus of the RAF School for POWs at Stalag Luft VI, Germany, designed, written and illuminated by Sgt. James W. Lambert with a foreword by Sgt. E. Alderton, 1943. **MS.Eng.misc.d.286.**

H. C. T. Stronge
Memorandum on the Czechoslovak Army at the time of the Munich Crisis, September 1938. **MS.Eng.hist.d.150, fols. 147-168.**

Capt. David Euan Wallace (1892-1941)
Secretary to the Ministry of Transport, 1939-40. Ts. copies of entries from his diary, August 1939 — October 1940. **MSS.Eng.hist.c.495-498.**

Commodore Humphrey Thomas Walwyn
Copy of a narrative of the battle of Jutland by Commodore Humphrey Thomas Walwyn of HMS *Warspite*. Extracts were published in H. W. Fawcett and G. W. W. Hooper, eds., *The Fighting at Jutland* (1929). **MS.Eng.hist.c.192.**

Sir Laming Worthington-Evans
Sir Laming Worthington-Evans, 1st Bt. (1868-1931). Parliamentary Secretary to the Ministry of Munitions, 1916-18, and Minister of Blockade, 1918-19. Uncatalogued papers, a few of which relate to Munitions but none to Blockade. **Ref. Worthington-Evans Papers.**

Sir Alfred Zimmern (1879-1957)
Service with the Political Intelligence Department, Foreign Office, 1918-19; Montagu Burton Professor of International Relations, University of Oxford, 1930-44; and Deputy Director, Research Department, Foreign Office, 1943-45. Uncatalogued papers.

Christ Church College, OXFORD

Geoffrey Drage (1860-1955)
Box 6 of these papers contains material relating to German propaganda in Europe and some diplomatic correspondence for Eastern Europe, as well as 20 letters from Sir Maurice Hankey, all concerning WWI.

Marshall of the Royal Air Force Sir Charles Portal (1893-1971)
Air Member for Personnel, 1939-40; AOC-in-C, Bomber Command, 1940; and Chief of Air Staff, 1940-5. The papers consist of copies of correspondence between Portal and Winston Churchill during WWII.

Corpus Christi College, OXFORD

Arthur Francis Hemming (1893-1964)
Principal Assistant Secretary, War Cabinet Offices, 1939-41; Administrative Head, Economic Section, War Cabinet Secretariat, 1939-40, and Central Statistical Office, 1941; Principal Assistant Secretary (Fire Guard), Ministry of Home Security, 1941-4; and Director of Petrol Rationing, Ministry of Fuel and Power, 1944-5. There are diaries for 1938-9, and papers concerning WWII and his secretaryship of the International Council for Non-Intervention in Spain, 1936-49.

Sir Robert C. K. Ensor (1877-1958)
Journalist, author and academic student of international affairs. Private papers relating to the study of British foreign policy in the 20th century.

Nuffield College, OXFORD OX1 1NF

G. D. H. Cole
One envelope of papers of the historian and journalist G. D. H. Cole.

Sir (Richard) Stafford Cripps (1889-1952)
Ambassador to the Soviet Union, 1940-2, and Minister of Aircraft Production, 1942-5. Subject and speech files covering his political life, 1930-50.

Hugh Dalton
Papers of (Edward) Hugh (John Neale) Dalton, Baron Dalton (1887-1962). Minister of Economic Warfare, 1940-2, and President of the

Board of Trade, 1942-5. His other papers are located in the British
Library of Political and Economic Science (see p. 96).

Alfred Emmott
Alfred Emmott, Baron Emmott (1858-1926). Under-Secretary of State
for the Colonies, 1911-14; 1st Commissioner of Works, 1914-15; and
Director, War Trade Department, 1915-19. There is correspondence for
1890-1927 and diaries, 1907-15.

Hugh Gaitskell (1906-63)
Principal Private Secretary to the Minister of Economic Warfare,
1940-2, and Principal Assistant Secretary, Board of Trade, 1942-5.

Frederick Lindemann
Frederick Alexander Lindemann, Viscount Cherwell (1886-1957).
Paymaster General, 1942-5). Private correspondence from 1895; one
box of papers regarding WWI work as a scientist with the RAF; and
papers relating to the war effort, including air offence and defence,
atomic energy, production, etc., 102 boxes.

Herbert Morrison
Herbert Stanley Morrison, Baron Morrison of Lambeth (1888-1965).
Minister of Supply, 1940, and Secretary of State for Home Affairs and
Home Security, 1940-5. There is a small collection of correspondence,
1940-5, and a ts. draft of his autobiography, including much which is
not in the published version. Students must make a written application
to the Warden of the college for use of these papers.

Joseph Pease
Joseph Albert Pease, 1st Baron Gainford (1860-1943). President of the
Board of Education, 1911-15, and Postmaster General, 1916. Correspondence, 1886-1943; diaries, 1908-15; and a few papers from the
work of the Claims Commission in France and Italy, 1915.

Maj. Gen. Francis Rennell Rodd
Maj. Gen. Francis James Rennell Rodd, 2nd Baron Rennell of Rodd
(b. 1895). Service in the Civil Affairs Administration, Middle East, East
Africa and Italy during WWII. There are seven boxes of papers regarding
relief work and agriculture in Somalia, 1943; personal correspondence,
1943; a survey of Madagascar, 1942-3; finances of the Civil Affairs
Branch, Middle East Forces, 1944; and reports relating to the British
military administration in Malaya, 1945-6, Eritrea, 1945, the
Dodecanese Islands, 1945, and Tripolitania, 1945.

John Seely
John Edward Bernard Seely, 1st Baron Mottistone (1868-1947). Secretary of State for War, 1912-14, and Parliamentary Under-Secretary of State to the Ministry of Munitions, 1918-19. 26 boxes including general correspondence, and political, official, literary and miscellaneous papers. There are also military papers concerning the administration of the Canadian Cavalry Brigade, of which Seely was commander, including battle reports, speeches, reports on officers, etc.

Oxfordshire County Record Office, County Hall, OXFORD OX1 1ND

Oxford Territorial and Auxiliary Forces Association, minute books, 1908-59, and committee minutes, agenda, papers, files, photographs, etc.

WORLD WAR I

Ts. notes on trench discipline, *c.* 1914-18. **CH.XL/i/7.**

WORLD WAR II

County Council records: Emergency Civil Defence Committee minutes, September 1939 – December 1941 and January 1942 – September 1945; immediate action file, 1939-45; air raids log book, 1940-4; wardens and other staff, register of addresses and ARP posts; invasion file; and ARP Committee reports, 1937-45.

Rhodes House Library, OXFORD

Rhodes House Library is a division of the Bodleian Library. In addition to its own collections of manuscripts, Rhodes House Library is the depository for the Oxford Colonial Records Project, launched in 1963 to discover and preserve papers in private possession relating to the history of the British colonial period. The two published catalogues are L. B. Frewer, *Manuscript Collections of Africana in Rhodes House Library, Oxford* (1968) and *ibid, Manuscript Collections (excluding Africana) in Rhodes House Library, Oxford* (1970). They each include the relevant Colonial Records Project deposits to date of publication.

Enquiries should be made to the Superintendent, Rhodes House Library.

Abyssinia
History of the Somaliland Scouts, 1941-52; Abyssinian affairs, 1916; the campaign against Italian East Africa, 1940; and intelligence reports, 1917-19. **MSS.Afr.s.551.**

Godfrey Allen
Report on the political situation in the Cameroons under French mandate, July – August 1940. **MSS.Afr.s.424, ff. 240-254.**

Robert K. Allen
War diaries of the Northern Frontier Police, Kenya 1940-4, and personal diaries, 1940-1 and 1943. **MSS.Afr.s.497-502.**

K. M. Anderson
Headmistress's notes and reports on kindergarten and transition classes, Stanley Internment Camp, Hong Kong, and reminiscences of service in Hong Kong, 1923-45. **MSS.Ind.Ocn.s.110.**

Arthur L. Armstrong
Copy of a minute to the Colonial Secretary, Fiji, referring to American forces in Tonga during WWII, ts., n.d. **MSS.Pac.s.35.**

Kenneth James Ball
Five vols. of diaries and other papers as a POW in Singapore, 1942-5. **MSS.Ind.Ocn.r.3.**

H. J. Barnard
Notes regarding the activities of the Nationalist Chinese Kuomintang in North Perak after the Japanese surrender, 1945. **MSS.Ind.Ocn.s.26.**

G. Lennox Barrow
Ts. of unpublished autobiography of life in the Solomon Islands during WWII, entitled 'Outlying Interlude'. **MSS.Pac.s.43.**

Basutoland Resident Commissioner
Enemy subjects, 1914-19, and miscellaneous despatches, 1909-19. **MSS.Afr.s.645.**

Marjorie Binne
Account of the mutiny of the 5th Light Infantry in Singapore, 1915.

Kenneth Ray Blackwell
Ts. of unpublished autobiography covering 1921-44, entitled 'Malay Curry', 1945. **MSS.Ind.Ocn.s.90.**

H. E. Bloxham
Record of meetings with and correspondence addressed to the Japanese authorities by the Central Committee, Changi Internment Camp, Singapore, March — November 1942. **MSS.Ind.Ocn.s.166.**

W. L. Blythe
Papers as Colonial Secretary, Singapore, including accounts of Changi Internment Camp, Singapore, 1942-5. **MSS.Ind.Ocn.s.116.**

I. C. Booth
A short history of the Field Survey Company, Federated Malay States Volunteer Force, ts., 1945. **MSS.Ind.Ocn.s.58.**

C. R. Bowden
Sime Road Internment Camp, Singapore, extracts and summaries from 'Standing Orders for the Civilian Internees', published by the Japanese authorities, 1 December 2604 (1942). **MSS.Ind.Ocn.s.147.**

B. L. Bremner
Letters from Nairobi, mainly concerning the war in East Africa, 1914-15, as Locomotive Superintendent on the Kenya Railway.

R. R. Cambridge
Photocopy of a letter describing his experiences at the evacuation of Singapore, 1942.

A. H. Peter Cardew
Papers relating to the Japanese capture of Singapore: a letter home; report of the Electrical Department; and account of his escape from Singapore, 1942. **MSS.Ind.Ocn.s.77.**

Michael J. P. Casserly
Diary as a POW in Singapore, 8 December 1941 — 11 August 1945; report on the condition of POWs in Thailand, May — December 1943; and extracts from British Army orders and Japanese internment camp orders, February 1942 — June 1943. **MSS.Ind.Ocn.s.212.**

E. G. Chapman
American Red Cross reports on Greek refugee camps in the Belgian Congo, 1944, with photographs.

Frances Fay Clarke
Diary in Malaya preceding the fall of Singapore, 1 January — 22 February 1942. **MSS.Ind.Ocn.s.175.**

H. E. Clayton
Ts. report for the Colonial Office, 'The Federated Malay States Railways, 1942-1945, during the Japanese occupation'. **MSS.Ind.Ocn.s.78.**

W. F. M. Clemens
Diary for 1942 as District Officer, Guadalcanal and fuller ts. copy with MS notes, January 1941 — December 1942, describing the evacuation of the Solomon Islands and operations against the Japanese, with photographs. **MSS.Pac.s.61.**

H. F. Clements
Ts. extract of a letter describing imprisonment in Changi Internment Camp, Singapore, June 1944. **MSS.Ind.Ocn.s.34.**

Dr S. Colbeck
Records from Changi POW Hospital, Singapore, 1942-4.

Herbert L. Cole
Original draft report for the acting British Consul at Duala concerning the introduction of Free French troops into the French Cameroons, then supporting the Vichy Government, 1940. **MSS.Afr.s.424, ff. 292-294.**

C. E. Collinge
Notices of the men's representative in Sime Road Internment Camp, Singapore, 1944-5, ts. **MSS.Ind.s.79.**

J. Coupland
Diaries for 1942-4 written while in Palembang Internment Camp, Sumatra, with 1945 calendars. **MSS.Ind.Ocn.r.9.**

Maj. Gen. Sir Gordon Covell (b. 1887)
Ts. reminiscences of the military campaign in East Africa, 1914-17; ts. copy of a journal with notes on the campaign; and letters home from Africa, 1914-20. **MSS.Afr.s.385-387.**

Hubert Russell Cowell
Personal diary of the war, 1939-45; miscellaneous reports on economic affairs in the colonies, 1939-46; and 12 files of letters. **MSS.Brit.Emp.s.359.**

A. Barry Cozens
Letters home from the East African campaign as subaltern, 3rd Battalion, Nigeria Regiment, 1940-2. **MSS.Afr.s.964.**

R. S. Davies
Report by G. J. F. Tomlinson of his and R. S. Davies' action against Bukr, ex-Mai Mandara, suspected of complicity with the Germans, including a minute of Lord Lugard, Cameroons, 1915. **MSS.Afr.s.424, ff. 116-124.**

J. R. C. Denny
Diary of a journey from Pulau Tekong, Singapore to Colombo, 1942. Restricted.

A. H. Dickenson
Photocopy of orders by the Inspector-General of Police to the Straits Settlement Police, February 1942, in the event of the surrender of Singapore. **MSS.Ind.Ocn.s.123.**

A. H. Dickinson
Account of and papers relating to the munity of the 5th Light Infantry in Singapore, 1915.

W. J. Donnelly
The story of the 5th (Garrison) Battalion, Northern Rhodesia Regiment, 1941-2, ts. **MSS.Afr.s.1009.**

John Gordon S. Drysdale
History of the Somaliland Camel Corps, ts., 1935. **MSS.Afr.s.552.**

J. P. Edwards
Malaya, internment documents, maps, etc., 1943-5. **MSS.Ind.Ocn.s.31.**

J. Fairweather
Surrender of the British garrison at Singapore, 1942: report of dialogue between Lt. Gen. A. E. Percival and Gen. T. Yamashita; findings of the commission to record evidence from internees arrested by the Japanese military police; and notices from Sime Road POW Camp after the Japanese surrender, 1945.

D. W. G. Faris
Reports on the working of the Government Health Department, Singapore, 1941-5, and reports on the hospital and nutrition at the civilian internment camp, ts. **MSS.Ind.Ocn.s.135.**

A. E. Fawcett
Personal memories of Malaya and internment in Singapore, 1941-5, two
ts. vols. **MSS.Ind.Ocn.r.1,2.**

Lancelot Forster
Papers of the Professor of Education, University of Hong Kong, relating
to the Stanley Internment Camp, 1942-5. **MSS.Ind.Ocn.s.177.**

Edmund Austin Gardiner
Notes on the work carried out by the Public Works Department, Perak,
during the Japanese occupation, 1942-5, and topographical intelligence
reports on central Kedah, 1943-4. **MSS.Ind.Ocn.s.172.**

F. H. Geake
Diary of internment, Singapore, 1942-5.

R. Gethin
Diary of impressions while with the 1st South African Division and the
East African Military Labour Corps, 1941.

Sir Franklin Gimson
Account of internment in Hong Kong, 1942-5.

Leslie Harold Gorsuch
Unpublished autobiography of life and internment in Malaya, 1940-5,
entitled 'Crooked Figure', ts. **MSS.Ind.Ocn.s.91.**

G. E. Griffiths
Ts. diary, 1941-2, relating to secondment from Kenya for police duties
in Ethiopia after its occupation by the British. **MSS.Afr.s.879.**

Theodor Gumzert
Extracts of memoirs, in German, dealing with service in German East
Africa and the German Foreign Office, 1902-33.**Micr.Afr.446.**

Malcolm Hailey, 1st Baron Hailey (1872-1969)
Correspondence and papers relating to his African journey, 1940-1;
papers concerning the Colonial Research Committee, 1940-3,
MSS.Brit.Emp.s.342; and papers regarding his American tour, 1942-3,
MSS.Amer.s.5.

Frank C. Hallier
Miscellaneous papers referring to the campaign in Ethiopia, 1940-1, and
his war diary, April — December 1941. **MSS.Afr.s.1072.**

J. Hardman
Singapore and Penang Harbour Board: evacuation of staff from Singapore, 1942; report on the evacuation of Malaya by W. F. Wegener; and operations of Malayan Command, 1941-2. **MSS.Ind.Ocn.s.29.**

C. A. Harness
Correspondence, cuttings, etc. regarding the internment of Miss C. A. Harness in Changi Civilian Camp, Singapore, 1943-5. **MSS.Ind.Ocn.s.25.**

Sir Charles Henry Harper (1876-1950)
Gold Coast diaries and correspondence, 1914-20. Harper served with the Togoland Field Force and was Senior Political Officer during the British occupation of Togoland until December 1914. **MSS.Brit.Emp.s.344.**

Sir T. C. Haskyns-Abrahall
Papers concerning the mission to the Free French in 1940 of the Acting Chief Secretary of Nigeria.

Mortimer Cecil Hay
Diary as Acting Chief Inspector of Mines, Malaya, 1941-2, and Chief Civil Affairs Officer, Johore, British Military Administration, 1945-6. **MSS.Ind.Ocn.s.45.**

G. M. Hector
Memoranda and papers relating to WWI service in Abyssinia and Madagascar.

Thomas D. Hewer
Correspondence and papers referring to the Sierra Leone Royal Garrison Artillery Volunteers, 1914-18. **MSS.Afr.s.992.**

A. Hill
The fall of Hong Kong, 25 December 1941; Stanley Civilian Internment Camp scrapbook, 1942-5; and press-cuttings and photographs. **MSS.Ind.Ocn.s.73.**

J. Hodder
Ts. copies of his diary as a POW in Malaya with his statement to, and the report of, the commission investigating Japanese brutality to internees. **MSS.Ind.Ocn.s.52.**

Sir (Alfred) Claud Hollis (1874-1961)
Twelve vols. of autobiography covering his service in the East Africa

Protectorate, Sierra Leone, German East Africa (where he was Secretary to the Provisional Administration, 1916-19), Tanganyika, Zanzibar, Trinidad and Tobago, 1874-1948. **MSS.Brit.Emp.s.293-304.**

Thomas Gibson Husband
Copy of his narrative as State Engineer, Public Works Department, Perak, of the escape from Singapore, February 1942. **MSS.Ind.Ocn.s.211.**

E. Roy Jerrim
Letters home during service with the 3rd Nigerian Regiment, 1914-18.

A. G. Johnson
Ts. appreciation of the situation from the Italians point of view at Wajir, 25 August 1940. **MSS.Afr.s.845.**

J. Rooke Johnston
Tanganyika, defence papers, 1940. **MSS.Afr.s.503.**

R. R. Johnston
American Red Cross reports on Polish refugee camps in Tanganyika and Northern and Southern Rhodesia, 1944.

J. Kellett
Diary as a POW in Malaya, 1942-5. **MSS.Ind.Ocn.r.5.**

H. G. Lacey
Diary of the Japanese invasion of Malaya, 1942. **MSS.Ind.Ocn.r.8.**

L. A. Laffan
Diary of the liberation of Malaya, 9-29 September 1945. **MSS.Ind.Ocn.s.182.**

Cyril D. Le Gros Clark
Correspondence prior to internment at Kuching in 1941, his camp note book, and correspondence relating to his murder by the Japanese at Keningau, North Borneo. Restricted.

H. A. L. Luckham
Miscellaneous papers and memoranda, including 'Some causes of the loss of Malaya, 1942'. **MSS.Ind.Ocn.s.169.**

Sir Lewis Heath Macclesfield
Lecture on the Malayan campaign, November 1941 — February 1942, given in Changi POW Camp, 1942. **MSS.Ind.Ocn.s.117.**

B. F. Macdona
East Africa in wartime, 1944.

Charles F. C. Macoskie
Correspondence concerning his work as Chief Civil Affairs Officer in British Borneo, following recapture from the Japanese, 1945-7. Restricted.

D. R. McPherson
Evacuation of the General Hospital, Seremban, 1942. **MSS.Ind.Ocn.s.132.**

Malaya
The evacuation of the Malayan Survey Department, military maps and mapping material from Singapore to Australia, February 1942; and Operation ZIPPER and the British Military Administration in Selangor, 1945-6. **MSS.Ind.Ocn.s.199,200.**

Col. William S. Marchant
Papers concerning service in the British Solomon Islands, 1942-3, and military administration in Tripolitania and British Somaliland, 1941-3. **MSS.Brit.Emp.s.292.**

Norman Frederick H. Mather
Diary and notes, 15-20 December 1941, as British Resident in Perak; Changi Guardian, personal recollections of the first bombing and evacuation of Taiping; progress of the Japanese campaign in Kedah; and résumé of events at Began Serai Buntar Mills, December 1941. **MSS.Ind.Ocn.s.205.**

T. Matthews
Miscellaneous reports by a Senior Evacuation Officer on refugees and repatriates, and the problems of organising transport and camps in Ethiopia, Somalia, Italy, Sicily, Germany and Malaya, 1941-7. **MSS.Brit.Emp.s.360-362.**

Richard Meinhertzhagen
Diaries as Military Adviser to the Colonial Office in India, Mauritius, East Africa and Palestine, 1899-1956, 76 vols. Restricted.

E. Melville
Ts. memorandum on the organisation and functions of the British Colonies Supply Mission, Washington 1943, with appendices. **MSS.Brit.Emp.s.358.**

S. J. Millen
Report on Port Swettenham and notes on its organisation and operation, compiled from memory in Changi Internment Camp, 1942. **MSS.Ind.Ocn.s.121.**

K. W. L. Miller
Papers relating to the Cameroons campaign, 1914-15, including medical operations orders and diary, November — December 1914; letter of 30 December (?)1914, with translation from H. E. Schmidt at Tehain to Herr Lehring, reporting on events; and diary of Lt. Nothnagel, July — September 1914. **MSS.Afr.s.1025.**

J. N. Milsum
Diaries as a POW in Malaya, 1944-5, three vols. **MSS.Ind.Ocn.r.4.**

Maj. Gen. Sir Philip Euen Mitchell (1890-1964)
Governor and C-in-C, Uganda, 1935-40; Deputy Chairman, Council of East African Governors, 1940; Political Adviser to Gen. Sir Archibald Wavell, 1941; British Plenipotentiary in Ethiopia and Chief Political Officer on the staff of the C-in-C, East Africa, 1942; Governor of Fiji and High Commissioner for the Western Pacific, 1942-4; and Governor and C-in-C, Kenya, 1944-52. 33 vols. of diaries, 1927-59. Restricted.

W. G. Morison
Ts. personal experiences during the Japanese occupation of Sarawak, 1942. **MSS.Ind.Ocn.s.155.**

A. H. Morley
Diaries of a Tanganyika medical officer during wartime service in Kenya, Somaliland and Ethiopia, 1939-42. **MSS.Afr.s.792.**

Eric L. Mort.
Seven pp. extracted from his personal diary of service with Gen. Cunliffe's column in the German Cameroons, 1915. **MSS.Afr.s.141, ff. 272-282.**

Charles F. Mummery
Papers referring to imprisonment in Seoul Internment Camp, Korea and the aftermath, 1942-5. **MSS.Ind.Ocn.s.136.**

Constance B. Murray
Transcript of a diary kept in Kowloon, Victoria and Stanley civilian internment camps, December 1941 — September 1945. MSS.Ind.Ocn.s.185.

Bertram Neyland
Introduction and drawings concerning imprisonment at Changi and Sime Road internment camps, Singapore, December 1942 — September 1945. MSS.Ind.Ocn.t.3.

Alexander Niven
Letters from Singapore, 1940-2, as a surveyor with the Public Works Department, including one describing his escape from Singapore in 1942.

J. L. Noakes
Report on defence measures adopted in Sarawak from June 1941 to the occupation in December 1941 by Imperial Japanese forces, with an appendix on personal experiences while interned, December 1941 — September 1945. MSS.Pac.s.62.

Martin Ogle
Ts. unpublished narrative, 'A "private's eye" view of an inglorious campaign, Penang 1 December 1941, Singapore 15 February 1942, escape from Singapore 1942'. MSS.Ind.Ocn.s.173.

J. T. I. Phillips
Ts. diary of service entitled 'Air Force blue and khaki', covering Kenya, Ethiopia, Somaliland and Madagascar, December 1941 — May 1945. MSS.Afr.r.50.

E. W. Pudney
Financial accounts of the British Community Council and the International Welfare Committee during internment in Stanley Camp, Hong Kong, 1942-5. MSS.Pac.s.51.

R. K. Rice
Correspondence from the Mombassa W/T station, 1914-15, and draft of an article by A. T. Matson, 'Wireless interception in the East African campaign 1914-1916'.

H. K. Rodgers
Singapore and Penang Harbour Boards, evacuation of staff from Singapore, February 1942, ts. MSS.Ind.Ocn.s.51.

Arthur F. Rowland
Central area bulletins, September 1945, and tables, lists and catering notes, 1946, relating to Singapore Internment Camp. **MSS.Ind.Ocn.s.137.**

Gordon A. Ryrie
Malayan diary as Medical Superintendent, Sungei Buloh Settlement during Japanese occupation, 1942-4. Restricted.

Charles R. Samuel
Diary of escape from Penang and Singapore, and experiences during internment, 1941-2. **MSS.Ind.Ocn.r.7.**

L. A. Searle
Diary, Stanley Gaol, Hong Kong, 1941-4. **MSS.Ind.Ocn.s.76.**

Singapore
Evacuation of Harbour Board staff from Singapore, demolition of port facilities, destruction of RAF oil dumps, civilian internees, and chart of the Japanese bombing of the harbour, 1942; and Operation SHACKLE, preliminary reconnaissance of Singapore, Operation TRIBUTE, 1945. **MSS.Ind.Ocn.s.46.**

Arthur Sleep
Ts. copy of account of life in Changi Internment Camp, Singapore, 23 August 1945, and Constance G. Sleep's diary in letter form written while in Changi Camp, 25 May 1942 – 30 October 1945. **MSS.Ind.Ocn.s.130.**

Somaliland Scouts
History of the Somaliland Scouts, 1941-52. **MSS.Afr.s.551.**

R. H. Steed
Ts. report on the activities of the Public Works Department in Malaya, from the outbreak of war with Japan, 1941-2. **MSS.Ind.Ocn.s.57.**

James S. Sturgess
Reminiscences of Malaya, 1937-57; diary compiled from rough notes, December 1941 – May 1942; rough diary notebook as a POW, 1942-5; and communications from home, 1943-5. **MSS.Ind.Ocn.s.142.**

Douglas Sturrock
Report of the situation in Penang up to the time of evacuation,

December 1941, as Deputy Registrar of Statistics, and a record of personal experiences, 16 December 1941. **MSS.Ind.Ocn.s.189.**

Maurice H. W. Swabey
Two vol. informal diary as District Commissioner, Cyprus, 28 May 1942 – 7 April 1943. **MSS.Med.s.13.**

J. E. Thomas
Tanganyika diary as a lieutenant in the (South African) Frontier Force, Intelligence Department, January 1915 – July 1919. **MSS.Afr.r.102.**

L. A. Thomas
Ts. reminiscences of the mutiny of the 5th Light (Indian) Infantry, Singapore 1915. **MSS.Ind.Ocn.s.106.**

Sir (Thomas) Shenton W. Thomas
Papers and correspondence as Governor of the Straits Settlements and High Commissioner for the Malay States, relating to the war effort in Malaya. Restricted.

Sir G. K. N. Trevaskis
Papers regarding service as Senior Divisional Officer with the British Military Administration in Eritrea, 1944-51.

Uganda Civil Defence Board
Minutes of meetings 1-36, 1942-4; developments in 1942; and annual report, 1943. **MSS.Afr.s.523.**

Rev Dr K. H. Uttley
Internment diary in Stanley Camp, Hong Kong, 1941-5.

E. Cyril Vardy
War diary in Malaya and subsequent internment. **MSS.Ind.Ocn.s.63.**

W. J. Watts
Chinese affairs in Malaya, review of the history of the Department of Chinese Affairs, and notes on Chinese secret societies, 1879-1956. Restricted.

George W. Webb.
Memorandum on the Chinese in Malaya as Acting Secretary for Chinese Affairs, Singapore, 1948, with a note on the memorandum by W. L. Blythe. Restricted.

W. F. Wegener
Ts. report on evacuation from Malaya, 1942. **MSS.Ind.Ocn.s.50.**

R. T. Wickham
Incomplete narrative of a civilian's attempted escape from the Germans in Tanganyika, 1916. **MSS.Afr.s.861.**

J. K. Willson-Pepper
Journals with the RAMC in West Africa, 1942-3. **MSS.Afr.s.45,46.**

Thomas Wilson
Photocopies of extracts from a diary kept in Changi POW Camp, January 1942 — October 1945, including the journey to the camp from Malacca. **MSS.Ind.Ocn.r.10.**

W. K. Wilton
Extracts from a diary of his escape from Singapore, with explanatory notes, 1942. **MSS.Ind.Ocn.s.56.**

R. M. Winston
Diary of a journey in Kenya and Uganda, 1943, and a summary of staff, equipment and organisation for BI section of the 5th (Kenya) Field Ambulance. **MSS.Afr.s.966, ff. 168-182.**

William P. Winston
Three ts. letters home, giving an account of the Japanese invasion of Malaya and his escape, 1942. **MSS.Ind.Ocn.s.122.**

Yesufu
Photocopy of a letter to the Chief Secretary to the Government from a Nigerian boatswain, covering *inter alia* his experiences in WWI. **MSS.Afr.s.424, ff. 305-311.**

St. Antony's College, OXFORD OX2 6JF

Henry Boyle (1863-1937)
Consul and Oriental Secretary, Cairo, 1899-1909, and Consul General, Berlin, 1909-14. The papers referring to his tenure in Berlin are mainly personal and family letters of little interest.

Carlile A. Maccartney (b. 1895)
Service with the Intelligence Department, League of Nations Union, 1928-36, and Research Department, Foreign Office, 1939-46. A large

collection of material deriving from his studies of Eastern Europe, including notes, drafts and printed material.

Maj. Gen. Sir Neill Malcolm (1869-1953)
British Military mission, Berlin, 1919-21, and High Commissioner for German Refugees, 1936-8. MS and ts. copies of his diary for April — August and September — December 1919, press-cuttings, ts. articles, papers relating to the peace conference, correspondence, reports concerning Germany and some correspondence for 1935-7.

Sir John Wheeler-Bennett
Historian and author. A collection of papers relating to German affairs, including photocopies of documents from the Auswärtiges Amt, *c.* 1936; the Nuremburg trials, where Wheeler-Bennett was attached to the British team; German—Japanese relations, 1941; and papers regarding 20 July 1944.

Italian Papers
Photocopies of Italian diplomatic files, *c.* 1920-40, assembled in Italy during the Allied advance northward. There are some files from the ministries of the Salo Republic which were collected in an arbitrary fashion from ministries in Rome, 1943-4. The collection also contains papers of Mussolini and Ciano. For greater detail see F. W. Deakin's commentaries in his *The Brutal Friendship* (1962), which utilized this material.

Germany: Auswärtiges Amt
German Foreign Office documents, located at Whaddon Hall in Buckinghamshire, relating to Italy from 1867-1920, reproduced on 25 reels of microfilm. See American Historical Association, Committee for the Study of War Documents, *A Catalogue of files and microfilms of the German Foreign Ministry Archives 1867-1920* (Oxford, 1959).

St. Antony's College, Middle East Library, 137 Banbury Road, OXFORD OX2 6JF

The Middle East Library contains a collection of papers and documents unique in Britain for Middle East Studies. Access is by appointment only and enquiries should be made to the Director of the Middle East Centre. The following selection covers most of the material relevant to the two world wars.

Richard Adamson
Notes on the Cairo Conspiracy Trial, 1919-20, by a member of the British Police in Cairo at the time.

Aden Protectorate
Order of 1940 and additional instructions of 23 November 1944.

Lord Allenby
Miscellaneous papers of Lord Allenby relating to the defeat of the Turkish Army, letters to Gen. Wavell, and diaries.

Aref El-Aref
Gaza diary, 20 July 1939 — 19 June 1940.

Nevill Barbour
Papers regarding service as a journalist in the Middle East during and after WWII.

Gertrude Bell
Many WWI letters, some of which are in the Philby Papers.

Norman Bentwich
Articles concerning Ethiopia, 1943-4, by an influential Zionist.

F. W. G. Blenkinsop
Private memoranda on the Arab—Zionist conflict by the District Commissioner of Beersheba in WWII. There is additional material in the Spears Papers.

Humphrey E. Bowman
Diaries, 1904-49, personal papers and photographs covering service with the 18th Battalion, Royal Fusiliers during WWI in France, India and Mesopotamia. Bowman was director of Education in Mesopotamia, 1918-20, and a member of the Advisory Council in the Palestine Government, 1920-36.

Henry Boyle
Papers mostly relating to his service as a diplomat in Egypt, 1899-1909, but including some material concerning his work in the Middle East during WWI. Other Boyle papers are held in St. Antony's college library (see p. 254).

Geoffrey Bridgeman
Recollections of the fall of Jerusalem, 9 December 1917.

British Bank of the Middle East
The bank was known as the Imperial Bank of Persia until 1950. The collection contains papers regarding French, German and Russian interests in Mesopotamia and the Persian Gulf, 1890-1924.

British Military Administration of Palestine
Assorted papers, 1918-19.

Sir Milne Cheetham (1869-1938)
Counsellor of the British Embassy in Cairo, 1911-19. Private letters to Sir Eldon Gorst and Lord Kitchener referring to British policy in Egypt, 1910-15, and telegrams sent and received, 1912-13.

Brig. Gen. Sir Gilbert Clayton (1875-1929)
Director of Intelligence, Egypt, 1914-17, and Brigadier General, General Staff, Hejaz operations, 1916-17. Letter to Sir Reginald Wingate, Governor General of the Sudan, 3 August 1916.

Col. Alfred Collard
Papers relating to service in WWI, 1915-18.

Dr N. L. Corkhill
Reports on health and diet in the Sudan, 1941-62.

P. C. Davey
Papers concerning service as ADC to the Resident, Aden and the Red Sea, 1936-38, and Political Officer, 1938-46.

Brig. Gen. Sir Wyndham Deedes (1883-1956)
Military Attaché, Constantinople, 1918-19. Copies of his letters home and diary during the Gallipoli and Palestine campaigns, and other papers regarding the conflict of British and French interests in the Middle East, 1916.

Gerald Delany
Papers of a correspondent in Cairo during both world wars.

A.G.M. Dickson
Memoirs of his banking career in Turkey, Greece and Egypt, 1890-1950. Of particular interest is the material on the moratorium declared in Egypt, August 1914, on his recommendation.

Lt. Col. H. R. P. Dickson (1881-1959)
Service in Mesopotamia, 1914-15; transfer to the Political Department,

1915; and Political Officer in Mesopotamia, 1917-19. Papers relating to various aspects of his service.

Col. Richard Doughty-Wylie
Extracts from letters concerning the negotiations on Lake Tsana, 1913-15.

A. E. H. Elkington
Memoranda and correspondence on economic conditions in Cyrenaica by an economic adviser to the British Military Administration, 1943.

Feisal, Emir of the Hejaz
Later he became King of Iraq. The papers include the 1919 agreement with Chaim Weizmann, al-Fatat Society material, his role in the Paris Peace Conference and notes on the Desert campaign.

Feisal II, King of Iraq
Series of personal letters to Stewart Perowne, 1943-57.

R. Fraser
Police papers and his diary, 1939-48, as a member of the Palestine Police.

Col. W. A. K. Fraser
Photocopies of diaries during service in Persia, 1912-19.

Gray, MacKenzie and Co Ltd.
Road concessions, Teheran-Kum-Khoramabad and related security problems, 1892-1924.

Margaret and Helen Haig
Accounts of a journey undertaken around Meshed, 1914-16, and Isfahan to Mohammerah, 1918.

Lt. Col. Sir Thomas Wolseley Haig (1865-1938)
Consul General and Agent of the Indian Government, Khivasah, Persia, 1914-16; Isfahan, 1916; and Teheran, 1919. Unpublished reminiscences of Persia before and during the war, 1913-18.

J. A. de Courcy Hamilton
Papers including his diary of events in Northwest Persia and Baku, 1918-19.

Lord Edward Hay (1888-1944)
Papers covering service during WWI in Europe; at the Paris Peace Conference, 1918-19; and on special missions to Austria, Hungary and Bulgaria, 1919-21. The collection also contains his personal diaries, 1916-36. In addition, there is material on the Persian Gulf and Baluchistan, 1920-33.

David G. Hogarth
Director of the Arab Bureau, Cairo, 1916-18. Letters on the war in the Middle East, 1914-18, including correspondence with T. E. Lawrence, Gertrude Bell, etc.

Sir Alexander W. Keown-Boyd (1884-1954).
Papers as a civil servant in the Sudan, 1907-16, and Oriental Secretary to the High Commissioner of Egypt, 1917-19.

Sir Arthur F. Kirkey
Papers referring to service as General Manager of the Palestine Railways and Ports Authority, 1942-8.

T. E. Lawrence
Miscellaneous letters to S. F. Newcombe, King Hussein and others, 1917-19. There is more Lawrence material in the Philby Papers.

Brig. Stephen Longrigg
Report on occupied enemy territory in Cyrenaica, 1 February – 31 March 1941 and 14 October 1941 – 31 January 1942.

Sir Donald MacGillivray (1906-66)
Papers concerning service as Administrative Officer in Palestine, 1938-42; Deputy District Commissioner, Galilee, 1942-4; and District Commissioner, Samaria in Palestine, 1944-6.

Sir Harold MacMichael (1882-1969)
Political and intelligence inspector with the expeditionary force capturing Darfur, 1916; High Commissioner, Palestine and Transjordan, 1938-44; and Special Representative, Malaya 1945. The papers cover various aspects of his career.

Brig. Gen. Sir H. Osborne Mance (1875-1966)
Technical Advisor to the Ottoman Bank, 1924-62. Papers regarding the Bank's operations, including details of railways, agreements, etc., 1911-60.

Middle East Supply Centre
Papers concerning land tenure and the possibility of land reform in the
Middle East, 1943-4.

Elizabeth Monroe
Historian and author. Minister of Information and Director of the
Middle East Division, 1940. Papers concerning her career.

Dr C. Stanley Mylrea
Copy of MS memoirs relating to work at the American Mission
Hospital, Kuwait, 1907-47. The material regarding the Saudi attack on
Kuwait and the British defence, 1920, is especially interesting.

Stewart Perowne
Papers regarding service as Information Officer, Aden, 1939; Public
Relations Attaché, Baghdad, 1941; and Oriental Counsellor, Baghdad,
1944.

Harry St. John Bridger Philby (1885-1960)
Philby had a long and distinguished career in the Middle East. He
started in the Punjab Secretariat in 1914; was Political Officer with the
Mesopotamian Forces from November 1915; Political Officer in charge
of the British Political Mission to Central Arabia, 1917-18; Advisor to
the Minister of the Interior, Mesopotamia, 1920-1; and Chief British
Representative in Transjordan, 1921-4. A large and very important
collection of papers covering various aspects of his career, including
diaries, drafts, notes, memoranda and correspondence.

James H. H. Pollock (b. 1893)
District Commissioner, Haifa, 1939-1942; Galilee, 1942-4; and Jerusalem, 1944-8. Correspondence and other papers.

Sir George Rendel (b. 1889)
Notes on the proposed Greek participation in WWI, 1914-15, relating
mainly to the conversations between members of the British Legation
and the Greek Government. They were made by Rendel as 3rd
Secretary of the British Legation in Athens.

Herbert Samuel
Sir Herbert Louis Samuel, 1st Viscount Samuel (1870-1963). An
important collection of papers gathered during his long involvement
with the creation of Israel. See the House of Lords Record Office for
the main collections of Samuel's papers (p. 101).

Sir Terence Shone (1894-1965)
Chargé d'Affaires, Yugoslavia, 1937-9; British Minister, Cairo, 1940-4; and Minister to the Republics of Syria and Lebanon, 1944-6. MS account by Prince Paul of events leading to the Tripartite Pact allying Yugoslavia with the Axis in 1941; and reports on the Levant states, April — September 1945, including reports and photographs of events in Damascus, May — June 1945.

Rev Hunter Smith
Two accounts of fighting in Gallipoli, 1915.

Maj. F. R. Somerset
Memoranda and letters referring to the Palestine problem, 1919-21. Some of this correspondence is in the Philby Papers.

Maj. Gen. Sir Edward Spears (1886-1974)
Head of the Spears Mission to Syria and Lebanon, July 1941. Papers relating to the mission and his service as First Minister to Syria and Lebanon, 1942-4. Papers referring to other aspects of Spears' career are located at Churchill College, Cambridge (see p. 20).

Sir Mark Sykes (1879-1919)
Advisor to Middle Eastern Policy to the Foreign Office in WWI. The collection contains microfilms of papers concerning the Middle East, 1915-19, including the Arab Revolt, the Sykes—Picot Agreement, the liberation of Baghdad, the Asia Minor Agreements, Zionism and the Palestine Settlement.

Sir Charles Tegart (1881-1946)
Papers, correspondence and diaries covering police and security matters as well as Palestine policy, 1937-9.

W. Tudor-Pole
Reminiscences on the launching of the Balfour Declaration and personalities in the Zionist Commission to Palestine, 1918.

Owen Tweedie
Papers as a journalist in the Middle East during WWI, including letters to Lord Allenby.

Sir Robert Wingate
Ts. copies of the British declaration of December 1914 regarding the deposition of the Khedive and the establishment of the British Protectorate.

William Yale
American diplomat in the Middle East during WWI, with particular
involvement in the Palestine question. There are papers referring to his
Middle Eastern service. Other papers concerning his life and career are
located at Yale and Boston Universities.

Sir Hubert W. Young (1884-1950)
Papers regarding service as Assistant Political Officer in Mesopotamia,
1915-17; Deputy Director, Local Resources in Mesopotamia, 1917-18;
in charge of operations in the Hejaz, 1918; and President of the Local
Resources Board, Damascus, 1918. He served at the Foreign Office,
1919-21, and was Assistant Secretary to the Middle East Department of
the Colonial Office, 1921-7.

University College, OXFORD

Atlee Papers
41 boxes of papers of Clement Richard Atlee, 1st Earl Atlee
(1883-1967). Lord Privy Seal, 1940-2; Secretary of State for Dominion
Affairs, 1942-3; Deputy Prime Minister, 1942-5; Lord President of the
Council, 1943-5; and Prime Minister, 1945-51. Most of the collection is
post-1945 but there is correspondence with Labour Party officials,
1939-44, and Labour Party Committee papers.

Black Watch Museum, Balhousie Castle, Hay Street, PERTH PH1 5HR

The documentary contents of the Museum are surveyed in *NRA–
Scotland 881*. Enquiries should initially be made to the *NRA–
Scotland*. In addition to the material listed below, the Museum contains
numerous albums of press-cuttings and photographs, mainly of WWI
but also some for WWII.

WORLD WAR I

Lance Cpl. W. M. D. Anderson, 42nd Regiment, diary entitled
'Captivity' relating his observations as a POW in Germany, 1918.
Lt. Col. John Stewart, Black Watch, ts. copy of his 'Private Diary' with
a description of the Grand Fleet at Scapa Flow, 1916. There are also ts.
copies of his diaries of day-to-day occurrences and descriptions of

places and events in France, South Africa and the Middle East, 1915-18.

Brig. Gen. C. E. Stewart, Black Watch, diaries of his service in France, 1914-18.

Maj. A. D. C. Kroak, 1st Battalion, Black Watch, ts. copy of his diary describing an action near Paissy, France, 1914.

Albert A. Hay, 1st Battalion, Black Watch, memoirs entitled 'Soldiering' recounting events in France and India, 1917-21, written in 1935.

Capt., later Brig. Gen., C. W. F. Gordon, copy letters describing daily events in the regiment's service in France, 1914-18. The collection also contains his diary for 1917 with brief references to day-to-day occurrences during the regiment's service in France.

S. Ray, four files of sketches of personnel in the 6th Battalion, Black Watch during WWI.

1st Battalion, Black Watch: burial book, 1914-18; nominal roll, 1914; binder containing 'Part II' orders recording grants of leave, 1918; and 'Historical Records' containing copy extracts of documents giving brief references to day-to-day occurrences in the regiment's history, 1910-39. Notebook containing details of next of kin for the officers of the 2nd Battalion, Black Watch, 1914-19.

2nd Battalion, Black Watch: 'Historical Record', with miscellaneous ts. notes on day-to-day occurrences, 1909-39; order books for April – September 1914 and February 1918 – May 1919.

'Historical records of 2nd Battalion, Black Watch', containing copy extracts from documents relating to day-to-day occurrences in the battalion's history, 1908-21.

Capt. R. N. Duke, 8th Battalion, Black Watch. 'What I did in the Great War', memoirs comprising accounts of events, places and persons on the Western Front, with descriptions of the battles of Loos and Somme, four vols., 1914-19. Vol. 2 contains an appendix of notes on sentry duties, communications, provision of water in trenches and other miscellaneous daily routines, 1916. Appendix 1 of vol. 4 comprises notes on the Gauche Wood sector defence scheme, 1918; appendix 2, orders for the Meteren attack, Hoogenacker Ridge, 1918; and appendix 3, orders for the advance in Flanders, 1918. There are also ts. notes on the history of the 8th Battalion in WWI.

10th (Service) Battalion, Black Watch: 'Historical records' containing a diary of brief references to daily events in the battalion's WWI service, with some photographs of personnel; and printed standing orders, Aldershot, 1915.

Vol. recording parchment discharges or transfer certificates for personnel in the Black Watch, 1909-17.

3rd (Reserve) Battalion, Black Watch, record of special reserve officers' service, 1908-1915.

8th Battalion, Black Watch, envelope containing loose-leaf lists of the nominal roll of wounded NCOs and men in the battalion and those receiving medals and awards, c. 1914 — c. 1917.

Black Watch POW Relief Fund: envelope containing miscellaneous balance sheets, minor correspondence and other papers referring to the fund's work, c. 1915 — c. 1918; and two vols. listing donors and donations, 1914-18.

1st Battalion, Black Watch, ts. copy of diary of day-to-day events in the battalion's WWI service.

Pvt. Harry J. Ogilvie, miscellaneous papers including diaries giving a brief account of daily occurrences in WWI, 1914-17.

42nd (Royal Highlanders) Regiment, record of service, 1873-1939.

1st Battalion, Black Watch, historical record, August 1914 — March 1919, two copies.

2nd Battalion, Black Watch, historical record, October 1914 — May 1919.

Highland Battalion, Black Watch, historical record, April — June 1916.

2nd Battalion, Black Watch, 'War diary or intelligence summary' giving a brief historical record of service and including memoranda, maps and other miscellaneous papers, August 1914 — October 1918.

1/4th Battalion, Black Watch, historical record, February 1915 — February 1916, two copies.

5th Battalion, Black Watch: historical record, July 1914 — March 1916 and September 1916 — January 1917, two copies; and 'Duplicate war diary' for July 1914 — April 1919.

4/5th Battalion, Black Watch, historical record, March 1916 — April 1919, two copies.

1/6th Battalion, Black Watch, historical record, May 1915 — September 1917 and October 1917 — August 1919, two copies of each.

7th Battalion, Black Watch, historical record, May 1915 — March 1919, two copies.

8th Battalion, Black Watch, historical record, May 1915 — August 1919, two copies.

9th Battalion, Black Watch, historical record, July 1915 — April 1919.

10th Battalion, Black Watch, historical records, September 1915 — September 1918.

13th Battalion, Black Watch, historical record, October 1916 — July 1919.

14th Battalion, Black Watch: historical record, January 1917 — May 1919, two copies; and 'Duplicate war diary' for May 1918 — May 1919.

42nd Regiment: roll of personnel examined for possible discharge by the Medical Board, 1915; roll of personnel giving names, ages, places and dates of attestation, 1914-16; and roll of personnel taking up employment in industry, 1915-16.

Vol. giving details of certain battalion postings and recruits to the Black Watch, *c.* 1913-17.

Anonymous diary with reminiscences of actions involving the Black Watch in WWI, including the battle of the Aisne.

Col. G. A. M. Sceales, commander of the 4th and 4/5th Battalions, Black Watch during WWI: in letters referring to his period of command, personal affairs and regimental life, with an index of correspondents, 1915-31.

Maj. Sir W. Stewart Dick-Cunyngham, Bt., 42nd Regiment: photographs, commission warrant and other miscellaneous papers regarding his military service, 1914-20.

Quartermaster Sgt. Adam Macgregor Wilson, 8th Battalion, Black Watch: diary giving personal reminiscences of daily events and actions at Steen-je and other places on the Western Front, May – October 1915.

Maj. A. R. Nairn, notes describing the invasion of German Southwest Africa by the 8th Infantry (Transvaal Scottish) during WWI.

WORLD WAR II

Maj. Gerald Barry, 'War diaries 1-4' with day-to-day occurrences and descriptions of events and people during campaigns with the Black Watch in East Africa, the Middle East and India, including photographs, 1939-43, ts. copies.

2nd Battalion, Black Watch, war diary in the Middle East and North Africa, 1 March 1941 – 16 June 1942, and in India, June 1942 – May 1944 and September 1944 – December 1946.

Folder containing a 'List of officers and other ranks who died in the 1939 World War while serving in the Black Watch Regiment in Burma'.

Maj. Rory Murray, account of the activities of the 4th Battalion, Black Watch, in France, Gibraltar, Britain and Palestine, 1940-6, ts. copy.

2nd Battalion, Black Watch, 'War diary' recording day-to-day events of the regiment in India, 1944, ts. copy.

Folder entitled 'Tobruk', containing miscellaneous ts. and MS notes on the regiment's participation in the battle of Tobruk, 1941.

Folder entitled 'Palestine' containing miscellaneous ts. notes on the service of the 2nd Battalion, Black Watch in Palestine, 1939-40.

Folder containing ts. notes on the participation of the 1st Battalion, Black Watch, in Operation OVERLORD and the invasion of Germany, 1944-5.

Folder containing ts. notes on the activities of the 1st Battalion, Black Watch in France, May – June 1940.

Folder containing ts. accounts of captivity by POWs in Germany, 1939-45.

Folder containing brief ts. and MS notes on the war service of the 9th and 10th Battalions, Black Watch in Britain, 1939-44.

Folder containing brief MS notes on the war service of the 8th Battalion, Black Watch, 1939-44.

Folder containing ts. notes on an engagement involving the 17th Platoon of D Company, 6th Battalion, Black Watch at Cassino, 22-25 April 1944.

Folder containing ts. notes on the war service of the 6th Battalion, Black Watch in Greece 1944.

Folder containing miscellaneous ts. 'war diaries' of the 6th Battalion, Black Watch, recording day-to-day events in Italy, March – November 1944.

Folders containing miscellaneous ts. notes on the war service of the 6th Battalion, Black Watch in North Africa and Europe, 1939-45.

Folder containing miscellaneous ts. notes on the war service of the 5th Battalion, Black Watch in North Africa, 1942-4.

Folder containing ts. notes on the history of the 154th Infantry Brigade in the Sicilian campaign, 1943.

Folder containing miscellaneous ts. notes on the war service of the 1st Battalion, Tyneside Scottish (Black Watch), including the regiment's participation in the Dunkirk evacuation and the later invasion of France, 1939-45; the New Zealand Scottish Regiment, 1939-43, compiled by Maj. Gen. H. E. Barrowclough; and the 30th Battalion, New South Wales Scottish Regiment, 1939-44.

Folder containing ts. notes on the history of the Black Watch of Canada in WWII, with photographs, 1939-45.

Two folders containing ts. notes on the history of the Transvaal Scottish in WWII.

2nd Battalion, Black Watch, folder containing ts. notes on 'regimental milestones' in the history of the battalion, 1939-45.

Folder containing miscellaneous formal and other papers concerning honours and awards gained by the 2nd Battalion, Black Watch in Palestine, 1937-45.

Roll of honour of the Black Watch (RHR) and the Tyneside Scottish, 1939-45.

Roll of honour of the 1st Battalion, Black Watch, listing those killed in action in North Africa and on the second front, 1942-4.

Field-Marshal Earl Wavell, letter of 1945 to Col. V. Holt giving the movements of the 2nd Battalion, 42nd Regiment, in India and briefly commenting on the political situation.

Archives Department, Plymouth City Libraries, Drakes Circus, PLYMOUTH, Devon PL4 8AL

WORLD WAR II

City of Plymouth records
13. Civil Defence:
Emergency and other committees, minutes, 1941-5.
Sub-Committee minutes, 1941.
Index to ARP Committee minutes, 1937-9.
Defence Committee minutes, 1941-2.
Invasion Committee, 1942-3.
Classified directory, etc., 1944.
Emergency bulletins, 1941.
Wardens: card index of personnel, plan of sectors, and *The Alert* Civil Defence magazine.
Fire Guards: plans, indexes, statistics, training and miscellaneous papers.
Correspondence regarding war damage to houses, air raid shelters, unexploded bombs, wardens' posts, etc.
18. City Treasurer, Plymouth City Council, Civil Defence correspondence, 1937-46.
19. Water Engineer's Department, Plymouth City Council: air raid and defence precautions, 1938-44; and air raid report books, 1939-43.

Portsmouth City Record Office, Guildhall, PORTSMOUTH, Hampshire PO1 2AL

WORLD WAR I

Committee minutes, 1897-1918 **CCM 10/3**: Committee regarding allowance of men with colours; Economy Expenditure Committee; Roll of Honour Committee; and War Bonus Committee.

WORLD WAR II

War Emergency Committee, minutes, 22 May 1940 — 28 October 1946, five vols. **CCM50.**
Correspondence and reports of chairmen, 1941-6. **108A/4/1.**
ARP controllers' personal log book, 1941-4. **107A.**
Civil Defence Department, records, 1938-45. **108A/1.**

Civilian war deaths and air raid casualties, 1938-45. **108A/1/1**.

WVS, 1942-6. **108/1/2**.

Committees, 1941-6 **108A/1/4**: correspondence and reports of the Chairman of the War Emergency Committee, 8 July 1941 — 27 August 1946; correspondence regarding Cosham Invasion and Defence Sub-Committee, 10 June 1942 — 21 November 1944; and minute book of Cosham Invasion and Defence Sub-Committee, 26 June 1942 — 1 July 1943.

Accommodation registers, 1940-5. **108A/1/5**.

War diaries, 1939-45. **108/1/6**:

Invasion Committee, constitution of HQ, and West Sector HQ, Gosport, n.d.

Civil Defence warden's service, war diary, n.d.

Health Report, abridged, for 1945 by A. B. Williamson, n.d.

Civil Defence Report and Control Service, draft copy, n.d.

Official Medical History of War, n.d.

History of the Fire Guard, n.d.

Cosham Divisional war diary, n.d.

War diary, narrative of work undertaken by the Piers, Beach and Publicity Departments, including diagrams and sketches of semi-mobile kitchens.

Reports from Northern Division Groups I-O, February 1945.

Group Reports from Cosham Division Groups P. S. T. and V, 6 March 1945.

Group Reports from Cosham Division Groups P. S. T. and V, 6 March — 27 April 1945.

Reports from Southern Division Groups A-H, 13 March — 27 April 1945.

Awards for gallantry and service, 1940-55. **108A/1/7**.

Maps, photographs and related matters, 1940-4. **108A/1/10**:

Two copies of map showing positions of bombs dropped, 11 July 1940 — 15 July 1944.

Map showing group area boundaries and warden's poses, 1 December 1941.

Map showing Fire Guard areas and sectors, 17 April 1944.

Three photographs with an explanation, n.d.

Roll of Honour, list of awards, copy.

Medical History of the War, see **108A/6/11**.

List of raids, general correspondence.

Home Security Operations Bulletins, nos. 27-154, 1941-3. **108A/1/11**.

Unexploded bombs, 1941-6 **108A/1/14**: booklet, correspondence and reports concerning the location of unexploded bombs, 4 March 1941 — 17 May 1946; and weekly statements of unexploded bombs, 9 May 1941 — 21 December 1942.

Lancashire Record Office, Bow Lane, PRESTON, Lancashire PR1 8ND

Lancashire Territorial Association, register of sealed documents, 1910-68.

Papers, 1912-73, of Thomas Hope Floyd, covering service as an officer, 1916-19 and 1940-2. Part of his diary for 1916-19 was published as *At Ypres with Best-Dunkley* (1920). His WWII service was in Britain. There are also home letters, 1940-2; many letters to Floyd written during and after each war by ex-comrades; and documents and papers relating to his military service. In addition, the papers of his mother and Thomas Earl Floyd contain letters from the war periods. **DDF1/1-13.**

WORLD WAR I

19 letters from Lancashire Territorials at home and in France, 1914-15. Thornton-Cleveleys UDC letter books, including War Tribunal, 1915-18, and National Service, 1917. **UDTh/3,23.**

Letters to 2nd Lt. Herbert B. Smith, killed in France, July 1916, and his private accounts. **DDX/2/46, 47.**

Preston Volunteer Training Corps, minutes, 1915-23. **DDX/11.**

WORLD WAR II

Lancashire Home Guard records:

5th (Preston County) Battalion, including orders, photographs, location and commanders of companies, defence works and a brief history.

8th (Preston) Battalion, including orders, instructional handbook, and final strength returns, for the Lancashire Territorial Army Association, 1944.

41st Battalion, nominal rolls of officers, 1941-4, and women, 1943-5.

42nd (Irlam) Battalion, nominal roll of B Company, 1942-3.

47th Battalion, nominal rolls of B and C Companies, 1944.

48th Battalion, casualty book of C Company, 1941-3; nominal rolls of B, H, and HQ Companies, 1940-2; nominal roll of women, 1943; and nominal roll of cadet messengers, 1943.

49th Battalion, nominal roll of officers, 1941-4.

51st (Ashton-under-Lyne) Battalion, nominal rolls of B and HQ Companies, 1941-4, and of various companies of industrial enterprises, 1942.

55th Battalion, No. 3 Company commander's record book and nominal rolls for Nos. 3 and 4 Companies.

63rd Battalion, nominal rolls of A Company, 1940-4.
Burnley Home Guard, nominal rolls of various companies, 1940-4.
Rawtenstall Home Guard, HQ Company attendance register, 1944.
In and out transfers, various battalions, 1942-5.
Preston Home Guard dispositions, c. 1940, and a file of Home Guard and Civil Defence instructions and circulars, 1944.
MS notebook of a private in the Gloucestershire Regiment, recording his capture and escape, 1940. **DDF1/15.**
Lancashire County Council records: ARP Committee records, including minute books, memoranda and circulars; and photographs and letters relating to war damage in nine areas, 1940-4.

The Queen's Lancashire Regiment Museum, Fulwood Barracks, PRESTON, Lancashire PR2 4AA

The Queen's Lancashire Regiment Museum incorporates that of the Loyal Regiment (North Lancashire). Enquiries should be made to the Curator.

WORLD WAR I

The Museum holds the following kinds of material: officers' and soldiers' documents; unit and trench standing orders; Army orders; telegrams from divisional commanders; handwritten gallantry citations; midnight charts for April and May 1918; enemy information; ts. accounts of various actions; a captured German code book; and diaries kept by the 2nd Battalion, The Loyal Regiment (North Lancashire) of campaigns in East Africa and against the Turks.

WORLD WAR II

The collection contains training manuals; regulations for daily life issued in a Japanese POW camp; account by a war correspondent of the action of the 1st Loyals at Kesskiss, North Africa; and a ts. history of the 1st Loyals in North Africa, December 1943-5, by the CO.

Berkshire Record Office, Shire Hall, READING, Berkshire RG1 3EE

Berkshire Territorial and Auxiliary Forces Association: minutes, 1922-67, and scrapbooks and press-cuttings, 1922-68. **D/TA 1-4.**

WORLD WAR I

Photographs of POWs in Germany, 1916. **D/EX 23 F22.**
Letter from a lieutenant in the RFC after his plane had landed behind German lines, 1916. **D/EX 23 F30/7.**
Lists of parishioners of East Shefford serving in the war, 1914-18. **D/P 107/8/1.**
Royal Berkshire Regiment, photographs and papers at Asiago, Italy, 1918. **D/EX 229/1-5.**
Lists of men from Stanford serving in the war, 1914-18. **D/P 118/28/11.**
Temporary commission of J. H. Benyon in the Berkshire Volunteer Regiment, 1916. **D/EBy F 44/3.**
Printed notice on the administration of Berkshire in the event of invasion, from J. H. Benyon as Lord Lieutenant, and three copies of letters on the Berkshire Yeomanry, 1915-21. **D/EBy 0 13.**

WORLD WAR II

Civil Defence records, including log book of casualties, incidents, etc., and casualty reports, 1940-72. **C/D 1-21.**
Sunninghill and Sunningdale Local Defence Committee, war book, 1942-4. **CPC 126/18/4.**
Press-cutting on the use of Bucklebury Common as a vehicle repair depot during WWII. **D/EX 227 Z4.**

Local History Department, Reference Library, Blagrave Street, READING, Berkshire RG1 1QL

WORLD WAR II

Reading Corporation.
ARP Sub-committee, *Summary of the air raid precautions scheme* (Reading, Parnells the Printers Ltd, 1937), 8 pp.
Civil Defence Emergency Committee, pocket guide to the ARP arrangements in Reading, *c.* 1940, 48 pp.
Reading Civil Defence Centre, Whitley Rise, 1945, ten photographs.
Civil Defence Emergency Committee, *Where to go, what to do, after a raid* (Reading, Charles Elsbury & Son, 1941).

Duke of Edinburgh's Royal Regiment (Berkshire and Wiltshire), Brock Barracks, READING, Berkshire RG3 1HW

The material held by the regiment is wholly uncatalogued and may be seen by appointment only. All the material listed below relates to the Royal Berkshire Regiment unless otherwise indicated. Enquiries should be made to the Regimental Secretary.

History of the recruitment of the Berkshire Regiment, 1911-50.
The China Dragon, chronicle of the Royal Berkshire Regiment, January 1907 – September 1959.

WORLD WAR I

War diaries: 1st Battalion, 1914-18; 2/4th Battalion, 25 May 1916 – 25 September 1919; 5th Battalion, 30 May 1915 – 31 May 1919; 6th Battalion, 24 July 1915 – 22 February 1919; 7th Battalion, 19 September 1915 – 17 October 1919; 8th Battalion, 7 August 1915 – 25 May 1919; and 2nd Battalion, The Royal Fusiliers Regiment, 1914-18.
G. W. H. Cruttwell, *The War Service of the 1/4th Battalion of the Royal Berkshire Regiment* (Oxford, Blackwell 1922), believed to be the only extant copy.
Personal recollections of G. W. H. Cruttwell, 1914-16, dedicated to the 4th Battalion, Royal Berkshire Regiment.
W. L. Arrowsmith, padre, account of the 2/4th Battalion, 21-28 March 1918.

WORLD WAR II

1st Battalion, transcript of some war diaries.
2nd Battalion, notes and accounts of activities before 1939 and in India during the war prior to involvement in the Burma campaign, and war diary of B Company in Burma, 20 October 1944 – 22 May 1945.
4th Battalion, history, 1939-40.
5th Battalion, notes and official history, September 1939 – May 1945.
6th Battalion, short history, 1939-46.
7th Battalion, short account of activities, 1940.
8th (Home Defence) Battalion, later the 30th Battalion, diary, 1939-45.
10th Battalion, personal notes on the battalion in Sicily, 1943, and miscellaneous documents referring to the battalion in Italy, 1944.

Department of Manuscripts, University Library, Whiteknights, READING, Berkshire RG6 2AE

R. A. Chell, short history of the 55th Infantry Brigade in WWI, 1919. **MS. 121.**

Papers of Waldorf Astor, 2nd Viscount Astor (1879-1964). Inspector of Quartermaster-General Services, 1914-1917; Parliamentary Secretary to the Prime Minister, 1918; and Parliamentary Secretary to the Ministry of Food, 1918. **MS. 1066.**

Reminiscences of Edith Morley, Professor of English at the University of Reading, who did much work for refugees in Reading and district during WWII. **MS. 528.**

War diaries of Miss C. M. Edwards, 1939-45, who did voluntary work for servicemen and women during WWII. **MS. 1211.**

University Archives

Munitions Committee records, 1915-18.

RFC School of Instruction, two files of correspondence, 1914-19.

RFC occupation of University College, Reading, 1918.

RFC proposals to take over the remainder of University College, Reading, 1918.

RFC occupation of Wantage Hall, correspondence, 1918-22.

Circulars and correspondence from the War Office, Air Ministry and other military organisations, 1937-55.

ARP report, January 1937.

Bute County Library, ROTHESAY, Bute, PA20 0BX

WORLD WAR I

Roll of Honour for the Isle of Bute of the Regular Army, Kitchener's Expeditionary Army, Territorial Force, Boy Scouts, Red Cross Nurses, Munition Workers, the Navy and the Mercantile Marine, engaged in 'the Great War abroad and at Home', 1914-19, compiled by James King Hewison.

University Library, The University, ST. ANDREWS, Fife

Col. Henry Alford (1878-1955)

His papers, including service diaries during WWI and papers relating to the 11th Battalion, Gordon Highlanders.

D'Arcy Wentworth Thompson Papers
Comments on both wars, *passim.*

WORLD WAR I

Navy Board papers, 1902-17.

WORLD WAR II

Col. Michael E. Lindsay, short history of Zone III, Fife and Kinross Home Guard, 1940-4.
Maj. Lionel Showds, letter of 13 May 1943 to his mother describing the capture of Gen. Jurgen von Arnim in North Africa.
Air Raid summary, St. Andrews district, 1940-4.

Department of Local History and Archives, Central Library, Surrey Street, SHEFFIELD S1 1XZ

WORLD WAR I

Diaries and letters of Lt. Col. Sir Henry Stephenson of Haasop Hall, while on active service with the 49th West Riding Division Artillery, 1915-18.
Oscar Holt, corporal and later sergeant in the RFA: letters to his fiancée while on service in France, August 1915, and Belgium, 1915-18. **M.D.6063.**
Capt. A. J. Ellison, 1st Battalion, York and Lancaster Regiment: letters, 1915-19, and war diaries, 1915-18. **M.D. 2198-2199.**
Sheffield Smelting Company, letters to and from and concerning employees serving in the Armed Forces, 1914-19. **S.S.C. 498-502.**

WORLD WAR II

4th Field Park, RAOC, Sheffield: war diary, 1939-43, and miscellaneous papers.
Records of the City Librarian as BBC liaison officer in case of air raids, invasion or other emergencies, 1941-3. **C.A. 44.**
Records of wartime activities undertaken by the staff of Sheffield City Libraries, 1938-46. **C.A. 45.**

Records of the Sheffield Information Committee, a branch of the Ministry of Information, 1940-4. **C.A. 43.**

Royal Marines Museum, SOUTHSEA, Hampshire PO4 9PX

The Library and Archives of the Royal Marines Museum contain a fair amount of original material, of which the following is a representative selection. Enquiries should be made to the Archivist.

GENERAL

Colour Sergeant N. J. Hiscock, 'Twenty-one Years Service Ashore and Afloat', ts. **143/69.**

Col. C. F. Jerram, 'The navy at the beginning of the 20th Century', ts.; some reminiscences of the Royal Marines Corps, ts.; and a miscellaneous collection of maps, letters, diagrams, magazines, press-cuttings and documents. **143-144/69.**

Sgt. A. G. King, ts. reminiscences, 'And see the World in Ease and Comfort', 1917-49. **256/68.**

H. J. Reed, photocopy of 'Memoirs of a Royal Marines Bandsman', 1913-45. **77/70.**

WORLD WAR I

Pvt. V. L. Parry, RMLI, diary of service as a gunner in merchant ships, 21 May 1917 — 4 June 1918. **227/69.**

Personal diary of Cpl. Ernest Eeles aboard HMS *Agamemnon*, 1914-18, **128/73.**

Miscellaneous documents relating to HMS *New Zealand*, including a narrative of events, 3 August 1914 — 18 May 1915, 288 pp.; a narrative of the Dogger Bank action, 24 January 1915; a narrative of the battle of Jutland, 30 May — 2 June 1916; MS information obtained from survivors of SMS *Blücher* by officers and men of HMS *King Edward VII*, 26 January 1915; MS concerning the conduct of the battle of Jutland; and the track of HMS *New Zealand* during the battle of Jutland. **42/72.**

Short personal diary of Colour Sergeant Albert Saunders, kept aboard HMS *Princess Royal*, 1st Battle Cruiser Squadron, covering the Heligoland Bight, Dogger Bank and Jutland, 1914-17, 180 pp. **147/68a.**

Diary of HMS *Vanguard* during the battle of Jutland, 31 May — 1 June 1916. **51/74.** Documents concerning HMS *Vanguard*, 1909-17. **29/73.**

Capt. H. C. Harrison, personal diary in Southwest Africa, 15 March —
13 September 1915. 6/71.

Pvt. C. J. Moynihan, RMLI, personal diary, 1914-19. 118/71.

Pvt. William Jolly, diary aboard the cruiser HMS *Doris,* 3 August 1914
— 25 June 1916, recording *inter alia* raids on the Syrian coast in
support of T. E. Lawrence, 204 pp. 131/74/A.

Col. C. F. Jerram, personal diaries in France, January 1917 — February
1919. 141/69.

CSM R. E. Payne, RMA, diary of service in France, 2 March — 24 April
and 29 June — 31 December 1916. 64/74/B.

Pvt. E. E. Rowland, MS account of service in Belgium, 12 September —
18 October 1914, and another ts. copy. 289/70/C.

Sgt. G. J. Russell, RMLI, account of 'My trip to the British Front in
Flanders, December 1915'.

Colour Sergeant Harry Wright, account of the Zeebrugge Raid, 23 April
1918, and part of his subsequent time as a POW, with MS notes, 96 pp.
It was published in *Globe & Laurel* XXVII, 136-138, 154-155; XXVIII,
6-8, 24-26, 36-37. D/2/103.

MS diary of the 31st Division in France, 21 January — 25 June 1917.
135/69/a.

MS notebook showing rounds fired by No. 12 gun, Howitzer Brigade,
RMA in France, September 1916 — September 1918, with a rough
diary of movements. 286/70.

Four maps of France. 130/72.

Battalion Maj. J. Allen, Royal Marine Brigade, diary during the Gallipoli
campaign, 1915. 21/75.

Capt. E. Boztin, RMLI, MS field service notebook kept during the
Gallipoli campaign, August — October 1915. 175/71.

Lt. Col. N. O. Burge, RMLI, miscellaneous papers regarding the
Dardanelles. 181/72.

Lt. Arthur R. Chater, war diary of Chatham Battalion, Royal Marine
Brigade, 28 April — 27 July 1915. B/1/84.

Lt. Col. G. P. Orde, diary kept during the Dardanelles campaign, 2 April
— 25 July 1915. An edited version was published in the *Naval Review,*
IV (1916), 270. 201/75(B).

Maj. R. Sinclair, chart of the Dardanelles area used by him as
commander of a gun turret aboard HMS *Inflexible,* 1915. 79/71.

Pvt. J. Vickers, RMN, personal diary, November 1914 — July 1915,
including an account of the Gallipoli landing. 238/69.

Pvt. Henry C. Wilcox, personal diary of service in the Dardanelles and
Gallipoli. 14/71.

Lt. E. Wilks, diaries of service in Gallipoli, the Dardanelles and the
Bosphorus, 1915-16 and 1918. 3/72.

Diary of service in the Dardanelles area, 23 November 1917 — 31 December 1918, probably of Maj. R. D. Ormsby. 7/17/12.

Framed maps: new section of the Royal Naval Division, 20 December 1915; and enemy trenches on 10 December 1915. 180/70.

Printed copy of the original Force Order issued by Gen. Sir Ian Hamilton on the eve of the Gallipoli landings, 21 April 1915. 85/70.

Anonymous MS notes on the arrangements at the 'Helles' Front in Gallipoli, 1915, and arrangements for the evacuation of the Royal Naval Division, 1916. 135/69/B.

Two scrapbooks referring to the Dardanelles and Gallipoli operations, 1915-16. 133/69.

Royal Marine Brigade, field message book, 1915, and MS list of Turkish guns in the Dardanelles. 71/74/C.

Three sketch maps of Gallipoli. 16/72.

WORLD WAR II

Diary of HMS *Indefatigable,* 8 December 1943 — 19 November 1944. 94/65.

Diary of HMS *Malaya,* 31 December 1939 — 30 July 1949. 94/65.

Royal Marines, Account of Admiralty Achievements 1939-43. 3/71/DD.

Col. J. C. Coke, diary of a landing company, October 1939 — October 1942. 245/66(3).

2nd Battalion, Royal Marines, miscellaneous operations orders and maps from Iceland, 1940. 94/69.

Madagascar, Order of the Day, 8 May 1942, and chart referring to an attack on Diego Suarez, 1942. 79/73.

Sgt. Arthur J. Bradley, MS diary of service aboard HMS *Penelope* in Malta, 25 March — 10 April 1942. 213/71.

Col. F. W. Dewhurst, personal notes on the 7th Battalion, Royal Marines in the Middle East and Sicily, September 1942 — July 1943. 213/711.

41 Royal Marine Commando, bound vol. of standing orders, *c.* 1942, in North Africa. 147/70.

R. Mitchell, 'With No. 41 Royal Marine Commando in Sicily and Salerno 1943', 144 pp. 2/14/16.

43 Royal Marine Commando, maps of Italy and the Adriatic, 1944. 2/14/18.

43 Royal Marine Commando, miscellaneous documents concerning the unit in Italy and Yugoslavia, 1944. 180/73.

43 Royal Marine Commando, miscellaneous maps and documents: the Yugoslav mainland with area of deployment based on Dubrovnik; seven

maps of Brač of Capt. R. B. Loudon; four Italian road maps; two maps of Vis; map of Mostar, showing the Adriatic island of Vis used as a base for raids on the German held islands of Hvar, Mljet, Solta, Brač and Korcula, 1944; three maps of Algiers, December 1943; X Troop, No. 43 Commando, standing orders; maps and papers regarding Operation ROAST, a raid in April 1945 against the Spit at Lago di Comacchio in northern Italy, and subsequent operations in the Argenta area; MS account of C Troop's activities with partisans on the Yugoslav mainland, December 1944; and report on reconnaissance operations on Mljet, 29-31 May, by Capt. R. B. Loudon. **18/72.**

1st Special Service Brigade, Admiralty plan for D-day landing and several war maps used by the 45 Royal Marine Commando. **261/71.**

HMS *Glenearn,* landing craft operations order, D-day. **82/73.**

Tidal and astronomical tables for Normandy, 1944. **1/74.**

Map of the defences of Deauville issued the night before D-day. **95/74.**

Miscellaneous documents and papers relating to the Royal Marine Armoured Support Group on D-day. **85/72, 157/72.**

Account of action at Walcheren, 1 November 1944, two files. **204/74.**

Two maps referring to crossing the Rhine River at Wessel, 1945. **134/72.**

47 Royal Marine Commando: original operations orders for Operations CUCKOO III and IV, 6 April 1945; extract from the diary of Capt./Lt. Langfritz of the German Army; and orders issued by Capt./Lt. Kappes for training reconnaissance patrols after the successful completion of Operation CUCKOO by the 47 Royal Marine Commando. **236/70.**

Burma and Malaya, reports on Japanese campaigns, Military Appendix No. 2, Colombo, 25 August 1942. **ARCH79/19/11.**

Capt. Charles Feely, 'Burma War Diary: Some Impressions of the Burma Campaign, 10 September 1942', 8 pp. MS. **ARCH7/19/2.**

Maj. D. Johnson, CO, Force 'Viper': narrative account of the operations of Force 'Viper' in the Burma campaign, February — May 1942, 24 pp. and photographs. **ARCH7/19/2.**

James Liason, 'Synopsis: The Marine from Mandalay', 17 pp. ts.

List of amphibious raids in the Far Eastern theatre, two pages in tabular form, n.d. **ARCH7/19/14.**

44 Royal Marine Commando: diary, 1 August 1943 — 31 December 1946; and report on Operation SCREWDRIVER II, involving landings on the Arakan coast, 1-21 March and 12-30 April 1944. **ARCH2/14/9.**

44 Royal Marine Commando, account of operations in the Arakan, 1944, 7 pp., ts.

Royal Marine Siege Regiment, five files of documents relating to the regiment in Burma and the Arakan, 1944-5, comprising: detailed narrative of actions in which the regiment was engaged, 1-20 September 1944; field message book and aerial photographs; papers referring to

the origin of the regiment, policy regarding super long range guns, gun log and record of 'Winnie' and 'Pooh', and book of targets; two nominal roll books of the regiment; assorted technical documents and a list of officers serving with Maj. Gen. H. D. Fellowes in the regiment. **55/71.**
Operations in Akyab, Myebon, Kangan and Ra-ywa, n.d., 6 pp. and 2 pp. appendices. **19/8.**
HMS *Kansa,* 2 pp. referring to Operation HANKEY, the establishment of the Chebda beachhead, 24 January 1944. **ARCH7/19/8.**
Capt. A. M. Burnford, report on a visit to Royal Marine landing craft flotillas in operations along the Burma coast, 5 March 1945.
Combined Operations in Southeast Asia: Arakan to Rangoon, January — May 1945, headed 'Most Secret' and dated December 1945, 22 pp. with diagrams, photographs, maps and 15 enclosures. **ARCH7/19/11.**
Reports on operations at Akyab, Kangaw and Hill 170, 7 pp. and two maps. **ARCH7/19/8.**
Account of the action fought at Hill 170 by Nos. 1 and 5 Commandos, and 42 Royal Marine Commando, 31 August 1945, 9 pp., ts.
Japanese diary found by a marine in a Japanese officer's billet, Hong Kong, September 1945. **177/70.**
P. G. Dunstan, diary with ts. copy kept as a POW in the Far East, December 1941 — September 1945, and five photographs taken from HMS *Prince of Wales,* 1941. **244/70/A.**
Miscellaneous maps of Burma and India. **Acq. D/2/67.**
40 Royal Marine Commando, map and chart catalogue, Far East Land Forces. **267/71.**

Staffordshire County Record Office, County Buildings, Eastgate Street, STAFFORD

Staffordshire Territorial Association, minutes, etc., 1912-67. **D969.**

WORLD WAR I

Scrapbooks of Col. A. E. Blizzard, covering 1914-18 and including details of recruiting and aerial photographs of trenches. **D797/2.**
Photographs of Uttoxeter volunteers, *c.* 1914. **D1145/1/49.**
Map of trenches at Bas-Warneton on the Belgian—French border, *c.* 1917. **D1315/12.**

WORLD WAR II

Photographs of Luftwaffe plans of Walsall and Wolverhampton, 1941.
105.
Civil Defence records, various. **C/DA.**
Miscellaneous correspondence, including the effect of the war on
Abbot's Bromley, 1941. **D1209/10/7.**
Leek Area ARP Committee minutes, 1938-44; and Leek Area Fire
Prevention Committee, 1942-4. **D1283/5-7.**
Staffordshire Yeomanry, Queens Own Royal Regiment, battle casual-
ties, etc., 1939-46. **D1300/3/11-12.**
Staffordshire Yeomanry: diaries, etc. referring to Syria and Europe; Lt.
Col. J. A. Eadie's diary concerning El Alamein; and C Squadron's diary
during D-day and the invasion of Germany, 1940-6. **D1300/4.**
Stafford, register of ARP premises, 1939-45. **D1033/10/5.**

*William Salt Library, 19 Eastgate Street, STAFFORD ST16
2LZ*

WORLD WAR I

Surgeon K. M. Dyott, account of the battle of Jutland. **89/46.**
Military installations on Cannock Chase, *c.* 1915, photocopy plan of
Brocton Camp. **CB/Brocton/1.**
Letter of Pvt. Reginald Lawrence, 16th? West Yorkshire Regiment GHQ,
Lewis Gun School, France, 11 November 1917. **58/71.**
Letter of Pvt. William Dolphin, 8th North Staffordshire Regiment,
France, 9 August 1916. **58/71.**

WORLD WAR II

WVS and Civil Defence, various papers.

*Regimental Museum, Argyll and Sutherland Highlanders,
Stirling Castle, STIRLING*

Enquiries should be made to the Curator.

WORLD WAR I

War diaries and related documents:
1st Battalion, war diary, 1914-19, and documents, 1914-16.
2nd Battalion, war diary, 1914-19, documents regarding the operation of 25 September 1915; and timetable and diary of events, August 1914 — February 1919.
5th Battalion, war diary, 1914-19.
1/5th Battalion, war diary, 1914-19.
6th Battalion, war diary, 1914-19.
7th Battalion, war diary, 1914-19.
8th Battalion, war diary, 1914-19.
9th Battalion, war diary, 1914-19.
10th Battalion, war diary, 1914-19, and casualties, honours, etc., 1914-19.
11th Battalion, war diary, 1914-19.
12th Battalion, war diary, 1914-19.
14th Battalion, war diary, 1914-19.

Other material:
Lt. R. L. Mackay, personal diary of service in France, 1916-19.
File of VC awards and photographs, 1914-19.
Argyll and Sutherland Highlanders, casualty list, 1914-19.

WORLD WAR II

War diaries and related documents:
1st Battalion, war diary, 1939-45, and documents, 1939-45.
2nd Battalion, war diary, 1939-45, and Malayan campaign, Japanese POW reports.
5th Battalion, documents, 1939-45.
6th Battalion, war diary, 1939-45.
7th Battalion, war diary, 1939-45, and documents, 1939-45.
8th Battalion, war diary, 1939-45, and documents, 1939-45.
10th Battalion, casualties.
11th Battalion, documents, 1939-45.
93rd Highlanders, Malayan campaign losses, claims, etc.

Army Aviation Museum, HQ, Army Aviation, Middle Wallop, STOCKBRIDGE, Hampshire

The Museum Library contains files of documentary and manuscript material under the following categories: Aviation History, 1914-39; Air Observation Post History, 1940-45; and the Glider Pilot Regiment. There is also a file for each of the squadrons numbered 650-666, some of which are further sub-divided into files on separate flights. Enquiries should be made to the Officer in charge of the Library.

Light Infantry Office (Somerset), 14 Mount Street, TAUNTON, Somerset TA1 3QB

The Somerset Light Infantry Museum is now part of the Somerset Military Wing of the Somerset County Museum, The Castle, Taunton. The archives and library of the Somerset Light Infantry remain at the Light Infantry Office. Enquiries should be made to the Regimental Secretary.

WORLD WAR I

Maj. Gen. Sir Henry Joseph Everett (1866-1951), personal diaries covering 1893-1937 and including his war diary, 1915-16.
7th (Service) Battalion, diaries, scrapbook, etc.
Capt. Prideau, diary, 1914-16, and 'A Soldier's Diary', 1914-17.
Capt. Whittuck, diary, 1914.
'Philby's War', account of a POW from the 1st Battalion, 1914.
H. W. Ewing, 1/5th Battalion, diary.
Pvt. C. H. Fussell, experiences in the war.
Maj. Prousse, and Cpls. Barrett and Bailey, letters home.
Lance Cpl. A. J. Morris, letters as a POW.
Capt. H. L. Milsom, operations in Palestine.
William Watson, diary, 1914.

WORLD WAR II

Lt. Col. C. G. Lipscomb, history of the 4th Battalion, Somerset Light Infantry, Northwest Europe, June 1944 – May 1945.
Col. J. R. I. Platt, 'Early days in Italy'.
7th Battalion papers, 1944.

Account and photographs of the visit, subsequent death and funeral of Gen. Wladislaw Sikorski, Gibraltar, 1943.

Somerset Record Office, Obridge Road, TAUNTON, Somerset TA2 7PU

WORLD WAR I

Letters of a soldier in the Somerset and Shropshire Light Infantry to his mother, 1915-19. **DD/X/DWL.**
Diaries of a soldier in the Royal Fusiliers serving on the Balkan Front, 1916-19. **DD/X/DWL.**

WORLD WAR II

Somerset Home Guard: ts. account, drawings, photographs, etc. of 'Somerset on Guard' by Capt. Bushell; and 12 files of correspondence and returns.
Somerset County Council: ARP records, Invasion Committee minutes, incident diaries, reports, etc. **C/CD.**

Wiltshire Record Office, County Hall, TROWBRIDGE, Wiltshire BA14 8JG

WORLD WAR I

Walter Hume Long, 1st Viscount Long of Wraxall (1854-1924).
President of the Local Government Board, 1915-16; Secretary of State for Colonial Affairs, 1916-19; and 1st Lord of the Admiralty, 1919-21. Political and private papers, including: correspondence and other papers relating to his involvement in the voluntary recruiting campaign, and discussion about conscription as President of the Local Government Board, 1915-16; Cabinet papers regarding the war and peace negotiations; a file of correspondence with Lord Derby in Paris, 1917-18; and 20 letters to Long from his eldest son, Maj. (later Brig. Gen.) Walter Long, written from the Western Front in 1915 and 1916-17. **WRO 947.**
Calne Borough Council, schedules and papers concerning conscription, 1916-18.

WORLD WAR II

Wiltshire Rifle Brigade, later the Wiltshire Territorials, minutes and reports, 1938-45. **WRO 961.**

Papers deposited by the County Council and urban and rural district councils: war books; files on Civil Defence, ARP, fire service, etc.; and Emergency and ARP Committee minutes, 1939-45.

Cornwall Record Office, County Hall, TRURO, Cornwall

Cornwall Territorial Forces records: minutes, attendance books, committee papers, etc., 1899-1968. **DDX.295/1-12.**

WORLD WAR I

Cornwall Munitions Committee, correspondence and reports, 1915-19. **DDX. 104/16.**

POW diary of Pvt. A. Betty of 7th Somerset Light Infantry, 1917-18, captured near the Hindenburg Line. **AD314.**

Printed record of *Women's Land Army in Cornwall during the Great War* (Truro, Jordan, 1919). **AD439.**

Mid-Cornwall Munitions Company, wages and accounts, 1917. **DD.CN.4052/1-4.**

Letter requesting the use of Tregrehan House, St. Blazey, by the Canadian Red Cross for convalescent officers, 1917. **DD.CN.1318.**

Papers concerning the use of timber at Tregrehan, St. Blazey, for national purposes, 1917-18. **DD.CN.1319/1-3.**

Family papers relating to the war service of conscientious objectors, Society of Friends, 1914-19. **DD.ST.367-382.**

WORLD WAR II

Pensilva, St. Cleer, Civil Defence Committee minutes, 1941-4 and HMSO pamphlet, 'Instruction to Invasion Committees', 1942. **DDX.31/2-4.**

Folder of minutes, notes, etc. of the Civil Defence Workers' Rest Service of the Red Cross, and St. John Cornwall Joint War Committee, 1941-4. **DDX.87/3.**

Camborne-Redruth district, village invasion committees; and book of sketch plans of meeting places and surrounding roads for the use of messengers, n.d., *c.* 1942. **DDX.215/2.**

Highertown Home Guard Patrol, Truro duty book, inspection of night guards' rifles, 1941-2. **DDX.298.**

Home Guard plans, Redruth area. **AD.437/1-6.**

File of papers relating to Civil Defence including St. Clement Invasion Committee minutes, 1942-4. **DDP.33/28/1.**

St. Ewe Parish war book and Invasion Committee minute book, 1941-4. **DDP.62/24/1,2.**

Lists of Invasion Committee members, messengers, etc., 1942; returns of equipment available in private households, c. 1940; and various Defence Committee papers, 1940-5. **PC/Altarnun/4/1-3.**

War book, including Civil Defence, ARP, lists of men and horses, letters, etc., 1941-2. **PC/St. Cleer/4/1.**

Civil Defence Committee papers, circulars, lists of men and horses, etc., 1941-4. **PC/Egloskerry/4/4-9.**

Bundle of Invasion Committee papers, 1941-5. **PC/Lansallos/3/1.**

Invasion book, Invasion Committee minutes, correspondence, 1941-4. **PC/St. Martin-in-Meneage/5/1-3.**

Invasion Committee file, 1941-2. **PC/Probus/4/5.**

Papers concerning war damaged property in Penryn, 1944-5. **PC/Pen./459-461.**

Borough of Truro Evacuation Committee records, Auxiliary Fire Service accounts, and issue of civilian steel helmets, 1940-5. **B/T/186-196.**

ARP records, 1939-45. **County Council Official.**

Royal Armoured Corps Tank Museum & Royal Tank Regiment Museum, Bovington Camp, WAREHAM, Dorset BH20 6JG

The Museum contains a variety of material, such as manuals, official operating instructions, training instructions, etc., concerning the design and performance of tanks from 1916 to 1918. There is a certain amount of similar material relating to armoured fighting vehicles of WWII. The Museum is also known to hold papers deposited by the following:

Maj. Gen. George Lindsay (1880-1956).
A specialist in machine guns, he commanded the 99th Infantry Brigade, 2nd Division, 1916-17; the 9th (Highland) Division, 1939-40; and was Regional Commissioner, Southwest Civil Defence Region, 1940-4.

Maj. Gen. Sir Ernest Swinton (1868-1951).
An originator of tanks, he raised the Heavy Machine Gun Corps, 1916,

and was Assistant Secretary in the War Cabinet during WWI.

Maj. Gen. Sir (Henry) Hugh Tudor (1871-1965).
Commander, RA, 9th Division; and Commander, 9th Division, 1918.

As the holdings of the Museum are in the process of being catalogued,
the Curator declined to permit further listing.

*The South Lancashire Regiment (PWV) Museum, Regimental
Headquarters (Increment), The Queen's Lancashire
Regiment, Peninsula Barracks, WARRINGTON, Cheshire
WA2 7BR*

Enquiries should be made to the Curator.
The collection contains MS war diaries for all battalions of the South
Lancashire Regiment and numerous personal diaries, letters and maps
for WWI. The only material relating to WWII comprises a few war
diaries, letters and orders.

*Regimental Museum of the Queen's Own Hussars, The Lord
Leycester Hospital, High Street, WARWICK*

Application to use the records should be made to the Regimental
Secretary. They are uncatalogued but contain *inter alia* the following:
3rd Hussars, operations in France, 1918; 7th Hussars, two files of war
records, 1939-45; and 3rd Hussars, MS history, 1940-5.

*The Royal Warwickshire Regimental Museum, St. John's
House, WARWICK CV34 4NF*

The Museum contains manuscript and photographic material which is as
yet uncatalogued. Applications to use the records should be made to
the Regimental Secretary.

Warwick County Record Office, Priory Park, Cape Road,
WARWICK CV34 4JS

WORLD WAR I

Warwick County Nursing Association, Queen's Institute of District
Nursing and War Agricultural Committee minute books and papers,
1909-49. **CR 815.**
War Relief Fund, Rugby RDC Local Committee minute book, 1914-16.
CR51/846.
Letter from G. N. May on the Western Front, 1918. **CR1382/10.**
Press-cuttings about WWI and war service of the sons of the 4th
Viscount Templeton, 1914-18. **CR426.**

WORLD WAR II

Seven files of records deposited by the Clerk to the County ARP
Committee. **CR20.**
Log book of the evacuee schools at Long Itchington, 1940-2. **CR914.**
Memoranda and circulars, many relating to WWII. **CR1348.**
Correspondence   and   wartime   verses   and   anecdotes,   1940.
CR114A/893.
Diary and record of watches at the ARP warden's post at Whitnash,
1942-4. **CR646.**
Midland War Zone courts, correspondence, 1940-5. **CR586.**
ARP records, WWII. **CR1499.**
Documents not on deposit in the County Record Office:
WWI correspondence, diaries, press-cuttings, accounts of events
between 1914-18, etc., still in the possession of the Earl of Denbigh,
whose papers are kept at Pailton House near Rugby, Warwickshire. The
9th Earl of Denbigh, his three sons and two of his daughters served
abroad during WWI, whilst the family's home, Newnham Paddox, was
converted into a hospital to care for the wounded. Members of the
family wrote home frequently and their letters have been preserved, as
have copies of the letters sent out from Newnham Paddox and the
correspondence received by Lord and Lady Denbigh from their friends
at this time. Enquiries about this material should be made to the
County Archivist.

City Record Office, 20 Southgate Street, WINCHESTER, Hampshire SO23 9EF

WORLD WAR I

Winchester War Service Tribunals, records.

WORLD WAR II

Evacuee records.

Hampshire Record Office, 20 Southgate Street, WINCHESTER, Hampshire SO23 9EF

Hampshire and Isle of Wight Territorial Army and Air Force Association: minute books, 1907-68, including quarterly reports and progress of the Home Guard, 1939-46. 37M 69.

WORLD WAR II

Lieutenancy records, letter books, January 1938 — February 1942. **LL. 127-128.**
Council records, WWII, containing varying quantities of information concerning ARP, Civil Defence, occasionally Home Guard, invasion committees, evacuation, and related home front activities. Winchester City, Alton UDC and Farnborough UDC are the fullest of these local records but material is found to a lesser extent in the records of Aldershot Borough, Andover RDC, Basingstoke RDC, Droxford RDC, Eastleigh Borough, Gosport Borough, Kingsclere and Whitchurch RDC, Lymington Borough, New Forest RDC, Petersfield RDC, Petersfield UDC, Romsey and Stockbridge RDC, Southampton Corporation, and Winchester RDC.

Royal Green Jackets Museum, Peninsula Barracks, Romsey Road, WINCHESTER, Hampshire

The Museum incorporates the museums of the Oxfordshire and Buckinghamshire Light Infantry, the King's Royal Rifle Corps and the Rifle Brigade. The library contains various personal diaries, maps, signals and related documents which are presently unlisted but can be made available to accredited researchers by appointment. Enquiries should be made to the Curator.

Hereford and Worcester Record Office, Shirehall, WORCESTER WR1 1TR

Worcestershire Territorial and Auxiliary Forces Association, approximately 340 minute books, accounts, ledgers, deeds, letters, plans and related papers, 1802-1965. These records are all administrative in nature and have no particular relevance to either world war, with the possible exception of the minutes of the association and its committees. **5204.**

WORLD WAR I

Gunner Gilbert Clements, four diaries, some 42 letters, photographs and other papers relating to service in France with the 241st Artillery Brigade, RFA, 1914-19. **5329.**

Maj. Gen. Henry R. Davies (1865-1955). Commanded the 3rd Brigade in France, 1915-16; 33rd Brigade, 1917; and the 11th Division, 1917-19. Collection of WWI letters and journals.

J. S. Preece, approximately 300 letters and other papers mainly from him to his mother and some 200 photographs and postcards referring to his service with the Worcestershire Yeomanry, 2519A Squadron in the UK and Egypt, 1914-19; and other miscellaneous related material. **5334.**

Lt. G. R. W. Woodward, field message book used in France during service with the 241st Artillery Brigade, RFA, containing notes on military movements, use of equipment and preparations for action, 1915. **5330.**

Sir Hugh Chance, 'Subaltern's Saga', an account of his WWI experiences with the 8th Worcesters and the RFC, 1968. **5225.**

G. Harvey, approximately 200 photographs gathered during service in Salonika, 1917-19. His unit is not known. **5517.**

WORLD WAR II

Flight Sgt. R. J. Collins, some 300 letters, various air force papers and other material referring to RAF service in the UK and Egypt, *c.* 1939-52. **3570.**

Malvern UDC, 5,500 letters relating to Civil Defence and ARP, 1937-50, including 25 items concerning defence against enemy landing, 1940-1. **2970.**

Fleet Air Arm Museum, RN Air Station, Yeovilton, YEOVIL, Somerset BA22 8HT

The Fleet Air Arm Museum records the history of the FAA and the RNAS from their inceptions. The recently formed Research Department holds a small but growing collection of original material.

WORLD WARS I AND II

1. Training Course Notes. The majority concern WWI engines, rigging, armaments and aircraft in general.
2. Photograph albums. There are over 60 private photograph albums of FAA and RNAS airmen.
3. Diaries, comprising a small collection of personal diaries, including diaries of Sgt. Wilson with 209 Squadron, 1916-18; W.O. Porter, Dunning Landing, 1917; and S. Ingles, service in France, 1917-19.
4. Personal documents. There is a collection of personal documents of FAA and RNAS airmen, including some private papers of Maj. W. G. Moore.
5. Flying log books. A collection of WWI flying log books including: two log books of Maj. W. G. Moore, part diary and part flight reports, with pencil notes on the East Africa campaign; log of R. A. Yates with 73 Squadron in France, 1917-18; B. Pretty, flying boat operations over the North Sea, Harwich and Felixtowe, 1917-18; S. Mossop, convoy patrols; (?)Usher, RNAS, Dardanelles and Chanak operations, 1918-19; B. G. Blampied, early carriers and the Russian campaign, 1919; F. Anderson, RNAS, anti-submarine work, 1916-18; and A. B. Hill, service in Turkey and Greece, 1916-17. The WWII logs contain the following combat records: A. P. Scott, 810, 836 and 842 Squadrons, shot down, taken prisoner and rescued by marines at Diego Suarez, Madagascar, 1941; V. A. Langman, Air to Surface Vessel patrols from Dekheila, 1942-3; J. S. Bailey, the invasion of Diego Suarez, 1941; R. S. Charlier, service with 767, 810, 819 and 811 Squadrons; and P. F. Manders, service on HMS *Argus* and with 821 Squadron, 1940-2.
6. Battles and actions, comprising reports, mostly in the form of letters home, including material concerning the following: Cuxhaven and Tondern raids, RNAS Daily Summaries, 1917; Operations DAKAR, LIBREVILLE, DARDANELLES, PEDESTAL and TUNGSTEN; the Constantinople Raid of 1916, the Taranto raid, Zeebrugge, Koenigsberg

in WWI, the Russian campaign, 1918; and Narvik, Middle East in WWI, *Tirpitz, Scharnhorst, Gneisenau, Prinz Eugen* and *Bismarck.*

13th/18th Royal Hussars (Q.M.O.), Home Headquarters, TA Centre, Tower Street, YORK YO1 1SB

Enquiries should be made to the Officer Commanding.

WORLD WAR I

Regimental mobilisation orders for the 18th Hussars.
MS accounts of actions fought by the 18th Hussars during 1914, prepared by the OC and Adjutant.
Copies of letters and messages relating to routine matters concerning the 18th Hussars during 1914.

WORLD WAR II

Personal diary of an NCO in the 13th/18th Hussars during the Dunkirk operations.
Personal diary of a Troup Leader in the 13th/18th Hussars, covering 1944-5.
War diary of the 13th/18th Hussars.

The West Yorkshire (Prince of Wales's Own) Regiment Museum, Regimental Headquarters, The Prince of Wales's Own Regiment of Yorkshire, Imphal Barracks, YORK YO1 4HD

Enquiries should be made to the Regimental Secretary. The material listed below relates only to the West Yorkshire Regiment.

WORLD WAR I

War diaries, regular battalions:
200. 1st Battalion, 1914-19, ts. copy.
201. 1st Battalion, 1915-19, MS copy.
202. 1st Battalion, October 1916 — May 1919, MS in Army Book 152.
203. 1st Battalion, October 1916 — May 1919, bound ts. copy.
204. 2nd Battalion, November 1914 — May 1919, ts. copy.

205. 2nd Battalion, 1914-17, MS in Army Book 152.
206. 2nd Battalion, 1916-17, MS in bound order book.
207. 2nd Battalion, 1914-19, MS copy.
208. 2nd Battalion, 1917-18, ts. copy.
War diaries, Territorial battalions:
209. 5th Battalion, 1915-19, ts. copy.
210. 5th Battalion, miscellaneous operations orders and war diaries, 1916-17, MS copies.
211. 1/5 Battalion, 1915-19, MS copy.
212. 2/5 Battalion, 1917-18, MS copy.
213. 2/5 Battalion, 1917, ts. copy.
214. 2/5 Battalion, January − July 1918, ts. copy.
215. 2/5 Battalion, January − August 1918, ts. copy.
216. 1/6 Battalion, 1914-19, MS copy.
217. 2/6 Battalion, 1915-18, MS copy.
218. 2/6 Battalion, 1917-18, ts. copy.
219. 1/7 Battalion (Leeds Rifles), 1915-19, MS copy.
220. 2/7 Battalion, (Leeds Rifles), 1917-18, MS copy.
221. 2/7 Battalion (Leeds Rifles), 1917-18, ts. copy.
222. 1/7 Battalion, 1915-19, and 1/8 Battalion, 1915-177, ts. copies.
223. 1/8 Battalion (Leeds Rifles), 1915-17, MS copy.
224. 2/8 Battalion (Leeds Rifles), 1917, MS copy.
225. 8th Battalion, (Leeds Rifles), 1918-19, MS copy.
226. 2/8 Battalion, 1917-18, and 8th Battalion, 1918-19, ts. copies.

War Diaries, service battalions:
227. 9th Battalion, 1915-19, ts. copy.
228. 9th Battalion, 1915-19, MS copy.
229. 10th Battalion, 1918-19, MS copy.
230. 11th Battalion, 1915-19, MS copy.
231. 12th Battalion, 1915-17, MS copy.
232. 15th Battalion (Leeds Pals) and 15/17 Battalion, 1915-19, MS copy.
233. 16th Battalion (Bradford Pals), 1915-18, MS copy.
234. 17th Battalion (Leeds Bantams), 1914-17, MS copy.
235. 18th Battalion (Bradford), 1915-18, MS copy.
236. 21st (Pioneers) Battalion, 1916-19, MS copy.
237. 22nd (Labour) Battalion, 1916-17, MS copy.
238. 52nd (Graduated) Battalion, 1914-19, MS copy, formerly 11th Battalion, South Staffordshire Regiment.
Other material:
239. Roll of Honour, officers, 1914-19, printed.
240. Roll of Honour, soldiers, 1914-19, printed.
241. Correspondence regarding West Yorkshire Regiment POWs.
251. A list of battalions of all categories: Regular, Special Reserve, Territorial, Service, Pioneer, Labour, Reserve, Garrison, etc.

252. Outline of service battalions, 1914-18.

253. 1st West Yorkshires in the first battle of the Aisne, Conan Doyle's account of the 6th Division in action, September 1914.

254. Major Lang, 1st Battalion, letter to his wife, 30 September 1914.

255. Lt. Henderson, 1st Battalion, diary, 6-28 September 1914, ts. copy.

256. Capt. Spence, 1st Battalion, letter referring to action of October 1914, ts. copy.

257. Map of route taken by the 1st Battalion into Germany, 1918.

258. Lt. Col. Lowry, 2nd Battalion, letters, press-cuttings and an appreciation by Capt. Rogerson.

259. Some written messages of the 2nd Battalion preserved by Maj. Hinchcliffe, 1917-18.

261. Account of the 'liquid fire' attack made by the Germans on the Leipzig Salient, 31 July 1916.

262. Diary of a corporal in the 2/7 (Leeds Rifles) Battalion, MS, 1917.

263. 2/8 (Leeds Rifles) Battalion, operation orders for an attack on Cambrai, November 1917, and 62nd Division's Order of the Day, July 1917.

264. Letter of Maj. James Leadbitter Knoll, 10th (Service) Battalion, killed on 1 July 1916 at the Somme, printed copy.

265. 11th (Service) Battalion, ts. record compiled by Brig. Hobday, 1914-18.

266. A short history of the 15th (Service) Battalion (Leeds Pals), written at the end of the war, ts.

267. A short history of the 21st (Service) Pioneer Battalion, written by Lt. Col. Hanson, ts.

269. Capt., later Brig. Gen., James L. Jack, commander of the 2nd Battalion, 1916-17, bound ts. copy of his war diary during this period. There is other material relating to Jack in the Imperial War Museum (see p. 106).

WORLD WAR II

1st Battalion:

400. 1st Battalion detachment in the Andaman Islands, ts. account, 1940.

401. Ts. narratives of the 1st Battalion by Brig. Marindin: India, September 1939 — January 1942; retreat from Burma, Pegu, 1942; retreat from Burma, Pegu to Imphal, 1942; and Lushai Scouts, 1944.

402. First action, D Company, Pegu, Burma, ts. account by ? Croft.

403. 1st Battalion in retreat from Burma, ts. narrative by Maj. Phillips, 1942.

404. 1st Battalion, The Manipur Road, 1942, ts. account by Cpl. Dent-Smith.

405. Two articles by Brig. Marindin, 'Burma 1942' and 'Meiktila 1942'

406. Retreat from Burma, 1942, by Capt. Dyson.

407. Unofficial war diary of the 1st Battalion in Burma, 1942.

408. The defence of Imphal, notes by Lt. Col. Crofton.

409. The Lushai Scouts, by Maj. Longbottom, 1st Battalion, 1944.

410. 1st Battalion, war diary in Burma, 1944-5, accounts of brigade and division operations, and press-cuttings of men decorated for gallantry.

2nd Battalion:

411. 2nd Battalion in the East African campaign, 1940-1: Gallabat, Keren and Ad Teclesan, by Maj. Osborn; Keren, an article by Maj. Osborn; Keren, 'Forgotten Fighting' by Swift; Keren, letter from Lt. Col. Barker; Keren, an appraisal by Lt. Col. Barker; Keren, a panorama and plan; Keren, message from the Prime Minister to Forces; and Order of the Day from Maj. Gen. Heath, 5th Indian Division, on relinquishing command, April 1941.

412. 2nd Battalion, 1940-2, by Capt. Wiberg: Gallabat, 1940-1; Knightsbridge to June 1942; and Eritrea, Cyprus, Iraq and the Western Desert, 1941-2.

413. 2nd Battalion, 1940-5, by Lt. Col. Newman: movements of 2nd Battalion; Gallabat; Abyssinia; the Western Desert, 1942; Iraq, India and Arakan, 1942-3; Arakan; and X Company, Tiddim Road, 1944.

414. 2nd Battalion, 1940-2, by Maj. Osborn: impressions of A Company Commander, Sudan — Eritrea, 1940-1; and A Company in the Cauldron, Western Desert, June 1942.

415. 2nd Battalion, 1942, by Brig. Langran: The Cauldron, Western Desert, 5 June 1942; and Iraq, Egypt and Cyprus.

416. 2nd Battalion, 1941-4, by Brig. Cree: Kirkuk, Cyprus, Egypt, Tobruk, Cauldron, Ruweissat Ridge, October 1941 — September 1942; Ruweissat Ridge, Western Desert, 30-31 August 1942; Egypt, Iraq, India, Arakan, October 1942 — December 1943; the Admin Box, Arakan; operations December 1943 — June 1944; Imphal reunion, 1st and 2nd Battalions, 7 April 1944; defence of Imphal; Tiddim Road operations, July — August 1944; and *Yorkshire Post* account, 12 June 1945, of the operations of the 2nd Battalion.

417. Articles from *Ca Ira* relating to Western Desert operations, June — July 1942, by Lt. Col. Steel and Col. Osborn.

418. Ruweissat Ridge, Western Desert and Burma, 1942-4, a note by Brig. Salomans, 9th Brigade.

419. Notes by Maj. Steel, 1942-5: Halfaya Pass, Western Desert, May 1942; operations, 5 June 1942; move to Arakan, March 1944; and Meiktila to Rangoon, 1945.

420. Pamphlet, 'A Command Study in North Africa of the Western Desert Operations 1942', 1945.

421. Burma, December 1943 – June 1944, account prepared by Field Marshal Sir Cyril Deverell, Colonel of the Regiment, ts. copy: Maungdaw, the Admin Box and Imphal.

422. Burma 1944, by Lt. Col. Cree: the Admin Box and Tiddim Road.

423. Burma and Indonesia, 1943-6, by Lt. Col. Green: Maungdaw, Admin Box, Kohima-Imphal Road, December 1943 – June 1944; Imphal, Tiddim Road, Kaley mo, July – December 1944; Meiktila to Pegu, December 1944 – August 1945; Singapore and Java, August 1945 – April 1946.

424. Burma 1944-5, by Capt. Roche: Maungdaw and Razabil; Admin Box; and Pegu, 1945.

425. Operations in the Western Arakan, consisting of enquiries by Brig. Lucas Phillips for his book on Arakan and answers from officers.

426. Ts. copy of 2nd Battalion war diary in Burma, 1-30 April 1944.

427. Burma, April 1944, panorama sketch by the Intelligence Section of Kanglatombi from Segemai to the north of Imphal, when the 2nd Battalion covered evacuation of the Lion Box.

428. Padre Thompson's sketch of the Tiddim Road 1944.

429. A Company on Tiddim Road, operations in August 1944, ts. account by Maj. Bishop.

430. Burma, 1944-5, ts. by Maj. Horsfall: Imphal incidents; Tiddim Road; completion of Tiddim Road, B echelon, etc.; Tiddim Road poem; newspaper extract; and Meiktila, 1945.

431. Burma and Meiktila, 1945, ts. by Maj. Lawson.

432. Burma and Indonesia, ts. by Brig. Brain: Burma, March 1945; and Java, 1945-6.

433. Indonesia, 1945-6, ts. by Capt. Myers.

434. Indonesia, 1945-6, ts. by Capt. Atkinson.

435. Ts. notes by CQMS Lawn as a POW of the Italians and Germans.

436. Maps of Burma, 1944-5.

Non-regular battalions:

437. Ts. record of service for non-regular battalions, 1939-45, by Brig. Cree.

438. Service battalions raised in WWII: 9th, 10th, 2/10th, 11th, 12th, 13th and 70th, ts.

439. '1st/5th Battalion in Iceland', article from *Ca Ira* by Brig. Morrison.

440. 1st/5th Battalion, 1939, ts. by Lt Col. Sabine.

441. 1st/5th Battalion in the UK and Iceland, 1939-42, ts. by Maj. Spencer.

442. 2nd/5th Battalion in France, April – May 1940, ts. by Lt. Col. Tighe.

443. 2nd/5th Battalion, 1939-40, ts. by Maj. Saunders.

444. 2nd/5th Battalion on active service, 1940: ts. by Maj. Park on France, 1940; and Brig. Cawthorpe on the 131st Infantry Brigade, 1940.

446. 11th Battalion in the Falkland Islands, 1942-4, ts. by Lt. Col. Green.

447. 11th Battalion in the Falkland Islands, 1942-4, ts. by Capt. Waud.

448. 70th Battalion, the disbandment and dispersal of drafts, 1943, ts. by Maj. Park.

York City Library and Archives Department, Museum Street, YORK YO1 2DS

WORLD WAR II

Civil Defence and ARP files, 1939-65.

Index